Globalisation

Australian-Asian Perspectives

Globalisation

Australian-Asian Perspectives

Edited by

Cynthia vanden Driesen

T. Vijay Kumar

ATLANTIC

PUBLISHERS & DISTRIBUTORS (P) LTD

Published by
ATLANTIC
PUBLISHERS & DISTRIBUTORS (P) LTD
7/22, Ansari Road, Darya Ganj, New Delhi-110002
Phones : +91-11-40775252, 23273880, 23275880, 23280451
Fax : +91-11-23285873
Web : www.atlanticbooks.com
E-mail : orders@atlanticbooks.com

Branch Office
5, Nallathambi Street, Wallajah Road, Chennai-600002
Phones : +91-44-64611085, 32413319
E-mail : chennai@atlanticbooks.com

ISBN: 978-81-269-1857-7

Printed in India at Glorious Printers, A-13, D.S.I.D.C., Jhilmil Industrial Area, Delhi-110095

This book is dedicated with affection and respect to the memory of

Dr C Vijayasree
(1953-2012)

Professor of English
Osmania University

and

Director
Osmania University Centre for International Programmes
(OUCIP)

and

A Dear Friend of ASAA

Contents

SECTION 2
Globalisation: Culture and Society

SECTION 3

Globalisation: Literary Insights

Introduction

This book is the fifth volume in a series of publications that have emerged over the past fifteen years (1998-2013) from the periodic international conferences organised by the Association for the Study of Australasia in Asia (ASAA), an Association which aims at promoting an international dialogue between Australia, New Zealand and their Asian neighbours. The essays contained in this publication are based on selected papers presented at the Fifth International ASAA conference held at Osmania University (December 2011) on the theme of globalisation.

The scope of the publication is wide-ranging since the membership of the Association, and the participants of the conference, are drawn from a range of different countries and cultures and a multiplicity of disciplines. Most of the contributors are academics who explore the conference theme from within their areas of specialisation. For example, while literary critics focus on how the theme is refracted through a particular literary text, historians explore its ramifications from the perspective of its impact on a particular historical phase or period. There are essays also by educators, a librarian, a medical doctor and even a distinguished member of the legal profession. These essays, based as they are on the personal and professional experiences of the presenters, offer unique insights into the conference theme.

This volume is dedicated, with affection and respect, to the memory of Dr Vijayasree Chaganti, Professor of English at Osmania University and Director of OUCIP (Osmania University Centre for International Programmes). ASAA owes her a special debt for the efficiency and grace with which the ASAA conference was organised at the Centre and the contribution she has made as a friend of the Association to the development of Australian studies in India. Her untimely passing in May 2012, a few months after the conference, was deeply mourned by colleagues and friends all over the world. Her contribution to the field of postcolonial studies and literature in general is too well-known to need rehearsing here. The dedication of this volume to her memory is only a fitting tribute.

For the manner in which external physical events and the multiple forces of globalisation have impacted simultaneously also on the inner awareness of the global community, it is difficult to improve on the succinct definition offered, in Section 1, by one of the earliest writers in the field, Roland Robinson, Professor of Sociology at University of Aberdeen. Robinson in his study *Globalization: Social Theory and Global Cultures* (1992) defined this phenomenon, in a mode most useful to the present volume, as "the compression of the world and the intensification of the consciousness of the world as a whole". Globalisation impacts people, institutions and societies all over the world. Some regard it as a negative force, an extension of the evils of imperialism and a mode of reinforcing Western capitalist domination over more regions of the world, while others see it as a beneficial force creating new economic opportunities, stimulating cultural diversity, and expanding educational horizons.

Globalisation is too complex a phenomenon to be comprehended through the prism of a single discipline. Multi-disciplinary approaches are perhaps the best way to grasp the implications of this dominant feature of contemporary life. The 'multi-disciplinarity' of approaches in Section One is evident from the professional backgrounds of the contributors: Abu Siddique and Ameer Ali are trained economists; Mohan Ramanan and Rita Tognini are educators from two different continents; Harish Mehta is a historian; Nicholas Hasluck is a legal expert (and a novelist); Serge Liberman is a doctor (and a creative writer); and Julia Gross is a librarian and knowledge management professional.

Siddique's carefully researched essay on SAARC, that iconic example of the impact of globalism, is juxtaposed with Ameer Ali's discussion of how a new importance can be bestowed on older economic institutions which display undiminished functionality in the new context. Hasluck's essay exploits his legal expertise and his knowledge of literature to show how in this age of 'globalism' there is a need for adoption of such statutes as the 1948 Universal Declaration of Rights, a suitable balance needs to be struck with appropriate weight given to local experience. The essay emphasises the importance of imaginative writers in showing things as they really are and revealing what human beings feel most deeply. Liberman explores the (largely) humane operation of the principles of globalism and the collapse of borders in the area of medical practice and preservation of human life. He also reflects on how the continued consciousness of borders can precipitate other global events which spark large-scale destruction and suffering. Harish Mehta traces the trajectory of an Australian journalist who moved beyond the geographical and ideological borders of his Australian context to support the justice of the South Vietnamese cause in the Vietnam War. Ramanan and Tognini reflect on the impact of globalisation on the field of education. Ramanan assesses the degree of self-questioning and adaptation required in conventional departments of English literature to prepare students for the demands of a globalised world. Tognini's essay offers an appraisal of the reforms in the Australian education system to make students more 'Asia literate' as Australia recognizes the need to acknowledge her geographical positioning in Asia. In the last essay of the section, Gross explores the exciting opportunities opened up by advances in technology. She considers the possibility of open access publishing being made accessible worldwide for the wider sharing of knowledge.

Section 2 examines in considerable detail an important feature of globalisation—border crossings triggered by migration across regions and the emergence, and at the same time interrogation, of trans-national identities. Ashcroft's characteristically thought-provoking essay notes that the question of territorial borders has more prominence today than ever before in history because the increase in the number of migrants, asylum seekers and refugees, and their global mobility "disturbs the authority of the nation". Ashcroft outlines two ways in which borders are disrupted both "ontologically and culturally": the strategies of inhabiting bounded spaces and the evolution of a transnation, which must lead to an awareness of the fluidity and instability of borders of all kinds. Singh's erudite essay explores the nuances of the situation of South Asian migrants in the United States. Riemenschneider's pioneering study draws on documentary evidence as well as literary works to offer a comprehensive assessment of a similar group but with later antecedents and a different history in New Zealand. Julie Mehta's incisive analysis of the fiction of Judy Fong Bates demonstrates how food habits and cuisine have become modes of resistance against the marginalisation of the Chinese community in Canada. Das's essay deals with the aboriginal song-dance ceremony—*corroboree*—and underlines how this 'essential' cultural element helps the indigenous people reclaim their 'ethnonation' and identity. Rani draws a comparison between the myths of Australian Aborigines and Indian Dalits to demonstrate how they project an empowered notion of selfhood and a rejection of the canonical accounts of the myths. Sharmistha De and Anjali Roy focus on a large and undocumented region of resettlement of migrants from Bangladesh. On the evidence of field work they argue that the constant inflows of migrants from Bangladesh exposes not only the porosity of national borders but also certain stereotypes about the causes of migration and the status of the migrants.

In Section 3, motifs of migration and other aspects of the impact of globalisation emerge through the explorations of varied literary works. The essays in this section would seem to illustrate the point that Nicholas Hasluck makes in his essay about the gift of the creative writer, in the context of globalisation, to capture the lived experience of displacement, the negative as well as the positive aspects of migration, and the evolution of new trans-national identities. Two essays in this section focus on two different novels by Amitav Ghosh. The commonalities that emerge from them show the writer's predilection for suggesting the need for breaking free of the territorial limits of nation-states to explore the dynamic nature of cultural identity as being fostered in fluid, open spaces. Metaphors of ships and boats and the symbolism of the sea show how peoples swept across global flows develop fluid notions of belonging, and concepts of citizenship that reach across cultural borderlands. Fernandez' analysis of *Sea of Poppies* shows how English greed is symbolised through the poppy plant and its contaminating power over the land. The life on sea offers to Deeti a freedom and an identity that is denied to her on land, corrupted as it is by the British presence and the opium trade. Bannerjee's discussion of *River of Smoke* examines how colonial expansion in the 19th century formed the background to globalisation and how the South China Sea became the location of the activities of a small Indian community which in turn dislocated their traditional notions of belonging and identity. Highland's essay explores the ambivalence in the attitude of the migrant who belongs neither to his original nor to his adoptive home. Simoes da

Silva scrutinizes closely the notion that all writers who take up the cause of the refugee create an empathy with this figure so representative of the homeless and the displaced in the globalised world. His comparison of the work of Nam Le and Keneally leads da Silva to declare that works such as the latter's could result in constructions which amount to a form of "representational waste".

The two essays by Phillips and Bindu offer an innovative departure. Together they indicate the capacity of 'regional' poetry to transcend the limitations of local borders, and seemingly limited cultural conditioning, to achieve a creative bonding between regions far removed from each other in terms of geographic and cultural locations. This interesting insight emerges from Phillips' analysis of Kinsella's work and of Bindu's interview/discussion with Phillips regarding facets of his own work. Ringo's analysis of Aravind Adiga's *The White Tiger* notes both the liberating as well as the destructive forces of globalisation. While it has seemingly created new opportunities, particularly for the socially and economically marginalized, globalisation has also brought in a new life ethic, and the ruthless logic of a market economy. Kulkarni's lively survey of the rise of the Chick Lit genre in India draws attention to the fact that though local products followed the global models, they did not merely imitate them. Instead, they adapted the model and infused it with local content. In the last essay of the volume, Lowe traces the trajectory of her experience from colonialist visitor to partner of indigenous artist Jimmy Pike. This deeply personal account draws the reader into a contemplation of the more benign facets of the process of globalisation, and the encounters between peoples, cultures and events that will continue to proliferate.

The contributors to the volume are drawn from a number of different countries and disciplines, and they explore the ramifications of globalisation from widely different regions, social contexts and historical backgrounds. The diversity of approaches will enable the scholars as well as the general reader to grasp the complexities of the seemingly universal phenomenon of globalisation. What emerges finally from the various studies is a sense of the commonalities of experience alongside the wide variations which subsist within and across different countries and regions.

Cynthia vanden Driesen
T. Vijay Kumar

SECTION 1

Globalisation: Multi-disciplinary Perspectives

CHAPTER

1

Vanishing Borders and the Visibility of Rights

Nicholas Hasluck
Writer, Australia

Franz Kafka's writings include a work of speculative fiction called *The Great Wall of China* in which the storyteller in a strange, unreal, self-doubting tone of voice describes the memorable moment when the Great Wall was 'finished off' at its northernmost corner. This was the point where the two great armies of labour—the eastern and western armies—were believed to have finally converged.

However, the storyteller goes on to say, it was well-known that as a consequence of the so-called 'piecemeal principle of construction' many gaps had been left along the way as supervisors transferred labouring groups from one neighbourhood to another in order to relieve the tedium of the vast undertaking. Indeed, the narrator confides—somewhat apologetically—it seems that a considerable number of the gaps were not actually filled in until after the official announcement was made that the Great Wall had been completed.

Having glanced over his shoulder and lowered his voice, the self-doubting narrator then feels obliged to confess that according to rumour there are in fact many gaps in the structure which have never been filled in at all! Rumours of this kind lie behind the myriad of legends to which the building of the Great Wall has given rise. Not surprisingly, these troublesome assertions cannot be verified by the evidence of any single witness owing to the size and extent of the famous wall, the mountain-buckled undulations of which seem to be always disappearing into the clouds.

In any event, the narrator declares, reverting to an authoritative tone, the important point is that the Great Wall is generally understood to be well and truly finished. And finished notwithstanding the instability of human nature that can endure no restraint and is inclined to tear things asunder, including walls and borders and its very self.

But could it be, the narrator suddenly asks himself, raising a pensive finger to his lips as if assailed by further doubts, that uncertainties about human nature of the kind he has just mentioned, which understandably weighed heavily against the building of the Great Wall in the first place, were taken into account by the 'High Command' when the principle of piecemeal construction was decided upon and allowance was made for gaps and omissions? Although where exactly the office of the High Command is, and who sits there, neither the narrator nor anyone he has ever met knew then or knows now.

At last, with a show of resolution, the patently unreliable narrator winds up his summary by affirming loudly that the main thing to remember about the Great Wall is this: if it were not for the wisdom of the High Command in allowing for the sizable number of gaps and omissions that are rumoured to exist, the Great Wall might not have been finished off, and might not be there in whatever is thought to be its final form—a splendid line of defence standing wherever it is in the public mind for the admiration of one and all!

I was reminded of Kafka's bizarre but prescient tale as I turned to the conference theme and the suggestion that contemporary times are characterised by vanishing borders and a belief that we now all live in a global marketplace which is indifferent to national boundaries. Has globalisation transformed the nature of nation states to such an extent that politicians and the people they represent have a greatly reduced capacity to influence events?

With such thoughts in mind, one can appreciate the force of Kafka's allegorical fantasy and its application to the twenty-first century. In many places, the High Command of the country in question may continue to draw upon local patriotism by pointing to the presumed presence of a magnificent wall to protect the country's borders—its individuality—while simultaneously securing a reputation for far-sighted wisdom by making it clear to the global market-place that free-traders will find enough gaps and omissions to move to and fro as they please.

Can Kafka's Great Wall be regarded as a paradigm of globalisation in post-modern times? Borders remain but are incomplete. Lines of defence are praised but are full of gaps. The Great Wall's counterpart in reality can be seen from space but seen online it can be reconfigured instantly by touching an iPad or a computer screen. We inhabit an information-saturated planet where most of what businessmen know will soon be stored in a new-fangled repository called 'the cloud'. One doesn't have to be Kafka or a digital whizz kid in order to accept that we are living in a surrealistic age in which hackers can unleash a pervasive virus and multi-national corporations can move funds across borders at the click of a mouse.

What are the implications of this? The field of inquiry is vast so I will confine myself to some observations about law and literature, and the way in which ambiguities about national sovereignty bear upon the upholding of human rights. I will argue that, notwithstanding the tendencies associated with globalisation—its indifference to borders, its ominous presence—talk about rights and the provision of related remedies can't be divorced from local ways and legal processes. The freedom to hold opinions and to speak freely may prove to be illusory unless human rights are properly understood in the community directly affected by what is thought and said. The customs and innate wisdom of the relevant community are likely to have a bearing upon rulings concerning such matters.

A wall of the kind envisaged by Kafka—an elastic barrier that is viewed as both strong and pliable—is a familiar concept in most advanced legal systems, for the law is accustomed to providing exceptions to a general rule and creating legal fictions that mask gradual changes to what appears to be an immutable custom. Moreover, in seeking to provide for the needs of society, by adhering to the never-ending quest for relevance, advanced legal systems have usually had to make provision for relations with the outside world. The Roman jurist Gaius, for example, began his famous *Institutiones* by saying that 'every people that is governed by statutes and customs applies partly its own peculiar law and partly law which is common to all mankind'. For Gaius and other jurists in ancient times 'natural' law was derived from the principle of order that is manifest in the physical universe and which is represented in mankind by its reason.

With the rise of the nation state any lingering belief in natural law was swept away by the dictates of national sovereignty. Legal systems in the modern world proceed from the premise that law consists of the rules made or approved by the state. International law and rules in treaties will only be fully effective if they are incorporated within and applied by the governmental agencies of the domestic system, although international law and related reasoning undoubtedly have an important influence upon the development of domestic law.

In the aftermath of the Second World War and with the founding of the United Nations, well before the era of globalisation, the sovereign nations of the world saw merit in the development of an international system of rights and responsibilities. And so the Universal Declaration of Human Rights, adopted unanimously by the General Assembly of the United Nations in 1948, gave expression to the undefined notion of human rights reflected in the UN Charter.

The Universal Declaration and later covenants, which deal with matters such as torture, treatment of prisoners and racial discrimination, are now replicated in the domestic law of many countries and seek to protect a significant range of civil and political entitlements. These rights for the most part are vested in individuals although the province of international law had traditionally been concerned with the relationship between countries.

The Universal Declaration, while not of itself legally binding, has been a template from which various charters of rights have been developed within domestic legal systems. Examples include the Canadian Charter of Rights and Freedoms 1982, the South African Constitution 1996 and the United Kingdom Human Rights Act 1998. Domestic legislation of this kind has been enacted in two Australian jurisdictions but it remains a matter of debate as to whether the federal parliament should follow suit. For the time being, pursuant to powers vested in it by the Australian constitution with respect to international affairs and treaties, the federal government attends to enforcement of statutes that draw upon certain facets of the Universal Declaration and other international instruments. The Racial Discrimination Act 1975 is a well-known example.

In this short essay I will not attempt to explore all the implications of the debate concerning the incorporation within domestic law of precepts derived from the Universal Declaration. It has been argued in certain quarters that such precepts run contrary to conventional views about state sovereignty, even though, as we noticed in earlier discussion, the very notion of state sovereignty in an age of globalisation is being called into question. It has been argued also that human rights law is essentially a construct of the western democracies and rights talk may simply mask or blunt the desire for change in countries with a different background.

These criticisms raise significant issues but I will put them to one side for present purposes in order to look at another important matter, namely, the contention that because human rights are usually defined by the use of abstract or general language they are difficult to interpret and do not always provide ready answers to specific controversies. There is considerable force in this critique. Astute law-makers have always been conscious that if rights are presented simply as a series of high-minded abstractions they may soon become invisible because their application to the ups and downs of daily life is not entirely clear. So let us pause to take a closer look at the Universal Declaration, bearing in mind that by and large its language is replicated in similar domestic instruments.

The preamble notes that disregard for human rights has resulted in barbarous acts. It foreshadows the advent of a world in which human beings will enjoy freedom of speech and freedom from fear and want. The text that follows begins with 11 articles that seem to echo the U.S. Constitution and the French Declaration of the Rights of Man in proclaiming the right of everyone to life, liberty and personal security. There are further articles dealing with rights in civil society such as the right to own property and the right to free movement. Other articles give effect to ideas drawn from the Athenian *polis* concerning democratic political rights. These articles include the right to participate in government through periodic and genuine elections.

Article 18 provides that everyone has the right to freedom of thought, conscience and religion. Article 19 states that 'everyone has the right to freedom of opinion and expression' which includes 'the freedom to hold opinions without interference and to seek, receive and impart information and ideas through any media and regardless of frontiers'. There are further rights concerning standards of living although some of these could be regarded as essentially aspirational assertions. Moreover, article 29 acknowledges that limitations on rights are permissible 'for the purposes of securing due recognition and respect for the rights and freedoms of others and of meeting the just requirements of morality, public order and the general welfare of democratic society'.

It is immediately obvious that there is room for disputation as to what activities are in fact protected by the right to freedom of expression. This is due to the generality of the language used and the prospect that rights may be curtailed to some extent by the presence of other equally important rights and limitations referable to communal needs. Are defamatory or pornographic publications protected by the right to freedom of expression? Is racial vilification protected? A host of examples can quickly be brought to mind of dubious utterances or activities on the borderline of legitimacy.

Inevitably, in countries professing an adherence to human rights, it will be left to a court or a tribunal to resolve controversies about such matters in the course of defining the ambit of the right. If a matter in contention is difficult in the sense that the governing text is too broad and there is no precedent applicable to the dispute, then the adjudicator may have to fall back on whatever line of reasoning that is available in order to arrive at a ruling that will be acceptable to others in the legal profession and can be explained to the ordinary citizen. It may be necessary to draw upon local knowledge and the adjudicator's own sense of justice. A discretionary approach of this kind arguably vests too much power in the judicial arm of government but, on the other hand, it serves to clarify the exact nature of the right.

It will be apparent from this overview that we live in a world that is being rapidly reconfigured by global finance (and related shenanigans). There is an increasing realisation that the economies of the world are inter-connected; that electronic gadgetry now makes it virtually impossible to impede the free flow of money and information. It is clear that what has happened on the international stage in times past has had a profound effect upon the rights of citizens throughout the world. Nonetheless we ought not to assume too readily that borders will disappear entirely. The international human rights system still relies upon national implementation for its validity. Nation states and local judges continue to bear the principal responsibility for working out how laws concerning human rights are to be applied.

If there be any merit in this analysis, some force in the suggestion that particular rights such as freedom of expression will only be truly visible so long as they are seen to have a specific content, a spirit consonant with local circumstances, then more will have to be said about the values underlying the right to think and speak freely. We must also look at the way in which issues of infringement are to be resolved in difficult cases.

There are various assumptions underlying the case for free speech. Freedom of expression is thought to be inherent in the process of advancing knowledge and discovering truth. It is said to be necessary for democratic participation in decision-making, with the result that change can be achieved openly and peacefully, rather than by clandestine activities and insurrection. Above all, free speech and the entitlement to think as one pleases are essential for individual fulfilment, the prospect of making the most of what one is, of standing up for one's self.

The reasons usually provided for favouring an individual's right to freedom of speech, as against a conflicting right or a communal need, bring us back to the question of infringement. The resolution of a dispute is often explained in terms of the balancing of competing rights, as if discrete but potentially conflicting rights—the right to freedom of expression and the right to due process, for example—are simply pushed up against each other until the resulting 'balance' miraculously appears. But, in truth, where exactly the balance is to be struck will sometimes depend upon attitudes deeply rooted in the traditions of the particular community, at times upon political necessity—what is thought to be permissible in a time of peace, to take an obvious example, may not be quite the same as what is appropriate in a state of emergency.

Limitations on free speech such as suppression orders or rules concerning contempt of court or libel are inseparable from community membership. The question of whether or not to regulate the freedom is bound to be a local one. The answer to a particular dispute about the extent of the right to freedom of speech will be less than sufficiently convincing if the adjudicator relies solely upon abstract principles that are either so broadly expressed as to be devoid of content or coloured by some ideological agenda from overseas. It is at this point that the nature of the narratives brought into existence by historians and storytellers can be seen to bear upon the marking out of the case for free expression.

Freedom of speech is thought to cover not just language used precisely by educated elites but also the utterances of those who may have important things to say but sometimes lack the skill to say them neatly. An old wife's tale may point to some piece of folklore passed down from one generation to the next, some clumsy piece of wisdom typical of that community, but evoking the presence of an ongoing partnership between the living and dead. The poet T.S. Eliot put it this way in *Four Quartets* (1943), his profound meditation upon the past and the folly of seeming to be wise: 'And what the dead had no speech for, when living/They can tell you, being dead: the communication/Of the dead is tongued with fire beyond the language of the living' ("Little Gidding").

Words jotted down in a diary or an old letter, the poet intimates, words that might have seemed ordinary or inconsequential when first uttered, may turn out to be revered beyond the grave if the author becomes famous or dies a martyr. A few old words in a dusty deed-box may finish up igniting fierce passions at the reading of a will. A tattered deed may reveal essential but seldom-mentioned truths about a family, or even a community.

Eliot's ruminations are a reminder also that in looking at words we are concerned with meaning. This is a matter not only of dictionaries and rules of grammar but also of context: what do the words convey to the mind of a reasonably well-informed audience with some background knowledge as to the ways of the community. We start with an assumption that people will use words and grammar in a conventional way but, quite often, it becomes apparent that possibly for want of education or local vernacular they are not doing so and we adjust our interpretation of what they say accordingly. This enables us not only to choose the intended meaning when a word has more than one dictionary meaning but also to understand the speaker's meaning when he or she has used the wrong words.

Mrs Malaprop, in Sheridan's *The Rivals* (1775), had a habit of using the wrong words but was still capable of conveying her meaning. When she says that the person in question is "as obstinate as an allegory on the banks of the Nile", we reject the conventional or literal meaning of allegory as making nonsense of the sentence and substitute 'alligator' by using our background knowledge of things likely to be found on the banks of the Nile and choosing one which sounds rather like "allegory".

Further, in seeking to interpret a contentious utterance that may or not be protected by the freedom to speak freely, we must also take account of the fact that meaning can be conveyed indirectly, by hints and silences, by the art of irony whereby what is said must be taken to imply some meaning to the contrary. As in Kafka's account of a recently completed 'Great Wall' which seems in fact to be far from complete, being principally renowned for its many gaps and omissions—a show of strength riddled with insecurities.

To a discerning literary critic, Kafka's allegory *The Great Wall of China* or other works from the same period such as *The Radetzky March* by Joseph Roth, may seem to reflect a deep historical pessimism related to the decay and ultimate collapse of the ramshackle pre-war Habsburg empire. The ironies in these works, the ambiguities and veiled humour, have to be construed accordingly. To a lawyer, these works, albeit fiction, ought to suggest, at the very least, that a writer with a middle European background might be inclined to speak in a guarded way, without the direct free-wheeling tone of a Mark Twain or some other boisterous product of American democracy, although the right to speak being exercised is essentially the same in both cases.

It seems to follow that judicial officers, even those with an extensive practical knowledge of their own legal system, will benefit by constantly pondering the ambiguities of language and the unpredictable ways in which meanings can be affected by tone and different cultural backgrounds.

But careful reading or listening will not be sufficient in all cases. Words and phrases are often laced with ironies or contradictions that can only be deciphered in a court of law by reference to the surrounding circumstances. A famous trial in England that led to a death sentence turned upon the meaning of a few words shouted out to a burglar brandishing a pistol on a London rooftop. 'Let him have it!' the burglar's accomplice shouted, whereupon the police officer confronting the burglar was shot dead (Eatock v Bolt 2011).

What did the words mean? Let him have it in the sense of 'let the police officer have the gun and we'll both surrender'? Or did the words mean, echoing the language of various comic books and gangster movies (which the evidence showed the two criminals were in the habit of reading), let him have it in the sense of 'pull the trigger and let him have a bullet in the chest'? And if it transpires that the words, properly construed, were meant in the latter sense—as indeed they were found to be—could the right to freedom of speech be thought to justify or excuse such an utterance, a command fraught with hazard and undeniably detrimental to the welfare of the community as a whole in challenging the authority of the police to make an arrest?

I will attempt to draw together these various observations about the distillation of meaning and limitations upon the right to speak freely by referring finally to a recently decided Australian case—the Andrew Bolt case—which neatly illustrates the way in which the right in question may be curtailed by countervailing rights or a need to consider the public interest. It highlights also the importance of understanding local circumstances: in this case facts and matters related to the so-called 'history wars' in Australia that might seem mystifying to a stranger.

The complainants contended that a Melbourne journalist Andrew Bolt had written a piece implying that, as lighter-skinned individuals of part-Aboriginal descent, they had 'chosen' to identify as Aboriginal because of the financial or career benefits such a choice conferred. This was said to infringe section 18C of the federal Racial Discrimination Act whereby it is unlawful for a person to do an act in public if the act is reasonably likely in the circumstances to offend or insult another person or a group of people, and is done because of the race, colour or ethnic origin of the other person or all of the people in the group.

Justice Mordecai Bromberg found that the words complained of amounted to a breach of the statute. He held that fair-skinned Aboriginal people, or some of them, were reasonably likely in all the circumstances to have been offended or insulted by the imputations. He said that Bolt's article included a liberal use of sarcasm of a kind that had "a heightened capacity to convey implications beyond the literal meaning of the words utilised. It is language which invites the reader to not only read the lines but also to read between the lines."

The judge then had to consider whether the breach was balanced by the protection of free speech in the exceptions contained in section 18D of the statute. These exceptions included statements made for 'any genuine purpose in the public interest' and fair comment that was 'an expression of a genuine belief held by the person making the comment'. The judge concluded that because certain of the facts underlying the journalist's views (albeit views genuinely held) had been distorted, a finding against the journalist was justified. His Honour held that the incursion into freedom of speech involved in such a ruling was no greater than that which might have been inspired by the law of defamation.

The judge's verdict gave rise to considerable controversy. The President of a civil liberties group, Liberty Victoria, noted that the judge was required to weigh in the balance the right to be free of racial intolerance and discrimination on the one hand and freedom of expression on the other. The ruling may have been justified in the particular circumstances of the case due to the degree of hurt experienced by the nine complainants. Nonetheless, his organisation's view was that the relevant statutory provision had been drafted too widely because the subjective test of whether certain individuals felt offended and insulted was too low a hurdle for the protections of the Act to be triggered.

The same commentator touched also upon another important issue. This concerned the public interest in the free communication of ideas and opinions as an avenue to truth and a form of involvement in democratic decision-making. He noted that the question of whether the provision in question might transgress the Australian constitutional protection of freedom of public and political communication has not yet been tested by the High Court. It could therefore be fairly assumed that 'this issue may not have run its race yet'.

In various ways the Andrew Bolt case raises the question of whether the racial vilification provisions of the relevant statute constitute too great an incursion on freedom of speech. It was, of course, that famous iconoclast of the French revolutionary era, Voltaire, who reportedly said two centuries ago: 'I disapprove of what you say, but I will defend to the death your right to say it.' The spirit of Voltaire's saying was reproduced eventually in the Universal Declaration. The French philosopher would argue, no doubt, that in seeking to protect freedom of speech, that which lies at the core of individuality and decision-making, there should be allowance for some degree of over-zealous or careless expression of thought, for we cannot expect every citizen to make his feelings known with the precision we have come to expect from a well-educated university professor or a judge. But, as I have attempted to show in earlier discussion, how the freedom is interpreted is likely to vary from place to place.

It emerges, then, that the Universal Declaration, which is sometimes loosely represented in contemporary rhetoric as a law 'common to mankind', has influenced domestic law in most countries of the world. To that extent, like the phenomenon known as globalisation, it has played a part in diminishing the effect of national sovereignty. Nonetheless, in the field of law, it is too early to suggest that borders between countries are steadily vanishing. The reality is that in strict analysis international covenants have to be incorporated within the domestic law of nation states in order to be fully effective, domestic legal systems are still governed by local rules and related judicial attitudes, the scope of each right will generally be conditioned by the context in which it is to be exercised.

Striking the right balance between freedom of speech and other considerations—such as countervailing human rights or the public interest—will usually be a complex and difficult exercise. In certain cases the adjudicator may finish up having to look at local habits and customs, and sometimes even at works of literature which shine a light upon the ways of the community. The vitality of the rights to think and speak freely depends upon this process of inquiry. For rights to be truly visible they must be generally respected and capable of enforcement in the place where enforcement counts.

Works Cited

Eatock v Bolt. 2011. FCA1103.

Eliot, T.S. 1943. *Four Quartets*. New York: Harcourt Brace.

Kafka, Franz. 1976. *The Great Wall of China*. London: Secker and Warburg/Octopus.

Roth, Joseph. 2000. *The Radetzky March* (1932). London: Penguin Classics.

CHAPTER 2

The Political Economy of Islamic Banking and Finance: A Faith-based Enterprise Growing in the Global Village

Ameer Ali
Murdoch University, Australia

Introduction

Islamic Banking and Finance (IB&F) was born as an alternative to the conventional financial industry. It emerged in the wake of an oil-based economic boom and a wave of religious resurgence in the Arab Middle East. Its birth also coincided with the collapse of the Keynesian-Neoclassical consensus and the rise of the Washington consensus in macroeconomic management. It is the latter that has reigned supreme in the current era of economic globalisation. In a global economy dominantly driven by secular rationalist ideologies the appearance of a faith-based financial sector to challenge the status quo was originally viewed as something bizarre and even ridiculous. Over the last four decades however, this new sector has grown to be a resilient alternative to conventional banking and finance and has captured a niche market both within and outside Muslim countries. What follows is a brief analysis of the political economy of the different phases in the history of IB&F. Surprisingly, in the post-2001 world of Islamo-phobia and banking and financial turmoil in Europe and America the nascent Islamic alternative appears to have won admiration from some unexpected quarters.

IB&F: The State of Play

Although the ideological debate about an Islamised economy and finance was first raised by Maulana Abul-ala

Maududi in pre-partition India, and although a few sporadic experiments in Islamic finance were tried out in Malaysia and Egypt in the 1950s and 1960s (Visser 2009), IB&F as an independent and novel model of money and credit business came into existence only in the mid-1970s with the establishment in Dubai the first private Islamic bank in 1975. Since that time the growth of IB&F has been robust and it has earned itself a unique identity and a niche market in an economic environment of tumultuous banking and financial activities. *The Banker* magazine of the *Financial Times* and Group HSBC Amanah, has listed in its November 2007 issue the top 500 Islamic financial institutions that were operating in forty-seven countries with a total *sharia*-compliant asset value of $500.5 billion at the end of the year 2006. According to the same source, in addition to 292 banks, both fully Islamic and those offering Islamic windows or selling Islamic products, there are 115 Islamic investment banks and finance companies, and 118 insurance companies, adding up to a global total of 525 institutions. According to a more recent publication the total value of the IBF industry has grown to $820 billion at the end of 2008 (IFSB *et al.*, 2010). The HSBC Group alone has a global network comprising "about 10,000 offices with almost 110 million customers in 77 countries and territories in Europe, the Asia-Pacific region, the Americas, the Middle East and Africa" (*The Banker* 2007).

In India too, due to the financial exclusion of a large section of the Muslim community "because of a certain mindset prevailing in the banking sector" the demand for Islamic banking appears to have won the sympathy of the Indian Banks' Association and is awaiting an amendment to the Banking Regulation Act to make Islamic banking and finance a reality (*Frontline* 2009). In Australia, there is already one private institution, the Muslim Community Cooperative Australia (MCCA) established in 1989 "to provide a comprehensive Islamic alternative for all financial needs of the Muslim community" (Saeed & Akbarzadeh

2001, 189), and within the conventional banking industry, the National Bank of Australia has recently announced its intention to engage in *sharia*-compliant financial business (Ali 2009).

Thus, in the 'global village' where conventional banking and financial institutions are grappling with periodic currency crises, financial meltdowns and institutional bankruptcies, the IB&F industry appears to be "Islam's collective answer to the failures of Adam Smith's invisible hand" (Napoleoni 2010, 17). A strong demand for *sharia*-compliant products in Muslim countries, the progressive strengthening of regulatory framework within IB&F, a growing demand from conventional investors in search of asset diversification, the relative resilience that the IB&F industry has shown during the 1997 financial crisis in Asia and the 2008 financial meltdown in the US and Europe, and the capacity of the industry to innovate and structure financial instruments to satisfy the needs of both corporate and individual investors have combined to provide the necessary impetus to the robustness of IB&F (Hasan and Dridi 2010). Yet, in terms of its size and scale IBF is still a minuscule. The entire $820 billion *sharia*-compliant assets cited above is not even one per cent of the $167 trillion worth of global financial assets, as reported in the MacKinsey & Co. report of 2008. Even in Malaysia where IB&F has the support of the government only 10 per cent of all banking assets were held in sharia-compliant accounts in 2005 (KPMG 2006).

The Faith-base

IB&F is a prohibition-driven industry. It is the religious ban on (a) *riba*, translated as usury by some and interest by many; (b) *gharar*, meaning risk and uncertainty; and (c) *maysir*, literally meaning games of chance where one party faces the possibility of total loss—and therefore, in general, referring to gambling—that provides the religious rationale for the IB&F industry. Jurists of all schools of

Islamic jurisprudence consider *riba*, *gharar*, and *maysir* immoral and unjust and therefore deem detrimental to the welfare of not only the individuals and institutions that indulge in them but also to the society as a whole in which they operate. In the jurists' view these activities contradict the Islamic principles and objectives of economic fairness and social justice.

Riba, the prohibition of which preceded long before the revelation of the Quran between the sixth and seventh centuries, is not confined to monetary transactions alone but covers a broad range of economic transactions including gold, silver, wheat, dates, barley, and so on, where the economic return to one party in the transaction exceeds what is considered to be a fair market norm. In this sense all monopoly profits would fall under the category of *riba*. In addition, and in the context of conventional bank lending however, it is argued that it is unfair and unethical for capital as a factor of production to claim a pre-determined rate of return before that factor enters the process of production and shares the consequence.

Historically the ban on *riba* that predates Islam was imposed by all Abrahamic faiths at a time when money was considered only a medium of exchange and therefore an unproductive asset. The modern interpreters of *sharia* and IB&F practitioners however accept that money is a productive resource and a store of value but adheres to the ethical principle that any resource should share equally in both the risks and benefits that accrue from an enterprise. Thus, while conventional banking intermediation is largely debt-based and allows for risk transfer, Islamic banking mediation is asset-based and risk-sharing. In short, IB&F activities are based on the principle of profit-loss-sharing (PLS). While Judaism and Christianity gave up the prohibition and surrendered totally to the forces of mammon (Tawney 1960), Islam, after centuries of silent resistance has now taken up the fight to a new level. IB&F is the present battleground on which this confrontation is taking place.

Political and Economic Environment of the 1970s

Internationally the IB&F industry emerged in the 1970s and grew in an environment of momentous economic and political changes; and within the Muslim world these developments overlapped with a new wave of religious awakening. The collapse of *dirigisme*, the rise of free market economics, and the revolution in communication technology set the international stage for the arrival in the 1980s of economic globalisation. The loosening of restrictions for capital to move across national borders coincided with a period of accelerated capital accumulation in parts of the Muslim world thanks to the financial bonanza flowed from petroleum products. The partial victory of Egypt in the 1973 Ramadan/Yomkippur War, and six years later in 1979, the Islamic Revolution in Iran, reinvigorated an Islamic religious fervour that hitherto lay dormant because of the political dominance of secular Arab nationalism and its pseudo-socialist manifestation in the 1950s and 1960s (Ahmad 2011). Lavishly funded and organisationally supported by several of the petroleum-rich Arab countries headed by Saudi Arabia, this rekindled religious awakening, apart from its outward expressions in the form of regularised religious rituals, construction of new and renovation of old mosques, establishment of religious schools, and strict consumption of *halal* food and Islamic attire, generated a series of Islamic conferences and colloquiums for Muslim intellectuals and academics with the specific purpose of producing a blueprint or program for Islamizing a perceived un-Islamic world order. The demand for an interest-free economic and financial system was the product of this grand Islamization project.

From the point of view of the history of IB&F industry the year 1979 was momentously significant for its political impact in the Muslim and Western worlds. The *shia*-Islamic revolution In Iran in February that year followed by the Mecca rebellion in Saudi Arabia in November and the Soviet invasion of Afghanistan in December created an international political ambience within which IB&F could operate quietly without provoking undue attention from any quarter. Khomeini's resolve to export the revolution to other parts of the Muslim world obviously sent shock waves to autocratic Muslim regimes and among them to the Saudi monarchy in particular. When a group of armed religious zealots occupied the mosque in Mecca and demanded the overthrow of the Saudi regime Khomeini's wish seemed to have almost come to fruition. Although the rebellion was brutally crushed the Saudi regime soon realised its vulnerability and sought to fortify its position by allying with the West more closely. Fortunately to the Saudis the Soviet invasion of Afghanistan and US's determination to drive out the 'Evil Empire' from Asia came as a blessing in disguise. The congruence of interests between the Saudi regime and the United States: oil and money in exchange for technology and protection, and their common interest against the Soviet threat created an opportunity for the forces of resurgent Islam with its Islamisation project to penetrate the West without much resistance.

The end of the 1970s and the beginning of the 1980s also witnessed another development which was to facilitate this penetration even further. This was the collapse of the Keynesian consensus in macroeconomic management which was structured on the basis of independent national economies governed internationally by the Bretton Wood arrangements. The 1970s stagflationary interregnum in the Western economies, the serial collapse of the command economies led by the former Soviet Union, and the revolutionary breakthrough in electronic and communication technologies set the stage for the re-emergence of unfettered economic liberalism that hitherto remained somewhat restrained by the Keynesian-Neoclassical consensus. Economic liberalism which rolled back the state from economic management and freed the invisible hand forced open the doors for economic globalisation. It was in this new global economic environment that the idea of an interest-free financial sector was to translate itself into reality.

Economic globalisation and the ensuing freedom for cross-border movement of finance capital meant a two-way traffic as far as the IB&F industry was concerned. While conventional banking and financial institutions could enter the hitherto 'unbanked' Muslim sector and compete with the nascent IB&F intermediaries the latter also had the same freedom to do likewise outside its home ground. Yet, in the 1980s and 1990s IB&F activities remained overwhelmingly a Muslim-country phenomenon. With accommodative regulatory arrangements by home governments and with flexible administrative arrangements by interested institutions even conventional banks operating in the Muslim countries entered the faith-based industry by opening 'Islamic windows'. Buy the end of the 1990s virtually every conventional bank in the Middle East was in IB&F business. While Malaysia was fast emerging as the IB&F hub international banks such as the Citicorp and HSBC had entered the field by the end of the century.

Diaspora Muslims, the Housing Market, and IB&F

The pre-1970 industrialization and economic affluence in the Western countries had a relaxed attitude towards immigration. The need for cheap labour and a political interest in keeping the former colonies under their influence made it desirable for the Western powers to grant at least temporary resident permits to Muslim migrants from the Middle East and South Asia. The size of the Muslim population living in the West increased significantly and the latest estimates of their number vary between 12 and 24 million (Pew Forum 2009; Kettani 2010). These diaspora Muslims living mostly in the United States, Canada, Britain, France, Germany, and Netherlands presented a potential target-niche-market for IB&F. The religious resurgence of the 1970s in the Muslim-majority countries and the rise of Islamism under the leadership of the Ikhwan-al Muslimeen in Egypt, Jama'at-e-Islami in Pakistan, and the Tablighi-Jamaat in India did not leave the immigrant Muslims in the West un-impacted (Ahmad 2011). A significant segment of these immigrants who flocked to the West in the sixties and seventies were already living in virtual parallel societies and remained largely disconnected socially and culturally from the mainstream communities. After the seventies however, the second generation of these immigrants came increasingly under the influence of resurgent Islam. A significant number of this community became members of several Islamic organisations like the Islamic Society of North America, and the Council on American-Islamic Relations, which were generously funded by Saudi Arabia and other Gulf countries and became centres for the propagation of Islamist ideals (Ahmad 2011).

The Islamic prohibition of interest kept many Muslim families in the West away from the housing-mortgage market. Many of them preferred to live in rental properties rather than to purchase their own through bank loans. Even though the European Council for Research and Fatwas and the League of Scholars for Sharia in the USA had allowed, on the basis of the Hanafi school of Islamic jurisprudence, interest-based borrowing from banks for financing homes, the more orthodox of the Muslims like the Moroccans in Netherlands and the *salafis* in the US and in other parts of Europe kept aloof from conventional mortgage markets (Visser 2009, 106 and 142-44). It was this unmet need within the immigrant Muslim community that initially offered a lucrative opportunity for IB&F to enter the West. Several so-called *shariah*-compliant financial products were devised, such as *murabaha* or cost-plus sale, where the financier buys the house and resells it to the ultimate buyer with a mark-up against periodic payments; *ijara wa iqtina* or deferred payment sale, where the client finds a home and asks the financier to buy it, the financier then sells the house to the client against deferred payment, possibly at the same price, but holds on to the title until the last payment is made; *musharaka mutanaqisah,* or partnership contract, where the financier and the home buyer jointly owns the home and over time the fancier's share diminishes continuously as the home buyer's share increases; and *istisna*, or sale with deferred delivery, which involves financing of home construction (Visser 2009, 107-12). Although these *sharia*-compliant products are more expensive and complex to transact than the conventional ones and were criticised by some as Islamic only in name (El-Gamal 2007), yet, to the pious, they are deemed qualitatively better and are therefore spiritually rewarding. The Al-Baraka Islamic Bank in Britain and, after its closure in 1993, the United Bank of Kuwait concentrated their business mainly in the housing market (Khan and Porzio 2010, 213-15).

Another *sharia*-compliant product, the *sukuk* or asset-backed Islamic bonds, which originated outside the immigrant communities, and which were to draw high demand after 2000 had its religious legitimation in the 1980s when the *Fiqh Academy* of the *Organization of the Islamic Conference* (OIC) gave its approval in 1988 (Jobst 2007). *Sukuks* are "certificates that represent ownership of an underlying pool of assets, or the usufruct...of such assets, and therefore, entitle their holders to return resulting from the sale or lease of the assets" (Warde 2010, 150). There are about fourteen different types of *sukuk* described a permissible in the AAOIFI (Accounting and Auditing Organization for Islamic Financial Institutions) *sharia* standards on *sukuk*. Most *sukuk* issues have been sponsored by sovereign and quasi-sovereign issuers in Islamic countries. Currently, Malaysia is the pacemaker and leader for the development of *sukuks* when in 2002 the Malaysian Government kick-started the market with a US$600 million issuance backed by lease payments (Jobst 2007). In 2003,

Qatar followed with an issuance of US$700 million. Bahrain and Pakistan did the same for US$250 million and US$600 million in 2004 and 2005 respectively (Jobst). According to the London based IFIS, Islamic Finance Information Service, the total value of *sukuk* issued in the first half of 2010 had exceeded US$20 billion Sukuk.me 2011).

Conventional insurance is another prohibited area for Muslims according to a majority of *sharia* experts. The Fiqh Council of the World Muslim League in 1978 and the Fiqh Academy of the OIC in 1985 declared conventional insurance as *haram* or prohibited. This led to the birth of *takaful* or cooperative or mutual insurance in which an insurer agrees with other participants in the fund to mutually help each other by way of providing financial assistance should any member of the fund suffer a catastrophe or disaster. The *takful* fund invests the contributions in a *sharia*-compliant manner. Any surplus earned will be distributed to the participants.

With these *sharia*-compliant innovations the IB&F industry, in spite of few financial scandals such as the international investigation into the money laundering activities of the Bank of Credit and Commercial International (BCCI) which led to its collapse in 1991. Later, with better standards of accounting and supervision carried out by AAOIFI, the Accounting and Auditing Organization for Islamic Financial Institutions set up in Algiers in 1990, it has operated as an alternative and well integrated financial institution within and outside many of the Muslim countries in the 1980s and 1990s.

The Impact of 9/11

The Al-Qaeda sponsored terrorist attack on New York and Washington in 2001 and the decision by President George Bush (Jr) to declare a War on Terrorism spelt disaster to the life and security of all Muslim communities living in the West. However, the President's declaration of a 'financial war on terror' became an unexpected blessing to the growth of IB&F. "This morning", announced President Bush on September 24, 2001, "a major thrust of our war on terrorism began with a stroke of a pen. Today, we have launched a strike on the financial foundation of the global terror network" (quoted in Warde 2007, vii). Following the President's announcement, the United Nations Security Council passed Resolution 1373 on September 28 requesting all nations to keep their financial system clean and free of terrorist funds. The G7 countries, the World Bank, and the International Monetary Fund introduced stringent measures of financial control to satisfy to meet the UN stipulated conditions (Warde 2007, 74).

The US Government's clamp-down on the operation of all Muslim charities and its close surveillance over the activities of Islamic banks (Warde 2007, 74), and similar actions by the British and European authorities was a blow to the IB&F industry. It was in this hostile atmosphere that Sheikh Saleh Kamel, the founder of the Al-Baraka International Bank called the Muslim financial institutions and individuals to withdraw their money from the West and invest in Muslim countries and develop the IB&F industry in the region (Warde 2010, 86). Thus began a short exodus of Muslim investments from the West to Asia and the Middle East. According to Napoleoni, Muslim investors who held about $1,000 trillion in the US deserted the greenback and switched to safer destinations which ultimately hurt the US dollar (Napoleoni 2010, 76). The rapid rise of Malaysia as the chief centre of Islamic banking coincides with this exodus.

In spite of the 9/11 catastrophe and subsequent clamp down on Islamic charities and finances, the rising disenchantment against the spread of a global turbo-capitalist economy, "liberated from government regulation, unchecked by effective trade unions, unfettered by sentimental concerns over the fate of employees or communities, unrestrained by customs barriers or investment restrictions, and unmolested as little as possible by taxation" (Luttwak 1999, 27), had already produced several anti-globalisation protests starting in Seattle in November 1999. The common cry in all such protests was 'economic justice'. In the world of banking and finance it meant a call for limits on investing in risky assets and making greedy profits.

The financial meltdown triggered by the sub-prime mortgage crisis in the United States in 2008 was only the severest of more than one hundred economic and financial crises over the last four decades. Excessive and imprudent lending by banks, high leverage which enables such lending, greed and speculation, lack of managerial and accounting transparency, and weak regulatory mechanisms are some of the reasons that may have contributed to these crises. However, even before the 2008 crisis there had been calls for ethical investments and socially responsible behaviour of investors and corporations, from economists like Joseph Stiglitz and financial experts like George Soros who had become increasingly critical of market fundamentalism. Above all and surprisingly, in a joint report authored by Loretta Napoleoni and Claudia Segre, the Abaxbank Spa fixed income strategist, published in the official newspaper of the Vatican *L'Osservatore Romano*, on 5 March 2009, Islamic finance was cited as the solution to the global financial crisis. "The ethical principles on which Islamic financed (are) based", said the authors, "may bring banks closer to their clients and to the true spirit which should mark every financial service". "Western banks", they continued, "could use tools such as the Islamic bonds, known as sukuk, as collateral". Giovanni Maria Vian, the editor of the paper in an effort to include Christianity also in the picture added that "great religions have always had a common attention to the human dimension of the economy". This endorsement from the most powerful Christian authority is another testimony to the changed global attitude towards the IB&F industry.

The participation of non Muslim governments and institutions in the IB&F industry is the most interesting development after 2001. Their participation is noteworthy in the property market and *sukuk* issuance. In the property market for example, the Singapore listed Cambridge Industrial Trust has been transformed into an Islamic property trust. The National Australia Bank has also shown interest to invest US$35 million for a stake in the world's first listed *sharia*-compliant industrial property trust. It will be the first publicly listed *sharia*-compliant Real Estate Investment Trust in Singapore. In *sukuk* issuance, the World Bank for example issued its first local-currency dominated 760 million Malaysian Ringgits *sukuk* in 2005. In Germany the provincial government of Saxony Anhalt raised €100 million from both Middle East and European investors through *sukuk*. In Japan, the Financial Services Authority has proposed an amendment to the banking law to allow Japanese banks to offer Islamic products through a subsidiary (*Sukuk.me* 2011).

Intellectual Debate on IBF

Between the 1970s, when IBF was at its experimental stage, and the 1990s, when it received recognition as a separate and unique entity by the global financial industry, intellectual debate on Islamic economics in general and IB&F in particular had swung from theological generalities and euphoric support to simplistic secular reductionism and outright condemnation. While the supporters were mainly concerned with implementing the *sharia*-prohibition of *riba*, *gharar*, and *maysir*, and therefore redesigned and renamed some of the conventional financial products to circumvent the religious prohibition, the opponents criticised those products solely on the basis of legal trickery and economic inefficiency. El-Gamal, a prominent critic of IB&F underlines this dichotomy when he writes that, "the primary emphasis in Islamic finance is not on efficiency and fair pricing. Rather, the emphasis is on contract mechanics and certification of Islamicity by "Shari'a Supervisory Boards" (El-Gamal 2006, 1). The entire IB&F industry, to another Muslim thinker, is "a prolonged exercise in artful delusion" and an "oxymoron" (Allawi 2009, 214-15). Even Ibrahim Warde, an expert on international business and a supporter of IB&F, concedes the fact that the industry "rather than being a different financial system, based on partnership finance...ha(s) generally mirrored conventional finance and concentrated on short-term financial transactions" (Warde 2010, 247). However, in the same article he attributes this shortcoming to the relative immaturity and therefore the growth pains of the industry. In spite of its double digit growth from an average of 14 per cent a year between 1994 and 2002 to 26 per cent a year between 2003 and 2009 the industry "did not...quite live up to its original billing".

The argument that IB&F products are expensive and therefore economically inefficient should be balanced against the fact that it is qualitatively a better product, at least in the eyes of the beholders. To the Muslim faithful who want to be guided by the *shariah* the higher cost is the price for keeping their financial matters clean of *riba*, *maysir*, and *gharar*. Still, one has to confront the other criticism of El-Gamal about the actual Islamicity of the products. With at least four different major schools of jurisprudence in *sunni* Islam namely, Shafii, Hanafii, Maliki and Hanbali and with an altogether separate *shia* school there is a multiplicity of legal opinion on every single issue that affects a Muslim. In matters of economics and finance the Islamicity or otherwise of a certain product or service will ultimately depend on the verdict of the board of scholars or *sharia* boards who advice various governments and financial institutions. Experts on Islamic *sharia* equipped with equal expertise on banking and finance are in short supply. According to a 2008 report there are only 60 such scholars worldwide (Devi 2008). On top of that there is also a serious shortage of skilled personnel who could innovate and introduce new *sharia*-compliant products and make them marketable. Conflict of interest and pecuniary motives among the innovators, approvers, and suppliers of *sharia*-compliant products may threaten the credibility of the industry and will make it supply-driven rather than demand-driven. Even though organisations like the Islamic Financial Services Board (IFSB) and AAOIFI are striving towards creating *sharia*-convergent standards the hardline Wahhabi school in Saudi Arabia and its supporters in other parts of the world may present a problem for the sustainability of some of the *sharia*-compliant products.

Mutual Accommodation and Convergence

When IB&F emerged as a possible alternative to conventional banking and finance in the 1970s it was like David challenging the Goliath. Even after four decades of respectable growth amidst a tumultuous political and economic environment IB&F, as pointed out at the beginning, is tiny in size and in no way a threat to the conventional sector. However, after the 2008 sub-prime mortgage collapse in the United States which triggered a banking and financial crisis worldwide and producing the "Great Recession" (Kolb 2011, 143) there had been an immense pressure from governments, inter-governmental organisations and NGOs for the banking and finance industry to radically change its business behaviour by making it socially responsible, less risky and more transparent and accountable. A worldwide demand for an efficient regulatory mechanism to control the reckless behaviour of mega-banks and other financial institutions, especially in the United States and Europe, is bound to impose limits on risky operations. The need to control leverage, to restructure banking and financial assets by shifting from asset-based to asset-backed assets, and to improve institutional governance are measures promoted as part of the banking and financial reforms. Ironically these are the pillars on which IB&F claims to have built itself.

On the side of IB&F it has been observed that a number of its products that are marketed as *sharia*-compliant differ only in their Arabised names but not in substance. For example, in the case of *murabaha* contracts in mortgage financing "the result looked a lot like interest, and some argue that murabaha is simply the thinly veiled version of it.... The bank officials argue that God is in the details" (Useem 2002). Similarly El-Gamal finds not much difference between the *sukuk* and conventional bonds (El-Gamal 2007, 97). In fact he agrees with other observers that there is "tension between attempts to be essentially similar to conventional finance...and attempts to preserve a distinctive Islamic character..." (El Gamal 2007, 2). In this tension the bank officials and fanciers who design and market various *sharia*-compliant products and the *sharia*-boards that approve those products are indulging in an age-old practice of *hiyal* or legal trickery in order to circumvent the religious prohibition of *riba, maysir,* and *gharar*.

Thus, what one finds in the development of the two sectors of the industry is a progressive movement towards accommodating each other. While the conventional banking and finance sector undertakes to reform itself by incorporating some of the ethical values enshrined in the Islamic Banking and Finance sector the latter on its part, by borrowing the conventional products and adding an Islamic veneer to them, is virtually blurring the line of demarcation between the two. In the global village in which they both operate this cross fertilization is unavoidable.

Works Cited

Ahmad, Leila. 2011. A Quiet Revolution. New Haven and London: Yale University Press.

Allawi, Ali A. 2009. *The Crisis of Islamic Civilization.* New Haven and London: Yale University Press.

Ali, Ameer. 2009. "NAB may lose interest but keep the faith". *The Australian Financial Review*, 1 July.

Devi, Sharmila. 2008. "Scholars and harmony in short supply". *Financial Times*, 18 June.

El-Gamal, Mahmoud A. 2007. *Islamic Finance: Law, Economics, and Practice*. New York: Cambridge University Press.

Frontline Oct. 10-23, 2009.

Hasan, Maher and Dridi Jemma. 2010. "The Effects of the Global Crisis on Islamic and Conventional Banks: A Comparative Study". IMF Working Paper, WP/10/201, September.

Islamic Financial Services Board, *www.ifsb.org*

Jobst, Andreas A. 2007. "The Economics of Islamic Finance and Securitization". IMF Working Paper, WP/07/117, August.

Kettani, Hussein. 2010. "2010 World Muslim Population". Proceedings of the 8th Hawaii International Conference on Arts and Humanities, Honolulu, Hawaii, January.

Khan, Fahim M. and Porzio Mario, eds. 2010. *Islamic Banking and Finance in the European Union: A Challenge*. Cheltenham, UK: Northampton, MA; USA: Edward Elgar.

Kolb, Robert W. 2011. *The Financial Crisis of Our Time*. New York: Oxford University Press. KPMG. 2006. "Making the transition from niche to mainstream; Islamic banking and finance: a snapshot of the industry and its challenges today". www.us.kpmg.com/microsite/ FSLibraryDotCom/ docs/Islamic%20Banking%20and%20Finance.

Luttwak, Edward. 1999. *Turbo Capitalism*. London: Orion Business Books.

Napoleoni, Loretta. 2010. *Terrorism And The Economy*. New York: Seven Stories Press.

Saeed, Abdullah & Akbarzadeh Shahram, eds. 2001. *Muslim Communities in Australia, Sydney:* UNSW Press.

Sukuk.me. 2011. www.sukuk.me/news/articles/73/Global-sukuk-markets.html

Tawney, R.H. 1926. *Religion and the Rise of Capitalism*. London: John Murray.

The Banker, November 2007.

The Pew Forum. 2009. "Mapping the Global Muslim Population". The Pew Forum on Religion and Public Life, Pew Research Centre.

Useem, J. 2002. "Banking on Allah". *Fortune*. June 10.

Warde, Ibrahim. 2007. *The Price of Fear*. London; New York: I.B. Tauris.

———. 2010. *Islamic Finance in the Global Ecomnomy*. Edinburgh: Edinburgh University Press.

CHAPTER

3

Globalisation and Economic Development in South Asian Association for Regional Co-operation Countries: Evidence from SAARC

M.A.B. Siddique
The University of Western Australia, Australia

1. Introduction

With the advancement of globalisation, the SAARC economies have experienced some important changes since the formation of this regional cooperation body in 1985. Key SAARC economies such as Bangladesh, India, Pakistan and Sri Lanka (hereafter referred to as SAARC-4) have gradually become globalised economies through numerous economic pro-globalisation measures. The impact of globalisation has been more pronounced in the areas of trade, foreign direct investment and information and communication sectors than in any other sector in these economies. These changes make these economies an interesting study on globalisation. The primary objective of this study is to assess the progress of globalisation in selected SAARC economies namely, Bangladesh, India, Pakistan and Sri Lanka. The study is divided into five main sections. The next section defines the concept of globalisation, and is followed by an examination of the progress of globalisation in the countries under focus in the section 3. Section 4 briefly examines the economic progress made in SAARC-4 countries; the last section brings the discussion to a conclusion.

2. Globalisation: The Concept and Measurement

Concept of Globalisation

The exact definition of globalisation is the subject of much debate as it is perceived in different ways by different people. Globalisation in this paper is defined as a process by which countries and peoples are integrated more closely with one another through 'free' and increased movement of goods and services including labour, capital, finance, technology and knowledge. Identifying when globalisation 'began' is a difficult task. It depends on the timing of steps taken by a country to remove various barriers that are considered as major obstacles to free movement of goods, services and factors of production. Unfortunately, "there is little consensus about identifying dates when countries may be said to have 'globalised' or 'liberalised'" (Round and Whalley 2003, 4). Dollar and Kraay (2001) identify the timing of globalisation of a number of countries which embarked on globalisation after the 1980s with the following trade related measures:

(a) Growth in trade relative to GDP; and

(b) Decline in average tariff rates.

Measurement of Globalisation

A.T. Kearney, in its annual Globalisation Index, ranks 62 countries of the world according to their level of globalisation. They use four main dimensions to measure globalisation:

(1) Economic integration—a measure of the volume of trade and foreign direct investment.

(2) Technological connectivity—a measure of the number of internet users, internet hosts and secure servers.

(3) Personal contact—a measure of the extent of connectivity of individuals in a country to the rest of the world. It includes international telephone

traffic, and remittance and personal transfers (including worker remittances, compensation to employees and other person-to-person and non-governmental transfers).

(4) Political engagement—this looks at countries membership in international organisations, personnel and financial contribution to UN peacekeeping missions, international treaties ratified and governmental transfers.

Globalisation impacts an economy in a number of ways, such as increasing economic growth through trade reforms, increasing demand for skilled workers, attracting foreign direct investment and improving the capacity of a country to adopt modern technology in the knowledge based sectors such as ICT, banking and finance.

Theories of Globalisation

Theories of globalisation are generally characterised by the emphasis on the increasing integration of peoples and cultures, and political and economic structures. Reyes (2001) underpins his reasoning on the theory of globalisation with identifying two increasing trends, (a) the increasing importance of worldwide active communication systems and (b) the improving fluency of economic conditions, particularly the high mobility of financial resources and trade. From this Reyes suggests that increasing global communications has allowed all countries, rich and poor, to integrate themselves into a 'global village'. This has created a new environment to carry out economic transactions and trade.

Scholte (2000) argued in his theory that globalisation transpired as a result of four factors: (a) the spread of rationalism as a dominant knowledge framework; (b) the development of capitalism; (c) technological innovation in communication and data processing; and (d) the formation of an enabling regulatory framework. Expanding on this, in relation to the spread of rationalism as a dominant knowledge framework, Scholte likens the process of globalisation to the pursuit of the 'secularist holy grail' in that the thought process of rationalism "encourages a belief that people can gain comprehensive knowledge when they access the terrestrial world as a whole". The focus then has been on the physical world as a whole providing the mentality for spurring on the globalisation process. The second element, capitalism focuses on the pursuit of global markets by organisations to expand production to maximise their production; this is a key element of capitalist thought. This quest to expand production has resulted in the rise of global mobility of productive forces and processes. Together these act as another force behind globalisation. This complements basic economic theory with increasing production resulting in the attainment of economies of scale and lower costs (Krugman and Obstfeld 2006).

The third factor is relatively straightforward. As in Reyes' analysis, technological innovation in communication and data processing have increased the ease of conducting financial transactions and international trade and has improved global marketing and accounting activities. In addition, Scholte suggests technology has been important in creating 'transworld social places' which has contributed to this process. Fourthly, the formation of a consistent regulatory framework such as standardising various legal and institutional arrangements has, according to Scholte, streamlined and facilitated the process of globalisation.

Is Globalisation a New Phenomenon?

Globalisation, in its widest meaning, is not really a new phenomenon. Baldwin and Martin (1999) point out that the two most recent spurts or waves of globalisation occurred between 1870 and 1914, and 1960 to the present. The former wave of globalisation began when the world was fairly homogeneous, that is, homogeneously poor and agrarian while the latter began when the world was sharply divided between rich industrial nations and poor primary producers. Nevertheless, these two periods are characterised by rapid technological change focused mainly in transport and communication. Between 1870 and 1914, the new technologies included the steamship, refrigeration, the telegraph and the telephone, whereas the 1960 to the present globalisation wave has been characterised by mobile phones, the internet and increased air travel. O'Rourke and Williamson (1999) argue that the expansion of trade during the present wave was driven by falling transport costs rather than trade liberalisation.

In contrast, James (2002) concludes that the driving force for increased trade between 1960 to the present has been the reduction in communication costs. Nayyar (1998) more specifically contrasts the two waves by stating that the 1870-1914 wave was dominated by imperial nations while the 1960—present wave is dominated by Multinational Corporations (MNCs) and International Financial Institutions (IFIs) namely: the World Bank, the International Monetary Fund (IMF) and the World Trade Organization (WTO).

The present wave of globalisation has received the most divergent views. No other issue has been as hotly debated as globalisation and its effects on different economies. One reason for this could be the fact that it lacks one clear definition. In addition, technology changes have led to a widespread increase of information which can be manipulated to support one's argument for or against globalisation.

3. Globalising SAARC

Background of SAARC

The South Asian Association for Regional Cooperation (SAARC) was formed in 1985 with member countries consisting of Sri Lanka, Bhutan, India, Maldives, Nepal, Pakistan and Bangladesh. Afghanistan joined two decades later in 2005. SAARC's key objectives on formation included:

promotion of welfare and increase of the quality of life in South Asia; acceleration of economic growth; and to strengthening of cooperation with other developing countries.

The objective of increased economic growth is of particular interest. Globalisation is often a product of economic growth. The SAARC region has a wide range of resources, in the form of both natural and human resources. Landscapes differ widely across regions offering potentially a large variety in production, mineral resources such as coal, iron, and natural gas as well as being home to a variety of animals, herbs and timber. Unfortunately, prior to the formation of SAARC the individual countries did not maximise the potential wealth that could be gained from these resources, despite having a combined population of more than 1.5 billion (Chowdhury 2005). In what follows, we look at the progress of globalisation in SAARC-4 countries.

Globalisation Initiatives and Progress in Globalisation

Depending on the scope of the analysis, there are many indicators that can be used to measure globalisation, but the most difficult task is finding relevant data to measure progress under each of the indicators. The following qualitative and quantitative indicators are used here to measure the progress of globalisation in SAARC-4: policy reforms in the areas of (a) economic integration; (b) trade and foreign direct investment (FDI); (c) growth in trade relative to GDP; (d) growth in FDI relative to GDP; (e) progress in the information and communication technology (ICT) sector; and (f) globalisation index. Improvements in any, and preferably, in all of these indicators in a country are expected to lead to global integration.

Economic Integration

Some of the initiatives set by SAARC to increase economic integration included setting up a group on customs cooperation in 1996 with the aim to ensure consistency between customs rules and regulations, make it easier for intra-regional exports and improve infrastructure. SAARC has also identified the need to improve transit facilities in order to increase trade within and outside of SAARC region.

In addition, SAARC has undergone negotiations with the World Trade Organization (WTO), World Customs Organization (WCO) and the World Intellectual Property Organization (WIPO). It is the hope of SAARC that through regular consultations it would be able to protect collective interests by increasing their negotiation power in multilateral forums. SAARC stands together in issues such as anti-dumping, anti-subsidy investigations and environmental standards.

The South Asian Preferential Trading Agreement (SAPTA) was formed in 1995 and aims for higher intra-regional trade liberalisation and economic cooperation between member countries. The most prominent goal of SAPTA is to have a free trade area within the trading bloc with preferential treatment given to the Least Developed Countries, that is, Bangladesh, Maldives, Bhutan and Nepal. By removing all tariff and non-tariff barriers to trade in the trading bloc, the free movement of goods and services between SAARC member countries will be allowed. The third round of negotiations of SAPTA saw India offering 1917 tariff concessions, contributing to an overall of 3456 tariff lines that were put under concessional tariffs. During the fourth round, the number of concessions increased to 4952 products with countries also making substantial decreases in tariff rates for selected products. While the non-trade barriers of member countries declined during the 1980s and 1990s by more than 85 per cent, removal of tariff and non-tariff barriers on intra SAARC trade still has a long way to go (Chowdhury 2005).

SAPTA was followed by establishment of free trade agreement in South Asia formally known as the South Asian

Free Trade Area (SAFTA) which was signed in Islamabad, Pakistan, on January 06, 2004. The main objective of SAFTA is to increase the level of trade and economic cooperation among the member countries by reducing trade and investment barriers as well as to provide special preference to the Least Developed Countries (LDCs) among the SAARC nations namely, Bangladesh, Bhutan, Maldives and Nepal.

Trade

Since the 1970s, Bangladesh has undergone many changes in its policy regime, with a particular emphasis in creating export-promoting incentives. Main changes include; reduction in tariffs levels, duty-free access to imported inputs: financial assistance to firms undertaking non-traditional exports; tax rebates on export income; and elimination of dual exchange rates and currency convertibility. In addition, fiscal incentives were also put in place and included accelerated depreciation allowances and income tax rebates of at least 30 per cent on export earnings. Industries in the Export Processing Zones (EPZ) benefited from additional incentives. Examples include the exemption of income tax for the first ten years of operation and a three-year tax exemption on the wages of foreign workers. Import policy changes were also made, with a large emphasis on a reduction of import duties. Major reforms include the reduction in the quantitative restrictions of imports as well as a simplification of trade procedures. The capital goods industry experienced the largest decrease in protection, with the rate of protection decreasing from 73 per cent in 1989 to 17 per cent in 1995 (Hossain and Alauddin 2005).

In the 1950s the Indian economy was heavily state-directed and had an emphasis on import substitution industrialisation. India's trade policy was extremely protectionist with increases restrictions on imports by intermediaries, only certain goods were able to exported and imported to the public sector as well as government purchase preferences for domestic producers (Topalova and Khandelwal 2011). Import-substitution seemed to be working in favour of the Indian economy, with industrial growth, according to Dutt (2003), reaching an average of 7 per cent per year, before falling during the period 1962-1980 with economic growth averaging 3.3 per cent. Facing an increase fiscal deficit in addition to other macroeconomic imbalances, the International Monetary Fund (IMF) introduced a structural adjustment program.

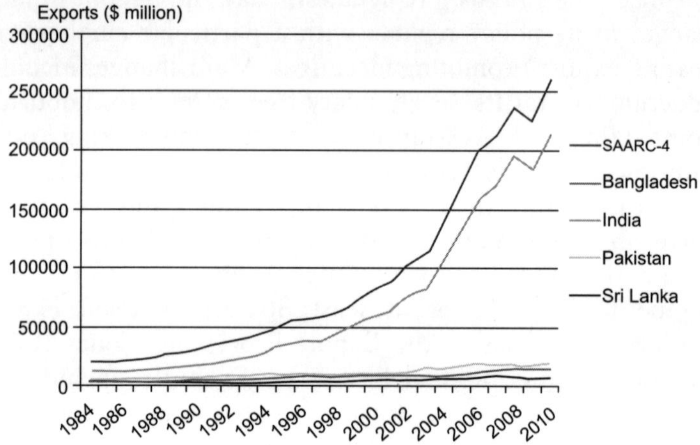

Fig. 3.1: Exports in US$ million (1984-2010)

Note: Data before 1984 for Sri Lanka is not available.

Source: World Data Bank (2012).

In July 1991, the Indian government announced the introduction of major trade reforms. Objectives as stated by Hasan, Mitra and Ramaswamy (2007) included the reduction and removal of licensing and other non-tariff barriers on intermediate and capital goods, the increase in export incentives (for example the removal of export restrictions), removal of state-owned export-trade monopolies as well as currency convertibility. The Eighth Five-Year Plan (1992-1997) resulted in a large change in India's trade policy by drastically reducing the control of imports and exports. According to Rakan and Sen (2002) the average tariff rate dropped from 128 per cent in 1991 to 34 per cent in 2000. In addition, the maximum tariff rate fell by 310 percentage points from 355 per cent in 1991.

The above reforms led to steady expansion in trade in SAARC-4 between 1984 and 2010 as demonstrated in Fig. 3.1 and 3.2.

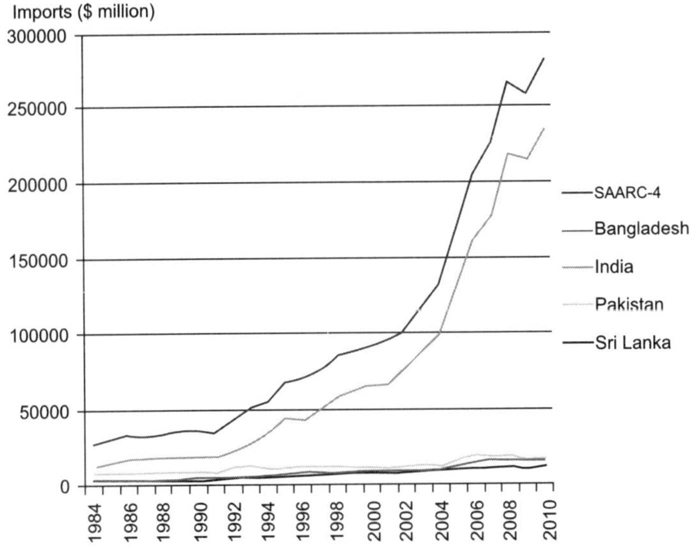

Fig. 3.2: Imports in US$ millions (1984-2010)

Note: Data before 1984 for Sri Lanka is not available.

Source: World Data Bank (2012).

Expansion of Exports

Figure 3.1 demonstrates that over the period, Bangladesh, Pakistan and Sri Lanka have experienced steady increases in their exports, with changes of 1039.75, 417.54 and 289.02 respectively. India has experienced the largest change in exports over the period, with a change of 1598.39 per cent. On average the SAARC-4 countries increased exports by 836.2 per cent. It is also observed that since 1999 Pakistan has experienced a growing export sector. This follows in conjunction with Pakistan's policy to gradually reduce tariffs since 1997. Between 1997 and 2001 the number of tariff bands decreased from 13 to 4. In the mid-1980s Bangladesh adopted trade policies that encouraged economic growth, contrasting to previous import-substitution policies. We can see this reflected in the data, with exports increasing by at least $3,806,569.35 (Constant 2000 US$) per year since 1985.

Expansion of Imports

Fig. 3.2 shows that similar to exports: Bangladesh, Pakistan and Sri Lanka have experienced steady increases in their imports with changes of 429, 113 and 268 per cent respectively. India experienced the largest increase, with a change of 1725 per cent. Imports in the SAARC-4 region increased by an average of 634 per cent. It also exhibits a huge increase in the quantity of imports that entered India in the period following 1991. In 1991, India underwent steps to ensure that its markets became more open. After 2004 there was a drastic increase in imports as a result in the reduction of the basic ceiling tariff rate from 25 per cent to 20 per cent (Fig. 3.2).

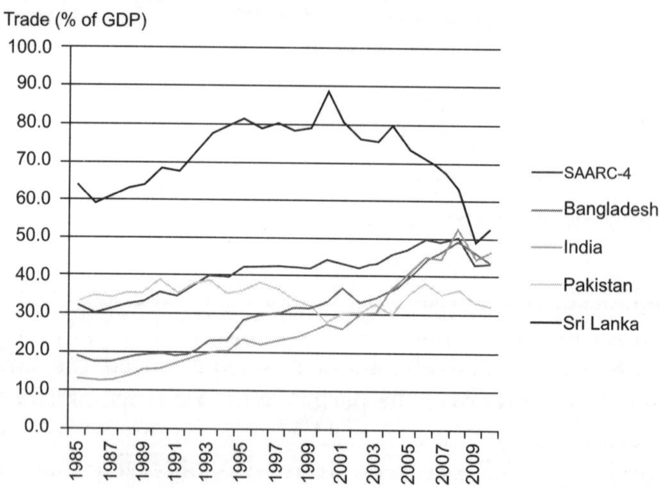

Fig. 3.3: Proportion of Trade in GDP (1985-2010)

Source: World Data Bank (2012).

Total Trade

Fig. 3.3 exhibits the trade (exports + imports) over GDP ratios in SAARC-4 during the period under consideration. It appears that Bangladesh and India have experienced an increase in the amount of trade as a percentage of GDP over the period, with a percentage point change of 24.6 and 33.33 respectively. Both Pakistan and Sri Lanka have experienced an overall decrease in the amount of trade as a proportion of GDP, with values falling by 0.9 and 11.5 percentage points respectively. On average, trade as a proportion of GDP has increased by 11.4 per cent for the SAARC-4 countries.

Foreign Direct Investment

India has come a long way with regards to its FDI policies. Currently India allows FDI in most of its sectors, excluding retail trading, atomic energy, lotteries and gambling and betting, and according to Sahoo (2006) equity limits range from 26 per cent to 100 per cent. As an incentive for future FDI, India has set up Special Economic Zones (SEZs). These SEZs are a place where foreign companies can take advantage of the lack of duties and tariffs. In addition, multi-national companies (MNCs) are able to take advantage of tax exemptions on any profit that arises from India. An issue that is becoming increasingly important for any MNC is how the receiving country protects intellectual property rights. While India does protect these rights to some extent, it is only to a limited extent.

In 1989, Pakistan introduced a new industrial policy package whose main aim was to attract FDI. Prior to 1997 FDI was limited to the manufacturing sector; it has, however, opened up now to other sectors, for example, services and agriculture. Pakistan has reduced or removed most of its tariff levels. Certain goods are currently exempt from tariffs, for example, imported raw materials used in the production of export goods. On the other hand, plants, machinery and equipment not manufactured locally have a 5 per cent customs duty charge. Pakistani labour laws contribute negatively to a company's decision to undertake FDI in that country. They are "overprotected and complicated" thus creating potential productivity loss.

There are two distinct periods during the evolution of FDI in Sri Lanka. The first was during 1948-1977 and was characterised by the public sector which controlled the country's resources. The second is the period following 1977 where economic reform encouraged a more outward looking export-oriented approach, including a more liberal view towards foreign direct investment. Unfortunately, in addition to Sri Lanka still having several sectors where FDI is not allowed, labour laws in Sri Lanka are prohibitive to foreign investment. The laws often favour the employee and restrict employers from dismissing employees except in the case of disciplinary transgressions.

Bangladesh has made considerable improvements with regards to encouraging FDI. Improvements since 1996 include the increasing number of sectors that have opened up to FDI, including telecommunications. The country has also provided many other incentives for foreign companies including tax incentives for power generation, import duty exemptions for export processing and exemption of import duties for export oriented industries. An increasing issue for companies globally, is the protection of intellectual property rights. How a country deals with these potential problems can determine whether a company undertakes FDI in that nation. Bangladesh understands this and is making continuous efforts to improve the protection of intellectual property rights.

The impact of the above reforms to attract FDI in SAARC-4 is illustrated in Fig. 3.4 which shows that there has been an upward trend in the ratio over FDI/GDP in SAARC-4 countries, with a deal of fluctuation. Altogether,

SAARC-4 has experienced a 410.7 per cent increase in the FDI received. Bangladesh, India, Pakistan and Sri Lanka experienced a 3329.0, 2932.0, 170.2 and 120.5 per cent increases in the amount of FDI received over the period (World Bank, World Data 2012).

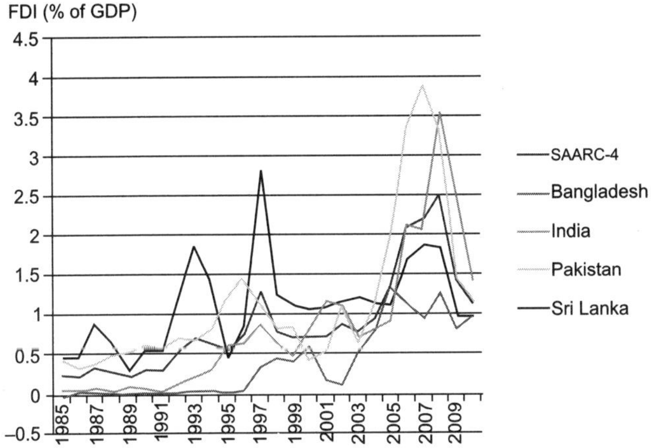

Fig. 3.4: Net Foreign Direct Investment as a Proportion of GDP (1985-2010)

Source: World Data Bank (2012)

Information Communication and Technology

The Information Communication and Technology (ICT) sector in India has undergone a drastic change and is responsible for the rapid expansion of service trade in India. According to Rajan and Sen (2002), the ICT sector accounted for almost 58 per cent of service exports and 16 per cent of total exports in 1998. The durability of the sector can be seen through India's performance during the crisis of 1998. India continued to increase its share of ICT goods and was only one of two countries to do this, the other being Indonesia, coming second to the Philippines in the highest share of ICT service exports.

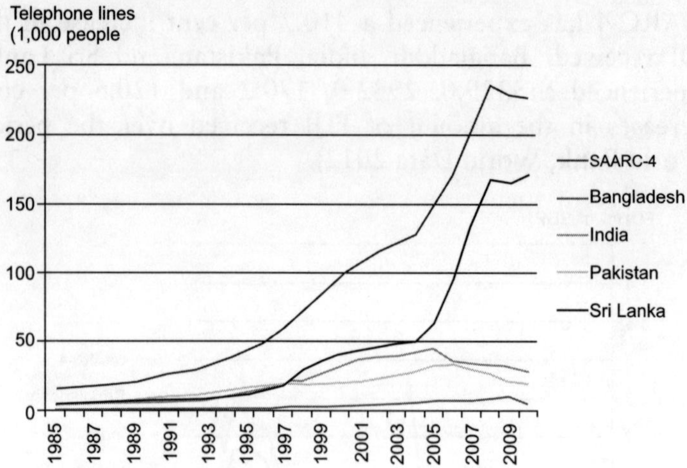

Fig. 3.5: Number of Telephones Lines per 1000 People (1985-2010)

Source: World Data Bank (2012)

As evident from Fig. 3.5, while Bangladesh, India and Pakistan have all experienced large increases in the number of telephone lines per 1000 people over the period (269.0, 624.0 and 313.0 per cent respectively), Sri Lanka has had exponential growth, with the number of telephone lines increasing by 3071 per cent. The SAARC-4 countries had an increase in 1324 per cent over the period.

There also has been a steady increase in the number of television sets in the 4 countries (Fig. 3.6). Bangladesh had the largest increase with a 2478.6 percentage rise. India also had a large change in the number of television sets with a 1500.0 per cent increase. Pakistan, Sri Lanka and SAARC-4 experienced an overall increase of 484.1, 329.6 and 618.9 per cent respectively.

Globalisation Index (GI)

We use the following globalisation index to measure progress of globalisation in South Asia:

$$GINDEX_{it} = \sum_{j=1}^{J} \omega_j \left(\sum_{m=1}^{M} \omega_m \left(\frac{X_{jmit} - X_{jmt}^{min}}{X_{jmt}^{max} - X_{jmt}^{min}} \right) \right)$$

Where i and t denote country and time periods respectively, m and j denote different component variables, ω_m and w_j are the weights attached to each contributing $\omega_m X$-variable within a component and the weights attached to each component respectively.

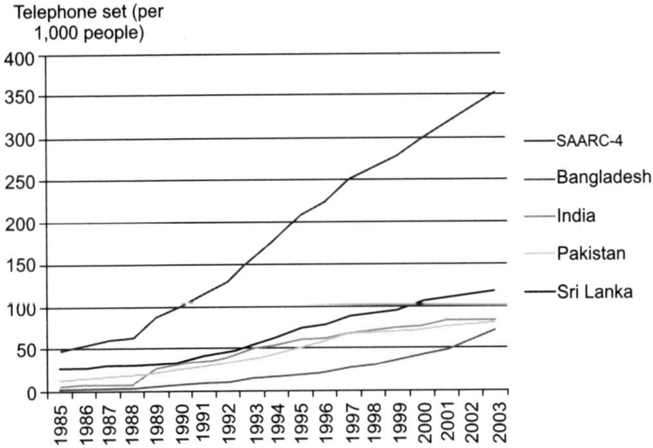

Fig. 3.6: Number of Television Sets per 1000 People (1985-2003)

Source: World Data Bank (2012).

The index looks at three components, Economic Integration, Technological Connectivity, and Personal Contact. The weights applied to Economic Integration, Technological Connectivity and Personal Contact is 1.00, 0.75 and 0.50 respectively. The variables, X, used in Economic Integration are trade and FDI net inflows as a percentage of GDP with weights 1.50 and 2.00 respectively. Personal Computers per 1000 people, Mobile phones per 1000 people, telephone mainlines per 1000 people and television sets per 1000 people are all variables for the Technological Connectivity and are given weights 1.50, 2.00, 0.50 and 1.00 respectively. If any data from one of the variables is missing at some point in time for at least one country, that variable is excluded from the analysis. These variables are aircraft departures, internet users, and personal computers per 1000 people and television sets per 1000 people.

It should be noted that commencement of the process of globalisation varies from country to country in SARC-4 region. It usually depends on the political decision of the government of the day to embrace globalisation by introducing and implementing necessary reforms in various sectors of the economy. Very often it faces strong opposition from various corners (such as trade unions, domestic industrial sector, etc.).

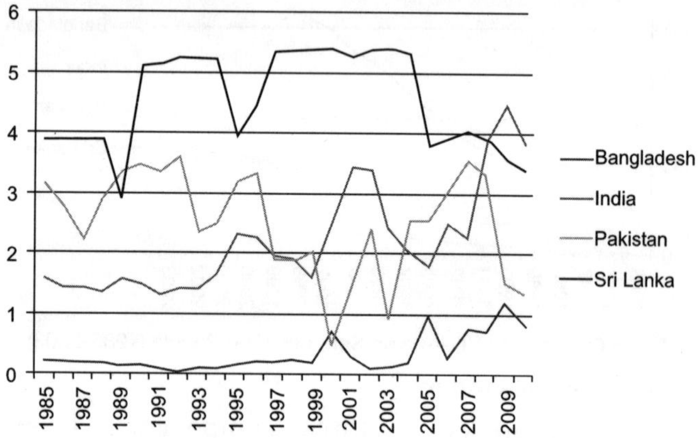

Fig. 3.7: Globalisation Index in Selected SAARC Countries: 1985-2009.

Source: Estimated relevant data collected from World Bank (2012), United Nations (2012) and the World Resources Institute (2012).

The process of globalisation for the four countries we are analysing, namely Bangladesh, India, Pakistan and Sri Lanka, started in the year 1990, 1991, late 1980's to early 1990's and 1977 respectively. Our analysis in this section is based on the starting dates of globalisation for the four countries. While Sri Lanka started the globalisation process before 1985, we decided that this year was appropriate to start the analysis as from this point we would expect to see a change in the globalisation index for all four countries.

Overall, all four countries experienced an upward trend in GI index during 1985-2009 although with wide fluctuations (Fig. 3.7). All four countries witnessed a downturn in the GI index in 2009. Possibly the global financial crisis is responsible for this. However, detailed analysis of the GI index for each country highlights some interesting features of the GI index for SAARC-4.

While there was an overall decreasing trend between 1985 and 2010 for globalisation in Sri Lanka, the country experienced a period, from 1990 to 2004, of increased globalisation. The sharp decrease in the index from 1988 to 1989 comes from the drop in Sri Lanka's FDI inflows as a percentage of GDP from 0.65 per cent to 0.28 per cent causing the Economic Integration variable to decrease in value. The drop in the globalisation index for Sri Lanka in 1994-95 was also due to fluctuations in the FDI inflows as a percentage of GDP, from 1.42 per cent in 1994 to 0.43 per cent in 1995 and increased again in 1996 maintaining a value of above 1 per cent from 1997 onwards. Trade as a percentage of GDP dropped substantially in 2005, from 79.48 per cent to 74.50 per cent in 2004 and 2005 respectively, causing a further drop in the globalisation index. Since 2005 it has been on a steady decreasing trend.

Pakistan has also experienced a decreasing trend in globalisation over the period 1985 to 2010, with large fluctuations in the index. A large decrease in the index is seen in 1996 to 2000 with substantial decreases seen over this 5-year period in all components. Over the period trade as a percentage of GDP decreased from 38.33 per cent to 28.12 per cent and FDI inflows as a percentage of GDP dropped 1.45 per cent to 0.42 per cent. From 2000 to 2007 Pakistan experienced an overall upward trend in its GI, despite a large drop in 2002-2003. The drop was a result of a large decrease in foreign direct inflows into Pakistan (from 1.14 per cent in 2002 to 0.64 per cent in 2003). After 2007 the upward trend of Pakistan's GI stopped and it experienced a steady decrease in the GI. The drop with the largest magnitude was between years 2008 and 2009, with

Pakistan undergoing huge decreases in the Economic Integration and Technological Connectivity variables. From the Economic Integration variable, the value of FDI as a percentage of GDP dropped from 3.32 per cent to 1.44 per cent. From the Technological Connectivity variable telephone lines per 1000 people experienced a decrease of 21.6 per cent. Over the period 1985-2010, Pakistan experienced an overall decreasing trend.

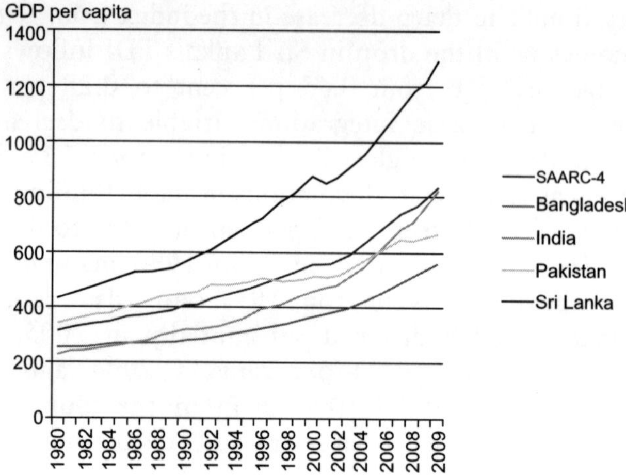

Fig. 3.8: GDP per capita (1980-2010)

Source: World Data Bank (2012).

As shown in Fig. 3.7, India has experienced an overall upward trend in its G.I. index, with most of its fluctuation coming from large spikes upwards. The first is in the year 2000-2001 with foreign direct investment as a proportion of GDP almost doubling from 0.78 per cent to 1.15 per cent. India's GI then underwent a sharp drop, so that it was only 0.18 points above original levels. This drop was largely contributed to by the decrease in the value of the Economic Integration variable. Between 2002 and 2005 foreign direct investment as a percentage of GDP decreased from 1.11 per cent to 0.91 per cent. The large increase in the GI between 2007 and 2009 was due to a large increase in the Technological Connectivity variable, despite a substantial drop in the value of the Economic Integration variable. This jump in the Technological Connectivity variable comes from the huge increase of 44.8 per cent in the number of mobile phone users per 1000 people over the period between 2007 between 2009.

From the Fig. 3.7 we can see that Bangladesh has had a significantly lower level of globalisation. Even in 2010, Bangladesh's level of globalisation is below all three other countries that are being analysed, but is only slightly lower than Pakistan. The sharp increase in the GI between 2000 and 2001 is due to a substantial increase in the amount of trade as a percentage of GDP, from 33.2 per cent to 36.9 per cent. In the subsequent year, the amount of trade decreased returns to close to original levels of 33.3 per cent, causing thc GI indcx to fall. In 2005, Bangladesh experienced a huge increase in the Economic Integration variable, causing the GI to increase substantially. This was a result of Bangladesh experiencing increases of 3.3 and 0.56 percentage points in the proportion of trade and foreign direct investment to GDP respectively. The gradual increase in the GI for Bangladesh from 2006 onwards can be attributed to the continuous rise in the value of the Economic Integration variable which results from trade as a proportion of GDP rising, reaching a peak of 49.1 per cent in 2008.

4. Globalisation and Economic Progress in SAARC-4

From Fig. 3.8 (below), we can observe that each member country has experienced tremendous growth in GDP per capital the three decades following 1981. Bangladesh, India, Pakistan and Sri Lanka have experienced a 119.90, 258.88, 96.96 and a 199.79 per cent increase in their GDP per capita respectively. SAARC-4 has increased its GDP per capita by an average 168.9 per cent.

We can also look at the increase in economic development of the member countries (Table 3.1). Mortality rates have dropped substantially for all, and literacy rates for those countries that had rates below 80 per cent experienced large increases. Sri Lanka had relatively high literacy rates in 1981-1990 which explains the small changes over the period.

Table 3.1. Mortality and Literacy Rates in SAARC-4

	1981-85	1986-90	1991-95	1996-2000	2001-2005	2006-2010	% change
Panel A: Mortality Rate**							
Bangladesh	120.4	104.50	88.3	69.7	54.2	42.2	-64.9
India	95.2	85.2	75.5	66.2	58.0	50.8	-46.6
Pakistan	108.4	99.6	92.1	82.8	76.7	71.8	-33.8
Sri Lanka	32.80	20.8	23.9	20.5	17.7	15.2	-53.7

Panel B: Literacy Rate***	1981-90	1991-2000	2001-10	% change
Bangladesh	29.2	35.3	51.7	76.9
India	40.8	48.2	61.9	51.8
Pakistan	25.7	42.7	53.2	106.7
Sri Lanka	86.8	0.0	90.7	4.5

Notes:

**. Number of infants per 1000 live births.

***. The percentage of literate people ages 15 and above. As the frequency at which the data becomes available varies for each of the countries, the values presented are the averages of the literacy rates that are published within the decade.

Source: World Bank (2011).

5. Conclusion

As stated earlier, one of the key objectives of establishing SAARC has been to enhance economic growth and development. Globalisation is often considered as an important vehicle to achieve this objective. While analysing the sources of growth in a country is a complex process and requires application of growth accounting process, what appears from the findings of this paper is that by looking at the progress of indicators of globalisation in SAARC-4, one can comfortably establish a strong link between globalisation and economic progress in SAARC-4 economies.

While each of the SAARC-4 countries has undergone economic growth, international trade has also increased, with all four countries experiencing an increase in both exports and imports over the period. Similarly foreign direct investment has also increased by a huge amount. Moreover, the information communication and technology (ICT) sector in these four countries has experienced significant changes. Establishments of SAFTA in 2004 and its enforcement in 2006 witnessed significant reductions in trade barriers. The Globalisation Index which is an important barometer to measure the progress of globalisation in a country is giving has also witnessed an upward trend in each of the four countries during the period under consideration with some fluctuations.

Works Cited

Baldwin, R. and P. Martin. 1999. "Two waves of globalisation: superficial similarities, fundamental differences". NBER Working Paper No. W6904.

Dollar, D. and Kraay, A. 2000. "Growth Is Good for the Poor", Development Research Group, *World Bank*, www.worldbank.org/research/growth/pdfiles/ growthgood forpoor.pdf, accessed on 29 July 2005.

Dutt, Pushan. 2003. "Labor Market Outcomes and Trade Reforms: The Case of India". In *The Impact of Trade on Labor: Issues, Perspectives, and Experiences from Developing Asia*, edited by Rana Hasan and Devashish Mitra. Amsterdam: Elsevier.

Hossain, A. and Alauddin, M. 2005. "Trade Liberalization in Bangladesh: The Process and Its Impact on Macro Variables Particularly Export Expansion". *The Journal of Developing Areas*, vol. 39 (1): 127-50

Kearney A.T. 2005. "Measuring Globalisation: The Global Top 20, Foreign Policy". www.atkearney.com/shared_res/ pdf/2005G-index.pdf. Accessed on 29 July 2005.

Kevin H. O'Rourke & Jeffrey G. Williamson, 1999. "The Heckscher-Ohlin Model Between 1400 and 2000: When It Explained Factor Price Convergence, When It Did Not, and Why". NBER Working Papers 7411.

Rajan, R.S. and Sen, R. 2002. "A Decade of Trade Reforms in India". *World Economics*, vol. 3(1).

Round, J. and J. Whalley. 2003. "Globalisation and Poverty: Implications of South Asian Experience for the Wider Debate". Available at: www.gapresearch. org/production/ JJoverview.pdf, Accessed on: 18/04/2004.

Sahoo, P. 2006. "Foreign Direct Investment in South Asia: Policy, trends impact and determinants". ADB Institute Discussion Papers, No. 56, http://hdl.handle.net/10419/ 53445

Topalova, P. and Khandelwal, A. 2011. "Trade Liberalization and Firm Productivity: The Case of India". *The Review of Economics and Statistics*, 93(3): 995-1009.

World Bank (2012). 'Data Indicators', *The World Bank*, Available at <http://data.worldbank.org/>. Accessed on 27 April 2012.

CHAPTER

4

Dr Jekyll and Mr Hyde: On Brotherhood and Flags— A Writer/Doctor's Reflections on "Vanishing Borders" in the Age of Globalism

Serge Liberman
Writer, Australia

Of globalism of other kinds—economic, political, corporate, cultural, religious, internet, ideological and so on—I will leave to other participants at this conference with more profound scholarly mastery of the theme to elaborate on. My intention is to present my personal reflections as a practising doctor and writer on how globalism appears to operate in medicine. It seems to me that while it mostly operates in the best of possible ways to secure the welfare of the needy worldwide, it is also beset by a paradox reflective of human behavioural traits. These are traits that, sadly have proven ineradicable ever since the stories of the sons of Adam and Eve, of the Biblical Abraham, and then of the twins of Isaac and Rebecca, were recorded in this world.

Those of you who are aficionados of Ludwig von Beethoven will surely know his choral setting to Friedrich Schiller's "Ode to Joy," of which the second group of four lines runs:

Freude, schöner Götterfunken
Tochter aus Elysium,
Wir betreten feuertrunken,
Himmlische, dein Heiligtum!
Deine Zauber binden wieder
Was die Mode streng geteilt;
Alle Menschen werden Brüder,
Wo dein sanfter Flügel weilt.

This eulogy to Joy, which the poet addresses as "you beautiful spark of divinity and daughter from Elysium", whose:

> ... magic reunites
> What custom strictly divided.
> All men become brothers,
> Wherever your gentle wing comes to rest.

"All men become brothers:" To a practising doctor like myself, all men (using the term as a generic one for all humanity) must be my brothers. Whoever is in need of my services, I must treat to the best of my abilities, whatever be his social or economic station, his origins, colour, race, religion, values, even criminality or sinfulness. And, as I sit in my clinic every working day tending to my patients, I cannot permit any borders or distinctions of any kind to affect either my judgement or counsel. That is my compact with every patient to whose welfare I am sworn in keeping with both the Hippocratic Oath after the Greek physician Hippocrates of the 5th century before the Common Era, and, less well-known, with the Oath of Moses Maimonides, a 12th century physician and most eminent of scholars in Jewish history.

Permit me here to extend the frame from the microcosmic—the individual doctor treating his patient in his globally miniscule clinic back home—to the macro scale and ask:

> What do diseases know about borders? What have they *ever* known about borders? Have not epidemics and pandemics frequently dogged humanity around the world? Among the first recorded was that which struck Athens from 430 to 427 BC while malaria, too, was already known around the same time in Rome.

Pandemics of plague made return visits between the years 541 and 747 of the Common Era and from 1346 to 1353, when it was known as the Black Death, which, arising in China, kept close to the Silk Road and passed through

India, Persia and Russia. It struck again in 1894, this time also beginning in China, and, through increasing public mobility around the world, appeared also in the Philippines, Hawaii and Japan, but, worst of all according my sources, ravaging India too, where, between 1896 and 1921, it was responsible for the deaths SPACE of some 10-12 million people.

In the 16th century, what came to be called the "French disease", syphilis, broke out among troops in northern Italy, reached as far as China, Africa and the recently-discovered land of America. Smallpox raged in 18th-century America and Europe and endured right through to the 20th century, in which century alone, it claimed some 300-500 million people—most of them children—world-wide. Then there have been measles, leprosy, influenza, yellow fever, poliomyelitis, tuberculosis, cholera and dysentery endemic in several regions of the world and, most recently, SARS or the Severe Acute Respiratory Syndrome of 2002 and the so-called 'swine flu' of 2009. The transmission of all of these have, over the centuries been propelled by the forces of globalisation: improved means of travel via steamers and sailing ships, ever more distant voyages of exploration, discoveries of land, colonisation and expanding trade, and increasing migration and settlement, particularly by Western travellers who introduced lethal and decimating diseases to the indigenous populations of newly-penetrated lands where these had not been known before.

In short, what may begin as local diseases can swiftly become global, there being no border guards able to halt their passage, nor obligation to carry passports or visas to enter countries anywhere and set about their ravenous damage. Nor should we forget malaria, of which, even today, there are still about 350 to 500 million cases reported annually, particularly in Africa, Asia and the Americas, although here the vectors are not people infecting each other, but the humble mosquito which carries the malaria parasite, a micro-organism endowed with the cunning to develop resistance against nearly all classes of anti-malarials currently known.

Among the newest and most deadly pandemics known to humankind worldwide has been AIDS, (acquired immune deficiency syndrome), caused by the human immunodeficiency virus or HIV, which, in the context of this paper, conveniently illustrates our subject of vanishing borders from two angles. Thought to have originated in Africa, AIDS was first recognised in the United States in 1981, particularly amongst homosexuals, intravenous drug users and haemophiliacs transfused with inadvertently contaminated blood.

Contributing to its rapid and vehement spread were such forces as the vastly increased volume of international travel, the large-scale transport of blood supplies to places of need, the re-use and sharing of contaminated syringes, and the availability of antibiotics against venereal diseases, while the use of contraceptive agents, by diminishing the risk of unwanted pregnancies, enhanced sexual freedom, facilitated casual sexual encounters and sidelined condom protection.

As a consequence, by 1997, sixteen years after its initial recognition, there were two million AIDS-related deaths worldwide each year. In the year 2000, 25 million were reported as infected with almost 3 million deaths. In 2003, there were an added 4.8 million new cases, their greatest number in sub-Saharan Africa, and in South Africa and Asia.

I must now deal with the second aspect of the particular phenomenon of vanishing borders to which I alluded earlier, namely that of the global mobilisation and convergence of medical personnel and measures set in motion to bring epidemics and their sequelae under control. Almost as soon as new epidemics become manifest, international relief agencies such as the World Health Organisation, the International Red Cross, the Save the Children teams, the

Medecins Sans Frontieres, World Vision, and so on are galvanised into action. Doctors, nurses, logistics experts, administrators and water and sanitation engineers converge where they are needed, while field hospitals are set up and food, equipment and medical supplies in bulk are delivered. And in laboratories worldwide, scientific research teams set to work on developing vaccines and medications to combat, contain and, where possible, eradicate the epidemics and reduce their mortality and morbidity.

To return briefly to AIDS, mercifully, effective medications have now become available against the condition, and as a consequence, some studies suggest that the mean survival time has risen from about 9 years to about 20 years in newly-diagnosed persons. Other success stories include smallpox, the last case recorded having been, I believe, an infection of a laboratory worker contaminated by a specimen held in storage there. There are hopes that polio may soon follow the way of smallpox: a vaccine is now available against cholera, although its effectiveness is still well short of ideal. In October 2011 the press reported the possible imminent advent of a vaccine against malaria. Communicable diseases are being progressively, if still slowly, ameliorated through international research, discoveries and new knowledge disseminated by means of medical publications, conferences and the electronic web.

I have now been a doctor for forty-four years and yet I find it mind boggling when I contemplate how far and fast medicine has, advanced in that time: in investigative and therapeutic radiological technology, surgical techniques, physiological understanding and pharmacological expansion. All of these enhance health and longevity unhampered by borders, and reflect as a non-negotiable principle, medicine's regard for the individual worth of individual worth, his well-being, dignity and his life above all as the most practical realisation of Friedrich Schiller's majestic celebration of the brotherhood of all humankind.

Yet, the theme of this Conference is that of vanishing borders in a global world, which, inherent in its very wording, juxtaposes two sides to the issue: the universal on the one hand and the delimited or bordered on the other.

Thus far, I have spoken of globalism in the context of medicine, both in terms of diseases and of the rapid mobilisation of aid from diverse agencies around the globe to contain them and counter their effects upon victims. It is also appropriate here to mention the natural catastrophes that plague our world, these too—droughts, famine, earthquakes, landslides, tidal waves and cyclones that ravage cities, towns and villages, care nought for national borders causing wholesale death, disease and displacement as refugee. Yet these too mobilise relief agencies and fine, caring, dedicated and ready doctors and nurses into expeditious action.

But: if only Schiller's words could be engraved in marble and honoured by universal observance. Alas, they are not; whereupon I must now depart a little from the strictly medical slant on this subject, my special area of expertise, and quote an excerpt from another song, a song that I first learned in Paris, where I lived for three years as a child of post- World War Two refugee parents and began my schooling. I do believe that you will recognise it:

Allons enfants de la Patrie,
Le jour de gloire est arrive !
Contre nous de la tyrannie,
L'étendard sanglant est levé, (bis)
Entendez-vous dans nos campagnes
Mugir ces féroces soldats?
Ils viennent jusque dans vos bras
Égorger vos fils, vos compagnes !
Aux armes, citoyens,
Formez vos bataillons,
Marchons, marchons !
Qu'un sang impur
Abreuve nos sillons !

Which translates as:

Arise, children of the Fatherland,
The day of glory has arrived!
Against us stands tyranny
The bloody banner is raised, (repeat)
Do you hear, in the countryside,
The roar of those ferocious soldiers?
They're coming right into our arms
To cut the throats of our sons and women!
To arms, citizens,
Form your battalions,
Let's march, let's march!
Let impure blood
Water our furrows!

Originally titled *Chant de guerre pour l'Armée du Rhin* (War Song for the Army of the Rhine), and subsequently re-titled as *La Marseillaise*, it was written and composed by Rouget de Lisle in 1792, adopted as the French national anthem in 1795 and endures as such to this day—a rousing war song if ever there was any.

La Patrie!—but one variant of *La Patria*, *Vaterland*, *Homeland* or *Motherland* of other nations—all of these terms are telling examples that nationalism, that loyalty to, and defence of, one's nation-state still beats strong in human hearts, the nation-state being an autonomous entity *de jure* distinguished from its neighbours by precisely established borders sacrosanct to that state.

Fairly benign examples of this kind of nationalism are the Olympic and Commonwealth Games, where teams march on the eve of the Games behind national flags, where medallists stand proudly on their victory podiums as their anthems are played in celebration of their victories around them, and where their respective national media are saturated with stories of these medallists and their exploits as if the rival contestants from rival countries barely existed.

This leads me to ask: in the realm of more serious international *realpolitik* within and between nations, do borders ever really vanish in our globalised world? Just contemplate the following:

> In the sixty-six years since the end of World War II in 1945, there have been some forty separate wars across the globe, years in which the major European powers, England, France, Belgium, Italy, Portugal and others, however begrudgingly, either granted their colonies independence or were forced, through rebellions by their subject peoples, to grant it to them, while in the 1990s alone, about 20 civil wars were taking place concurrently in every average year. What did such serial gaining of independence lead to if not *more* states, very real new sovereign states within clearly-defined borders, their number having since WWII risen from 51 nations represented at the first meeting of the General Assembly of the newly-formed United Nations on October 24th, 1945, to the present 193, all of them, large and small, being autonomous political and economic structures venerated by their citizens with pride, allegiance, flags, mottos, anthems and laws of their own?

One would have liked to believe that with such acquired sovereignty, each nation would have reached a state of harmony within itself and peace with its neighbours which would work to the advantage of each, enhance their regional wealth, resources and economic, scientific, political and cultural development and technological know-how.

But what have we seen instead? A rash of territorial disputes and civil wars. In the case of civil wars, there was an increase in the 1990s to about ten times the historical average in the 19th century and a tripling of the average duration of civil wars to over four year. There have been wars about borders: in a chronological order of sorts—the four Israel-Palestinian wars since 1947, the recurring Indo-

Pakistani wars also dating from that time, the 1950 Korean War, the Sino-Indian War of 1962, the 1959-1974 Vietnam War, the 1974 Turkish invasion of Cyprus, and the wars between the USSR and Afghanistan, Iran and Iraq, the Anglo-Portuguese War over the Falklands, the Gulf War, Balkan wars, the war between Russia and Chechnya, and the current one in Afghanistan which has been raging since 2001 (and who knows how and when that will end?).

Some of these have been compounded by the incursion of Western nations such as America, England and Australia, variously into, Korea, Vietnam, Saudi Arabia, Iraq and Afghanistan. Their motives have been variously again, to hold back Communism, ostensibly to destroy supposed weapons of mass destruction, introduce Western-type democracy into regions that have not the most basic conception of the notion. The consequences of these interventions have been more terrorist acts, longer wars, more destruction, more casualties, more deaths, more refugees, more international animosities, and, of course, more work for the Doctors Without Frontiers, International Red Cross, World Health Organisation, International Refugee Organisation and more need for reconstruction.

And here, from a doctor's perspective, lies a profoundly disconcerting, dismaying, even ugly and tragic paradox:

> Where, on the one hand, the doctor treats each man, woman and child one by one by one, because, to him, every human life is precious, unique, indispensable and unquestioningly meriting the best that he can offer, politicians, soldiers, military pilots and terrorists with one commanding word, one signature on an order, one grenade, one salvo of machine-gun fire, one bomb, one suicidal bombing or execution alongside an excavated pit in some nondescript field or forest, kills in the tens, the hundreds, the thousands, tens of thousands or more. Witness Hiroshima August 6, 1945 where a single atomic bomb caused the instant death of 80,000

Japanese. It hurts when the daily press, the radio newscast and television newsreel bring home how perverse humankind can be when in pursuit of ideological, sectarian or self-interested national, political or economic ends.

In this light, the notion of 'vanishing borders' is merely conceptual, metaphoric, and illusionary. If borders do vanish—truly vanish—the reasons are ages old: they do so either through conquest as the outcome of political disputes either fabricated or justified; by one nation's thrust for aggrandisement at the expense of another, and for whatever other web of selfish motives that historians have teased out throughout history's long, volatile and bloodied corpse-ridden course.

But even as we juxtapose the issue of borders with that of their vanishing, as I read it, we are talking about them in two widely different contexts, between which, however contrary they may be to one another, neither incompatibility, nor conflict nor confrontation need necessarily exist: the one being strictly political, geographic, territorial, discrete and sharply-defined into nation-states clearly marked in any up-to-date atlas of the world; the other being of a more porous kind across which, for good or for ill, traverse the so-called acts of God—epidemics and *tsunamis* among them—and swiftly mobilised medical, nursing, humanitarian emergency aid, and economic, ideological, philosophical, artistic and cultic vogues, in tandem with new technologies, discoveries and extended knowledge—the issue of transmissible human inventiveness around the globe leaving actual borders not one whit altered, let alone made to vanish in any discernible way.

So, here you have it—what I call the Dr Jekyll and Mr Hyde sides of humanity: the moral, duty-conscious, well-intentioned doctor and other unselfish and heroic humanitarian workers who emerge in numbers it seems in times of natural disasters in particular and on the other, his darker, callous and abominable *doppelganger* who maims, kills and destroys *his* brothers in their multitudes there being no indication that this will ever change. May time, the spread of wisdom and the growth of an awareness of a shared heightened humanity prove me wrong, but the record thus far and the realities of the present gives scant cause for faith. Mr Hyde pursues his destructive bent on a scale of ever greater in magnitude, more widely encompassing in range and more inventively efficient in execution; while more quietly, soberly and cordially, Dr Jekyll in his clinic tends to each successive patient in turn, from beyond whichever border he may hail—as would-be brother or sister of flesh, blood, mind and bone—knowing, as does Shakespeare's sorely-maligned Shylock:

> Hath not all humanity eyes? Hath not all people hands, organs, dimensions, senses, affections, passions? Is not every man fed with the same food, hurt with the same weapons, subject to the same diseases, heal'd by the same means, warmed and cooled by the same winter and summer as his fellow is? If any of us be pricked, do we not bleed? If any of us are tickled, do we not laugh? If we are poisoned, do we not all die?

Works Cited

de Lisle, Claude Joseph Rouget '*La Marsellaise*'. Wikipedia online, access through search heading, *La Marsellaise*.

Hays, J.N. 2005. "Epidemics and Pandemics: Their Impacts on Human History". Santa Barbara California: ABC-CLIO, Inc.

Schiller, Friedrich *The Ode to Joy*, 1785. Wikipedia online, access through Symphony No. 9 (Beethoven).

Shakespeare, William. 1937, *The Merchant of Venice*, from *The Complete Works of Shakespeare*. New York: Walter J. Black, Inc., Roslyn.

Stevenson, Robert Louis. 1972. "The Strange Case of Dr Jekyll and Mr Hyde" (1886), from *Dr Jekyll and Mr Hyde, The Merry Men and Other Tales*. London: Everyman's Library.

CHAPTER 5

Reconfiguring the Colonial Gaze: The Cross-Border Itineraries of Wilfred Burchett during the Vietnam War

Harish C. Mehta
McMaster University, Canada

In many of his thirty-five books, including nine on Vietnam, the Australian author-journalist Wilfred Burchett argued that Western imperialism was destroying by force the Vietnamese peoples' aspiration for self-determination. Yet many Westerners travelling to Vietnam were unconcerned about these national aspirations. The Australian government gave military and diplomatic support to the United States' war in Vietnam in order to halt Communist expansion in Southeast Asia during the Cold War, and demonstrate solidarity with the United States. Within Australia, opponents of the US and Australian military interventions in Vietnam were restricted to the Australian Communist Party, peace activists, and a comparatively small number of concerned citizens, while a vast majority supported their government's involvement in Vietnam. Between the two World Wars, many US missionaries, travel writers, and scholars described the Vietnamese as "primitive" and "lazy" (Bradley 2000, 13-14, and 47-48).

Many US and Australian officials viewed Burchett as a Communist sympathiser whose writings bordered on treason because he opposed US and Australian war policy in Vietnam. But what was Burchett really like? True, he sympathised with countries struggling against Western imperialism, but his writings were far from treasonous. He espoused values of peace, anti-colonialism, and non-intervention in the affairs of countries such as Vietnam—the very same values that most Australian workers, farmers, and peace activists of the 1960s believed in. Burchett evoked strong reactions in his readers, causing scholars and journalists to write books and articles about his controversial career. These books have provided the political and social context within which he operated, but they have not critically analysed his work in the framework of theories and discourses of hegemony, resistance, Orientalism, neocolonialism, and the idea of real and artificial place, space, and borders.

A critical reading of Burchett's works shows that this frequent traveller to Indochina reversed and reconfigured the colonial gaze. From Indochina Burchett gazed back at the West: he adopted a new identity as an anti-colonial writer who perceived Vietnam as an imagined community, free of imperial control. Scholarly understanding of Burchett must start by examining if it is possible to locate him as an Orientalist. Burchett was deeply disturbed by the savaging of Vietnam's geography by the colonial powers. He was appalled at the South Vietnamese policy of using epistemic violence to divide and destroy Vietnam's tribal communities. And when the United States and its client regime in South Vietnam corralled villagers into fortified Strategic Hamlets to keep them separate from the Communists, Burchett saw the strategic hamlets as "non-spaces". These spaces existed within artificial borders wherein US/South Vietnamese policymakers attempted to create a new non-Communist community. But the villagers who were forced to live within these artificial spaces rejected and destroyed the hamlets by force in their effort to turn them into "real" spaces, free from colonial and neo-colonial control. Throughout their long war of resistance against imperialism, the Vietnamese revolutionaries considered Burchett to be one of their own, a revolutionary brother and an ally whose powerful writings enabled their side of the story to be carried to Western readers.

Owing to his closeness with the revolutionaries, Burchett was able to travel across Indochinese borders at will: from Hanoi he made frequent visits to South Vietnam, Cambodia, and Laos. Travelling with Vietnamese guerrilla armies meant that he did not need to carry a passport in order to cross territorial borders. His inclusive globalist worldview and deep respect for human life made it easy for him to also cross ideological borders: a democrat at heart, he observed that Ho Chi Minh's efforts to create an independent country were sincere, and that Vietnamese society contained elements of participatory democracy. Above all, he witnessed the human face of Vietnamese Communists whom the Australian and US government were quick to denounce.

Fellow Australian news correspondents described this itinerant traveller as a "pocket handkerchief-sized" person (Vine 1945). Although he was diminutive in height, Burchett bulked large in the influence he commanded over readers and policymakers in the West and at home in Australia. Burchett challenged the "imperial" policies of the governments of Australia and the United States, and went on to become an unrelenting critic of their intervention in Vietnam. In turn these governments, and many Australians and US citizens who had bought into their governments' foreign policy line, responded by denouncing Burchett. Yet his detractors valued his opinions, his closeness to the leadership of the Democratic Republic of Vietnam (DRV, or North Vietnam) and the National Liberation Front of South Vietnam (NLF), and his vast knowledge of Indochinese politics and society. Not surprisingly, US officials such as Secretary of State Henry Kissinger sought meetings with Burchett in order to gain knowledge of Vietnam, but he and other US officials described him as a Communist "devil" that left a "bad taste in our mouths" (Kissinger Memorandum 1971).

How did a child born into a family of Australian farmers and labourers, who worked as a "cow cocky" (dairy farmer), carpenter, cane cutter, vacuum cleaner salesman, and one that lacked formal education, become one of Australia's most formidable foreign correspondents and prolific writer of books that challenged colonialism and 20th century US and Australian policy? (McCormack 2007, xv). Born in 1911, Wilfred Burchett educated himself, learned languages, and travelled widely. After his death in 1983, scholars and journalists wrote books about his journalistic career in which they explored why he would defy Australian foreign policy to support Communist parties in North Vietnam, the Soviet Union, China, and North Korea. Some, like the British author-journalist John Pilger, who tried to unravel the truth about Burchett, found him in Vietnam "pounding on that ancient typewriter, surrounded by screwed up balls of paper...festoons of washing and cans of beer cooling on equally ancient air conditioners" (Pilger 2007, xiv).

Keeping an Eye on "Burchette"

Burchett was not a Communist. He was not a member of the Communist Party of Australia, or of any Communist party. Yet he subscribed to an earthy "Australian bush socialism", not informed by formal ideology but driven by overwhelming desire to stand up against oppression (McCormack 2007, xvi). In David Bradbury's 1981 documentary film on Burchett's career, *Public Enemy Number One,* Burchett remarked: "I'm not a member of the communist party" (Bradbury 2004). Burchett has clarified in his autobiography that he had filled a membership form of the Communist Party of Australia and had come close to joining, but he had chosen not to because he was repelled by the "violent language" of Karl Marx and Friedrich Engels' *Communist Manifesto*, a free copy of which he was given by the party. "I returned it after futile struggle with the first chapter, explaining as best I could in a brief note my incompetence to comment. There was no follow up to my application!" (Burchett 1981, 47-48).

Yet, his critics did not believe him. Robert Manne, who has attempted to catalogue Burchett's connections with Communist parties in Australia, the Soviet Union, China, Korea, and Vietnam, does not provide evidence of Burchett's membership of any of these parties. The closest Manne comes to linking Burchett to the Communist Party of Australia is his remark that in 1950 Burchett "toured Australia for the Communist Party front organisations, the Australian Peace Council and Democratic Rights Council" (Manne 1989, 12). Touring Australia on behalf of the Communist Party was only indicative of Burchett's sympathy for global Communist revolutions and his desire to present to Australian audiences the progressive face of Asian communism: did not show that he was a member of the party. Yet, Burchett had much in common with both the New Left and the peace activism that was flourishing in the West in the 1960s. It was natural for him to oppose US interventions abroad. As a result, the Australian government maintained voluminous intelligence files on Burchett. US government archives also contain much evidence of how successive presidents since Dwight D. Eisenhower kept close tabs on his writings, and his contacts within the Communist world.

A telephone conversation between Kissinger and CBS White House correspondent Robert Pierpoint, on 23 December 1971, reveals much about how US officials viewed Burchett (Kissinger 1971):

> Pierpoint: ...I gather you confirm you met with Burchette [sic]. Is that on the record?
>
> Kissinger: Yes....
>
> ...
>
> P: Did you know of his background?
> K: Yes.

> P: That he is considered a traitor by the Australian govt?
> K: It's not morale abrobation [sic, moral approbation]. I will take information for peace from the devil.

In Australia, Burchett was accused—without evidence—of (1) being an agent of the Soviet intelligence agency, the KGB, China, North Korea, and North Vietnam; (2) making false allegations of US use of chemical weapons during the Korean War (1950-1953); and (3) interrogating and torturing Australian, British, and US prisoners of war in Korea. Burchett sued the government for defamation, and won. The Australian government had 'othered' Burchett. But Burchett had already seceded from Australian policy, which he openly denounced. In a Foucauldian sense the Australian authorities were behaving like earlier European states in creating normative as well as abnormal subjects—within the confines of the European space—in order to police both, and to distance the other in the form of a madman or a leper (Loomba 2005, 49). The Australian authorities constructed Burchett as a traitor. The construction was false. Burchett returned the favour by denouncing US-Australian policy in Vietnam as criminal and illegal. It is not surprising that Burchett's Communist itineraries have kept writers of scholarly and journalistic books occupied for several years. Australian scholars and journalists on the left wing have praised Burchett's journalism (Ben Kiernan, John Pilger, David Marr, Alex Carey, Gavan McCormack), and those on the political right wing have denounced him (Vince Gair, Jack Kane, Phillip Greville, Denis Warner, Rober Manne). After having studied both wings, Tom Heenan has detailed the insubstantial nature of the allegations against Burchett (Heenan 2006, 1-14).

Burchett deeply sympathised with the NLF, and he made clear as early as 1965 that the NLF was a powerful entity in its own right and could not be eliminated by bombing North Vietnam (Burchett 1965, 5-6). Burchett gave ample coverage to the DRV claim that captured US pilots were "common criminals", not prisoners of war because the United States had never declared war against the DRV. Burchett's interview with Pham Van Bach, the President of the Supreme Court of the DRV, was broadcast over world television networks. Burchett reported that North Vietnam considered itself the victim of "piratical" air attacks similar to those waged from the sea by the Barbary Corsairs and others like them (Burchett 1966, 47-49).

Like the British philosopher, peace activist Bertrand Russell, Burchett excused DRV/NLF revolutionary violence as necessary for the self-defence of a country under attack by an imperialist power. This lucid idea formed the foundation of his journalistic beliefs. Very rarely did he use political science theory in his writing; he did not need to because he had internalised theory. Moreover, none of the books and essays about his life analyse his work in the context of discourses of hegemony and resistance (Kiernan 1986, Meray 2008, Manne 2004). Yet, on at least one occasion Burchett cited political science theory, the "repression-resistance principle", arguing that Vietnam demonstrated that "repression generates resistance, resistance in turn generates more repression, and then comes more resistance at a higher level. There is a continuous upward spiral from police repression of political struggle to the highest stage with a foreign expeditionary force trying to protect a satellite government from people's war" (Burchett 1968, 112). Burchett traced "the complete cycle of the repression-resistance principle" from 1 August 1954 when police fired on a Saigon crowd demonstrating approval of the Geneva Agreements, to 8 March 1965 when the first detachment of US Marines landed in Danang. He considered a people's wars the "highest form of resistance", and the US expeditionary force as the "highest form of repression."

This theory enabled him to construct his anti-colonialism. It helped him to create formulations such as: "those described as guerrillas and 'Viet Cong' were simply people resorting to mankind's oldest privilege—the right to defend home and family", and that the Vietnamese were "forced to wage" a "people's war" because their alternatives were "to live as concentration camp slaves, die under the guillotine, or fight back" (Burchett 1963, 26). His anti-colonialism was also based on his firm belief in the resistance ideology of the North Vietnamese: that the regular Vietnam People's Army, regional troops, village guerrillas, and the people were united, and that "the people as a whole actively participated in the armed struggle. How otherwise could a few dozen men armed with flintlocks, cross-bows, and bamboo spears in mid-1940: develop into the force which defeated France's mighty expeditionary force and the cream of her generals 14 years later?" (Burchett 1963, 39).

The Orientalist, the Gazer

I situate Burchett as a peace activist belonging, in spirit, to the New Left; an outsider in Vietnam gazing in, becoming revolutionary, and casting his eye, now as a Communist Party insider, on his homeland, Australia. The outsider gazing at Vietnam becomes an insider, and the son of the Australian soil becomes an outsider in his country of birth. In the 1960s and 1970s, when Burchett travelled to Vietnam, the country was geographically brutalised by the colonial powers: North Vietnam had declared independence in 1945, and then waged war against France and the new colonial power, the United States, while South Vietnam remained under US occupation. The north, thus, was a postcolonial state fighting for its own survival and the survival of a unified Vietnam. The south was a neocolonial state with all the trappings of foreign intervention: a rightwing dictatorship in Saigon propped up by foreign financing, and maintained in power through massive electoral and fiscal corruption. Burchett aimed to convince readers to lend moral support to the Vietnamese revolutionaries who were struggling to defeat the US intervention. His description of life in both halves of Vietnam, and the harmful policies of French and US occupation forces are considered accurate and valuable resources for policymakers and scholars (Marr 1986, 214). Burchett's analysis and reportage has given scholars a deeper understanding of the symbiotic relationship between the NLF and the government of South Vietnam than any other Western author in those days (Marr 1986, 221). For instance, Burchett has revealed how ordinary South Vietnamese soldiers and officers made tacit arrangements with the NLF, which the South Vietnamese hid from their US allies because they feared US officials might fire or transfer them for talking to the enemy. One of these arrangements was the NLF policy not to destroy certain roads because both the NLF and the South Vietnamese regime depended on these roads.

Scholarly understanding of Burchett must start by examining if it is possible to locate him as an Orientalist. Here we have a white male, an outsider to the region he is writing about, a region whose specific location is explicated by the kind of narrative voice he adopts, the structure of arguments he builds, and the thematic motifs that pervade his work (Said 1991, 20-21). As Edward Said saw it, the Orientalist stood outside the Orient, both as an existential and moral fact. But while orthodox Orientalists of the 18th to 20th centuries usually exaggerated the threat of Orientals and even denounced them as lustful, lazy, and untrustworthy, Burchett transformed the dreaded Vietnamese Communist revolutionaries into a cast of warm, likeable characters, who were fighting an illegal, evil, and violent foreign occupation. So far so good, but the Orientalist garment comes loose as we confront the truism that if the Orient could represent itself, it would, but since it cannot, the representer does the job for the West.

As a representer, Burchett was, of course, doing a fine job of keeping secret service operatives in the United States and Australia working overtime just to keep tabs on his latest columns and books, and his whereabouts. Nor were his representations the only ones. The Vietnamese were actually representing themselves. But Western government officials dismissed their words as Communist propaganda that bore little resemblance to the reality of life under authoritarian rule. It was not so easy to dismiss the discourses of Burchett and the Vietnamese revolutionaries because they were being read and believed by people in many Western countries who were appalled at US brutality, and the corruption and state-sponsored violence rampant within the US client state of South Vietnam. Because the Orientalist gazer stands outside as an exterior entity, what the gazer produces is not truth but representation. Yet, Burchett swam against the tide of this idea because he had interiorised himself and embedded himself ideologically, culturally, and morally within the cause of the Vietnamese revolutionaries. He was not a casual intellectual dilettante that observed from the outside.

The widely used formulation of non-violent resistance obviously does not fit the resistance of Burchett, the DRV, and the NLF. These resistances must be distinguished from the variegated resistances Mahatma Gandhi and Martin Luther King were practising. Gandhi and King appealed to the conscience of the imperial powers. Burchett believed that the imperial powers had no conscience, and that their intervention in Vietnam was "illegal", "immoral", and impossible to restrain. Burchett lent his support to Ho Chi Minh's dual tactic to expel the imperial powers from his country—a combination of military force and diplomatic pressure through a worldwide diplomatic front sympathetic to his cause. "People's war" coexisted with Ho's "people's diplomacy" idea. Ho Chi Minh symbolised war and peace—the militant Subhas Chandra Bose and the pacifist Gandhi in the body of a single resistor.

In his long gaze, Burchett not only constructs knowledge of the Vietnamese Revolution, but also constructs himself—in a Foucauldian sense—as resistor, sympathiser, and fellow traveller. Burchett globalised the resistance struggle through his writings as a "peace correspondent", a title he used in order to deliberately distinguish himself from the vast numbers of embedded "war correspondents". But it is not possible to retrieve the peace correspondent without dragging in the war correspondent. Burchett was in effect a "people's war" correspondent. He truly belonged to the "other side". Yet, he never ceased being Australian, as seen in his lengthy struggle to get back his Australian passport that Canberra had denied him, and his emotional solidarity with Australian peace activists, workers, and farmers.

Faced with overwhelmingly violent colonial power, anti-colonial movements had to create new and powerful identities for colonised people, and the North Vietnamese used the idea of the nation in order to harness the energies of their indigenous anti-colonial struggle. Anti-colonial nationalism in Asia and Africa was not built on an imitation of the colonial power, but on highlighting its difference from Western ideals of freedom and human dignity. The difference lay in Ho Chi Minh's vision of a world free of colonialism, which was at odds with the idea of empire espoused by France and the United States.

In October 1945, Ho Chi Minh addressed the French population of Indochina "not as the president of the Democratic Republic of Vietnam, but as a sincere friend of the honest Frenchmen". Just as they loved France and cherished its independence, the Vietnamese loved their fatherland and wished it to be free. Ho said, "We neither dislike nor hate the French people", adding that he respected them for propagating their ideals of liberty, equality, and fraternity. Yet, he pointed out that the Vietnamese struggle was not directed against France or against honest Frenchmen, but 'against the cruel domination of French colonialism in Indochina'" (Ho Chi Minh 1961, 36-39).

When the United States began its intervention in Vietnam in 1961, Burchett argued that "US policy was to black out as far as possible what it is up to in South Vietnam" (Burchett 1963, 16). And again, Burchett wrote about the US State Department's "Blue Book"(released on 8 December 1961) "As a diplomatic document it must rank among the most primitive of its kind and it must be taken as a sign of the times that the State Department would lend its name to such a spurious effort" (Burchett 1963, 52). He argued that the United States was attempting to "justify open violation of the Geneva Agreement". Burchett argued that the "threat to peace", which the Blue Book claimed had existed, came not from the north but the US: "The real threat comes from 10,000 miles away—in Washington's Pentagon building" (Burchett 1963, 74). He argued that US "special warfare" was "nothing less than the military expression of American neo-colonialism, just as the Expeditionary Force was the military expression of classical colonialism". Burchett believed that "neo-colonialism tries to present a different face to old-style colonialism, ruling up to a certain point by remote control, through a Synghman Rhee, a Ngo Dinh Diem, or a Tsombe. But when that fails, the military machine moves in, 'invited' of course by a complaisant puppet." Under US, neo-colonialism "the Americans supply the arms and dollars, the planes and pilots", in fact everything short of US troops (Burchett 1965, 9).

Strategic Hamlets as "Non-Spaces"

The Diem regime and the US government created Strategic Hamlets, or fortified villages, in order to separate the people within the villages from the Vietnamese Communists, and to deny the Communists the ability to recruit villagers and use village resources. Strategic Hamlets were "non-spaces" such as airports, national highways, and supermarkets because they did not arouse "membership passions" like cultures did within their spaces (Gupta 2000, 22).

After witnessing the construction of such non-spaces on a massive scale, Burchett commented that US actions were aimed at "carving South Vietnam up into huge concentration camps, isolated from each other by 'white zones' in which every village and hut and every plot of food crops would be destroyed". And within these "prosperity zones", the euphemism coined for the major units of concentration, would be established "strategic hamlets", villages surrounded by high bamboo walls and penned within mine-filled moats (Burchett 1963, 19). Almost spontaneously, South Vietnamese peasants began destroying most of the Strategic Hamlets, and began constructing their own "fortified villages". Burchett visited several fortified villages that were linked together by tunnel systems, and had more than 500 firing positions. Burchett counted about "4800 such fortified villages in South Vietnam at that time, mostly in the Mekong Delta region, but they were being added every day in Central Vietnam" (Burchett 1965, 45). Burchett lived in ambiguous space. He often asked if he was in "liberated" or "controlled" territory, and if troops were around were "theirs" or "yours". On many occasions, he stayed in hamlets that were "liberated" while on the other side of a river was another hamlet belonging to the same village which was "enemy controlled" (Burchett 1965, 59).

When Australia began supporting the US war in Vietnam, Burchett was appalled. He argued that the Australian dockers' gesture to oppose the war would not be forgotten in South Vietnam

> How right were the Melbourne dockers who, in June 1962, refused to load barbed wire when they found it was bound for South Vietnam. 'Barbed wire! Concentration camp!' said the first docker who

noticed the destination. How correct his suspicions! (Burchett 1963, 27)

There are many examples of Burchett serving willingly as a voice of Hanoi. He accepted Ho Chi Minh's explanation of the role of North Vietnam in the southern revolution: that it was up to the people of the south to decide whether to have a neutral regime, or any other sort of regime. Ho told Burchett that the "historical, geographic, economic, cultural, social, and national" reality is that Vietnam "is a united country which definitely no force can partition" (Burchett 1963, 110). Burchett professed a "special sympathy for the South Vietnamese people in their heroic struggle" in the face of a "new type of warfare in South Vietnam, so-called 'special warfare'" in which US troops were not involved and the fighting was done by the "US puppet South Vietnamese forces" (Burchett 1965, 7). Burchett also acted more like a Vietnamese revolutionary than a journalist when he met US military personnel captured by the DRV/NLF. He has been criticised for his interviews with captured US pilots because he questioned their participation in the war. He asked Lawrence Guarino, a 44-year-old US military major, how he felt about participating in "this sort of action" when there was no state of war between the United States and North Vietnam. Guarino replied that he hoped US military and leaders were doing the right thing (Burchett 1966, 35). Burchett gave worldwide coverage to Hanoi's views that "captured U.S. pilots would be tried as criminals" because there was no state of war between the two parties, and Hanoi considered itself the "victim of piratical air attacks, similar to those waged from the sea by the Barbary Corsairs and others of their ilk in the days of organized piracy" (Burchett 1966, 49).

While Western journalists reported the sensational bombardment of Diem's palace by South Vietnamese Air Force pilot Nguyen Van Cu, Burchett went much further: he celebrated the rebellious airman. The pilot had bombed Diem's palace from his Skyraider aircraft on 27 February 1962 in order to show his dissent from Diem's repressive policies. Burchett wrote that the pilot was "brave as a lion", and had hit his target but missed Diem, who had taken shelter in his personal air raid shelter (Burchett 1963, 79). The pilot, who had fled in his plane to the Cambodian capital of Phnom Penh, told Burchett: "I am not a Communist at all. But I am an ardent nationalist" (Burchett 1963, 113). By espousing the very same positions and policies held by the DRV/NLF, Burchett had crossed both physical and ideological borders to become himself a revolutionary.

Tran Thi Nham and the Tortured Geo-Body of the Nation

Burchett creates a powerful postcolonial narrative on the mutilated body of a young South Vietnamese woman who was tortured repeatedly and jailed by Diem's police on suspicion of being a Communist agent. Tran Thi Nham, who Burchett described as a "perfect, flawless beauty", whose right shoulder was covered in "small cauliflower-like eruptions where the flesh had been torn out with red-hot pincers" (Burchett 1963, 33). Diem's mobile police had arrested and tortured her in 1955. When they dumped her body outside for prison workers to bury. As they were about to bury her, they found her heart beating and smuggled her out to some local villagers who nursed her back to health. To Burchett, the mutilated body of Tran Thi Nham symbolised the tormented body of the nation of Vietnam.

The independent Vietnamese nation was formed literally by the demarcation of its body, that is, the territoriality of a nation (Winichakul 1996, 67-92). For the Vietnamese, territory was the most solid foundation of their nation. It was an expression of their collective self, and was the geo-body of their imagined nation, an entity which is both a political and cultural construction. So, when Tran Thi Nam dies on the geo-body of the nation, her weeping body sores and still bleeding wounds remind Burchett that this is a nation worth dying for. Her near-dead body serves as a living archive—of the body as a text—which provides evidence of a nation being tortured by the Diem regime and its US backers (Ramaswamy 2010, 284).

Burchett emerges in his writing as an early proponent of eco-criticism, lamenting the unconscionable harm done to the geo-body of the nation by US chemical weapons. In conversation with Burchett, Cambodian Prince Norodom Sihanouk denounced the US use of chemicals to destroy forests: "they even make war against the trees now" (Burchett 1963, 60). Burchett used Sihanouk's words as a chapter title: "War Against Trees". Burchett wrote that US planes were spraying chemicals onto trees and food crops with the "deliberate intent of starving the peasantry into entering the 'prosperity zones' and 'strategic villages'". The South Vietnamese people had become guinea pigs for testing new weapons for their local wars. Burchett's explication of Sihanouk's formulation of the "war on trees" suggests that the US military was not just defoliating the physical environment, but was also misleading the South Vietnamese people with the false promise of democracy and prosperity in a neocolonial space where dictatorship and poverty existed under US supervision.

Exposing Epistemic Violence by the Southern Regime

Colonial violence included attacks on the culture, ideas, and value systems of the colonised people. Burchett was distressed that Diem made a desperate effort to "tame" the ethnic minorities of the Central Highlands, such as the Rhade, Jarai, Bhanar, and Van Kieu. In Dac Lac province, Diem agents spread the word among the Thuot clan that the Rak Clay clan was preparing to attack them and wipe them out. The same rumour was spread among the Rak Clay. Diem agents offered modern weapons to both clans, leading to a major battle in which many clansmen were killed on both sides before Rhade leaders found out what was happening and stopped the fighting. The Chams also suffered under Diem because they were Muslim, and Diem was Catholic.

Burchett "created" characters in his news reports, and gave them voice. "The parallel with the American Indians", he wrote, is "too painfully obvious". The Diemists had "started the old-type extermination...tribal lands gone, hunting finished, customs trampled on, their way of life turned upside down, they would die out anyway!" But the tribespeople were not resigned to their fate. One of them described what was left of their lives as "ash". But "underneath the ash are glowing coals. We await the day when the wind will come and blow away the ash and fan the coals into life" (Burchett 1965, 160-61).

The US/Diem policy of "divide and rule" was powerfully answered by the NLF's "unite and resist" programme. Divide and rule policy was based on fomenting hatred between the Vietnamese and the tribespeople by setting up "agricultural colonies" of conscripted Vietnamese workers on the richest of the tribal lands, "bulldozing out of existence the forests on which the existence of the tribes people depended, carving out coffee and rubber plantations, and condemning the tribes people to living death in concentration camp villages in the plains which were intolerably stifling and humid for them" (Burchett 1968, 124-30).

Notwithstanding his many critics on the right wing, many Vietnam scholars and veteran Indochina correspondents have celebrated Burchett's work on Vietnam as being the best in classic war correspondent tradition, for being where the action is, and interviewing people in the line of fire, or close to it. He also freely crossed the border into South Vietnam, Laos and Cambodia to attend press conferences and talk to the leaders of the other side. It would be unfair to criticise him for his non-academic language because he was not trying to write for that kind of an audience. The true value of the Burchett archive is that is provides scholars and others with a rich primary source. His Australian childhood and affinity for workers and the poor led him to sympathise with the plight of the North Vietnamese and the NLF, and to oppose US policy. He developed an early hatred for "bullies, landlords and moneylenders", and despised US Secretary of State John Foster Dulles's performance at the Geneva Conference. He wrote that Dulles's "very appearance, bullying, cynical, crafty and predatory, fits him for his role of chief representative of a class and system condemned by humanity on the march to die, a system and class already moribund and putrefying" (Burchett 1956, 56-57).

In his wholehearted support for the oppressed Vietnamese his reporting sometimes appeared to lack objectivity. But that was because he did not want to write anything that might cause the Vietnamese revolutionaries' morale to weaken. Given his heartfelt sympathy for the Vietnamese Revolution, it is not surprising that Burchett is revered in present-day Vietnam as much more than a close friend, or a wartime ally. In 2011, a photo exhibition of Burchett's wartime photographs was held at the Ho Chi Minh Museum in Hanoi to mark Burchett's 100th birthday. The Vietnamese see him as a part of their diplomatic front, and a true Australian friend.

The Burchett story could be regarded as one in which borders truly collapsed under the pressure of humanitarian sympathy and political idealism; a white male European identified completely with the struggles of a non-European nation against the massed power of the Imperialist world.

Works Cited

Bradley, Mark. 2000. *Imagining Vietnam and America: The Making of Postcolonial Vietnam*, 1919-1950. Chapel Hill: University of North Carolina Press.

———. 2000. "Slouching toward Bethlehem: Culture, Diplomacy, and the Origins of the Cold War in Vietnam." In *Cold War Constructions: The Political Culture of the United States Imperialism, 1945-1966*. Ed. Christian G. Appy. Amherst: University of Massachusetts Press.

Bradbury, David. Interview with Wilfred Burchett. Broadcast on February 23, 2004 on Australian Broadcasting Corporation. www.abc.net.au/gnt/history/Transcripts/s1051042.htm

Burchett, George, and Nick Shimmin, eds. 2005. *Memoirs of a Rebel Journalist: The Autobiography of Wilfred Burchett*. Sydney: University of New South Wales Press.

———. 2007. *Rebel Journalism: The Writings of Wilfred Burchett*. Cambridge: Cambridge University Press.

Burchett, Wilfred, G. 1956. *North of the Seventeenth Parallel*. New Delhi: People's Publishing House.

———. 1963. "Operation Sunrise." *The Furtive War: The United States in Vietnam and Laos*. New York: International Publishers.

———. 1965. *Vietnam: Inside Story of the Guerilla War*. New York: International Publishers.

———. 1966. *Vietnam North*. London: Lawrence and Wishart.

———. 1968. *Vietnam Will Win*. New York: Guardian.

———. 1977. *Grasshoppers and Elephants: Why Viet Nam Fell*. New York: Urizen Books.

———. 1981. *At the Barricades*. London: Quartet.

Edwards, Peter. 2003. "Australia's Involvement in the Vietnam War." In *America, the Vietnam War and the World: Comparative and International Perspectives*. Ed. Andreas W. Daum, et al. Cambridge: Cambridge University Press.

Grey, Jeffrey. 2002. "Protest and Dissent: Anti-Vietnam War Activism in Australia." In *Australia's Vietnam War*. College Station, TX: Texas A&M University Press.

Gupta, Dipankar. 2000. *Culture, Space and the Nation-state: From Sentiment to Structure*. New Delhi: Sage.

Heenan, Tom. 2006. *From Traveller to Traitor: The Life of Wilfred Burchett.* Melbourne: Melbourne University Publishing.

Ho Chi Minh. 1961. "Address to the Frenchmen in Indochina." *Selected Works*, Vol. 3. Hanoi: Foreign Languages Publishing House.

Kiernan, Ben, ed. 1986. *Burchett Reporting the Other Side of the World*, 1939-1983. London: Quartet.

Kissinger. Memorandum of Telephone Conversation. December 23, 1971. Collection: Kissinger Telephone Conversations. Item Number: KA07202. Digital National Security Archive.

Loomba, Ania. 2005. *Colonialism/Postcolonialism: The New Critical Idiom*. London: Routledge.

Manne, Robert. 1989. *Agent of Influence: The Life and Times of Wilfred Burchett*. Toronto: The Mackenzie Institute for the Study of Terrorism, Revolution and Propaganda.

———. 2004. *Left Right Left: Political Essays, 1977-2005*. Melbourne: Black Inc.

Marr, David G. 1986. "Burchett on Vietnam." In *Burchett Reporting the Other Side of the World, 1939-1983*. Ed. Ben Kiernan. London: Quartet.

McCormack, Gavan. 2007. Foreword. In *Rebel Journalism: The Writings of Wilfred Burchett*. Ed. George Burchett and Nick Shimmin. Cambridge: Cambridge University Press.

Meray, Tibor. 2008. *On Burchett*. Victoria: Callistemon.

Pilger, John. 2007. "Foreword." In *Rebel Journalism: The Writings of Wilfred Burchett*. Ed. George Burchett and Nick Shimmin. Cambridge: Cambridge University Press.

Ramaswamy, Sumathi. 2010. *The Goddess and the Nation: Mapping Mother India*. Durham: Duke University Press.

Said, Edward W. 1991. *Orientalism: Western Conceptions of the Orient*. London: Penguin.

Vine Jim. 1945. *Courier Mail,* Brisbane. September 11, 1945.

Williams, Raymond. 1989. *Resources of Hope*. London: Verso.

Winichakul, Thongchai. 1996. "Maps and the formation of the geo-body of Siam." In *Asian Forms of the Nation*. Ed. Stein Tonnesson and Hans Antlov. Surrey: Curzon.

CHAPTER 6

The Local, the Global and the English Department

Mohan Ramanan
University of Hyderabad, India

We are living in precarious times and there is little doubt that institutions are being interrogated and nothing can be taken for granted. This is poignantly the case with the Departments of English in universities, and in our globalized times their relevance is being called into question in a variety of ways. First in erstwhile colonies like India, the very existence of the English Department is an often raised question and English is seen in rivalry with the *Bhashas* (languages) of India. Why should we be reading English literature or literature in English when we have a rich *Bhasha* literature in Telugu, Tamil, Hindi, Urdu and so on? This is a contemporary variation of the debate between the Anglicists and Vernacularists during the 1830s when Lord Macaulay's Minute settled the question in favour of English. For those Indians who consider themselves 'upper class' and 'upper caste', Macaulay is some kind of a demon and is chiefly responsible for what some perceive as a "willed amnesia" , to use G.N. Devy's term (1992) about our rich cultural past. English is seen as an obstacle to authenticity.

Ask Dalit activists today, however, and you will be told that Macaulay is a hero and that English is very much an issue of survival and even self-respect for them. Thus the question of English is very much open and requires the kind of debate that Ngugi and his colleagues subjected it to in Kenya. Further, we in English Departments in India are very vulnerable, in these globalized times, to suggestions that we are not doing the kind of work expected of us. What on earth is the use of Shakespeare or Dickens when the big IT workforce and the Corporates are waiting for us to genuflect in their direction and take up the cause of accent neutralization, soft skills, communication and report writing! In this, some of us have found salvation and we have been prepared to make those fast bucks at the cost of our dedication to literature. But many of us have not 'copped out' and we are still as dedicated as ever.

What is our relevance in an age when the internet has taken over, when Kindle, I-Pad and other gadgets rule the roost and when our children are immersed in Facebook, Twitter, and the SMS? The English Department, at least the one in which I serve, has found a way to come to terms with this sort of thing by making it the object of study. This is a dimension of Cultural Studies which cares little for the distinction between literary and non literary because such a distinction is anathema in the first place. So the Department of English is quite resilient and does reinvent itself in keeping with the exigencies of our times. My essay is an attempt, conservative rearguard if you like, to ask some fundamental questions and to suggest a reinvention of ourselves without sacrificing the core of what we used to do as literary scholars and attempts to suggest that in a slippery global context, we perhaps should stand our ground, be rooted in our local realities and still gesture towards a globalism divested of some of the pejorative ideas which are associated with the term.

Antonio Gramsci in his *Prison Notebooks* (1971) poignantly remarks that all criticism has to be based on personal location in a cultural and ideological context. Only then would it have legitimacy. Taking a cue from him let me describe myself as an upper caste, upper class anti-colonial teacher of English. I cannot help this background and will not make an apology for the circumstances of my birth and upbringing. It was in a middle class Tamil Brahmin family. We were diasporic and lived in a somewhat hostile Bengali

Para (locality) in Kolkata where my father was employee in a multinational Company. I learnt enough Bengali to bandy words with my Bengali tormentors who could not stomach our Otherness though they drank cups and cups of the *Tetul pani* (Sambar) which they made fun of. I learnt enough Hindi to be able to communicate with my friends in different parts of India where the literate classes by and large understand Hindi but I was sufficiently South Indian and Tamil to resent Hindi domination. It is quite remarkable how North Indians easily slip into Hindi as though it is their birth right to do so and as though it is incumbent on us *Madrasis,* as they call us, to know and speak that language. Due to the circumstances of my birth I am afraid I have not quite acquired literacy in Tamil but I do have a sense of the language because I speak it at home or at least a version of it because we are *Palghat* people and the Tamils of the mainland make fun of our Tamil which is heavily tinged with Malayalam accents. I speak Maltam and am familiar with Malayalam and in any case Kerala is a second home to me because the great temples of our culture like Sabarimala and Guruvayur are situated in that blessed State. Since I have accidentally strayed into English literature and studied English in wonderful institutions, I believe I have a competence in it.

I have, perhaps immodestly, revealed personal details; but they have a point. My life has ensured that I can be comfortable in any part of my great country because I can communicate in different languages. At the same time I am also quite committed to my Tamil ways. This is deeply implicated with English education. The Tamil diaspora in Kolkata was a class apart. It had its identity and it differentiated itself from the Bengalis partly because of its fluency in English. My father's experience with the American Consulate where he was Senior Economic Analyst and with other multinational institutions, and his own brilliance as a student of English for which he won awards, and my grandfather's reputation in Coimbatore, Calicut,

Bangalore and Rangoon as a teacher of English, I suppose, ingrained in me almost from the womb, so to speak, a love of English. This was only strengthened by the innumerable English movies, including musicals, which I saw over the years. I learnt to admire British English and even today I will never spell 'labour' or 'favour' without the u. Along with this has also emerged a healthy distrust of America and American adventurism. Somehow British Imperialism seems a lesser evil than American intervention in Vietnam, Korea, Iraq and Afghanistan. The Indian encounter with Britain is responsible for the English Departments of our colleges and universities.

When I accepted a place in Loyola College, Chennai, in the English Department, I did not know then that I would be specializing in that subject. The teachers were very good—Fr Pinto, Fr Sequiera, Fr Lourduswamy, Fr Jerome d Souza, Fr Murphy, Mr Raja, Mr Ramamurty, Mr Irudayaraja. Reading Shakespeare and Lord Macaulay under their guidance was a seductive experience and I could not avoid the inevitable—an MA from MCC (Madras Christian College), Tambaram, to be followed by a PhD on the Movement Poets. I chose English rather than Indian or American poetry for my doctoral dissertation. In finding a job in Hyderabad University, I discovered American Literature not without much help from the then ASRC (now OUCIP) and Professor William Mulder and Isaac Sequeira. Soon I was publishing steadily and teaching American literature. Some ten years ago, I began to review my progress and I realized that I should really be getting closer to my culture as an Indian scholar of English. Indian Writing in English was a necessary concern but one could not read this literature without a wide awareness of the larger Indian context and that meant understanding the *Bhashas* and the whole context of English in India. That is where I find myself today.

Increasingly my work is on National Discourse embodied in *Bhasha* texts, many of which were profoundly influenced by English and Englishness. Thus we see that the study of literature is never something done in isolation. It is not solitude at all, as is claimed sometimes, but rather a community involvement. There is after all an Interpretive Community. The point, if it is not already sufficiently clear, is that this incursion into the personal experience of one teacher of English in India is, by and large, the trajectory of many others. If there is one thing which my experience implies, it is that one cannot be simply local or nativist, nor can one be so Anglicized that one is unaware of one's roots. The middle path is to be both local and global or as the catchword goes—be glocal. Therefore, the future of an English department in India, staffed by people with my experience, and I do believe, we still constitute a majority, cannot but break down boundaries, cannot but be "Universal" in a special sense. Universality is not the prerogative of the Enlightenment or of Europe. It can have Indian resonances.

In what follows, I want to consider some moments in my experience as a teacher of English, not because I have any egotistical desire to foreground myself, but because those moments in which I was an active participant along with my colleagues had the effect of changing my perceptions and I dare say of others about our profession, about English Studies and about ourselves. As Gerald Graff (1987) has asserted, we as English scholars have been very good at representing literature but not done enough to represent ourselves. This essay then is about self-representation. The camera pans out to the scenario in my English Department when the Administration is asking University Postgraduate teachers of English to now engage with first year undergraduate students of our Five-Year Integrated MA/MSc Programme. The Department is distinctly uncomfortable. We have Language Specialists in the Department but they are wary of committing themselves to an unending demand on their time and they ask quite legitimately, what would happen to their research in Language Studies? The Literature teachers have two responses: one, they are hired to teach literature and the language people should face the burden; the other group claim they have long ago stopped teaching basic language skills because now they are in a University and cannot be expected to teach school-leavers. The English Department opposes the Integrated Programme on other grounds because it cannot afford to admit that its faculty feel that they are not capable of teaching these students or will find the burden too heavy.

Over a period, the Administration manages to create an ELT Cell which at first is part of the English Department and administered by it but soon this arrangement breaks down and it is separated from the English Department through a Professor from the English Department who is asked to manage the show without becoming involved in teaching in the Integrated Programme. Two permanent Lecturers are appointed and they bear the burden of teaching Basic English or English 1 or Communicative English semester after semester. The situation is getting impossible. How can two lecturers do so much work even if they are helped by Guest faculty? How can they progress in their careers if they are not allowed to supervise M Phil or PhD students or teach a variety of courses in Language? The solution is either for the English Department to merge itself with the Cell and take up the burden of the Integrated Programme by designating some faculty (numbers will be added, it is promised) to teach at the Integrated level. That way the Department would involve itself with an important University initiative besides perhaps gaining an accretion of strength. Besides, a full-fledged Language stream MA could be introduced in addition to an MA in Literature and an MA in Culture Studies. The English Department, it is argued, would become a formidable force and could even aspire to be a School of Studies given its wide range of activities and its engagement with so many levels of English teaching and its expansive understanding of English to include Literature, Language, and Culture.

But the English Department will have none of it. It still voices its opposition to the Integrated Programme. It will not accept responsibility for two lecturers who are deprived of full status, indeed are second class citizens because they were not appointed to the English Department in the first place, it will not move in the direction of introducing an MA in Language Studies because it is now argued by the Language teachers in the English Department that they do not have the numbers to do so. If an MA in Language Studies had been introduced in the English Department, then the Department would perhaps have got the numbers, but that was not to be.

The scene shifts to the Administration and a decision is taken to float the idea of a Centre for English Language Studies which will be the new avatar of the Cell and which will be decisively *apart* from the English Department. Faculty from English engaged in language teaching will be free to transfer to the new Centre and some positions will be made available to the Centre to make it viable. The split or partition takes place and we now have a curious phenomenon—An English Department which has to reinvent itself and a Centre for English Language Studies which will do the service work shunned by the English Department and which in addition is mandated to research at the MPhil and PhD levels on Language matters.

This is, in the main, the contours of the developments which led to two English Departments in the same University. What lessons should we learn from this? First, is it the job of the English teacher to teach basic language skills in a University? I confine myself to institutions of higher learning. Is not the teacher of English supposed to be also qualified in Linguistics in English as well as Literature in English? Is the Integrated requirement a dilution of the work of an English teacher? Let me straight-away say that an English teacher should be able to teach Basic English and a Department of English should be the largest in the University because it both serves and researches. You need many graduate assistants in addition to core faculty and a sizeable number of teachers in an English Department which must engage with this basic task of teaching Basic English. In our globalised scenario we now have many demands on teachers of English. In our country we are now expected to teach soft skills to our young people and it is my belief that a good University Department of English should meet this challenge from globalisation by offering "service" to the huge number of people who want a competence in English. That way lies prestige and relevance for our Departments and once we have satisfied the need of society we will always be able to plough some of the money we garner with such service into humanistic research.

A competence in English among our youth in a globalised world will be to the advantage of both Language and Literature research because by attending to these students early we will ensure a broad competence in English when these students come to us for Graduate Study. Further, I am of the opinion that this Language/Literature divide is artificial and induced by a turf war to the detriment of a holistic understanding of English. How, I ask, can you possible understand a literary text if you are not sensitive to the nuances, the idioms and the syntax and diction of a language and how, I ask again, can you possibly be a good linguist if you are insensitive to the best expression in that language which happens only in good literature? This observation takes me to what is widely called the linguistic turn in criticism widely seen as something which happened with the Russian Formalists and Ferdinand Saussure and their spiritual heirs the Post-structuralists and the Deconstructionists.

Contemporary thinking about literature is informed by this linguistic turn and it raises some very important issues. Should an English Department be in the thrall of a political or ideological agenda and speak about everything and anything under the sun instead of concentrating on the main thing—the verbal artefact. I am, of course, alluding to New Critical terminology, but the New Critics with their distrust of the author's intention and the effect of a work on the audience, and their emphasis mainly on poems as spatial metaphors, or inclusive, tension-filled, ironic or structurally or texturally organic, were after all taking their lead from the Russian Formalists who introduced ideas like literariness and defamiliarisation. It seems to me that we cannot have an exclusive attention to the formal aspects of literature and the concerns of people in English Studies with matters like nation and narration, gender, caste and class need to be interpellated into our engagement with works of literature. However, what we now see in our typical English Departments is an exclusive concern with extra literary matters of the kind just listed.

Please don't get me wrong. Much has happened in the last twenty years and we cannot pretend ignorance of these factors and talk as though the literary work is some innocent, pure essence. But it seems to me that while our concerns with caste, class, gender and nation are valuable, they must not be confused with literary study. After all, what differentiates us from people in Philosophy or History—the two traditional disciplines with which Literature is compared—is that we, as literary scholars, attend to words, images, symbols, tropes and figures. In this, as J.L. Austin or Hayden White knew, the literary scholar is nonpareil and it is certainly the first and foremost contribution of people in Literature to the Humanities. It is that we know how language works and can preach to the philosopher and the historian, not to speak of the anthropologist or political scientist. In any reconstruction of the English department (and I speak from an Indian point of view) we must resurrect this love for words and reading habits! Language as performance and language as gesture, not to speak of its fictionality are important emphases for English teachers anywhere in the world and most particularly in this country where English is often held hostage to all kinds of identity politics.

A concern with words means that we need to have some sense of the way words are used well and this implies that we can make judgements about good, better and the best writing and also have the courage to say that some work is downright bad. This is something we are coy about and a kind of academic laissez faire has affected us. Is it too much to ask of our literary scholars to discriminate between two poems by say the same writer, or two poems by two different writers and express preferences and opinions? All critics, we must remember, are concerned with the way words combine and make or do not make meaning, make for closure and satisfaction or aporia and deferral of meaning. Whether there is poetic closure or aperture the insistence is on the formal properties of a work. That in my opinion is fundamental and as literary scholars we ought to be paying a greater deal of attention to it. A work of literature is both artefact and communiqué, both a thing made and a thing said, even if the saying refuses itself. After we have savoured the formal properties of a work, and internalized its effects we are ready to move centrifugally. But the centripetal urge is important and it is a bulwark against the proliferation of our discipline of English Studies, a proliferation brought on by globalisation and its concomitant, the ability, as Walter Benjam has affirmed, to mechanically reproduce (1936). One of the tasks of the English teacher in the age of globalisation is to resist this dilution of the aura and restore to public discourse a sense of the mystery of literary creativity.

I shall now move to a theme that is central to the globalized context we are in. It concerns nativity and identity. Once again I shall concentrate on India. Is India a nation? Undoubtedly in a political sense it is but there the idea founders. Partha Chatterjee's thesis of nationalism being a derivative discourse and his view that we must also attend to the fragments of the nation (1986) is apropos to what I want to say. In India, which is a *Dharmic* civilization, we have had a loose understanding of *Desh* (or country). The old view of *Bharat* as extending from the Himalayas to Kanyakumari and from Khandahar (Gandhara) to Khambuja (Kampuchea), is still a psychological reality to the traditional Indian mind and refuses to disappear in relation to a more secular and modern understanding of nationhood as determined in our case primarily by territory. The other markers of nationhood are ethnicity, language, and religion. India can be recognized as a nation neither from the point of view of ethnicity, language or religion nor the linguistic boundaries imposed on us by the Partition which can at the most only provide a secular consolation that we are also a nation. This is buttressed when the cricketer Sachin Tendulkar succeeds on a spectacular scale or when our hockey team disgraces itself. This is a kind of spiritual principle, if 'spiritual' could be translated as Dharma, and Dharmic civilizations have an edge over centralized, foundational religious cultures as in Europe by virtue of their inherent capacity to manage difference. Rajiv Malhotra (2011) speaks in Obama fashion of the audacity of difference and I believe he is onto something valuable from the point of view of the shifting boundaries a global world entails.

India in herself is a global order, what with its teeming millions, its bewildering variety of languages, religious traditions, ethnic groups, its peasantry and its forest and tribal peoples. We cannot formulate India in a phrase and it is difficult to define her. And that precisely is the strength of the literary scholar who professes English in a multi linguistic context. Built into our blood stream is not just tolerance (which is a passive virtue) but understanding and acceptance of difference. I say this because in literary studies and in English Departments today there is a clamour for interpellating gender, caste and class identities in every context. While I understand the importance of these particularities I cannot help feeling that what we now are treated to in Departments of English Studies is a new hegemony. Ostensibly it is against our colonial masters, it is against Brahmanical domination, it is also against the dominance of English. So we have the spectacle of English graduates being persuaded to study *Bhasha* texts, sometimes in the original if the class has a demographic character which is linguistically homogenous, but mostly in translation. Indian writing in English is seen as an opportunity to intervene decisively with the specious plea that all writing is translation and therefore a Hindi, Telugu or Urdu text must be added to the original writing in English.

I am with Amit Choudhury in his riposte to Salman Rushdie's astounding claim that the only good literature from India is that written in English (2001). But I am still in an English Department and I do believe that we cannot permit our students to graduate if they have not been exposed to the best that has been thought and said in English be it from England, Ireland, Australia, New Zealand, Canada or India. Ngugi wanted Gikuyu to be at the centre of his department of English and he pleaded for the abolition of the English department. I don't think we can go so far particularly since we have in India flourishing Departments of Hindi, Telugu, Urdu and other languages. Why should English alone be abolished? Is it not incumbent on us to give our students the benefit of the education we received which allows us to discriminate between good and bad writing, and enables us to savour the minds of excellent writers in the English language which incidentally is not Telugu or Hindi or Urdu. Are we going to send our students out asking who Wordsworth is or what the Dickens is

Dickens? Our concern with identity is important but it must be filtered through our engagement with English texts.

After attending to the verbal dexterity of a work it becomes necessary for us to move beyond meaning to significance. It is at this stage that our gender, caste and class concerns can come into play and clearly there is much to be learnt from a head- on collision between ourselves and the work. But what one observes is that our 'Identitians' approach each and every work, irrespective of its location in culture, without any effort to contextualize the work, with a supreme contempt for the historical dimension of the work, and subject it to two or three reductive questions. These go like this—"What is this writer's attitude to Women/Dalits? Why has he not specifically dealt with the Woman or Dalit question? Is this writer upper class? If so why has he not dealt with the lower classes?" A perfectly legitimate endeavour to enrich reading by bringing in your subject position into play in your engagement with a verbal artefact can degenerate into this reductionism.

I will now move to another dimension alluded to at the beginning of my essay, to what passes for literary study. It is the result of a heady postmodern mix of Foucault, Barthes, Derrida and Guattari. The conscious effort is to question the canon, the Ur narratives, the Foundational texts. The margin rather than the centre is now the focus. The minority discourse must displace the hegemonic majority. The cultured and the popular must now be mixed and there is to be a confusion of genres, styles, and hybridity and mixture (*Misra* in Sanskrit) must result. It is after all the age of remixes, of revisiting the classics (so many *Ramayanas!*), of fusion music and hard rock which is not music at all.

Thus we see in English Departments the focus shifting from the verbal to the visual, from words to images and sound, from books to comics and paintings and what have you. I must again say that some of this is legitimate activity and has its own place in the general scheme of things. But if you are trying to educate graduates into being learned and this is itself a stupendous task in our globalised environment where mediocrity and triviality rule, I fail to see how all this distraction will help. We are not teaching our children how to read. There is no foundation to their learning and it becomes a part of an academic cafeteria where anything goes and good English skills are not at a premium. This sort of thing passes for culture study and it is sexy and jazzy and has a hedonistic and seductive pull for young people. But we want young people to become full-grown adults, mature, capable of facing up to life's challenges. How is this possible if we are going to encourage this kind of circus?

If English Departments have to survive in any meaningful way, I am afraid we have to make some hard choices. These choices are: (1) To read carefully and write carefully. This would mean that SMS messages are a strict no no, that even if you are on e-mail (something I suppose we can't really get rid of) we had better attend to grammar and syntax and punctuation—all those aids to proper communication; (2) Read a book first for its verbal artistry and then interpellate your subject position, but for heaven's sake do this intelligently, not in the reductive fashion already described; (3) Accept that Culture is finally a whole way of life, but having said that we must make our choices of books on the basis of a proper discrimination—and finally; (4) a lesson for Indians—we belong to a *Dharmic* civilization, that we have the capacity to manage chaos, contradiction and difference and that this *samskara* should become part of our profession as English teachers. We should attend to meaning and then significance; to the paraphraseable core before we impose our interpretive desires; that we will accept the play of difference, even poetic aperture in the secure *Dharmic* belief that it is all part of the play of Providence, that chaos has a place along with order.

In our English departments then, we must resist reductionism, accept the genuine play of difference, and manage it intelligently. That way lies democracy and a proper engagement with the Global. In advancing such a view, I believe I am in the company of men like Gandhi, Tagore and Sri Aurobindo, all of whom were acutely aware of the reality of India but not so chauvinistic as to reject the necessary gesture towards Europe, which would make their Indianness, so much more passionate, so much more genuine and so much more meaningful.

Works Cited

Austin, J.L. 1979. "Performative Utterances" in *Philosophical Papers*. Ed. J.O. Urmson and G.J. Warnock. Oxford: Oxford University Press.

Benjamin, Walter. 1936. "The Work of Art in the Age of Mechanical Reproduction". In *Illuminations: Essays and Reflections*. Ed. Hannah Arendt. New York: Harwood, Brace & Butter, 1968.

Chatterjee, Partha. 1986. *Nationalist Thought and the Colonial World*. London: Zed Books.

Chaudhury, Amit, Ed. 2001. *The Picalor Book of Modern Indian Literature*. Delhi: Picador India.

Devy, G.N. 1992. *After Amnesia: Tradition & Change in Indian Literature*. New Delhi: Orient Longman.

Gandhi, M.K. 1997. *Hind Swaraj*. Ed. Antony J. Parel. Cambridge: Cambridge University Press.

Graft, Gerald. 1987. *Professing Literature: An Institutional History*. Chicago: Chicago Univ. Press.

Gramsci, Antonio. 1971. *Prison Notebooks*. International Publishers.

Malhotra, Rajiv. 2011. *Being Different: An Indian Challenge to Western Universalism*. New Delhi: Harper Collins India.

Ngugi wa Thiongo. 1986. *The Decolonization of the Mind: The Politics of Language in African Literature*.

Rushdie, Salman and Elizabeth West. 1998. *The Vintage Book of Indian Writing 1947-1997*. London: Vintage Publishers.

Said, Edward. 1978. *Orientalism*. New York: Vintage Books.

Sri Aurobindo. 1968. *Foundations of Indian Culture*. Pondicherry: Sri Aurobindo Ashram.

Tagore, Rabindranath. 1917. *Nationalism*. New Delhi: Rupa.

White, Hayden. 1978. *Tropics of Discourse: Essays in Cultural Criticism*. Baltimore: Johns Hopkins University Press.

CHAPTER 7

Educating Young Australians About Asia in an Age of Globalism

Rita Tognini
Western Australian Department of Education, Australia

Introduction

Amongst the many new challenges, confronting Australia in a globalised world is the need to incorporate awareness of its proximity to Asia in its educational curriculum. This essay explores the use of terms such as 'engagement with Asia' and 'Asia literacy' in these policy and program documents. The paper examines commitments to promote 'engagement with Asia' by young people through the development of the Australian Curriculum. It also examines and evaluates programs implemented through the *National Asian Languages and Studies in Schools Program* (NALSSP) that aim to develop 'Asia literacy' through expansion of Asian language programs and studies of Asia projects. The need to educate young people about Asia has been a recurring theme in Australian education in the latter part of the 20th century. In the first decade of the 21st century, factors related to the perceived need to respond to global issues have resulted in this matter being taken up in a systematic way. This paper describes policies and programs that aim to educate young Australians about Asia by ensuring that the curriculum for primary and secondary schools more fully reflects Australia's Asian regional identity.

Background

Asia is now recognised as the world's emerging economic powerhouse and there is talk of a shift of economic and cultural power and influence from the west to the east. The colonial origins of Australian society resulted in its economic, political and cultural orientation being aligned to England and Europe. Over the past 50 years, however, Australia has increasingly acknowledged its regional identity and has become a more active participant in the political, economic and cultural life of the region. Australia has developed economic and other partnerships with nations throughout the region and in particular with Japan, Indonesia and more recently China. These developments have been reflected in school education by a growing recognition of the need to educate young people about Asia. They have led to initiatives to enable students to develop understandings, knowledge and skills they are likely to need as future citizens of the region. The initiatives have concentrated on two main areas: the inclusion of studies of Asia in the curriculum and the teaching of Asian languages.

The inclusion of some aspects of the studies of Asia in the curriculum of Australian primary and secondary schools commenced in the early sixties. In the mid to late seventies, Asian languages (notably Japanese and Indonesian) were introduced in secondary schools. Despite these earlier initiatives, systematic incorporation of the studies of Asia and Asian languages into the school curriculum did not occur until the mid 1990s. The catalyst for this development was the introduction of the *National Asian Languages and Studies in Australian Schools* (NALSAS) strategy. The strategy was a recommendation of the *Asian Languages and Australia's Economic Future Report* (1994), prepared for the Council of Australian Government under the chairmanship of Kevin Rudd.

The NALSAS strategy was implemented nationwide from 1995-2002 and was supported by over $208 million of Commonwealth funding to states and territories. The strategy set ambitious targets for an expansion in the teaching four languages: Chinese (Mandarin), Indonesian,

Japanese and Korean. It also promoted the inclusion of Studies of Asia in learning areas such as Studies of Society and Environment, English and the Arts. An evaluation of the strategy in 2002 found an increase in the number of schools teaching the four NALSAS languages and the number of students learning them, with 49 per cent of all schools offering one of these languages. The most significant growth in enrolments was in Japanese, which had replaced French as the language with the largest number of students completing Year 12, and in Indonesian. The evaluation also found that the number of schools including Studies of Asia in their curriculum had increased from 82 in 1993 to 1864 in 2001.

Despite the achievements of the NALSAS strategy and sustained protest from the education and wider community, funding ceased in 2002. This was a setback for teaching of Asian languages and Studies of Asia in Australian schools as some programs were curtailed or cut. The *National Statement for Engaging Young People in Asia* (MCEETYA 2005) was subsequently developed to provide a rationale and framework for the continuation of studies of Asia and Asian languages programs in schools, but had no funding attached to it.

The election of the Rudd Labor Government in November 2007 resulted in renewed financial support for Asian languages and studies of Asia through the introduction of the *National Asian Languages and Studies in Schools Program* (NALSSP). Funding of $62.4 million over four years (2008-2011) was allocated to NALSSP, which was modelled on NALSAS, but not funded as generously. NALSSP similarly aimed to increase "opportunities for school students to become familiar with the languages and cultures of Australia's key regional neighbours, namely China, Indonesia, Japan and Korea" and to increase the number of studying these countries' languages to Year 12 level (Department of Education

2010). The decision not to extend the countries and languages addressed by NALSSP to include India appeared to ignore the increasing economic and cultural importance of that country to Australia. The growing importance of India was mentioned in the *Melbourne Declaration* (2008) alongside the acknowledgement of China's self-evident importance. This decision may be a function of the significantly smaller budget for NALSSP in comparison to NALSAS as well as NALSSP highly derivative nature.

As well as providing funding to maintain and significantly expand programs in Chinese, Indonesian, Japanese and Korean, NALSSP also funded grants to schools for projects that foster understanding of Asian cultures and learning of the designated Asian languages. Two other components (which are not examined in this paper) provided grants to promote strategic collaboration and partnerships between universities, higher education providers, businesses and Asian communities for the same purpose.

In 2008 it was decided to develop a comprehensive national curriculum (the Australian Curriculum) that "sets out the core knowledge, understanding, skills and general capabilities for all Australian students" (Retrieved from: www.australiancurriculum.edu.au). This provided an opportunity to address the issue of educating primary and secondary students about Asia through the mainstream curriculum. The strategy adopted by the Australian Curriculum Assessment and Reporting Authority (ACARA) was to identify three Cross Curriculum Priorities that each Learning Area had to address. They included Asia and Australia's engagement with Asia, along with Aboriginal and Torres Strait Islander histories and cultures, and sustainability.

As identified by the *Melbourne Declaration* (2008), the need to respond to global integration and mobility has been a factor that has influenced the development of the policies and programs described above, including NALSSP and the Australian Curriculum. These initiatives respond to globalism by strengthening and providing a comprehensive, cohesive, yet flexible school curriculum nationally. At the same time, they help ensure young people look outward, understand their region and world and are equipped to engage with it effectively, creatively and productively.

'Engagement with Asia' and 'Asia Literacy'

Over the last decade, the discourse surrounding the need to educate young people about Asia as part of their schooling has been broadly in terms of 'engagement in/with Asia' and 'Asia literacy'. The former refers to a process and the latter to an outcome. They have been used singly, in combination and sometimes interchangeably in key policy, curriculum and funding documents during this period. The *National Statement for Engaging Young People in Asia* (MCEETYA 2005) focused on process and announced 'engagement in Asia' focus in its title. It then identified six interlinked elements through which the engagement with Asia could be achieved. The elements mainly involved strategies to promote the studies of Asia in schools, but also included an acknowledgement that, "students will increasingly be able to communicate in one or more Asian languages" (MCEETYA 2005, 9).

The 2008 *Melbourne Declaration on Educational Goals for Young Australians* connected the two terms in its preamble by arguing that, "Australians need to become 'Asia literate', engaging and building strong relationships with Asia" (MCEETYA 2008). Building on the *National Statement,* the Australian Curriculum Cross Curriculum Priority includes 'engagement with Asia', but draws attention to 'Asia' as an object of study in its own right and emphasises the need to examine Australia's relationship with it. The description of the Priority outlines its desired impact on young people:

> Asia and Australia's engagement with Asia will allow all young Australians to develop a better understanding of the countries and cultures of the Asia region. Students will develop an appreciation of the economic, political and cultural interconnections that Australia has with the region. (Retrieved from: www.acara.edu.au/cross_curriculum_perspectives.html)

The Australian Curriculum will include the development of curricula for a number of Asian languages (Chinese, Hindi, Indonesian, Japanese, Korean, Vietnamese), thus affirming the importance of learning at least one of these languages as part of developing an understanding of the countries and cultures of Asia. The Australian Curriculum: History defines Asia as "the territorial area that extends from the western border of Pakistan to the northern border of Mongolia, to the eastern border of Japan, and that extends to the southern border of Indonesia."

'Asia literacy' was as a key concept and major outcome for NALSSP. It consisted of two related components for the school sector. The first component, the expansion of teaching programs for Mandarin, Japanese, Indonesian or Korean in primary and secondary schools, was allocated 70 per cent of program funds. The second component, the 'Becoming Asia Literate: Grants to Schools', provided direct grants of up to $20,000 for culture or language projects for this purpose and had 10 per cent of program funding. Schools did not necessarily have access to funding from both components.

The description of 'Asia literacy' in the NALSSP school grants information pack is puzzling:

> Asia Literacy is the specific literacy that supports knowledge, skills and understandings about the histories, geographies, societies, cultures, and languages in the diverse countries in the Asian region. (Schooling/NALSSP/FurtherInformation/)

This description seems to present 'Asia literacy' as an almost pre-existing skill that supports the acquisition of 'knowledge, skills and understandings' of the countries and cultures of Asia, rather than an outcome of the experience of learning about Asian countries and/or the language of one of these countries.

For the *National Statement on Asia Literacy in Schools 2011-12,* 'Asia literacy' is an outcome of the acquisition of knowledge, skills and understandings about the region gained from schooling. The document sets out to identify "the broad knowledge, skills and understandings required by all students to achieve Asia literacy in the context of existing policies and practices in teaching and learning" (asiaeducation.edu.au/partnerships/national_statement_2011-12). The knowledge, skills and understandings will be foundational and in-depth and will encompass the histories, geographies, societies, arts, literatures and languages of many Asian countries. Three areas need to be addressed to achieve 'Asia literacy': Asia and its diversity; achievements and contributions of the peoples of Asia; and, Asia-Australia engagement. The proposed strategies for achieving Asia literacy, for the first time, give prominence to the role of learning an Asian language in reaching this outcome.

In the document discussed, there is a degree of consistency and clarity in the concept and use of 'engagement with Asia'. 'Asia literacy', on the other hand, remains problematic in a number of ways. This is partly because the current notion of literacy includes both broad general understanding of an area as in 'computer literacy' or 'financial literacy' as well as the more specific language focused skills of ability to communicate, to decode and encode text and understand how it is used to influence the listener/reader. Use of the term does not always clarify (or is deliberately vague about) whether one or both literacies are to be achieved. Because of the vast geographical coverage of the region, 'Asia literacy' is inevitably panoramic in scope and seems to imply that students will develop knowledge, understandings and skills about 'Asia' (however defined) in its totality, rather than about specific Asian countries, cultures and/or languages. This tendency to hyperbole ignores the fact that studying the history, geography or culture of India, for example, does not necessarily develop knowledge, understandings and skills about China. Learning Indonesian has the potential to make students literate in that language and 'Indonesia literate', but not 'China literate' or 'Japan literate', even though students will acquire intercultural skills and understandings that are transferable to other Asian cultures. This raises the question of whether making young people 'Asia literate' is achievable or whether what can be realistically achieved is country/culture and language specific. If that is the case, is the term 'Asia literacy' actually useful in the educational context? Or is it just a slogan that creates less than feasible expectations and obscures the actual knowledge, understanding and skills that young people can acquire through participation in well developed, excitingly presented and sustained studies of Asia and Asian language programs?

The remaining part of the essay examines the type of programs implemented with NALSSP funding to educate young people about Asia. It also shows how the 'Asia and Australia's Engagement with Asia' Cross Curriculum Priority is incorporated into three learning areas of the Australian Curriculum: English, History and Languages.

NALSSP Funding to Expand the Teaching of Asian Languages

The ways that states and territories have used the funds made available through NALSSP to expand the teaching of Asian languages is examined in this section. It also outlines the number of schools and types of projects funded through the *Becoming Asia Literate—Grants to Schools* between 2009 and 2011. The data reported below have been extrapolated from information about NALSSP made available on the web site of the Department of Education, Employment and Workplace Relations (DEEWR).

The achievement targets for the end of Year 12 were an aspect of NALSAS that NALSSP set out to improve. The NALSAS Evaluation (2002) found that the increase in the number of students learning all four NALSAS languages between 1994 and 2000 did not translate into increases in the percentage of students completing these languages to the end of Year 12. NALSSP funding addressed these targets by requiring states and territories to submit strategic plans outlining how they intended to expand the teaching of Asian languages and achieve the 2020 target of 12 per cent of students continuing their Asian language study to the end of Year 12. The strategic plans addressed three key result areas: flexible pathways and delivery; increasing teacher supply and support; and, stimulating student demand.

Table 7.1 provides information on the number of proposals for each key result area from analysis of state and territories' Strategic Plan summaries on the DEEWR web site. The scope, complexity and focus of proposals varied, reflecting the needs and goals of different states and territories. Victoria and New South Wales' Strategic Plans were cross-sectoral and proposals identified broad initiatives. In contrast, each sector in Queensland submitted separate Strategic Plans. This partly explains why Queensland had two to four times more proposals than other states and the high number of proposals in the flexible pathways and delivery area. All states and territories, except the Northern Terrritory, included proposals for all three key result areas. Most states and territories had the greatest number of proposals in Key Result Area 2, indicating the importance of increasing teacher supply and support to the expansion of Asian language programs. Only the NSW, Victorian and South Australian proposals encompassed all four NALSSP languages.

Table 7.1: Summary of Strategic Plans—No. of Proposals for Chinese by State and Territory

State and Territories (All jurisdictions)	Proposals Key Result Area 1: Flexible Pathways and Delivery	Proposals Key Result Area 2: Increasing Teacher Supply and Support	Proposal Key Result Area 3: Stimulating Student Demand	Language(s) *Chinese (C)* *Indonesian (I)* *Japanese (J)* *Korean (K)*	Total No. Strategic Plan Proposals for all Languages
ACT	0	7	5	I, J & C	12
NSW	5	9	13	C, I, J & K	27
QLD	26	11	8	C, J & I	45
SA	13	13	5	C, I, J & K	31
TAS	2	12	2	J & C	16
VIC	4	10	6	C, I, J & K	20
WA	2	11	5	C, J & I	18
Total	52	73	44		169

Source: www.deewr.gov.au/Schooling/NALSSP/FurtherInformation/Pages/FundingInformation.aspx#asia

To give a sense of the different types of proposals made by state and territories, a brief description of a small selection of them, for each Key Result Area, is provided in Fig. 7.1.

NALSSP: Becoming Asia Literate—Grants to Schools

The *Becoming Asia Literate—Grants to Schools* aimed to support schools wishing to implement projects promoting Asian cultures and/or languages. Individual or clusters of schools could apply for a grant for this purpose of up to $20,000 per school.

Data about the grants on the DEEWR web site were collated and grouped into six categories: the four NALSSP languages; and, a general culture and a general language category. There was insufficient information about general culture and general language projects on the DEEWR web site to determine which Asian language(s) and/or culture(s) was being focused on. The number of grant projects funded in 2009, 2010 and 2011 is presented in Tables 7.2, 7.3 and 7.4 respectively. For each year, total project numbers are given for the six categories. The projects in the language categories are further broken down to reflect a mainly cultural or language orientation.

Fig. 7.1: Examples of Proposals from State and Territory Strategic Plans

Key Result Area	Examples
1. Flexible Pathways and Delivery	• Develop distance education materials for online delivery of Stage 6 Chinese, Indonesian, Japanese & Korean (NSW) • Strengthening partnerships with sister schools Asian communities that enable real world language experiences (QLD) • Implement the VET/Asian languages project: facilitate the provision of VET/Asian languages pathways in schools and flexible alternative pathways to link language learning to an accredited VET certificate. (SA)
2. Increasing Teacher Supply and Support	• The University of Tasmania will provide post-graduate programs for Asian languages teachers to support professional development of existing teachers and to train new teachers. (TAS) • Establish a Chinese Teacher Training Centre (CTTC) in partnership with The Office of the Chinese Language Council International, China (Hanban). (VIC) • By 2012, establish eight to ten Asian Language Hubs at secondary schools to support teachers and students at that school, partner primary schools and other schools. (WA)
3. Stimulating Student Demand	• Fund a pilot school to offer Community Languages programs in Chinese, including after-hours courses for Year 12 students. (WA) • The Department of Education will upskill their Languages teachers in the use of Digital technology and encourage students to enter the digital Stories Competition (ACT) • A rich languages learning website offering digital resources in Chinese, Indonesian and Japanese will be provided to students in Years 7-12 in all schools. (VIC)

Source: www.deewr.gov.au/Schooling/NALSSP/FurtherInformation/Pages/FundingInformation.aspx#asia

Table 7.2: Number of Becoming Asia Literate Grants in 2009

Year	Chinese		Indonesian		Korean		Japanese		Gen Cult.	Gen Lang.	Total
	Cult.	Lang.	Cult.	Lang.	Cult.	Lang.	Cult.	Lang.			
2009	9	17	2	19	0	0	7	20	43	24	
Total	26		21		0		27		43	24	141

Source: www.deewr.gov.au/Schooling/NALSSP/FurtherInformation/Pages/FundingInformation.aspx#strategic

Table 7.3: Number of Becoming Asia Literate Grants in 2010

Year	Chinese		Indonesian		Korean		Japanese		Gen Cult.	Gen Lang	Total
	Cult.	Lang.	Cult.	Lang.	Cult.	Lang.	Cult.	Lang.			
2010	3	18	13	14	9	3	6	45	59	21	
Total	21		27		12		51		59	21	191

Source: www.deewr.gov.au/Schooling/NALSSP/FurtherInformation/Pages/FundingInformation.aspx#strategic

Table 7.4: Number of Becoming Asia Literate Grants in 2011

Year	Chinese		Indonesian		Korean		Japanese		Gen Cult	Gen Lang.	Total
	Cult.	Lang.	Cult	Lang.	Cult	Lang.	Cult	Lang			
2011	16	16	10	22	2	0	7	22	75	13	
Total	32		32		2		29		75	13	190

Source: www.deewr.gov.au/Schooling/NALSSP/FurtherInformation/Pages/FundingInformation.aspx#strategic

The tables 7.2, 7.3 and 7.4 show an increase in the total number of projects funded over the three years, especially from 2009 to 2010 (141 to 191). There was a minimal overall decrease in the number of projects from 2010 to 2011 (191 to 190), but increases in projects related to Chinese, Indonesian and General Culture, in particular. The number of projects for the other categories decreased markedly. Projects with a general cultural focus predominated in all three years, increasing from 43 or 30 per cent of the total in 2009 to 75 or almost 40 per cent of the total in 2011. In contrast, projects with a general language focus decreased from 24 or 17 per cent in 2009 to 13 or almost 7 per cent in 2011.

The majority of projects for specific languages were for the three languages with an established presence in the curriculum in all states—Chinese, Indonesian and Japanese. The number of projects for Chinese dropped slightly from 2009 to 2010, but increased overall in 2011, especially those focusing on Chinese culture. Indonesian projects increased overall over the three years and Japanese projects spiked in 2010. There were notably more language oriented than culturally oriented projects for Japanese in all three years, but especially in 2010. This possibly reflects the established place of Japanese in the curriculum. Korean projects were few. There were none in 2009 and only two in 2011, making the 12 in 2010 seem an anomaly. Eleven of the total 14 Korean projects funded over the three years had a cultural orientation and 10 were in NSW schools, reflecting fact that the Korean is taught mainly in NSW.

Projects in the four language areas with a language orientation involved the introduction of a teaching program for a particular language, the creation of language materials for groups of students or levels of learning and/or innovative curriculum approaches to the teaching the identified language, especially involving ICT and online learning. For example:

- Jia You!—Chinese continuers Year 12 curriculum materials (2009);
- Engaging students in Korean language learning (2010); and
- Intercultural language learning in a networked hub—Indonesian (2011).

Language specific projects with a cultural orientation often focused on study of a particular aspect of the culture. For example:

- Student exchange with sister schools in China and Japan (2009);
- Learning community of schools engaging students in Korean Studies (2010); and
- Exploring Balinese dance and music—a creative IT-based approach (2011).

General language projects usually had a pedagogical or organisational focus. For example:

- Establishing a language laboratory and a sister school program (2009);
- Language acquisition and enhancement through the use of emerging technologies (2010); and
- Creating lifelong language learners: The need for LOTE transition (2011).

General cultural projects often involved the development of cultural understandings about Asia across the learning area, student exchanges to relevant Asian countries and so on. For example:

- Creating new pathways in a globalised world (2009);
- Enriching Asian awareness through collaborative practices within the humanities domain (2010); and
- Using Interactive Technologies to engage young Australians with Asia (2011).

Only a very small number of schools across Australia received *Becoming Asia Literate* grants each year—about 1.5 per cent in 2009 and around 2 per cent in 2010 and 2011. Given the program's short life, this raises questions about the adequacy of the level of funding for this program and its impact on stimulating student interest and developing their knowledge about Asian countries, cultures and languages.

The 2002 *NALSAS* Evaluation suggested that lack of integration in the teaching of Asian languages and studies of Asia was a factor in the strategy's failure to meet targets for increases in the percentage of students completing Asian languages to the end of Year 12. It is difficult to tell from the limited information available on individual NALSSP *Becoming Asia Literate* grants whether projects are a one-off initiative or part of a school's long-term and integrated approach involving a number of learning areas and possibly including language study. If the latter, a project could have a notable impact, despite a relatively low level of funding for limited time; if the former, its impact is likely to be more ephemeral.

The extent to which NALSSP met its objectives, especially in relation to 'Asia literacy' is yet to be formally evaluated. Whatever its impact, funding for NALSSP was not extended beyond 2011. States and territories that did not expend all of their funds by the end of 2011 have been given permission by DEEWR to continue their initiatives in 2012 using the remaining funding.

The advent of the Australian Curriculum with its Cross Curriculum Priority of Asia and Australia's engagement with Asia is likely to have influenced the decision not to extend NALSSP. The Priority gives studies of Asia a formal and systematic presence in the curriculum overall that they have not had before. Moreover, the Australian Curriculum: Languages will encourage a consistent approach to provision for and teaching of Languages F-12 across all jurisdictions. The Australian Curriculum: Languages is still in development. However, work carried out to date indicates support for the continued expansion of programs in the four NALSSP languages and advocates the introduction of Hindi and Vietnamese. Small candidature Asian languages taught mainly outside mainstream schooling such as Hindi, Khmer, Malay, Punjabi, Sinhala and Tamil, will continue to be nationally assessed at Year 12 level, thus provide formal recognition for students who learn these languages through programs taught outside mainstream schools.

Research in science education suggests that a transformative approach which focuses on the transformation of qualities such as values, attitudes and perceptions rather than solely on transmitting predetermined and measurable information to students may be crucial to ensuring deep-level student learning (Pugh, Linnerbrink-Garcia, Koskey, Stewart and Manzey 2010). This approach was likely to result in higher levels of student engagement and conceptual change and development. The emphasis of the transformative approach on engagement that extends beyond the classroom through the application of learning in context, on seeing and understanding aspects of the world in new ways and valuing of content for its usefulness to immediate everyday experience (Pugh et al., 2010, 3) could provide a framework for integration and thereby support the long-term success of the study of Asian languages to the end of Year 12 and a broader engagement with Asia in other areas of the curriculum.

The Australian Curriculum

This section of the paper explores how the 'Asia and Australia's engagement with Asia' Cross Curriculum Priority is incorporated into the Australian Curriculum: English and History, and how it is reflected in the recently released *The Shape of the Australian Curriculum: Languages* (ACARA 2011).

Fig. 7.2: Asia and Australia's engagement with Asia in the Australian Curriculum: English

> The Australian Curriculum: English enables students to explore and appreciate the rich traditions of texts from and about the people and countries of Asia, including texts written by Asian Australians. They develop an understanding of the many languages used in Australia and how they have influenced Australian Culture.
>
> In this learning area, students develop communication skills that reflect cultural awareness and intercultural understanding. They are encouraged to draw on knowledge of the arts and literature of the Asia region to influence their own creative pursuits and to express themselves through different media and genre.

Retrieved from: www.australiancurriculum.edu.au/English/ Curriculum/F-10

The Fig. 7.2 reproduces the description of the 'Asia and Australia's engagement with Asia' Cross Curriculum Priority found in the Australian Curriculum: English.

The content structure of the English Learning Area is made up of three strands: Language, Literature and Literacy. The introduction to the content for each year level indicates that 'texts from and about Asia' form part of the 'range of literary texts for Foundation to Year 10'. Strands for some of the year levels make explicit reference to Asia-related content. There are also opportunities for inclusion of Asia in many other strands across the year levels. The Asia Education Foundation has produced a resource for teachers that identifies explicit and other references to Asia-related content in the English Curriculum. A few examples from this resource of explicit references to Asia-related content in the English Curriculum are presented in Fig. 7.3:

Fig. 7.3: Examples of explicit Asia-related content—
Australian Curriculum: English

Year	Explicit Asia-related content	Strand
1	Exploring performance poetry, chants and songs from Asian Cultures.	Literature
3	Exploring the ways that the same story can be told in many cultures, identifying variations in the storyline and music—e.g., *The Ramayana,* which is told to children in India, Burma, Thailand, Cambodia, Laos.	Literature
6	Using display advertising as a topic vehicle for close analysis of the ways images and words combine for deliberate effect—e.g., comparing Hollywood and Bollywood film posters.	Literacy
8	Exploring examples of Singlish from a Singlish dictionary.	Language
9	Analysing how issues are debated and reported in the media in different countries—e.g., 'whaling' in Japan and Australia	Literacy

Source: www.asiaeducation.edu.au/resource/australian_curriculum_audit.html

Ensuring that teachers have easy access to appropriate teaching materials will be a key issue in the effective implementation of the Asia and Australia's engagement with Asia, Cross Curriculum Priority of the Australian Curriculum. Much material is already available. The Asia Education Foundation has produced a range of support materials for teachers for English (and the other Stage I curricula of History, Science and Mathematics) that can be accessed on their web site. *Asia-related literary texts to support the Australian Curriculum for English* is one such resource available online. Texts about China, Indonesia, India, Japan, Korea, Malaysia, Nepal, Tibet, Pakistan, Thailand and Vietnam are included. Examples of some of the texts recommended for the Indian subcontinent are provided in Fig. 7.4:

Fig. 7.4: Texts with Indian subcontinent content

Year	Title and Author	Text type	Further information
3 & 4 (8 & 9 year olds)	*Snapshots of Asia—India*, Richard Ledger and Sue Ledger	Range of text	Big book format with information about India in the form of photos, fact files, games, pictorial stories

5 & 6 (10 & 11 year olds)	*Kalpana's Dream,* Judith Clarke	Novel	Story of an Indian girl adjusting to life in Year 7 and 8 in an Australian school.
	Village by the Sea, Anita Desai	Story	A moving story showing some of the problems facing families trying to escape from the poverty of village life in India.
7 & 8 (12 & 13 year olds)	*Three Cups of Tea,* Greg Mortensen	Auto-biography	About setting up schools in Pakistan.
	The Cup, Khyentse Norbu	Feature Film	About soccer and Tibetan monks.
9 & 10 (14 & 15 year olds)	*City of Ghosts,* Bali Rai	Historical novel	Set in Amritsar in the Punjab region in 1919. It places young characters amongst events that resulted in a British military atrocity
	Chalkline, Jane Mitchell	Novel	Set in Kashmir, this is the story of a Muslim boy, Rafiq, who becomes a child soldier in the India-Pakistan conflict over Kashmir.

Source: www.asiaeducation.edu.au/verve/_resources/F10eltCOMaf23112010.pdf

The Fig. 7.5 reproduces the description of the 'Asia and Australia's engagement with Asia' Cross Curriculum Priority found in the Australian Curriculum: History.

The Australian Curriculum: History is organised in two interrelated strands: Historical Knowledge and Understanding (K & U) and Historical Skills (HS). Asia-related content is well represented in an explicit way in History. The curriculum also offers other opportunities to explore Asia-related themes. Explicit content about China, India, Vietnam, Indonesia is included. Not surprisingly, the History Curriculum has a substantial amount of explicit

Asia-related content. The Fig. 7.6 provides examples of some of this content as identified by the on-line resource developed for this purpose by the Asia Education Foundation.

Fig. 7.5: Asia and Australia's engagement with Asia in the Australian Curriculum: History

In the Australian Curriculum: History, students develop an understanding of the diversity of the people of Asia and their contributions to the region and the world, and an appreciation of the importance of the region for Australia and the world. Students understand the dynamic nature of socio-political relationships within the region over time, and the role that individuals, governments and other organisations play in shaping relationships between peoples and countries. Students develop an appreciation of the history of Australia-Asian engagement and how this influences contemporary Australian society and relationships with the countries of Asia. They understand the long history of migration to Australia by people from Asia and appreciate the contributions made over time by Asian Australians to the development of Australia's culture and society. They also understand the ongoing role played by Australia and individual Australians in major events and developments in the Asia regions.

(Retrieved from: www.australiancurriculum.edu.au/History/ Curriculum/F-10)

Fig. 7.6: Examples of explicit Asia-related content—Australian Curriculum: History

Year	Explicit Asia-related content	Strand
1	Discussing how some cultures, for example Chinese, describe a child as being one year old on the day that they are born.	K & U
3	Celebrations and commemorations in other places around the world: for example, Bastille Day in France; Independence Day in the USA; those observed in Australia such as Christmas, Easter, Chinese New Year; Diwali, Moon Festival and Ramadan.	K & U
5	Investigating the experiences and contributions of particular migrant groups within a colony (for example the Japanese in Broome; Chinese at Palmer River; Afghan Cameleers in the a Northern Territory.	K & U; HS
7	Identifying major civilisations of the ancient world, including India and China. The Asian world: India Option or China Option—including physical features, roles of key groups in each society, significant beliefs, contacts and conflicts within and/or with other societies, the role of significant individuals.	K & U
8	The Asia-Pacific World: Ankor/Khmer Empire Option or Shogunate Japan Option	K & U; HS

	or Mongol Expansion Option	
9	The extent of European imperial expansion, including in the Asian region	K & U
10	The impact of at least ONE world event or development and its significance for Australia such as the Vietnam War and Indochinese refugees.	

Source: www.asiaeducation.edu.au/resource/australian_curriculum_audit.html

The *Shape of the Australian Curriculum: Languages*, released by ACARA in late 2011, is the first stage in the development of this curriculum. It provides a rationale for language learning and a common conceptual framework for the development of specific curricula for identified languages and for the different types of learners (L1, Background and L2). These languages are: Arabic; Auslan; Chinese; Classical Languages; French; German; Hindi; Indonesian; Italian; Japanese; Korean; Modern Greek; Spanish; Turkish; and, Vietnamese. The centrality of Aboriginal languages is recognised for the first time and a framework for curriculum development for Aboriginal languages and Torres Strait Island languages is being designed.

The Fig. 7.7 reproduces the description of the 'Asia and Australia's engagement with Asia' Cross Curriculum Priority included in the *Shape of the Australian Curriculum: Languages*.

Fig. 7.7: Asia and Australia's engagement with Asia in the Shape of the Australian Curriculum: Languages

A direct means for learning about and engaging with the diverse countries and people within the Asian region is to learn an Asian language. Learning to communicate and to interact with intercultural sensitivity are fundamental to this engagement. When learning an Asian language students can explore concepts, experiences, and perspectives from within and across Asian cultures.

Retrieved from: www.acara.edu.au/verve/_resources/Languages_Shape_of_the_Australian_ Curriculum.pdf

Although the Languages Shape Paper acknowledges Australia's linguistic diversity, the practicalities of curriculum development and implementation mean that curricula/ syllabuses may be developed for a limited number of languages, rather than all of those identified. Work has commenced on the development of curricula for L1, L2 and Background speakers of Chinese and for L2 Italian. This will test the proposed model and allow opportunities for revision and adaption to ensure its effectiveness.

Conclusion

This essay has described the contribution of educational initiatives such as the *National Asian Languages and Studies in Schools Program* (NALSSP) and the Australian Curriculum to educating young Australians about Asia and noted the influence of factors related to global integration and mobility on their emergence. It has examined how these initiatives have been reflected in educational discourse through use of terms such as 'engagement with Asia' and 'Asia Literacy'. These terms are now part of the educational and even wider discourse. The term 'Asia Literacy' in particular has entered the general discourse. While this has benefits, as the paper has show, 'Asia literacy' is rather problematic in nature and how it is used. It raises expectations that may be hard to meet and possibly deflects attention from the knowledge, understandings and skills that young people gain from the variety of programs that engage them with Asia. It also tends to underplay the commitment and hard work required of individual students and schools in order to develop deep knowledge, understandings and skills about individual Asian countries.

Funding for NALSSP formally ceased at the end of 2011. An evaluation is required to document its impact on the development of 'Asia Literacy' and the expansion in the teaching of the four designated languages. The limited funding for NALSSP (especially in comparison to NALSAS) raises questions about the extent of its possible impact. The experience with NALSAS suggests that without significant integration of Asian language and Studies of Asia programs, the targets set for students completing an Asian language to

Year 12 may be hard to achieve. The development of the Australian Curriculum is likely to have influenced the decision not to continue NALSSP funding beyond 2011. The Australian Curriculum may, in the long run, be a more effective and systematic way of educating young Australians about Asia, both broadly and in-depth through integrated languages and studies of Asia programs.

The Australian Curriculum is still 'in progress' as only curricula for Stage I have been completed and implementation of Stage I in most states will not begin until 2012 and beyond. This paper has demonstrated connections made to Asia and the explicit Asia-related content in English and History. There are also many other opportunities to address Asian themes in these two learning areas that have been documented in support material provided by the Asia Education Foundation. The *Shape of the Australian Curriculum: Languages* confirms the presence of the four Asian languages promoted through NALSSP and provides the opportunity to add Hindi and Vietnamese, while supporting the continued offering Year 12 examinations in other low candidature Asian languages through existing structures.

The success of the 'Asia and Australia's engagement with Asia' Cross Curriculum Priority is likely depend on teachers' capacity to make their students' learning a transformative experience so that its relevance extends beyond the classroom. This will depend crucially on teacher knowledge, expertise and enthusiasm. Wilkinson and Milgate (2009) in their study of take-up of Asia-related topics in Year 12 History suggest that this take-up may not be particularly high, partly because of lack of teacher familiarity with this material. This points to the need to stimulate teacher interest in this area through opportunities for professional learning. Lack of well-qualified teachers has been an ongoing impediment to the expansion of the teaching of Asian languages since the introduction of NALSAS in 1996. The economic importance of Asia to

Australia, growing cultural, personal and educational ties and increased tourism affirms the importance of this particular educational enterprise to Australia in an increasingly globalised world.

Works Cited

Australian Curriculum Assessment and Reporting Authority (ACARA), *The Australian Curriculum*, 2009. Retrieved August 5, 2010 from: www.acara.edu.au/curriculum/development_of_ the_australian_curriculum.html www.acara.edu.au/cross_curriculum_perspectives.html www.australiancurriculum.edu.au

Australian Curriculum Assessment and Reporting Authority (ACARA), *The Australian Curriculum: English F-10*. Retrieved December 2, 2011 from: www.australian curriculum.edu.au/ English/Curriculum/F-10

Australian Curriculum Assessment and Reporting Authority (ACARA), *The Australian Curriculum History F-10*. Retrieved November 28, 2011 from: www.australiancurriculum.edu.au/History/Curriculum/F-10

Australian Curriculum Assessment and Reporting Authority (ACARA), *Shape of the Australian Curriculum: Languages*. Retrieved November 23, 2011. www.acara.edu.au/verve/_resources/Languages_Shape_of_the_Australian_Curriculum.pdf

Asia Education Foundation, *Asia Content in the Australian Curriculum*. Retrieved November 30, 2011 from: www.asiaeducation.edu.au/resource/australian_curriculum_audit.html

Asia Education Foundation, *Asia-related Literary Texts to Support Australian Curriculum for English*. Retrieved November 30, 2011 from: www.asiaeducation.edu.au/verve/_resources/ F10eltCOMaf23112010.pdf

Asia Education Foundation, *Call for National Action Plan for Asia Literacy in Schools*, 2010. Retrieved August 25, 2010 from: www.asiaeducation.edu.au/verve/_resources/AEF_AsiaLiteracy_22Dec10.pdf

Asia Education Foundation, *National Statement on Asia Literacy in Australian Schools 2011-2012*. Retrieved February 3,

2012 from: www. asiaeducation.edu.au/partnerships/national_ statement_2011-12.html

Council of Australian Governments, Asian Languages and Australia's Economic Future; Report prepared for the Council of Australian Government on a Proposed National Asian Language/Studies Strategy for Australian Schools, Brisbane, Australia: Queensland Government Printer, 1994.

Department of Education, Employment and Workplace Relations (DEEWR), *National Asian Languages and Studies in Schools Program* (NALSSP). Retrieved 24 September, 2010.DEEWR Web site: www.deewr.gov.au/Schooling/NALSSP/ FurtherInformation/Pages/FundingInformation.aspx#asia

Department of Education, Employment and Workplace Relations (DEEWR), *Summaries of Becoming Asia-Literate Grants to Schools for 2009, 2010, 2011*. Retrieved, November 4, 2011. www.deewr.gov.au/Schooling/NALSSP/Further Information/Pages/FundingInformation.aspx#strategic

Erebus Consulting Partners, *Evaluation of the National Asian Languages and Studies in Australian Schools (NALSAS) Strategy,* 2002. Retrieved July 10, 2010 from the Department of Education, Employment and Workplace Relations (DEEWR) Website: www1.curriculum.edu.au/nalsas/pdf/evaluation.pdf

Ministerial Council on Education, Employment, Training and Youth Affairs (MCEETYA), *National Statement for Engaging Young Australians with Asia in Australian Schools*. Melbourne: Curriculum Corporation, 2005.

Ministerial Council on Education, Employment, Training and Youth Affairs (MCEETYA), *Melbourne Declaration on Educational Goals for Young Australians*. Melbourne: Curriculum Corporation, 2008.

Pugh, Kevin, J., Linnerbrink-Garcia, L., Koskey, L.K., Stewart, Victoria, C., and Manzey, Christine. (2010). Motivation, Learning and Transformative Experience: A Study of Deep Engagement in Science. *Science Education, 1,* (94): 1-28.

Jenny Wilkinson and Gina Milgate. 2009. *Research Report Studies of Asia in Year 12*, ACER, Melbourne.

CHAPTER 8

Moving Beyond Borders: Open Access Publishing in the Age of Globalism

Julia Gross
Edith Cowan University, Australia

Introduction

Since the mid 1990s, the publication of academic journals in digital format has grown dramatically and academic libraries spend increasing amounts of their acquisitions budgets on digital materials. Digital publication is so ubiquitous that many scholars now make the assumption that most of their research needs will be met by online resources. In this essay, I will argue that despite the explosion of digital publication worldwide, much quality scholarly literature in digital format is inaccessible to global researchers and is on "virtual closed access", locked away behind institutional logins and pay walls. In tune with the theme of this conference one could say that much scholarly information in the age of globalism is still behind "borders", for reasons that will be explained below.

With the growth in digital format, publications in academic libraries have moved from the 20th century acquisitions model whereby they purchased and owned the printed materials (books, journals, etc.) held in the library's collection, to a complex arrangement whereby they subscribe to digital content. This shift has fundamentally altered the way libraries acquire and manage their collections. Libraries now need to negotiate access licences with numerous publishers and vendors, and pay access fees to the publishers. In this new paradigm some of the control over what is purchased has moved away from librarians and scholars, to the publishers.

Publishers, particularly in the areas of Science, Technology and Medicine (STM), are in control in the current publishing model which is skewed in their favour. While academic authors mostly give away their intellectual property in writing for the journals, academic publishers reap large profits. Libraries are caught in the middle, faced with rising subscription costs and budget pressures. This unique publishing model is unsustainable, resulting in what has become known as the "scholarly communication crisis" (Johnson 2002; Oppenheim 2008). This essay outlines the nature of the scholarly communication crisis and looks into the promise of new publishing models that would provide free and open access to research outputs in the digital realm.

The Scholarly Communication Crisis

The scholarly communication crisis manifests itself most acutely in the sciences, where journal publication is the mode of published output and where journal prices are high. However it has implications for humanities researchers too, as I will describe below. Most research is publicly funded and therefore there is a moral argument that the results of that research, including published outputs should be available to the public. In most cases the authors are not paid and many of them freely participate in the editing and peer review process of academic publications. On the other hand publishers get the content for free and they retain copyright in most cases.

The key stakeholders in scholarly communication are publishers, authors, libraries and scholars. It could also be argued that research funders and taxpayers have an interest, given that much research is publically funded. I will present the positions of each of the four key players: publishers, authors, libraries and scholars.

The Role of Publishers in Scholarly Communication

In August 2011 an article by George Monbiot appeared in the online version of *The Guardian* (UK). Monbiot took academic STM publishers to task over what he perceived as their excessive profit margins, claiming that "academic publishers make <Rupert> Murdoch look like a socialist" (Monbiot 2011). This criticism of scholarly publishers captured the attention of open access advocates, including many librarians, as it moved the decade-long debate about the scholarly communication crisis, into the mainstream media (Monbiot 2011; Guttenplan 2011).

Who are these publishers? STM publishing is a global business dominated by three main players: Elsevier, Springer and Wiley-Blackwells. These three publishers together account for 42 per cent of STM journal publication, so they have considerable clout (Peekhaus 2012). However Monbiot's polemic did present just one side of the argument. Publishers would argue that they provide a vital outlet for research; they mediate between authors and libraries to enable the distribution of published research; they manage the whole publication process; and they manage the peer review process which helps to ensure the quality and validity of research findings. They would also maintain that these services provide critical checks and balances and screen for plagiarism. Publishers argue that these are costly processes for the business to undertake. On the other hand an economic analysis of the business model of the STM journal publishing industry found that profits are excessive and cannot be justified (McGuigan 2008).

The Role of Authors in Scholarly Communication

To a certain extent the authors have a vested interest in the status quo in the current scholarly communication process. Authors may be researchers, academic staff and students and they are interested in creating new knowledge and in having their research find a wide audience. Being active in publishing papers is a career imperative in academia. It provides a path towards promotion, tenure, the receipt of research grant funding and awards. In the sciences, researchers are focused on enhancing their research impact which is often measured via the number of journal citations and journal impact factors. In the humanities and social sciences a number of research impact and quality measures are in use such as peer review. However, all of these involve being an active writer. Many authors also participate in editing, and in the peer review and quality control processes of academic publishing. So the current system is well entrenched and "publish or perish" is still a reality as far as authors are concerned.

The Role of Libraries in Scholarly Communication

Prior to the late 1990s all journals were published in print form and libraries subscribed and unsubscribed to individual journal titles on a title by title basis. When digital journals started appearing they were often published as a bundled collection of titles from a publisher. Libraries were now required to sign an access licence for a bundle of journals, some of which they used to have in print and some they did not. The paradigm shift for libraries was from ownership to access. Most libraries set up online access by IP (Internet Protocol) address range to ensure that only the institution's students and staff could gain access. Additionally, over the last decade, journal price subscription costs have increased above inflation. In the five years, 2007-2011, there has been an increase of 33 per cent for academic journals (EBSCO 2011). Many libraries have seen their budgets being "eaten up" by increasing subscription costs. Most Australian university libraries would now spend around 80 per cent of the acquisitions budget on journals and other subscription materials, such as databases and packages of ebooks. Funds available for books are being squeezed, resulting in a negative impact on book-dependant disciples in the humanities. Libraries are trying to confront the problem, mostly by embarking on a journal cancellation program.

The Role of Scholars in Scholarly Communication

Scholars need to be able to access the current literature in their field. On the one hand the growth in digital content has been a boon for scholars, particularly those in the developed world. However, only staff and students of the subscribing institution can gain access to content under the digital access model. The plight of scholars in poorer institutions and in the developing world highlights this issue. For example the graduating international research student from a developing country may find that on returning home, his or her own research will be unavailable locally as the local library may not subscribe.

Neylon argues that academic publishers and scholars (researchers) hold "two utterly incompatible world views of scholarly communication" (2012, 2). One needs unfettered access to scholarly literature, the other needs to operate a profitable business by publishing scholarly literature.

Open Access

Do these access barriers need to exist? The so-called "open access movement" has arisen out of a collective frustration with the existing publishing model and a quest to find an alternative. The Budapest Open Access Initiative (BOAI 2002) brought like-minded people together to come to an agreement to find another way forward. The BOAI challenged the status quo by re-framing how scholarly literature could be published. Open access has focused on the strong moral argument that open access to publicly funded research should be mandatory. When taxpayers pay for research funding, for the salaries of academics to do research and peer review and for libraries to purchase the journals, then surely they should have a say in how published research results are disseminated. Under the open access model the goal is that everyone in the world should share knowledge freely and openly.

In recent years the position of the research funding bodies on the open access question is changing. The main Australian government research funding bodies, the Australian Research Council and National Health and Medical Research Council, have begun to move towards endorsing open access in their research grant agreements (Lane 2006). However there has recently been a backlash against open access, with the drafting of a bill in the US, The Research Works Act (Neylon 2012).

Since 2002 two roads to open access have emerged: the so-called Green Road and the Gold Road (Wolfson Research Exchange 2011). By following the Green Road to open access, authors self-archive on a website, in an institutional repository or in a discipline-specific repository. Open access institutional repositories contain published research outputs, among other things. With the Gold Road the author publishes directly in an open access journal. Gold open access journal publishing has seen rapid growth and now encompasses many dedicated open access journals (Whitfield 2011). There are several models of Gold Road open access journals, with some charging authors an open access publication fee. Many open access journals are also peer reviewed.

How have authors reacted to the possibility of alternate forms of publishing, such as open access? Interestingly, author attitudes towards open access publishing are largely positive. Authors do not see open access as lessening the quality of the final product as many open access journals are peer reviewed. In a survey undertaken by InTech Open Access, 75 per cent of authors rated open access as important (Kenneway 2011).

Institutional Repositories

Institutional repositories or e-repositories are digital storage sites where the published research assets of an institution are collected, preserved and made available on open access. In the last decade institutional repositories have been established within many academic and research institutions around the world and they are usually managed by the library. Some advantages of repositories are that they showcase the institution's research, preserve research online, store and organise research and therefore enhance and promote scholarly communication. Repositories challenge the closed publishing model by providing fast global access to research with no requirement to log in to the site. Records are readily retrieved via a Google search and this ensures the paper will be found and enhances the possibility that it will be cited by others.

In order to place copies of published research papers in a repository, libraries must negotiate copyright clearance with publishers. Each publisher will have a different position on this, but many will allow the library to place a copy of the pre-print or post-print version of the journal article, conference paper and/or book chapter in the repository. Once in the repository these works can be freely accessed by scholars worldwide.

Since 2003 there has been an increase in institutional repositories and there are now over 2000 repositories listed in the OpenDOAR (2011) online registry of repositories. Of those 46 per cent are located in libraries or research institutions in Europe, 23 per cent in America, 17 per cent in Asia with the remaining 14 per cent elsewhere, including Australia. There are currently about 47 institutional repositories in India (OpenDOAR 2011).

Open Access in the Humanities

While the open access debate resonates most strongly among scientific researchers, the open access movement applies in the humanities too (Suber 2005). Organisations such as the UK Arts and Humanities Research Council (AHRC) are championing the cause of e-publication and open access in the humanities in the UK (Heath, Jubb and Robey 2008). A number of open access publishers cover humanities subjects. For example the Open Humanities

Press is an international open access publishing collective whose mission is to make leading works of contemporary critical thought freely available worldwide. One humanities open access electronic journal, Postmodern Culture, was established in the very early days of e-publishing. In addition, the works of humanities researchers are appearing in institutional repositories and the repositories themselves are agile enough to cater for digital media (audio, video, images) used in some creative and humanities research.

Recent Developments in Open Access

Ten years on from the Budapest Open Access Initiative the ideals of open access are still on the scholarly publishing agenda. Despite the gains made over the last few years, with repositories making available pre-print or post-print copies of articles, conference papers and book chapters, these developments are still subject to publishers giving libraries the copyright approval for a repository copy to be made accessible online. In late 2011 a bill known as the Research Works Act was introduced into the United States Congress. The Association of American Publishers, including commercial publishers such as Elsevier, are supporting the bill, one outcome of which would be to "forbid federal agencies to do anything that would result in the sharing of privately published research...unless the publisher of the work agrees first" (Howard 2012). Clearly some commercial publishers feel they are losing ground to open access and want to seize back control of the provision of access to published research. Subsequently there has been an international call for science researchers to boycott Elsevier since "its pricing and policies restrict access to work that should be much more easily available" (Fischman 2012). As of mid February 2012, some thousands of researchers worldwide have pledged not to publish, referee, or do editorial work for any Elsevier journal (The Cost of Knowledge 2012). It is by no means certain that the bill will pass into law. Leading thinkers in this debate predict that the future decade will bring many changes, with research funding bodies driving much of this change and mandating open access to the published outputs of publicly funded research:

> Within ten years all major funders will mandate CC-BY <Creative Commons> Open Access on publications arising from work they fund immediately on publication. Several major publishers will not survive the transition. A few will and a whole set of new players will spring up to fill the spaces. The next ten years look to be very interesting. (Neylon 2012, 3)

Thanks to the possibilities that open access enables we are seeing vanishing borders in the age of globalism, bringing a promise to the developing world that research benefits will be shared. However the saga of the US Research Works Act in 2012 demonstrates that open access cannot be taken for granted; STM publishers are prepared to apply influence on governments and fight for their turf. A wide-scale disruption of the academic publishing model is taking place. For those who care about a fair and equitable model of scholarly publishing it is surely a case of "watch this space".

Works Cited

Budapest Open Access Initiative (BOAI). 2002 [cited 23 September 2011]. Available from http://www.soros.org/openaccess.

The Cost of Knowledge: Researchers taking a stand against Elsevier (website). 2012 [cited 8 February 2012]. Available from http://thecostofknowledge.com/.

EBSCO. 2011. Five Year Journal Price Increase History (2007-2011) [cited 26 November 2011]. Available from www2. ebsco.com/ en-us/InfoProfs/academic/ Pages/budgetingtools.aspx

Fischman, Josh. Elsevier publishing boycott gathers steam among academics [cited February 1, 2012]. Available from http:// chronicle.com/blogs/wiredcampus/elsevier-publishing-boycott-gathers-steam-among-academics/35216

Guttenplan, D.D. 2011. Internet ruffles pricey scholarly journals. New York Times, September 18, 2011 [cited 16 November 2011]. Available from www.nytimes.com/2011/09/19/world/europe/19ihteducLede19.html?_r=1&pagewanted=all

Heath, M., M. Jubb, and D. Robey. 2011. E-Publication and open access in the arts and humanities in the UK 2008 [cited 1 December 2011]. Available from www.ariadne.ac.uk/issue54/heath-et-al/

Howard, Jennifer. 2012. Who Gets to See Published Research? [cited 7 February 2012]. Available from http://chronicle.com/article/Who-Gets-to-See-Published/ 130403/

Johnson, Rick. 2002. SPARC and ACRL: Working together to reform scholarly communication. College and Research Libraries News 63(9). [cited 16 November 2011]. Available http://www.ala.org/acrl/issues/scholcomm/crlnews/ sparcacrl

Kenneway, Melinda. 2011. Author attitudes towards open access publishing 2011 [cited 16 November 2011]. Available from www.intechweb.org/public_files/Intech_OA_Apr11.pdf

Lane, Bernard. 2012. ARC sold on open access to research (online), December 13 2006 [cited 10 February 2012]. Available from www.theaustralian.com.au/higher-education/arc-sold-on-open-access-to-research/story-e6frgcjx-1111112676725

McGuigan, Glenn S. 2008. The Business of academic publishing: a strategic analysis of the academic journal publishing industry and its impact on the future of scholarly publishing. E-JASL: The Electronic Journal of Academic and Special Librarianship 9(3). [cited 28 November 2011]. http://southernlibrarianship.icaap.org/content/v09n03/mcguigan_g01.html

Monbiot, George. 2011. Academic publishers make Murdoch look like a socialist [cited 1 September 2011]. Available from www. guardian.co.uk/commentisfree/2011/aug/29/academic-publishers-murdoch-socialist

Neylon, Cameron. 2012. The Research Works Act and the breakdown of mutual incomprehension [cited 8 February

2012]. http://cameronneylon.net/blog/the-research-works-act-and-the-breakdown-of-mutual-incomprehension/

Peekhaus, Wilhelm. 2012. The Enclosure and alienation of academic publishing: Lessons for the professoriate. tripleC 10(2): 577-99. [cited 23 July 2012]. Available from www.triplec.at/index.php/tripleC/article/download/395/380

OpenDOAR. 2011. The Directory of open access repositories—OpenDOAR [cited 1 December 2011]. Available from http:// www.opendoar.org/index.html.

Oppenheim, Charles. 2008. Electronic scholarly publishing and open access. Journal of Information Science 34(4): 577-90.

Suber, Peter. 2011. Promoting open access in the humanities 2005 [cited 28 November 2011]. Available from www.earlham.edu/ ~peters/writing/apa.htm.

Whitfield, John. 2011. Open access comes of age. Nature 474 (7354): 428.

Wolfson Research Exchange. 2011. Open Access: What's in it for you? [cited 7 October 2011]. Available from www2.warwick.ac.uk/services/library/researchexchange/topics/gd0006/#overview.

SECTION 2
Globalisation: Culture and Society

CHAPTER 9 Vanishing Borders: Boundaries, Habitation and Transnation

Bill Ashcroft
University of New South Wales, Australia

What would the world look like without borders? How might the utopian dream of a borderless world come about? Could rich nations open their borders with no regard for the control of migration? Could some nations and not others open their borders? These questions make us realise how recalcitrant borders are in political life. Borders could only be dissolved if the distinction that holds them in place—between rich and poor nations, democratic and undemocratic, colonised and colonising, the nation and its others, us and them—was itself dissolved. In other words borders maintain the system of inequality without which modern global capitalism (and national antipathy) could not function. If rich nations opened their borders the poor would flood in putting untenable demands on resources. Like a racial melting pot "big enough to take the world and all its got" as the song goes, a borderless world might lead to equality, increase the wealth of the poor, and reduce the wealth of the wealthy. But at what level of economic and cultural security would it settle?

Borders, Nation and Nationalism

The reason it is impossible to imagine a world without borders is that the first act performed by a people that wants to call itself a nation is to put borders around itself. For Australia the borders of the island nation were already established waiting for a nation to fill it. But in whatever way borders are constructed the link between borders, nation and identity is so pathological that any incursion induces panic. The increasing mobility of the global population, the growth of diasporas, the growing number of people in need of escape to lives of reasonable safety leads to a corresponding panic as borders of nations are ever more hysterically protected. What will become of us without asylum seekers to threaten our borders? The impossibility of a borderless world is due not only to this frightening mobility of people, but to the most destructive force of modern times, the force that keeps borders in place—nationalism. Nationalism is *always* complicated by ethnocentrism and racism and as nationalism proliferates, violence increases.

We appear to need borders to know who we are. Signs mean not by referring but by their difference from other signs. How else can we discover who we are than by determining who is other? As the poet Cavafy wrote in "Waiting for the Barbarians" at the end of a poem in which nothing had occurred in the city because the barbarians were coming

> Why this sudden restlessness and confusion
> (How serious people's faces have become)
> Why are the streets and squares emptying so rapidly,
> everyone going home so lost in thought?
> Because night has fallen and the barbarians have not come.
> And some who have just returned from the border say
> there are no barbarians any longer.
> Now what will become of us without barbarians?
> They were, those people, a kind of solution. (Cavafy 1992)

The need for barbarians is demonstrated every night on the news. During the 1990s in Australia, the barbarians, in the form of a trickle of desperate asylum seekers returned the conservative party to government three times. What will become of us without barbarians? This question underlies Coetzee's *Waiting for the Barbarians* in which Colonel Joll of the Third Bureau, arrives to extract, by torture, any information about the "barbarians" that can be gathered from a ragtag collection of old men, women and children, who are captured on a prisoner-gathering foray. The fact that the whole enterprise is manifestly absurd, that there is no threat from the barbarians, a nomadic people who come to town from time to time to trade, that there were no "border troubles" before the arrival of the "Third Bureau" (Coetzee 1980, 114) does not deter Colonel Joll. For clearly the Colonel is in the business of creating the enemy, of delineating that opposition which *must* exist, in order that the Empire might define itself by its geographical and racial others.

The reference to Cavafy's poem is apposite here because the thought of barbarians introduces us to a legal expedient created in Rome to deal with times of extreme emergency. The term *iustitium*—which is constructed exactly like *solstitium*—literally means 'standstill' or 'suspension of the *ius*—the law', not just the suspension of the administration of justice, but of the law itself (Agamben 2005, 41). Giorgio Agamben sees in this the paradigmatic form of the state of exception, which emerged in European politics in the 19th century, became the underpinning of totalitarian states in the 20th, and has become, through the paradigm of security, virtually the normal technique of government in the 21st (SE 14). The state of exception—*stato di eccezione*—is usually understood in English as state of emergency, a term that might have a benign use in times of disaster as 'bureaucratic expediency'. But state of exception captures more explicitly the way in which the *iustitium* creates a border that logically cannot exist. The state of exception is 'not a "state of law" but a space without law', a 'zone of anomie' (Agamben 2005, 50-51)—anomie from the Greek *anomia* meaning lawlessness.

By suspending the law in times of emergency the *iustitium* places the subject beyond the boundary of the law, thus reducing the subject to an object in a state of 'bare life,'—*homo sacer*—outside the law. But the state of exception presents a profound paradox that cuts to the heart of the democratic society.

> If the state of exception's characteristic property is a (total or partial) suspension of the juridical order, how can such a suspension still be contained within it? How can an anomie be inscribed within the juridical order? (23)

This is the same as asking: How can reason prescribe its own irrationality? Or, how can justice prescribe a zone of injustice outside itself and yet authorized and contained by it? How can the law inscribe something that is essentially exterior to it, that is, the suspension of the juridical order itself? (SE 33). What is the nature of such a border between this inside and outside? Agamben answers this question by declaring that the state of exception is neither internal nor external to the juridical order, and its difficulty "concerns precisely a threshold, a zone of indifference, where inside and outside do not exclude each other but rather blur with each other" (SE 23). In short the state of exception makes the border between law and lawlessness vanish.

The classic example of this paradox was the military order issued by George W. Bush on November 13th 2001 that subjected non-citizens suspected of terrorist activities to special jurisdiction that would include 'indefinite detention' and military tribunals.

> Those Talibans captured in Afghanistan are not only excluded from the status as Prisoners of War defined by the Geneva Conventions, they do not correspond to any jurisdiction set by American law: neither prisoners nor accused, they are simply detainees, they are subjected to pure de facto sovereignty, to a detention that is indefinite not only in its temporal sense, but also in its nature, since it is outside of the law and of all forms of legal control. With the detainees at Guantamo Bay, naked life returns to its most extreme indetermination. (Emergency)

In 1978 an estimated 30 countries were in some form of a state of emergency, by 1986 the number was 70, by 1996 this had increased to 147 (Humphreys 2006, 683) with the establishment of detention camps proliferating. In what now looks to be an uncanny prophecy Agamben stated in his 1997 essay "The Camp as *Nomos* of the Modern" that

> The birth of the camp in our time appears as an event which decisively signals the political space of modernity itself. It is produced at the point at which the political system of the modern nation-state...enters into a lasting crisis, and the State decides to assume directly the care of the nation's biological life as one of its proper tasks....
>
> The camp as dislocating localization is the hidden matrix of the politics in which we are still living, and it is this structure of the camp which we must learn to recognise in all its metamorphoses into the zones d'attentes of our airports and certain outskirts of our cities. The camp is the fourth inseparable element which has now added itself to—and so broken—the old trinity composed of the state, the nation (birth), and land. (1997, 113-14)

The camp has become the way in which the state has been able to place subjects outside its borders yet within its carceral jurisdiction. Guantanamo Bay is the prime example of this but Australia and many other countries have established the camp as the fourth element, outside the state, the nation and the continent, the space of not-Australia in which asylum seekers can be offered (not) asylum.

Refugees and asylum seekers may be the barbarians of the moment—as 'other' as the terrorists for whom the state of exception has become the norm. But as the millions spent on inland security confirm, to the state we are all potential barbarians. Airports themselves may be seen to have become zones d'attentes of modernity. The Australian Customs and Immigration Department. has morphed into the Customs and Border Protection Service. When lining up to go through customs in an Australian airport, you form a queue within a taped border on which are stamped the words "protecting our borders". I'm sure the enormous irony of this metonymy is lost on the Government Service—the borders being protected are also the borders keeping the population literally and metaphorically "in line". 'Protection' means limit and control.

Understandably perhaps, Agamben is essentially Eurocentric in his analysis. He developed his thesis of *Homo Sacer* from Carl Schmidt whose *Political Theology* (1922) established the essential proximity between the state of emergency and sovereignty—'sovereign is he who decides on the exception'. Agamben is deeply interested in the debate between Schmidt and Walter Benjamin that ensued from 1928 to 1940 circulating around the critique of violence, because this debate and the issues of violence and state of exception were particularly topical in this period of European history. The state of exception characterising the Nazi Reich and the appalling phenomenon of the Nazi camps provide Agamben with his prime examples and his motivation.

However, Agamben does locate the origins of the twentieth-century European concentration camp in Spanish *campos de concentraciones* in Cuba and British camps for Afrikaaner prisoners in the Boer War. In this genealogy the initial *raison d'etre* of the camp is colonial war, with an implicit racial/ethnic difference in the interned population, and the invocation of a 'state of exception' based on considerations of 'national security' rather than criminal behaviour on the part of those imprisoned. However, this raises the question of the exceptional state of the occupied colonial space itself, exposing the colonial state as a state in which the law, if not exactly suspended, is applied selectively. The colony is, at least in metaphoric terms, a state of exception.

By means of mapping and naming colonised space was brought into the European world by imposing the doctrine of property developed from agricultural Europe. 'Primitives' who did not 'develop' the land and its resources were invariably viewed as having no right of possession. This attitude, formalised in maps that provided the colonised with borders but without sovereignty, is repeated throughout the world in the progress of imperial expansion. The paradox of borders *without* sovereignty constituted colonial space as a state of exception, in essence a giant camp in which 'states of emergency' were a regular occurrence. Colonial space was brought into the European world yet kept out of it at the same time. This has been, in extreme and continuing form, the case with indigenous societies of settler colonies.

Therefore, the ability of colonial subjects to inhabit colonial space became a crucial, though informal strategy of resistance, and it provides an interesting model for the strategies of contemporary subjectivity. Neither detention camp nor colony is officially designated as a prison. But when we observe the dramatic effects of imprisonment as a tool of colonial dominance, and the discursive response to incarceration by the colonized, we see the prison, and the representation of imprisonment by the incarcerated, as the most extreme metonym of colonial occupation.

J.U. Jacobs examined the memoirs of prisoners in South African prisons and found the ways in which they were regularly deprived of their identity were surveillance, stripping, interrogation and torture. Astonishingly, the prison memoirs appropriated and transformed each one of these processes into a form of resistance. (a) Whereas surveillance is designed to produce a subject who identifies with the imprisoning power by seeing him or herself as a prisoner, in prison memoirs this identity becomes the authoring subject, the focus of a discursive resistance. (b) The writer engages in a stripping down, a baring of the soul, in a curious rehearsal of the dehumanizing experience of physical stripping, which *re-establishes* the humanity negated by that process. (c) The writer interrogates him—or herself as well as the prison system and the social structure for which it stands. (d) Whereas torture is designed to produce radical isolation the writer speaks for a community, not only to present a collective subject but to re-install that sense of communal experience which is explicitly removed by torture.

Inhabiting the Nation

We can see these processes as metonymic of the controlled subject's capacity for resistance through transformation. The purpose of using the state of exception example is not to diminish the depressing, sinister and outrageous development of the incarceration of asylum seekers. Neither do I want to make a simplistic identification between the prison, the detention camp, and the colonial state, but rather I want to emphasize the tenacious and innovative nature of the processes and techniques by which subjects inhabit borders of all kinds. Exception comes from the Latin *ex+capere*, to take hold of. "Exceptionality supposes a seizing rather than a passive acceptance of a state of being" (Pinkus 2006, 4). In turn the practice of habitation must be seen as equally active.If, as Agamben asserts, the declaration of the state of exception has been "replaced by an unprecedented generalization of the paradigm of security as the normal technique of government" (SE 14) and further, that the camp as dislocating localisation is the hidden matrix of the politics in which we are still living, we see that the institution of the nation itself is put in question as it becomes a form of carceral space by virtue of its sovereign power to create a state of exception. The techniques for inhabiting the space of the nation become all the more topical and urgent, and these techniques have been nowhere more strategically developed than in colonial states.

Africa is a particularly instructive example of the ambivalence of the nation-state. Perhaps no other continent has been so radically fragmented by colonial boundaries. Newly independent postcolonial states simply occupied the spaces negotiated between colonial powers during European expansion, and thus have no more cultural and communal logic than they had as colonies. As Wole Soyinka put it, the colonial powers carved up the continent "like some demented tailor who paid no attention to the fabric, colour or pattern of the quilt he was patching together" (1994, 31). Where state boundaries have cut through the territories of ethnic groups, these boundaries have remained, institutionalizing ethnic tension and communal violence. The problem for postcolonial societies has been that "the continuity of colonial boundaries served to indigenize colonized space rather than to rectify it" (Gotlieb 1992, 462). The boundary of the post-independence state remains an arbitrary but inescapable trace of a colonial past. As Verhelst says:

> Nowadays, it has become obvious that most Africans hardly recognise themselves in the states their colonizers have bequeathed to them.... An artificial entity, from the points of view of both its frontiers and history, the African state, far from being the product of a long and spontaneous process of nation-building, exists in itself, and very often for itself and for the bourgeoisie which has taken control of it. The people are elsewhere and define themselves by a sub- or trans-state identity.... As an elderly Mossi man put it, "To me Mali is just tax." Nothing more. (1990, 38)

The question of how postcolonial peoples are to inhabit the space defined by these boundaries, how they are to retrieve the 'place-ness' of such a space lies at the heart of the political realities of the postcolonial state.

For the ordinary people who cross borders every day in African states the reality of the national boundary is already being transformed because it is accorded a very different meaning. The boundaries of the state are inhabited differently by different people, different groups, at different times. For whom do these boundaries exist in Africa? Not for the local fishmonger who walks across the border each day to trade, nor for the family visiting relatives in the next country. For ordinary people, the national border means nothing and the traffic of local people, who may not even have heard of passports, is rarely policed. At the level of ordinary experience, the boundary is already vanishing. It is kept in place by the set of global requirements and still has a material reality at the level of international politics (and indeed as a source of tourist income), but as a definition of self, or a description of one's "life-place" it is less significant.

When does the issue of nationality matter? The meaning of nation for individuals is intermittent, fragmentary, variable, depending on their situation. People are drawn into the nation automatically when they enter the exchange economy. Money is, apart from anything else, a signifier of national distinctiveness. People may also choose to identify themselves with the nation at times such as war or international sport. But the activity of ordinary life at any "Third-World" border shows that the pattern of nations is a matrix, a boundary network regulating what is in fact a rhizomic pattern of habitation. This rhizome offers many disjunctive points at which the idea of nation might be appropriated for some purpose. But it also shows many other arborescences which push the boundary of nation back behind a dense network of other exigent realities. If the boundaries of states are provisional the boundaries around such concepts as 'Africanness' or 'Indianness' or 'Australianness' are even more so. Diasporic contributions to various forms of identity potentially deconstruct geographical and racial boundaries.

Transnation

The concept of habitation, which accepts the politically impermeable nature of national boundaries and yet reveals their porosity when the life practices of people are taken into account, allows us to conceive a 'transnational' reality that extends from within and goes beyond national borders. Such a reality allows us to address an increasingly pressing question: What are the limits of borders in this global age? There is no question that refugee and asylum seekers must cross borders and in a very material way: borders retain their hold over diasporic populations in the form of border patrols and incarceration. The ubiquitous 'border protection' becomes more and more hysterical the more fluid and mobile, (and the more desperate) these populations become. It is not Guantanamo Bay but Nauru and Christmas Island that become the models of the state of exception. It is important to remember that most illegal immigrants in Australia simply overstay their tourist visas. Since 1976 boat people have made up less than 1% of Australia's immigration intake. So the hysteria raised about them emphasizes the pathological symbolism of national borders.

This is why borders haunt our theoretical understanding of the global flow of populations—just as they haunt our discussion of national identity—and for this reason I want to extend the concept of habitation to national subjects in a way that addresses their experiential blurring and imaginative crossing of borders. Refugees and asylum seekers move from one bordered space to another and now may end up in a state of exception outside the law. But global populations are *transitive* without necessarily being transnational in the usual sense of this word. Within every nation state lies another 'imagined community' we can call "Transnation". The proliferation of states of exception reveals that the sovereignty of the state is ever more inimical to the freedom of national subjects and the fluidity of the transnation becomes an important element of hope for the nation living around the structures of the state.

Subjects in the transnation may at various times identify with the nation, with ethnicity, religion, family or tribe; they may know nothing of the workings of the state except for their experience of local officials; they may travel beyond national borders or stay within them, and never be in contact with other cultural subjects. But their experience provides the constant theme of the ambiguous relation between the nation and the state. Transnation is the fluid, migrating *outside* of the state that begins *within* the nation. This is possibly most obvious in countries with massive populations such as India and China where the 'nation' is the perpetual scene of migration and of various forms of *translation*. But translation is but one example of the movement, the 'betweenness' by which the subjects of the transnation are constituted. The transnation is a way of talking about subjects in their ordinary lives, subjects who live in-between the categories by which subjectivity is normally constituted. But it also reminds us that one of the most insistent categories with which people must negotiate is the nation.

If we think of the 'transnation' extending beyond the geographical, cultural, religious and imaginative boundaries of the state, both within and beyond the boundaries of the nation, we discover it as a space in which those boundaries are disrupted, in which national and cultural affiliations are superseded, in which binaries of centre and periphery, national self and other are dissolved. The transnation refers to something more than diaspora, since it is both internal and external, more than cosmopolitanism, because the transnation may include monocultures.

The transnation reveals that all subjects have at least some level of ability to move between the structures of the state. It is precisely this mobility, and in particular its symbolic threat to borders that has led nations to create states of exception—camps outside yet within their borders. Millions of people have been trapped by the hysteria of xenophobia and 'border protection'. But the mobility of the transnation *need not* be a permanent condition of displacement, loss and exile. On the other hand, exile, as a condition of displacement begins *within* the nation, it does not begin once borders have been crossed. The mobility and in-betweenness of the transnation injects the principle of hope into the equation.

At the end of *State of Exception* Agamben says:

> To show law in its nonrelation to life and life in its nonrelation to law means to open a space between them for human action, which once claimed for itself the name of 'politics'. Politics has suffered a lasting eclipse because it has been contaminated by law, seeing itself, at best, as constituent power (that is, violence that makes law), when it is not reduced to merely the power to negotiate with the law. (2005, 88)

While this might show insufficient attention to the separation of powers, Agamben follows Foucault in identifying law with the sovereignty, and hence the borders of the state. For him politics "has suffered a lasting eclipse" from its contamination by law. But my contention here is that the space of the political, the space opened between life and law, is occupied by the transnation, that proliferation of subjects who live what may be called the 'politics of the quotidian'. This may include the transgression of border crossers who evade the camps but it refers to *all* subjects of the state, those subjects who represent the exorbitant proliferation of the nation's subjects.

There are groups who live in the perpetual space of the border, who can say in the words sung by the Chicano group Los Tigres del Norte—"I didn't cross the border, the border crossed me." Borders continue to cross the transnational subject born into competing ideologies. The borders from which we might be free are therefore not simply the boundaries of the nation but those of nationness, and ultimately of identity itself. It is the strange contrapuntal relationship between identity, history, and nation that needs to be unravelled. For the Chicana writer Gloria Anzaldua the US-Mexican border, the "chainlink fence crowned with rolled barbed wire", is an "open wound" some 1,950 miles long. Such a line divides a people and their culture on both sides of the border. But it is not just a border in space, it is a lived border "running down the length of my body" splitting her very being (Anzaldúa 1987, 193). The concept of the border is disrupted in many ways in postcolonial literatures, but most powerfully in the relationship between memory and place: memory rather than nostalgia and place rather than nation.

The Space of the Transnation

On a global scale transnation is composed of subjects who occupy a space within and beyond the state, a distinction nicely captured by Deleuze and Guattari's comparison between smooth and striated space, which they explain by contrasting woven textile and felt. A textile fabric is composed of interwoven vertical and horizontal components, warp and woof, a delimited and organised structure that Plato used as a paradigm for 'royal science' "the art of governing people or operating the state's apparatus" (2004, 475). Felt, on the other hand is a supple solid, more like an 'anti-fabric'. It is an entanglement of fibres rather than a weave, one obtained by rolling the block of fibres back and forth, entangling, rather than weaving them. It is 'smooth' without being 'homogeneous'. We can see immediately the relevance of this to the practices of habitation, which may be *located* in the striated space of the state but find their *place* within, around and beyond its borders.

But what is the relation between smooth space and striated space when we use these terms to describe the political *institution* of the nation? Let us think for a minute of establishment of the Indian Constitution. If we think of the smooth space of the nation circulating around the striated space of the state, it continued its heterogeneous life regardless of nationalism, regardless of internationalism, in what we can understand as an alternative modernity that had little to do with the state's management. Ironically, the in-between subjects of the transnation can also participate in the state. A good example is the *harijan* or 'untouchable', Dr B.R. Ambedkar, chair of the Constitution committee and instrumental in confirming Article 17, which abolished untouchability. But there is a dual irony here: a person from the margins of national society participates in framing state legislation; but that legislation has little effect on attitudes to caste in the nation.

Dr Ambedkar shows us that smooth spacc is not separate from striated space. The smooth space of the nation exists alongside, between, even within the striated space of the state. But it is not necessarily liberatory. "Never believe that a smooth space will suffice to save us" (2004, 500), urge Deleuze and Guattari, and we see this very clearly in the case of the Untouchables. Despite national regulation, caste attitudes continue unabated. Smooth space may be the space of habit, prejudice and hostility. Yet by its very existence the smooth space of the transnation challenges, because it mostly ignores, exceeds, surrounds and interpenetrates, the striated space of the state. It is not in itself liberatory but it is the medium of liberation, because it is the medium of the glocal.

The concept of the 'transnation', however, while incorporating the separation of state and nation, and endorsing the utopian potentiality of the state's transformation, accommodates the constant, ubiquitous, oppressive and combative discourse of particular nation-states. It emphasizes the fact that the transnation is a product not only of the nation, existing as a kind of 'smooth space' running through it, but also a product of movement, displacement, relocation. The transnation is both global and local. It not only interpenetrates the State, it interpenetrates the multiplicity of states in their international and global relationality. The terms "global" and "local" are usually placed in a binary relation, even when the global is seen to be something under constant transformation at the local level. The transnation, by seeing the *movement* of peoples in globalization as a fundamental feature of spatiality, accentuates the *circulation* of the local in the global.

Literatures in Transnation

While the nation reasserted itself in global economics after the Global Financial Crisis, it has never really been under any threat in the identification of literatures. National literatures, despite the historical baggage of nationalist, nativist and chauvinist ideologies, still hold sway in the institutionalisation of the discourse. Print capitalism, which Benedict Anderson linked to the development of the 'imagined communities' of nations, also applies, particularly at the level of myth, to imaginative literature, and even more so to the categorization of that literature. Indeed the distinction is important: writers do not set out to 'write the nation' but are invariably held to do so within critical discourse. Jameson's notorious declaration that all Third World texts are national allegories (Jameson 1986, 69) is the most obvious example, but it is repeated in different ways almost universally in the discipline of literary study. Although a relatively subtle version of the concept of national literatures, 'national allegory' fails to embrace the complexity of the relationship between literature and the idea of nation. In particular, it "fails to adequately describe the dissolution of the idea of nation and the continuous persistence of national concerns" (Franco 1989, 211).

Far from being 'national' in execution, literary works emerge from the *transnation*, constantly projecting themselves into the realm of possibility. This is the dimension of literature that Ernst Bloch refers to as its utopian function. Literature, according to Bloch, is inherently utopian because its *raison d'etre* is the imaging of a different world. Its connection to reality is like that of fulfillment to lack. It is by narrative, by the stories we tell, that we have a world and it is by utopian thinking, utopian forms, utopian narrative, that we may have a conception of a radically changeable world. Literature is utopian because "its reference point is the future". In post-colonial writing this future is almost always mediated by memory, by a particular view of the past. J.M. Coetzee puts this in a more sombre, but no less utopian way in *Age of Iron,* when he describes man as:

> the only creature with a part of his existence in the unknown, in the future, like a shadow cast before him. Trying continually to catch up with that moving shadow, to inhabit the image of his hope. (1990, 155)

It is through narrative, through the stories we tell, that we best inhabit the image of this hope. It is through literature that we may best imagine a radically changeable world. This doesn't mean, of course that literary works are inevitably optimistic or even hopeful, but that their orientation to the future gives shape to the possibilities conceived in the human imagination. Literature is about possibility, about potentiality. 'Utopia', after all, refers to 'no place' rather than 'good place', but it is the place that defines the imaginative reach of literature.

In the context of the transnation, then, we are compelled to ask the question: to what extent is the utopian function of literature released when the boundaries of the nation are breached? Certainly postcolonial theory in its critique of the nation has seen the transformative possibilities of a literature unbound by nationalism, even if that sometimes involves a different kind of categorization in region or race or forms of colonial relationship. But there is considerable interest among philosophers in the capacity of literature to embody potentiality. For Casarino, "to write of a liberation beyond measure is to love potentiality" (2002, 79). To love potentiality means, among other things, to write, to experiment with forms and narratives that allow subjects to surpass their limits. Conversely one could say that 'to write is to love potentiality, which is to imagine a liberation without measure'. This is the utopian dimension of writing, of literature—its horizon of absolute potentiality—liberation without *telos*. What is expressed in writing, according to Agamben, is "an absolute writing that no one writes: a potential to be written". Thus, he stresses, "pure actuality, that is, the actuality of an act, is (also) pure potentiality, that is, potentiality of a potentiality" (1999, 216). Or, as Blanchot puts it: "To write is to surrender to the interminable" (1982, 27).

Curiously, the presence in literature of its utopian dimension, of pure potentiality, may be more attractive to philosophers than literary critics. But in postcolonial literatures the issue of language and its transformative potentiality becomes prominent, leading to a question that for various political reasons is virtually unaskable: 'to what extent does a common literary language—the colonial language, the appropriated and transformed English, the language of power and subjection—become the space of potentiality because it releases the writing subject from the myth of a fixed identity'? To what extent does the language become the medium by which the past transforms the present? These questions are 'unaskable' because they seem to undermine the necessity of resistance. But on the contrary, they show that the most effective resistance is the transformation of the imperial discourse in whatever form it takes. The question then becomes: 'to what extent are these potentialities realised in the transnation, which in its perpetually articulated subjects and the possibilities of its smooth space reveals itself to be a scene of potentiality, even of pure potentiality'? Theoretically, the combination of literature and transnational subjectivity should lead to an exorbitant potentiality. The reasons such literature doesn't always achieve this lie both in the institution of literature and in the constant pull of political, ethnic and cultural identification. It is not just the framework of the nation that resists the horizon of possibility in the literary text.

The horizonality of literature is peculiarly suited to the smooth space of the transnation. The utopian potentiality of literature is towards a future without dimensions. But something crucial happens to the concept of time in the literature of the transnation. In the displaced postcolonial world of diasporic subjectivity utopia is the constant horizon of the present, the horizon *that is at the same time* the horizon of the past. Edouard Glissant captures this perfectly when he proposes a view of the past that projects into the future, *a prophetic vision of the past* (Glissant 1989, 64). He says: "The past, to which we were subjected, which has not yet emerged as history for us, is, however, obsessively present. In this utopian space the border between memory and the future dissolves.

Horizon

This horizonal space, the space of transformation, the space of literature, lies in the smooth space of the transnation. There is a conjunction between the concepts of transnation and utopian transformation that exceeds the term 'diasporic literatures', or even the term 'cosmopolitanism'. This is a conjunction of dissolving borders, both of space and time. Just as the transnation can no longer be conceived of as lying beyond the borders of the nation, but also of extending within, so postcolonial reading shows us that the utopian dimension of its literatures is not simply located in its capacity to cross borders, or even to imagine a borderless future, but in its capacity to dissolve the boundary between past and future through acts of memory that paradoxically imagine a different world.

Works Cited

Agamben, Giorgio. 1997. "The Camp as *Nomos* of the Modern" in Hent de Vries and Samuel Weber (eds.), *Violence, Identity and Self-Determination.* Stanford: Stanford Univ Press: 106-18.

——— 1999. *Potentialities: Collected Essays in Philosophy*, ed. and trans. D. Heller-Roazen. Stanford: Stanford University Press.

——— 2005. *State of Exception,* trans. Kevin Attell. Chicago: University of Chicago Press.

——— 2006. "The State of Emergency" Extract from a lecture given at the Centre Rokand Barthes, Univerite Paris VII Denis-Diderot. www.generation-online.org/p/fpagambenschmitt.htm (accessed Dec 2011)

Anzaldúa, Gloria. 1987. Borderlands/La Frontera: The New Mestiza, San Francisco: Aunt Lute.

Blanchot, Maurice (1982). *The Space of Literature,* trans. A. Smock, Lincoln. NE and London: University of Nebraska Press.

Casarino, Cesare. 2002. 'Philipoesis: A Theoretico Methodological Manifesto' *Boundary 2*, 29: 1 (Spring): 65-96.

Cavafy, C.P. 1992. *Collected Poems.* Trans. Edmund Keeley and Philip Sherrard. Ed. Goeorge Savidis. Princeton: Princeton University Press.

Coetzee, J.M. 1980. *Waiting for the Barbarians*. Harmondsworth: Penguin.

——— 1990 *Age of Iron*. London: Secker and Warburg.

Deleuze, Gilles and Guattari, Felix. 2004. *A Thousand Plateaus—Capitalism and Schizophrenia,* trans. B. Massumi. London & New York: Continuum Books.

Franco, Jean 1989. "The Nation as Imagined Community" in H. Aram Veeser ed. *The New Historicism*. London: Routledge.

Glissant, Edouard. 1989. *Caribbean Discourse: Selected Essays* trans. with introd. by J. Michael. Dash Charlottesville: University Press of Virginia.

Gotlieb Yosef. 1992. "Retrieving Life-Place from Colonized Space: Transcending the Encumbrances of the Post-Colonial State." *Political Geography*. 11(5) (September): 461-74.

Humphreys, Stephen. 2006. "Legalizing Lawlessness: On Giorgio Agamben's *State of Exception*" *The European Journal of International Law*, Vol. 17, No. 3: 677-87.

Jacobs, J.U. 1991. "Confession, Interrogation and Self-interrogation in the New South African Prison Writing" in Kirsten Holst-Petersen and Anna Rutherford (eds.), *On Shifting Sands: New Art and Literature from South Africa*. Portsmouth NH: Heinemann (1992).

Pinkus, Karen. 2006. "$, Anomie, State of Exception" in Elena Bellina and Paolo Bonifazio, *State of Exception: Cultural responses to the Rhetoric of Fear*. Newcastle: Cambridge Scholars: 2-11.

Schmitt, Carl. 1922. *Political Theology: Four Chapters on the Concept of Sovereignty*, trans. George Schwab. Cambridge Mass.: MIT Press 1985.

Soyinka, Wole. 1994. Interview with Nathan Gardels, "Bloodsoaked Quilt of Africa," *Weekly Mail and Guardian* (South African) 20-26 May: 31.

Verhelst, Thierry, G. 1990. *No Life Without Roots: Culture and Development* (trans. Bob Cumming). London & New Jersey: Zed Books.

CHAPTER 10

Not Alone in the Diaspora: Reflections on South Asians in North America

Amritjit Singh
Ohio University, USA

Border Crossings: Diaspora and Globalisation

The concept of *Diaspora*, in its multivalence and evolving uses, continues to cause ripples in the studies of migration, culture, and identity. Like globalisation in theory and practice, diaspora as a paradigm and in the diverse realities it signifies cannot only illumine ongoing individual and group experiences, but also brings much-needed historical understandings of men and women who have been on the move throughout human history. In its extended and creative applications, the concept can sometimes clarify migratory or colonising phenomena and at other times cast an intriguing veil of confusion over debates about the processes of assimilation, agency, invisibility, and marginalisation that are often at play among populations displaced from their "homeland" territories. The concept, when flexibly used, can result in engaging interpretations of elusive global and transnational historical events and cultural phenomena.

Today, *diaspora* embraces the many globalised phenomena that continue to shape the economic realities in many parts of the world. The strong presence of diasporic populations in Europe, North America, Australia, or New Zealand signals just one aspect of the massive labor migrations that accompany the straddling of capital across nations. These populations also draw special attention to the difficult and life-changing journeys that millions of migrants undertake. The vanishing borders shaped by technology, multinationals, and jet travel, are counterbalanced by the reality of fences and borders that still divide nations, especially between the North and the South. In fact, in an ironical twist, globalisation has exposed, more than ever before, the continuing faultlines of class, race, gender, and nation all across the globe.

Still, Jana Evans Braziel and Anita Mannur view globalisation and transnationalism as "homogenising" and "impersonal," and they regard diaspora, in counterpoint, as a more humane and inclusive discourse that remains, "above all a human phenomenon—lived and experienced." However, in their extended discussion of these issues in their Introduction to *Transforming Diaspora* (2011, xiv-xvi), Robin E. Field and Parmita Kapadia posit that globalisation and transnationalism in fact invigorate diasporic communities. They argue that globalisation, and especially its attendant multiple communication technologies, allow for individual voices to shape the communal diasporic identity. In their view, the role that individual members and coalitions play in and around a particular diaspora must take precedence over the concepts of place and homeland as the primary foundation of a diasporic community. They also note how transnationalism too productively downplays the importance of the nation-state, with its prioritised originary connection to the diasporic communities, and instead allows other connections—such as race, religion, ethnicity, gender, and sexuality—to form between distinct diasporic communities.

Consider, for instance, the situation of gay Asian Americans, who, as Dana Y. Takagi has noted, view themselves "as on the margins of both communities,...[and] experience the worlds of Asian America and gay America as separate places—emotionally, physically, intellectually" (Takagi 1996, 22-25). Scholars such as Gayatri Gopinath, Martin Manalansan, and Chandan Reddy have demonstrated in divergent ways how the very experience of diaspora is profoundly shaped by sexuality and influences the shimmering mobility of individuals between diaspora communities. Moreover, the assumption that membership in a diasporic ethnic community entails full acceptance overdetermines the very histories of gender and sexuality bigotry. For example, a gay South Asian may feel "at home" with other South Asians given their shared connections to language, food, customs, etc., but still feel excluded, given the marginality of queer sexualities in India and in diasporic South Asian communities around the globe. Diasporas are thus complex migrant groups whose identities do not lend themselves to easy generalizations.

Broadly speaking, the term diaspora is applied to groups who form minorities in their new locations, even as they feel the pressure to preserve homeland cultures and languages and to defend them against intentional and unintentional assaults from the surrounding majority communities. Such formations involve the challenges of learning new ways of doing things at work and in social situations, as well as in language acquisition, against the backdrop of a growing awareness of cultural creolization. These processes represent a slow but sure development of transnational attitudes, practices, and habits that shape the need to come to terms with fresh identifications and new identities, as well as with the complications of individual growth, family, sexuality, racial constructions, and community in the growing familiarity of what was once alien and alienating.

But attempting to jump out of the crab-basket of narrow nationalist discourses is not simply a function and responsibility of the diaspora condition. Many popular immigrant destinations, such as the U.S., have also nourished long traditions of debate and dissent within their borders. Diasporic individuals might feel empowered through identifying and engaging such revisionist discourses that counter the provincialism and exceptionalism of pervasive cultural myths and symbols that surround

American identity. In short, to learn to think transnationally today would require a study of the evolution of hybrid identities both within and outside the U.S. borders. Within the U.S., for example, the homogenizing rhetoric of Frederick Jackson Turner's 1893 Frontier Thesis has received a direct or indirect rebuttal not only from W.E.B. Du Bois in *Souls of Black Folk* (1903), but also from José Marti's essays gathered in *Inside the Monster* (1975), Charles W. Chesnutt's *The Future American* (1900), and the critique of American provincialism in Randolph Bourne's *Trans-National America* (1916).

Diasporas are often comprised of refugee populations. Examples include Palestinians in many countries in the Middle East and around the world; Cuban, South Vietnamese and the Hmong immigrants in the U.S.; South Asians from Uganda in the U.K. and elsewhere in the 1970s; Rwandans in neighboring countries in the mid-1990s; and currently Zimbabweans in South Africa, as well as the refugees from the Democratic Republic of the Congo (formerly Zaire) in many neighboring central African nations. Members of a group who enjoyed the privilege of belonging to a majority community at home (such as Hindus in India, or Muslims in Pakistan or Iran) might be forced to wrestle with their minority status in their new homelands. Again, a particular group—such as South Asians or Filipinos—may feel sidelined in Asian American discourses even as they recognize the *realpolitik* imperative of merging into such coalitions in their new situations. In fact, as Shankar and Srikanth observe in the Introduction to their co-edited volume, *A Part Yet Apart* (1998), the equivocal position of South Asian American culture and art within Asian American Studies explains many South Asians' desire to be a part of, yet remain apart from, the rest of Asian America, even as they embrace and sustain multiple transnational locations for identity and culture. At the same time, driven by nostalgia, nationalist discourses, and a very human need for connection, South Asians and other diaspora groups may allow homeland ideologies and hegemonies to dominate or distort their lives in their new locations. In fact, their power of global connection and hard currency remittances can either impede or advance homeland goals centered in education, diversity, human rights, and environment.

Field and Kapadia explore such possibilities and much more through their careful engagement with transnational texts and phenomena. By pursuing unusual trajectories in Diaspora Studies, their work expands the meaning of diaspora as it conveys the term's capacious uses in critical discourses on art and culture. The volume achieves its goals by focusing especially on communities—*beyond national boundaries*—that do not fit the general expectations surrounding the diaspora paradigm. It recognises the value of flexibility in definition and approach to read and evaluate atypical historical and cultural contexts.

Azade Seyhan has demonstrated in *Writing Outside the Nation* (2000)—through her examination of the literary scene and transnational poetics in both Germany and the U.S.—some of the most innovative contemporary writers in the diaspora are writing in their second or third language. The work of such bilingual and bicultural writers as Oscar Hijuelos, Maxine Hong Kingston, and Eva Hoffman in the U.S., as well as Libuše Moníková, Rafik Schami, and E.S. Özdamar in Germany, calls for a new framework of cultural and linguistic memory to explore the relationships among displacement, memory, and language.

In the U.S., intense debates on "same sex marriage" represent a debate about equal access to legal rights and societal privileges. New scholarship in the field has already challenged those presuppositions of postcolonial and diaspora studies that elide the deep incidence of gender and sexuality in issues of identity and community. Scholars such as Gayatri Gopinath, Chandan Reddy, and Rahul K. Gairola have joined questions of sexuality to the already influential debates around alternative epistemologies, migration, exile, hybridity, and alienhood associated with names such as Edward Said, Gayatri Chakravorty Spivak, Homi Bhabha, Rey Chow, Ella Shohat, and Katarzyna Marciniak.

It is only since the 1990s that South Asians have registered their presence on the collective American consciousness in any significant way. It is no mere coincidence that this new recognition has been accompanied in the past two decades by the growing global importance of India as an economic power. While the earliest arrivals from the Indian subcontinent in the U.S. can be traced back to 1790, they reached the United States and Canada in noticeable numbers only between the 1890s and 1920s, when both countries found their own distinctive ways of preventing new South Asian migrants from becoming part of their predominantly European populations. On October 3, 1965, President Lyndon B. Johnson signed the Immigration Act of 1965 (Hart-Cellar Act) that opened up immigration from around the world and since then there has been a steady flow of immigrants from all South Asian countries to the United States.

It is worth noting that President Johnson signed this immigration reform legislation, barely three months after he signed into law the Voting Rights Act and less than a year after the historic Civil Rights Act of 1964. The Civil Rights Act and Voting Rights Act together resuscitated the long-ignored provisions of the 15th Amendment of 1870 and restored the civil rights denied to African Americans by Jim Crow laws and practices since the 1880s. Between 1962 and 1966, Canada too re-fashioned its immigration policies to ensure that prospective immigrants would no longer be denied entry on the basis of color, race, or nationality, welcoming instead skilled immigrants of all backgrounds. Since the 1960s, there has been a steady flow of new immigrants to both Canada and the US from India and other parts of Asia. Today South Asians in North America form a vibrant and visible community that is making important economic and political gains and they are also becoming vocal in various regions and spheres of society in important if uneven ways. While the totality of South Asian American experience invites a multiplicity of critical frameworks, diasporic and transnational perspectives lend us many valuable insights.

Homeland and Diaspora: A Palimpsest Relationship

In many ways, the diasporic populations and their "imaginary homelands" remind us of how culture and identity are reconstituted as they travel to new places. In, "Imaginary Homelands," Salman Rushdie views his own and other diaspora writings in adversarial terms: "Writers and politicians are natural rivals.... And the novel is one way of defying the official, politicians' version of truth" (1912, 14). He also acknowledges the influence upon him of the black American novelist, Richard Wright. Rushdie was helped by Wright's early recognition that black and white Americans were engaged in a war over the nature of reality: "their descriptions [of the world] were incompatible. So it is clear that re-describing a world is the necessary first step towards changing it" (Rushdie 1992, 13-14). In counterpoint, diaspora theory also opens up the possibility of viewing, say, Chineseness in China or Indianness in India as something always in flux, and not just a fixed or essentialized category—despite the preferred official or ideological narratives in these supposedly stable civilizations. Homeland and diasporic cultures mirror each other in a symbiosis of co-dependency but they also have the capacity to engage and nudge each other in various directions in a healthy, dialogic relationship.

In fact, this potential of mutuality and close connection has been reinforced in today's globalised world by the ease of jet travel and technological advances that allow persons to stay in touch across oceans on a daily basis through e-mail, internet phone, and inexpensive international calling plans. It is in relation to this contemporary context that Rajini Srikanth claims how "the South Asian American writers' not insignificant contribution to American literature and to the American imagination is the delineation of narratives and spaces that enable the conception of a nation as discrete and entwined within the folds of other nations" (Srikanth 2004, 11). Diaspora populations today often know that distance no longer signifies exile and that both diaspora and homeland are fluid, porous, unstable categories.

I personally know of at least a dozen American and Canadian individuals of Indian and Chinese descent who own apartments back in their homelands and visit there regularly for annual or biannual sojourns. There are thousands, probably millions, more who have embraced some notion of double citizenship in the past decade or so. In fact, for Shirley Geok-lin Lim, these new realities provide grounds enough to prefer the notion of transnationality over diaspora—writing with both Southeast Asian and American audiences in mind and facing the concomitant challenges of cross-cultural and multi-dialectal literary expression. For others such as Fiona Cheong, the notion of "transnational" is problematic, because then "the focus is on the nation. I'm not keen on national identities right now, because they are being used to justify committing atrocious crimes" (2002, 25).

Many self-conscious diasporic individuals who straddle two or more identities may feel implicated as global citizens not only in the continuing patterns of violence and human rights violations in their ancestral lands, but also in the contradictory and complex histories of their adoptive homelands. This double cross of knowledge and responsibility might make them suspicious of their new homeland's master narratives, even as they learn to view their originary homelands with a sharply critical affection untainted by nostalgia, guilt, or misplaced patriotism. This point about diaspora's potential to trouble homeland attitudes and mores merits some further explanation with reference to some recent debates regarding representational issues in diasporic writing, especially in relation to South Asian writers. The diasporic imagination's capacity to interrogate and refashion homeland realities manifests itself not only in the magic realism of Salman Rushdie's *Midnight's Children* as well as the writings of Rohinton Mistry and several others—novels, poetry and memoirs.

Many South Asian works demonstrate that regardless of whether the diaspora writers write about their adoptive homeland, or about the originary homeland through memories colored by their new experience of cultural hybridity, their art emerges inescapably out of a palimpsest-like continuum of feelings, thoughts, images and memories that comprise a writer's personal history and psyche. Mistry's *A Fine Balance* exposes the disagreeable realities of contemporary urban life that many in India would prefer not to disclose. Mistry's well-researched novel chronicles the lives of the outcast in the underbelly of a nameless metropolis, and his choice of situating his novel in the mid-1970s during Mrs. Indira Gandhi's Internal Emergency serves Mistry well to issue his quietly passionate indictment of authoritarianism, casteism, and political corruption. In bringing his sensibility to bear on ugly homeland realities (maybe he feels homeland writers are not doing enough on this front), Mistry has earned the irritation of his critics in India and elsewhere who want to zealously guard the new image of India as a globalised, rising economic power.[1] On the other hand, Mistry continues to provoke the ire of his Canadian critics by choosing not to write exclusively or even primarily about Canada, even though he has now lived in Canada for well over 35 years. In 1991, in response to a Canadian reporter's question about when he might write his first novel about Canada, Mistry responded, "I'll write a novel set in Canada if it comes to me. I have no policies on this" (cited in Singh 1992, 208).

For diaspora writers in North America, for example, whether they are originally from South Asia, Eastern Europe, or the Caribbean, self-definitions are often not shaped by their easy embrace of one or the other of the many assimilationalist formulas supplied by First World cultures. Instead, their self-image and their creative output are the result of their own individualistic struggles with the messy complexities of their moves from the homeland, as well as by their (in)ability to engage with the many historical group experiences that comprise the collective memory, the master narratives, and the counter-narratives of their new homelands. Poets and novelists are as likely to feel the same pressure as historians and literary scholars do to participate in the often explosive debates on race, ethnicity, identity, and citizenship—not out of their raw nerves or career agendas, but through a responsible sense of interconnectedness, as well as a careful attention to specific cultural and historical realities. Viewed thus, a diaspora writer's oeuvre is stripped of some of its alleged novelty and exoticism and it can take its legitimate place in "the existing order," *à la* T.S. Eliot, of all cultural productions in both their homeland and adoptive homelands—as one rendition among many of human quandaries and conflicts.

Diasporic populations often experience indifference and hostility, as well as negative stereotyping and more insidious forms of marginalization in their new sites. In North America, even in 2012, when people use the word "American" or "Canadian," they generally mean a white person. Lydia Kwa, an openly gay Canadian writer originally from Singapore, points to the curse of the phenotype (the automatic "visual misrecognition," as she terms it) that dogs the steps of all those who are not part of majority populations: "Here when some people see me they assume I'm not a Canadian writer, exposing what their racist conditioning and their beliefs about national identity can or cannot include" (Cheong et al. 2002, 24-25). The ability of diasporic individuals to fight back in such situations in their adoptive homelands, or even the impulse to resist the caricatures and exoticized renditions of their traditional cultures or faith traditions, may indeed clash with the practical necessity of blending in and moving up socially and economically.

Old Baggage, New Destinations

Having arrived in, say, North America, with a gunny sack of powerful media images of African Americans or American Indians, new immigrants may indeed reinforce the deep-seated racial constructions of such non-immigrant populations and in the process miss out on significant lessons of strategy, survival, community formation, and citizenship embedded in the historical experiences of these and other minorities. Consider, for example, the relative paucity and opacity of Asian American interactions with Chicanos, Blacks and American Indians.[2] Asian immigrants who have arrived in North America since the mid-1960s have generally failed to disengage themselves from the well-established historical pattern by which the European immigrants around 1900 had empowered themselves as "whites". The new Asian immigrants cannot become "white" in the same way as the Irish, Italians, and Jews did, so they seek overcompensation in real estate, material acquisitions, and other investments in class privilege. Despite the post-9/11 phenotype jolt received by many (South) Asian Americans, a vast majority of Asian Americans still attempt to make up for their lack of whiteness by acquiring a consciousness that is often quite "white" and assimilationist. Thus, diaspora populations can either deepen the existing fault lines of ideology, race/caste, class, and gender in both their old and adoptive homelands, or they can allow the potential strength of their imagination and lived experience to weigh on local and global issues through self-conscious acts of responsible citizenship.

As an illustration of how survival and strategy run the whole gamut of immigrant and non-immigrant racialized communities, it would be useful to compare diaspora writers' perspectives on issues of identity, community, and responsibility with the view of these matters that reverberates throughout the rejection of group solutions to the challenges of marginalization in Ralph Ellison's classic novel, *Invisible Man* (1952). In discussing James Joyce's young protagonist, Stephen Dedalus, Mr. Woodridge, the nameless protagonist's English teacher, exclaims, "Stephen's problem, like ours, was not actually of creating the uncreated conscience of his race, but of creating the uncreated features of his face. Our task is that of making ourselves individuals. The conscience of a race is the gift of its individuals who see, evaluate, record" (1981, 345-46). Ellison's complex perspectives on individualism and community, citizenship and responsibility—as expressed in his fiction, essays, and interviews speak resonantly to similar issues faced by diasporic and immigrant communities.

As Shu-mei Shih illustrates in her essay, "Against Diaspora," using a diasporic framework in a multiplicity of contexts has the potential of highlighting the power and expanse of border-crossings to examine phenomena and texts that would be seen as lying outside the more conventional domain of diaspora theory. Official agencies and/or political parties in emerging economic powers such as China and India are fully cognizant of the rich resource of revenue and influence their diaspora populations represent and are eager too to win them over to their own preferred ideologies and hegemonic discourses. Shih documents how Beijing's current privileging of Mandarin/ Hanyu, the language of the majority Han people in China, projects its preferred definition of Sinophone and how such a homogenising maneuver goes against the grain of established Chinese communities in Southeast Asia and North America that have localized culturally and speak a wide variety of Sinitic languages.

Likewise, although India's official narratives at home and abroad are anchored firmly in multiculturalism, her *realpolitik* manages to export to the diasporic populations in the West not only broadly nationalist discourses, but also narrow and sectarian right-wing Hindu and Sikh ideologies that clash with the generally more tolerant, First Amendment political culture and constitutional modalities of nations such as Canada, the U.K. and the U.S. Indian Hindus or Pakistani Muslims in North America, a small minority, might cry foul at any evidence of discrimination against them, but some of the same people display disturbing levels of insensitivity to the basic citizenship rights of minority groups back home. Within one body and mind, a middle-class Hindu living in Canada or the U.S. may cherish the constitutional protections for minorities in North America, but resent and oppose similar protections given to Muslims, Christians, Dalits, and other minorities in the Indian constitution.

Conclusion

Since the 1970s, new developments in postcolonial/transnational theory and American Studies have sharpened our sense of significant movements of many human populations: those from Africa, China, and India that were triggered by slave trade and indentured labor ("coolie") contracts; forced migrations of American Indians and other indigenous groups within North America; European imperialist activity around the world since the 1400s; and U.S. imperialist and neo-colonial ventures since mid-nineteenth century. The term diaspora meant "the scattered" in Ancient Greece and referred to those citizens of a dominant city-state who moved to a defeated territory to colonize and assimilate it into the empire. So, can we regard the colonizing and settler European populations across the globe as a kind of diasporic phenomenon to which the still unfinished narratives of the African, Chinese and South Asian diasporas provide a valuable counterpoint?

In fact, when we consider the nexus between indigeneity and diaspora (as Jean-Paul Restoule has done in his essay, "Urban Aboriginal Migration in North America"), diaspora theory might illumine in new ways the often involuntary internal migrations of indigenous populations in North America, Australia, or India. In doing so, Restoule's essay draws attention to other areas where the readings of race and ethnicity in U.S. Studies or Transatlantic Studies might shake hands with postcoloniality at diasporic or meta-diasporic crossroads. For example, what new insights would the diaspora paradigm bring to the Great Migration in which millions of African Americans moved from the South to the North between the 1880s and the 1960s? And how might diaspora help us to make sense of what is sometimes called the New Great Migration, in which large numbers of African Americans have, since the 1970s chosen to move back to the South, preferring to live in closer proximity to their kin, roots, and familiar Southern ways, as long as those ways are no more racist than those of the colder, more alienating North? And what about the "twice migrants" that comprise diaspora populations who have moved more than once from their original "national" site—such as the Chinese of Southeast Asian background who live now in Canada or the U.S., or South Asians from East Africa or Fiji or the Caribbean who have moved since 1960 to U.K. or North America or more recently from U.K. to Canada or the U.S., making them "thrice migrants"[3]?

Today, there is a growing awareness that culture, identity and geopolitics meet at the critical *intersections* of multiple major and minor diasporas—establishing the necessity of understanding the world beyond a Eurocentric, First World-centered, masculinist lens. Our knowledge of global histories and hybrid transnational cultures is being enriched not only by the enduring legacy of deconstructionist and anti-Orientalist projects, but also by more recent feminist and queer interventions by scholars who have argued for alternative epistemologies and critical frameworks, as well as by the urgency of exploring the intersections of the diasporic with the migrant, the transnational, the exilic, and the hybrid. Such interventions from the "Borders School" scholars and by others have begun to enrich the already considerable scholarship on a wide variety of diaspora communities, internal migration and immigration, ethnic history, and racial constructions (Schmidt and Singh 2000).

[An earlier version of this essay appeared as an Afterword to *Transforming Diaspora: Communities Beyond National Boundaries*, ed. Robin E. Field and Parmita Kapadia. Madison, NJ: Fairleigh Dickinson University Press, 2011].

Notes

1. See a recent debate relating to South Asian diaspora writers at www.independent.co.uk/arts-entertainment/books/reviews/ the-white-tiger-by-aravind-adiga-807509.html. Also relevant to the context of representational debates in relation to the South Asian diaspora writers is the debate between novelist Vikram Chandra and the late literary critic Meenakshi Mukherjee, originally published in the Sunday editions of the Indian newspaper, *The Hindu*, in December 1999 and January 2000. The conversation was later joined by Rajeshwari Sunder Rajan. As is clear from the two links below, this remains an unfinished and inconclusive debate: http://bostonreview.net/ BR25.1/chandra.html; www. thehindu.com/thehindu/2001/02/25/stories/ 1325067a.htm.
2. See a more detailed comment on misperceptions between African Americans and Asian Americans in Amritjit Singh, "The Possibilities of a Radical Consciousness: African Americans and New Immigrants," in *MultiAmerica*, ed.

Ishmael Reed (New York: Viking Penguin, 1997). A version of the essay is also available in *Between the Lines: South Asians and Postcoloniality* ed. Deepika Bahri and Mary Vasudeva. Philadelphia: Temple University Press, 1996.

3. "Twice migrants," a term first applied by Parminder Bhachu in *Twice Migrants* (1985) to East African Sikh migrants in U.K. refers to people whose family histories include more than one migration, within the South or from the South to the North or within the North. Family histories of direct migrants can also involve the experience of multiple locations through their children.

Works Cited

Braziel, Jana Evens, and Anita Mannur. 2003. "Nation, Migration, Globalization: Points of Contention in Diaspora Studies," in *Theorizing Diaspora* ed. Jana Evans Braziel and Anita Mannur. Oxford: Blackwell.

Cheong, Fiona, Lydia Kwa, and Shirley Geok-Lin Lim. 2002. "Singapore on My Mind: Fiona Cheong, Lydia Kwa, and Shirley Geok-lin Lim Compare Notes." *The Women's Review of Books* 19, nos. 10-11 (July 2002): 24-25.

Ellison, Ralph. 1952. *Invisible Man.* New York: Vintage, 1952; rpt. 1981.

Field, Robin E., and Parmita Kapadia, eds. 2011. *Transforming Diaspora: Communities Beyond National Boundaries.* Madison, NJ: Fairleigh Dickinson University Press.

Gopinath, Gayatri. 2005. *Impossible Desires: Queer Diasporas and South Asian Public Cultures.* Durham: Duke University Press.

Kapadia, Parmita. 2011. "Domestic Liminality: Intermarriage in the Diaspora." In *Transforming Diaspora,* edited by Field and Kapadia, 89-104.

Manalansan, Martin. 2003. *Global Divas: Filipino Gay Men in the Diaspora.* Durham: Duke University Press.

Mistry, Rohinton. 1995. *A Fine Balance.* Toronto: McClelland and Stewart.

Reddy, Chandan. 2011. *Freedom With Violence: Race, Sexuality, and the US State.* Durham: Duke University Press.

Restoule, Jean-Paule. 2011. "Urban Aboriginal Migration in North America: A Diasporic Identity." In *Transforming Diaspora,* edited by Field and Kapadia, 21-36.

Rushdie, Salman. 1992. "Imaginary Homelands." In *Imaginary Homelands: Essays and Criticism 1981-1991*, 9-21. New York: Penguin.

Seyhan, Azade. 2001. *Writing Outside the Nation*. Princeton: Princeton University Press.

Shankar, Lavina Dhingra and Rajini Srikanth. 2000. "South Asian American Literature: 'Off the Turnpike' of Asian America." In *Postcolonial Theory and the United States,* edited by Singh and Schmidt, 370-87.

——, eds. 1998. *A Part Yet Apart: South Asians in Asian America*. Philadelphia: Temple University Press.

Shih, Shu-mei. 2011. "Against Diaspora: The Sinophone as Places of Cultural Production." In *Transforming Diaspora,* edited by Field and Kapadia, 3-20.

Singh, Amritjit. 1992. "Rohinton Mistry." In *Writers of the Indian Diaspora*, ed. Emmanuel Nelson, 207-18. Westport, CT: Greenwood Press.

Singh, Amritjit and Peter Schmidt, eds. 2000. *Postcolonial Theory and the United States: Race, Ethnicity, and Literature*. Jackson, MS: University Press of Mississippi.

Srikanth, Rajini. 2004. *The World Next Door: South Asian American Literature*. Philadelphia: Temple University Press.

Takagi, Dana Y. 1996. "Maiden Voyage: Excursion into Sexuality and Identity Politics in Asian America," 21-35. In *Asian American Sexualities: Dimensions of Gay and Lesbian Experience*. New York: Routledge.

CHAPTER 11

The Persistence and Creation of Internal Borders: Indians in Aotearoa/New Zealand

Dieter Riemenschneider
Goethe University, Germany

> A more cautious view is that stereotypes, whether specially directed at Chinese and Indians, or more generally at Asians, still persist within contemporary New Zealand [...]. These may not be the insulting caricatures of the earlier Hindoo or Chinaman, but continued resistance remains in some quarters to New Zealand's localized Asian identity.
>
> (Ip and Leckie 2011, 183)

> People might have their own very different and complex ideas about nation and nationalism, about language and religion, about 'identity' and cultural meanings or symbols, and about their personal relationships to all these categories. This is what public discourse and certain kinds of diaspora studies overlook or sideline, and what a new kind of scholarship is attempting to retrieve or recuperate.
>
> (Fuchs, Linkenbach, Malik 2010, 105)

These two quotations chosen from recently published studies on Indians and Asians in Aotearoa New Zealand point at two major issues that I want to address in this essay though I will concentrate on the latter. These are the perception of immigrants as the 'other' of a nation's understanding of its own culture, and the immigrant people's self-perception of their identity—as individuals and as members of a community. Both are not necessarily grounded in the "race relations paradigm" discussed by

Stuart Hall or Homi Bhabha (Favell 2007, 265) but in ethnic, geographic, religious, linguistic, gender and generational relations, as will be demonstrated in the course of this essay. At the same time, to speak of 'vanishing borders' in spite of the noticeably increased mobility of Indians in the 'Age of Globalism', appears misleading because a strong tendency prevails of maintaining if not drawing 'internal' border lines between and among Indian settlers in New Zealand. Following a brief historically oriented introduction meant to point out when and how perceptions of one's group identity have evolved over a period of nearly a century of migration and settlement, my essay will focus on the present situation—and on self-perceptions—of Indian settlers in Aotearoa New Zealand. That is, I am less concerned with the critical discourse on migration as addressed by, among others, Cohen (1997), Massey (1998), Castles (1998) or Favell (2007) than with the nature of a specific diaspora as a discursive, empirical and aesthetic figure.

India in New Zealand: Local Identities, Global Relations, a collection of a dozen essays edited by Sekhar Bandhopadhyay, contains a wide-ranging bibliography (2010, 255-69), which however includes references to merely three books, a small number of essays and a few unpublished papers as well as B.A. and M.A. theses written before the mid-1990s on Indians in New Zealand. They are either of an introductory nature or pay attention to single ethnic or religious groups, for example Gujaratis, Punbjabis and Muslims, or to regional Indian settlements, e.g. in Christchurch and the Waikato. More comprehensive and analytical investigations started only towards the end of the 20th century.

One of the reasons for this scant attention is of a quantitative nature. Although dating back to 1809 and 1814 when a few Indian sailors jumped ship, respectively in the Bay of Islands and Otago Harbour, the first half dozen 'legal' Indian immigrants arrived in 1881. Forty years later, their population counted no more than 671 which increased fourfold to 2452 by 1951. Yet another thirty years later 15810 Indians lived in the country. In contrast and according to the 2006 census (Zodgekar 2010, 66), the last quarter of the 20th century showed an increase by 660 per cent to a total of 104,582 people of Indian descent. Making up more than 2 per cent of the New Zealand population, Indians had finally become a visible minority (Leckie 2007, 177) and, perhaps not unexpectedly, now the object of a series of investigations and analyses from various research angles.

Jacqueline Leckie's pioneering *Indian Settlers: The Story of a New Zealand South Asian Community* (2007) offers a comprehensive history of Indian migration and settlement over more than a century in a book that combines historical documentation from archival resources with narratives by and interviews with a large number of individuals, complemented by reproduced photographs, many of which were contributed by her interviewees. As the most knowledgeable scholar in the field, Leckie also co-edited with Paola Voci a volume of essays entitled *Localizing Asia in Aotearoa* (2011). Focusing on "micro or local histories and cultural spaces", these essays, as the editors claim, are intended to contribute to "understand[ing] diversity not just via an examination of cultural belongings that are defined by macro-national entities" (Voci/Leckie 2011, 9): a pertinent reference towards a methodological negotiation that sets out to interrogate conceptions of cultural community on the one hand and identity on the other. As it becomes immediately obvious, this shift from the macro to the micro level of immigrant/diasporan studies is basically grounded in the increasingly multi-ethnic character of New Zealand in the 21st century, and more specifically in Indians constituting a large and heterogeneous group (Leckie 2007, 177-78).

As Bandyopadhyay remarks 'Kiwi-Indians' do not only constitute the southernmost group in the Indian global diaspora (8), but this group's internal cultural diversity includes intergenerational differentiation as well as different linguistic, religious and cultural backgrounds since Indians "come from practically all the regions of India and from previous destinations of Indian migration" (2010, 11): a statement substantiated by figures of the 2006 New Zealand census.

The number of Fiji-born Indians increased from less than one thousand in 1981 to near 20,000 in 2001, a change mainly due to the exodus of the descendants of the *Girmitiyas,* former indentured Indian labourers, from their home for more than a century (Leckie 2007, 173) after the 1987 and 2000 military coups on the islands. Belonging mainly to business and professional groups, Fiji-Indians added to the social tapestry of New Zealand Indians among whom the largest majority till the 1990s had been made up of petty traders. Leckie equalized the Indian diaspora in the 20th century with retailing (Bandyopadhyay, 53), with Pukekohe, a small town south of Auckland, forming the centre of the Indian settlement (55). Janet McAllister has added that by the mid-1990s 85 per cent of Auckland's dairies were owned by Indians (McAllister 2002, 70).

The diversity of the social set-up of immigrants from Fiji has since been complemented by members of a newly emerging middle class from India that has arrived over the last two to three decades. By 2001 the percentage of Indian retailers had decreased to twenty-four while the number in white-collar occupations had increased to 44 per cent (Leckie 2010, 58); and whereas in 1991 only about fourteen per cent of the male Indian population had a university qualification, this figure had more than doubled by 2001 to 29.4 per cent. Indeed, "the Indian community [if one can really employ this term any longer] today is no longer a socially homogeneous group" (Zodgekar 2010, 70).

Concomitant with these social changes, to which political changes, like the election victory of the Labour Party in 1984 and the passing of the 1987 Immigration Act were also crucial, the selection of migrants was facilitated according to their professional qualifications and the economic requirements in New Zealand (Leckie 2007, 172). The religious and linguistic diversity increased while the gender map came to differ radically from that of the past. The majority of Indians remained Hindu, but the numbers of Christians and Muslims began to rise. Side by side with the languages of Hindi, Gujarati and Punjabi, still spoken by more than fifty per cent of the Indian population, other Indian languages have made their appearance on the linguistic map, as has English, spoken by three out of ten Indians, while ninety per cent attest to knowledge of the language.

Finally, the increasing role of women with tertiary qualifications needs to be mentioned (Zodgekar 2010, 73; Leckie 2007, 172). Considering that till the mid-20th century it was mainly males who had migrated the gender imbalance began gradually to shift. Initially, women had mainly remained attached to their families (Leckie 2007, 109-23), while figures relating to the time- span between 1996 and 2006 bear evidence not only of an increased number of educationally qualified Indian women in New Zealand but also of their faster percentile growth rate in higher education in comparison with European New Zealand women (Zodgekar 2010, 73).

I would like to draw several conclusions from my brief survey of these carefully researched statistical figures on Indians in New Zealand—people severally referred to as hyphenated New Zealand-Indians, Indo-New Zealanders, Kiwi-Indians, Indo-Fijians or Fiji-born Indians. (The number of Indian migrants from Africa, the US, Europe, Canada, or even Australia is still too small to have earned them another hyphenated real and discursive existence).

First, the historical, social, linguistic, generational, educational, gender and religious diversity as well as the differing geographical/national backgrounds of Indians in New Zealand necessitates reflections on the understanding of the terms 'diaspora' and 'community' since Indian people in New Zealand are closely linked by these variables (Voci/Leckie 2011, 9) in locally defined contexts and experiences. The recognition of such specifically coloured meanings of the 'Indian' community and diaspora will avoid generalizations that strain or even distort their lived reality.

Second and intimately connected, is the question of cultural identity, a many-layered term that is to be approached both, from the subjective or psychological perspective of an individual's self-perception as a private being, and as someone perceived by others in his/her role as a public person within his/her experiences of meeting/confronting culturally diverse 'worlds'.

As I have mentioned, these issues have been addressed over the last decade in essays and in interviews conducted by historians, sociologists, anthropologists, educationists as well as by scholars of cultural, media and community studies—not to forget, also by artists living or residing in New Zealand. I shall briefly summarize the main points they have arrived at before turning to several—and as yet very few—literary representations of Indian migrants in Mallika Krishnamurthy's novel *Six Yards of Silk* (2005) and the theatre plays written and performed by Jacob Rajan and Justin Lewis.

Jacqueline Leckie calls the Indian settlement "a long diaspora" and wonders whether the term diaspora is at all "applicable to the complex waves of Indian settlement and re-settlement" (2010, 61). She appears receptive to Carmen Voigt-Graf's distinction between diaspora and transcultural community, the former characterised solely as a migrant community with "sentimental and symbolic ties to the ancestral homeland", while the latter also includes its material and real links to the homeland (Leckie 2010, 47). These modifications are backed up by other scholars who prefer to distinguish between 'labour', 'trade', 'cultural' and 'imperial'" as well as 'victim' diasporas, because the notion in the present discourse, they argue, has assumed a form of essentialism and has become the "carrier of ideas and cultural continuity *across* national boundaries...[evoking] images of a transnational bond" (Fuchs, Linkenbach, Malik 2010, 82).

Field work or micro studies conducted in New Zealand thus illustrates how problematic the term diaspora is when examined at the micro level or 'from the inside'. In contrast, to the Indian historian Sekhar Bandyopadhyay Pakeha-New Zealand attitudes to the country's Indian population appear to be determined by an essentialising definition of diaspora. Having been ruled—and continuing to be ruled—by the country's global or imperial connections (to the erstwhile Western, imperial 'motherland'), these attitudes are shaped, he says, largely though not exclusively "by a postcolonial public discourse on underdevelopment and backwardness that owed its origins to imperial stereotypes...of India" (Bandyopadhyay, 169). As a piece of documentary evidence Bandyopadhyay quotes the headline of an issue of the *The New Zealand Herald* proclaiming, "They are hungry but they have the bomb", and he also relates to responses of interviewees who complained that professional qualifications from abroad are not recognized, nor had Bandyopadhaya's informants ever been promoted in New Zealand (168).

Concluding that over a period of more than eighty years the situation for many Indian migrants does not appear to have changed significantly (168), he blames Pakeha New Zealanders for still being unable to understand "middle India" (185). Leckie has also pointed out that "Stereotypes

…still persist within contemporary New Zealand […and] continued resistance remains in some quarters to New Zealand's localized Asian identity" (Ip/Leckie2011, 183). The term Asian, incidentally, points at the authors' essay on "Chinamen" and "Hindoos". Which is to say that they simply fail to take note of and grasp the scale of global social and economic changes as also those in the field of education that have occurred in India over at least the last two decades. In many quarters in New Zealand there exists an unwillingness, Bandyopadhyay feels, to revise the outdated postcolonial discussion on underdevelopment and backwardness.

The insights presented here and gained from studying Indian diasporan and community structures in New Zealand are, of course, based on a large number of individual case studies centring on the issue of Indian people constructing their selves and of grappling with an understanding of their cultural identities. As has been pointed out, defining oneself in New Zealand occurs much less at a national or ethnic level—although this also happens, of course—than in local contexts with multiple cultural surroundings and social, religious, generational, gender and educational variables. Bandyopadhyay comes to the conclusion that "Indian-ness" in New Zealand means different things to different people within the community, and that identities are negotiated by individuals on an everyday basis (2010, 12).

This is to say that we come across a wide range of self-perceptions marked at one end by the collapsing of one's individual cultural identity with tradition-guided agencies which, for example, insist on caste-marriage, strict loyalty to the regional-linguistic-cultural world of one's family and its background, and accordingly on the feeling of belonging to a specific socio-cultural network: a network often in the guise of a regional-ethnic (Auckland Marathi Association) or merely ethnic association (Sikh Society).

However, researchers have more frequently come across the experience of an in-between position of identity construction; for example, the belief that one's efforts in having made New Zealand your home had enriched one's life and enabled you to enjoy "a double identity" (Fuchs et al. 2010, 99); or, in more problematic terms, relating one's self to two worlds that were inextricably intertwined (Gilbertson 2010, 137) and perhaps even uncertain (Gilbertson, 133). Interlocked with such sentiments is the conviction of many interviewees and respondents, of their own agency, of looking at their own attitudes, decisions and actions as determined by an autonomous and choosing self (Gilbertson, 139)—which turns them, as several scholars have said, into "accomplished artists of *bricolage* [...] of skilfully handling and putting together diverse fragments of culture" (Fuchs et al. 101). And this is done in a pragmatic rather than a programmatic manner (Gilbertson, 138). Accordingly, negotiating one's position in a community is discerned as an ongoing process which precludes an ultimate definition of an individual's cultural identity.

Observing these processes over a period of time has, besides, given reason to assume that the more often it is noticeable that personal agency is insisted on and executed the more we have reason to speak of people shifting from perceiving themselves in collective and communal terms to identifying themselves in individual terms. National, ethnic and other supra-individual notions of identity are losing ground by shifting towards individual self-portraits (Singh & Singh 2011, 215), and perhaps even to seeing oneself as global citizen—as one respondent put it: "'I am proud of India, India has developed so much, but it is no longer a place where I can live. I belong neither to India nor to New Zealand—I am in between, I am a global citizen'" (Fuchs et al. 2010, 98). Whether they are guided by "certain basic universalist ideas, derived from religion [...] or secular humanist ideas", as Martin Fuchs and his colleagues suggest (103), remains to be further explored—apart from the neglect of material considerations of an economic nature which certainly also play a role in defining oneself as a global citizen.

Let me now turn first to the novel *Six Yards of Silk* and then to the plays, so I may analyse the creative treatment of Indian diaspora and cultural identity in New Zealand against the findings of the foregoing studies. Thirty-five-year-old Sharmila, married to the Pakeha New Zealander Keith and mother of three little boys, had emigrated from South India with her parents and younger brother Ramesh when she was still a child. Deeply disturbed after the sudden disappearance of her brother—who, as it turns out, had drowned himself—, she begins to distance herself from her family and her everyday life, becomes more and more depressed and retreats into the world of her childhood and adolescence which she had closely shared with Ramesh. Both had often rebelled against their more tradition-oriented parents' many strictures from which the boy had suffered more than his sister. His absence now means the loss of Sharmila's mainstay which her family obviously cannot immediately replace.

The psychological struggle she faces undergoes a cultural turn of events with her aunt's visit from South India. Meant to help and support her with her daily chores, Meenama, her mother's sister, who is deeply rooted in her Indian heritage, reawakens her niece's memories of her childhood and relatives, of the family's Kerala home and its local surroundings with their colours, smells, sounds and bright light, the heat and monsoon rains, the food, clothes and stories—and the traumatic event of her little sister's death by lightning. The past that had receded over the years—exemplified by Sharmila's total neglect of "the gods", the bronze idols in the cabinet on a shelf—gradually gains the upper hand in her mind and causes her to literally shut the present out by spending more and more time in her bedroom. Her cultural identity attained while growing up and having her own family in New Zealand is seriously challenged now with the world of her parents and aunt reasserting itself paradoxically through Sharmila's simultaneous experience of loss and reunion.

In contrast, her brother, very conscious of the culture conflict he found himself in as an adolescent and a young man, becomes increasingly ill suffering from psychosis as the reader learns from Ramesh's thoughts and outbursts conveyed through indirect free speech in untitled chapters strewn through the novel. Both, his parents' traditional ideas of living like a young Indian male forced onto him and the obstacles he had faced during his school days and in the labour market, in other words, the clash between the two worlds Ramesh had grown up in, proves insoluble and finally destroys him.

The issue then of cultural identity in Krishnamurthy's fictional rendering of two young Indian migrants is treated from a gender-differing perspective. Sharmila finally manages to cope pragmatically with the pull of tradition without denying it but Ramesh succumbs to the conflicting pulls of his Indian parents and Pakeha New Zealand's prejudices against migrants. Apart from the cultural side of the siblings' predicament we should not overlook its basically psychological fabric. Both characters are portrayed as highly sensitive and individualized human beings who minutely register 'the world's' demands and attitudes, their own feelings and individual responses and ascribe them existential importance—a configuration of fictional characters to which the writer's own personal make-up and biographical background may have contributed significantly. General conclusions as to Indian migrants' living in India and the issue of cultural identity thus must not be drawn from merely one literary text. Still, *Six Yards of Silk* certainly reflects and highlights salient points of migrants' predicaments.

Looking at the novel's literary-aesthetic achievement, the Ramesh chapters impress because the single narrative point of view shapes and controls a cohesiveness of content and form, of Ramesh's talking about his sensory hallucinations, the vanishing borders between the internal and external world and the sustained mood of strain and tone of presentation. The 'sari chapters', on the other hand, entitled with references to the garment's parts and ways of dressing in it and wearing it, are less cohesive, at times surprising the reader with unexpected and unwarranted shifts of perspective from present to past and back and from one character to the next (95-106, 108-16, 132-37). Here it seems that Krishnamurthy has not yet found a way of fully integrating the different time levels and character studies into a narrative that unfolds as densely as Ramesh's story.

Jacob Rajan and Justin Lewis's *Indian Ink* (2005), the trilogy, *Krishnan's Dairy* (first performed in 1997), *The Candlestickmaker* (first performed in 2000), and *The Pickle King* (first performed in 2002) are of a very different aesthetic calibre. Though each play is centred on the interaction of a few characters the plots are of very slender proportion and besides focus on different social segments within the Indian diaspora in New Zealand. As the title suggests, Krishnan runs a dairy and he works long hours to just make a living for his small family. Echoing the hard and not always safe life of many lower middle class migrants who continue to make up a considerable proportion of Indians in New Zealand, the play foregrounds their often confrontational existence and contain echoes of the violent attacks on them that have occurred from time to time (Leckie 2007, 174; Leckie 2010, 60). Though meant with reference to the more recent play *Guru of Chai*, Rajan's words that "the play you are about to see was born of a real life connection" (www.indianink.co.nz/Guru of Chai/Reviews), holds true also of *Krishnan's Dairy*. [Two more plays have been performed since: *The Dentist's*

Chair (2007) and *The Chai Guru* (2010). See www.indinanink.co.nz]

Compared to the novel, character delineation in the plays is thin and contents itself with roughly sketching the hard working, responsible dairy owner and, in contrast, his more traditionally anchored Indian wife who is full of stories and 'beliefs' and has a sweet tooth. This kind of attribution reveals a very characteristic feature not only of this play: introducing humour and a light touch that counterpoints the serious portrayal of characters and events and employs the contrast between two differing cultural identities as a means of comic relief. In *The Candlestickmaker* a similar effect is brought about by the rhetoric of a retired professor of astrophysics facing his aged female servant and cook's feisty retorts in Malayalam and broken English. This character constellation bears similarities to the outspoken and business-minded widowed matriarch running a small hotel in *The Pickle King* and the educated and demure heart surgeon who is forced to make his living as the hotel's porter. In this play Rajan and Lewis call attention to the neglect of "precious human capital" not being utilized by New Zealand employers (Zodgekar 2010, 76).

Altogether, the three plays take a very different course when compared with the novel. Combining the serious side of Indian migrants making a living in New Zealand with comic elements derived from contradictions in character and style, the playwrights do not shun theatre's rationale to entertain. It is furthermore enhanced by the use of theatrical forms like masks (referred to by Rajan as "Indian caricature masks"), thereby drawing on an element of Commedia del'Arte (Rajan/Lewis 2005, 19) with its concomitant effects of allegory, but also of Brechtian 'alienation'. (Masks identify the various characters, but in performance are, as a rule, only worn by Rajan who thus plays different roles). As Rajan put it "I think that Jacob and I are somehow drawn to old theatrical forms and we take great pleasure from rediscovering them in a contemporary context" (Qtd in Hayl 2011). Finally, music and various other devices (a duck, for example, manipulated by a puppeteer in *The Candlestickmaker*) add to the entertainment factor. These plays which have succeeded in drawing huge audiences in New Zealand over nearly two decades and have won critical acclaim in both Europe and the US, are located at the interface of the local, the diasporan and the global and are meant not just for a local Indian-New Zealand but an international audience.

Six Yards of Silk and the five plays by Rajan and Lewis indicate the beginnings of yet another literary tradition in English created by one of the more recent migrant groups in Aotearoa New Zealand. It may well contribute new patches, each necessarily bordered, to the patchwork of the country's modern literature; an increasingly polycultural body of work to which Pacific Islanders, Chinese, European migrants and Indians have added, and because of which the perception of a 'national' literature takes on new meaning. As Jan Kemp in her eponymous poem, "We are all newcomers" says:

> On Long Bay beach the languages
> of sky of sea of land, and of the newest
> comers speaking Samoan, Croatian,
> Hindi, Italian, Afrikaans, Arabic, Mandarin
> overheard in just one swim
> from three to seven pines and back—
> in a half hour Maori and English
> made plankton shoaling through
> the incoming whale tide of costumes and custom
>
> (2006, 15)

Works Cited

Bandyopadhyay, Sekhar. 2010. "Introduction". In Sekhar Bandyopadhyay, ed. *India in New Zealand: Local

Identities, Global Relations. Dunedin: Otago University Press. 7-20.

———. 2010. "In the Shadow of the Empire: India-New Zealand Relations since 1947". In Sekhar Bandyopadhyay, ed. *op. cit.*, 167-85.

Bhabha, Homi. 1996. "Culture's In-Between". In Stuart Hall and Paul du Gay, eds. *Questions of Cultural Identity*. 53-60.

Castles, Stephen, and Mark Miller. 1998. *The Age of Migration*. London: Macmillan.

Cohen, Robert, Ed. 1996. *Theories of Migration*. Edward Elgan: Cheltenham.

Favell, Adrian. 2007. "Rebooting Migration Theory: Inter-disciplinarity, Globality, and Post-disciplinarity in Migration Studies". In Caroline Brettell et James Hollifield, ed. *Migration theory: talking across disciplines*. London: Routlcdgc. 259-78.

Fuchs, Martin, Antje Linkenbach, Aditya Malik. 2010. "What does it mean to be Indian? A View from Christchurch." In Sekhar Bandyopadhyay, ed. *India in New Zealand: Local Identities, Global Relations*. Dunedin: Otago University Press. 81-106.

Gilbertson, Amanda. 2010. "Choosing Indian and Kiwi Identities: The Ethnic Options of New Zealand-born Gujaratis". In Sekhar Bandyopadhyay, ed. *India in New Zealand: Local Identities, Global Relations*. Dunedin: Otago University Press., 123-40.

Hayl, Natasha. 2011. "Indian Ink. Interview". *The Listener* (June 18, 2011).

Ip, Manying and Jacqueline Leckie. 2011. "'Chinamen' and 'Hindoos': Beyond Stereotypes to Kiwi Asians". In Voci, Paola & Jacqueline Leckie, eds. *op. cit.*, 159-86.

Justin Lewis. 2005. Indian Ink: Krishnan's Dairy. The Candlestickmaker. The Pickle King. Wellington: Victoria University Press.

Kemp, Jan. 2006. *Dante's Heaven*. Auckland: Puriri Press.

Krishnamurthy, Mallika. 2005. *Six Yards of Silk*. Wellington: Steele Roberts.

Leckie, Jacqueline. 2007. Indian Settlers: The Story of a New Zealand South Asian Community. Dunedin: Otago University Press.

———. 2010. "A Long Diaspora: Indian Settlement". In Sekhar Bandyopadhyay, ed. *India in New Zealand: Local Identities, Global Relations*. Dunedin: Otago University Press 45-64.

Massey, Douglas S. et al. 1998. Worlds in Motion: Understanding International Migration at the End of the Millennium. Oxford: Clarendon Press.

McAllister, Janet. 2002. "Passages from India." *Metro* (November 2002): 68-73.

Singh, Gurjet and Verpal Singh. 2011. "Changing identities among Kiwi Sikhs: Local, individual or world citizenship?" In Voci, Paola and Jacqueline Leckie, eds. *op. cit.*, 204-17.

Voci, Paola and Jacqueline Leckie. 2011. Eds. *Localizing Asia in Aotearoa*. Wellington: Dunmore Publishing.

———. 2011. "Introduction: Beyond nations and ethnicities: Localizing Asia in New Zealand". In Voci, Paola & Jacqueline Leckie, eds. *op. cit.*, 7-23.

Watson, Geoff. 2011. "'Indians Show the Way': Sport and Localization among Indians in New Zealand." In Voci, Paola and Jacqueline Leckie, eds. *op. cit.*, 50-67.

Zodgekar, Arvind. 2010. "Indian Presence: A Demographic Profile". In Sekhar Bandyopadhyay,ed. *India in New Zealand: Local Identities, Global Relations*. Dunedin: Otago University Press. 65-78.

CHAPTER 12

Sweet-Sour Pork and Boston Cream Pie: Chinese Immigrant Subversion and Citizenship in Judy Fong Bates' *Midnight at the Dragon Café*

Julie Mehta
University of Toronto, Canada

> I wanted my father to grow *lo fon* vegetables—things like carrots, radishes, tomatoes and beets. Instead, we harvested bok choy.... My parents soaked their last crop of bok choy in a smelly, brown salty brine and then hung the drooping vegetables on the backyard clotheslines to dry...allowed all the neigbours to see the limp, wrinkled greens...the few adolescent boys in our neighbourhood...would run through our backyard...and knock the stringy bok choy to the ground.... When my father ran after them cursing,...the scrawny boys would turn around and laugh, taunting him with cries of *Chinky, Chinky Chinaman*. But in the winter, when my mother made soup with pork bones, red dates, carrots and dried bok choy.... I knew that *lo fon* food could never be this good.
>
> —*The Year of Finding Memory*, Judy Fong Bates (2010, 147)

This essay explores how food is represented in the works of Asian-Canadian diasporic novelists as a trope for the secret domain of desire, raising community consciousness, and demanding social justice, often implicating the Canadian

State with insidious intent and evincing remarkable literary alacrity in a world of vanishing borders. These writers are infusing a new oeuvre into the Canadian literary canon, and though the seepage of Asian-Canadian identity might be slow, like strong Oolong tea, it is potent and irreversible. In an earlier study (Mehta 2012), I have explored the complexities of race and Canada's blotchy history of immigration, as reflected in culinary acts or encounters in the multi-genre works by South Asian diasporic writers in an age of globalisms. The current project is punctuated, as was the earlier one, by long classroom conversations with second and third generation Asian immigrants, undergraduates who have lived transnational and diasporic lives. Diasporic Asian-Canadian writers Judy Fong Bates, Anar Ali, Kwai-yun Li, Shyam Selvadurai, and Sheniz Janmohamed are regular visitors to my classroom at the University of Toronto and enrich the experience of the students. The course has become popular as more young Canadians become interested in seeking out their own hyphenated identities and configuring their place in the quickly evolving Canada which reflects transplanetary connections in a world with vanishing borders.

In this essay, I turn my attention to the politics of power and discourses of race, as represented in Judy Fong Bates' *Midnight at the Dragon Café*. I argue that in this work of fiction, articulations of food and the performative acts of cooking and eating are much more than markers of felicitous and celebratory cultural identity in the Chinese-Canadian diaspora. On the contrary, culinary fictions are increasingly employed to establish discourses of struggle and subversion by Fong Bates. They enable her to embed her narrative with resonant contextualities of imperialism and domination her people had once encountered as colonial subjects and which they must still endure, much in the way that Edward Said posits in *Culture and Imperialism:* "The power to narrate, or to block other narratives from forming and emerging, is very important to culture and imperialism, and constitutes one of the main connections between them" (Said 1993, xiii). In this essay I track the rise of Chinese immigrant foodways in a *lo fun* (Anglo-Canadian) landscape, explore the generational conflicts embedded in culinary encounters at home, and trace the evidence of preservation and invention of tradition through cultural hybridity and creolisation, which are strong forces of resistance.

It would seem that Chinese-Canadians have turned kitchens and public spaces of food consumption into sites of vigorous activism against racial and gendered patriarchy, as in the case of Su-Jen's mother Lai Jiang and Su-Jen's step-brother Lee Kung in Fong Bates' *Midnight at the Dragon Café*. Through their performance in foodways they resist exclusionary dynamics by battling forces of domination within and without the home. It illustrates the usefulness of Homi Bhabha's dictum in *The Location of Culture* of the necessity to pay close attention to "the transmutations and the translations of indigenous traditions in their opposition to colonial authority" as these "demonstrate how the desire of the signifier, the indeterminacy of intertextuality, can be deeply embedded in the postcolonial struggle against dominant relations of power and knowledge" (1994, 9).

This exploration is problematised further by the fact that Fong Bates is female, and her narratives challenge masculinist projects and attempt to establish feminine agency. I posit that in her fictive construction, Fong Bates is often irreverent, provocative and she challenges (although her criticism is nuanced) the accepted norms of the "multiculture" perspective projected by the patriarchal Canadian State. The representations of foodways in her fiction frequently interrogate issues of power, perception and identity within the spatial dynamics of a "new homeland". By destabilising domestic spaces, where food is meant to signify a certain zone of "belonging and comfort",

Fong Bates, constantly blurs racial, sexual and generational borders to suggest a muddying of purity and homogeneity.

What seems to emerge is a highly complex, Asian-Canadian "chutnified" identity which is constantly in flux, and in a state of becoming rather than being. Like the very idea of being "Canadian", diasporic Asian identity is being revisited, reconfigured and constantly contested in the writer's articulations of home. Informed by the vexed historical context of immigration in Canada, I focus in this essay on literary representations of racialised, non-Western immigrants whose cultural presence on the contemporary culinary and literary landscape of Canada has created a palpable tension across the genres. It is also configuring a new definition of a Canadian diasporic cosmopolitanism on the one hand, and essentialism, on the other. The immigrants are also rewriting the Canadian literary canon, where names like Michael Ondaatje, Rohinton Mistry and Shyam Selvadurai as well as Judy Fong Bates, Anita Rau Badami and Shani Mootoo are making more than cameo appearances. These stories from the fringes talk back to the centre and these voices, in their own tongues, are breaking through the ceiling of a White Canadian literary canon. Brown and yellow, curried and "chopsueyed", they are all asserting their identity as Canadian writers, much in the way that Homi Bhabha had configured nearly two decades ago when he wrote: "The political and theoretical genealogy of modernity lies not only in the origins of the idea of civility, but in the history of the colonial moment. It is to be found in the resistance of the colonised populations to the Word of God and Man-Christianity and the English language" (1994, 56).

The Empire Strikes Back (Ashcroft et al., 2002) remains an excellent theoretical scaffolding on which to build the literary impulses of a newly emerging Asian-Canadian diasporic literary phenomenon as we begin to grapple with the connections that suture language to cultural agency.

When Chinese diasporic writers like Fong Bates invoke and evoke a distinctive culinary litany, they frequently omit detailed explanations of unfamiliar terms—thus *bok choy* is given no English explication in Fong-Bates' *Midnight*; *Chum-chum* is not described by Mootoo even once in the short story "Out on Main Street"; nor *chholey bhaturey* explained by Rau Badami in "Can you Hear the Nightbird Call?" Many of the Asian-Canadian writers are doing away with glossing, when they speak of unfamiliar dishes, often challenging the reader to figure out what the untranslated/ untranslatable words mean in the text, making the linguistic opaqueness an act of resistance in itself:

> The gradual discarding of glossing...has...released language from the myth of cultural authenticity, and demonstrated the fundamental importance of the situating context in according meaning. While the untranslated word remains metonymic and thus emphasizes the (posited) experiential gap which lies at the heart of any cross-cultural text, it also demonstrates quite clearly that the use of the word, even in an English-language context, confers the meaning, rather than any culturally hermetic referentiality. Ultimately the choice of leaving words untranslated in post-colonial texts is a political act, because while translation is not inadmissible in itself, glossing gives the translated word and thus the receptor culture, the higher status (Ashcroft 2002, 65)

Judy Fong Bates is an author of three books—a collection of short stories, *China Dog and Other Stories* (1997); a novel, *Midnight at the Dragon Café* (2004); and her most recent book, a memoir, *The Year of Finding Memory* (2010). It is *Midnight at the Dragon Café,* however, which caught the public imagination with its strong anchors in Chinese-Canadian identity. The novel directly confronts the dislocation and dysfunction that was symptomatic of implementing an exclusionist immigration policy by deploying the Chinese head tax.... The Chinese head tax (about $500) was a fixed fee charged to each Chinese person entering Canadian territory. It was the amount a Chinese worker earned in a whole year. The tax was purposefully kept high so fewer Chinese would be able to enter Canada. When Fong Bates' father, Fong Wah Yent committed suicide by hanging himself in his basement, she found amongst his papers a green certificate with the words 'Dominion of Canada': "For thirty-three years when he travelled between China and Canada, his head-tax certificate reminded him that he was unwanted in this country" (Fong Bates 2010, 5).

The infamous head-tax was first levied after the Canadian Parliament passed the Chinese Immigration Act of 1885 and it was meant to discourage Chinese people from entering Canada after the completion of the Canadian Pacific Railway. The tax prevented Chinese workers from immigrating altogether, but did not deter business people, clergy, educators, students, and other categories. Although the Chinese Exclusion Act was repealed in 1947, regulations prohibiting families with children over the age of eighteen from joining fathers in Canada remained in place. Fong Bates recalls that her father spoke to her many times about the head-tax and was extremely bitter about it: "...his voice bitter. '*Only the Chinese had to pay this money. No one else. Five hundred dollars to get into this country. Five hundred dollars I had to borrow*'" (Fong Bates 2010, 6).

Midnight at the Dragon Café is a *bildungsroman* of the young girl Su-Jen/Annie, who comes to Canada as a new immigrant and grows up in the small town of Irvine, Ontario in the 1950s and 1960s. This is also an account of a Chinese girl who is renamed and struggles to find her hyphenated identity. Swinging between a Canadian identity during the day (Annie, while at school and learning to speak English), and Su-Jen, a Chinese persona at home, Annie-Su-

Jen has to cope with her inflexible Chinese mother's deep dark secret of an affair with her stepbrother, even as Su-Jen witnesses her old, Chinese father's earnest efforts to give her a better life in Canada. Her mother, Lai-Jing is the personification of cultural rejection and exile. Su-Jen's stepbrother, in his twenties, Lee Kung, is a son born of a common father, Hing-Wun Chou (the owner-partner of Dragon Café, the provincial Chinese restaurant), but a different mother, who died during the Maoist Revolution, while in China.

Wenying Xu writes:

> Each culture's foodways always already function in its system of representation as signs of sophistication or civilisation over against others engaged in 'crude and barbaric' food practices. In its variant ways of transferring Nature to Culture, therefore, cuisine inculcates eaters with a deep-seated (corporeal) sense of diversity and hierarchy within their social group and over against other groups. (2008, 4)

There are several different subversions being practised in this story of alienation and diasporic dilemmas about identity and empowerment. One of the most compelling tropes is how food is used by the woman Lai-Jing to powerfully critique White Canadian hegemony and fight any attempts of forcible acculturation. Young Lee-Kung's coming from Owen Sound to Irvine follows close on the heels of Lai-Jing's arrival at her husband's restaurant with Su-Jen/Annie, from China. What follows is a remarkable battle that Lai-Jing fights on several fronts, when confronted by White Canadian culinary culture.

Lee-Kung joins their father Chou, and begins to manage the "Chinese" kitchen that made ubiquitous Chinese food and the White-Canadian staples which most of the *lo fon* (White Canadian) customers devoured:

> Lee-Kung carried on in the kitchen, cooking the same fish and chips, clubhouse sandwiches, hot chicken and

> hot beef, and the Chinese dishes like sweet and sour chicken balls and egg foo yongs and chow meins. When we first arrived and my mother saw the "Chinese" food that was served to the customers, she was shocked. 'The *lo fons*', she said, 'I guess they don't know much about food.' She didn't think much of Canadian food either. It took her a long time to get used to seeing a big slab of meat served on a plate for one person.... (Fong Bates 2004, 78)

In her seminal study on issues that beleaguer Chinese identity in Canada and its problematic cultural history *Eating Chinese: Culture on the Menu in Small town Canada,* Lily Cho points out that in the context of Chinese identity and identification in Canada, eating Chinese food signposts the importance of "a moment of violent incorporation with all of the cannibalistic connotations that accompany the moment of consumption" (2010). Honing on the idea of sweet and sour pork, she claims that eating Chinese in Canada "is a repetition of the cannibalistic scene where the desire for violence is both preserved and repressed. It is at once an enactment and a disavowal of violence."

Sweet and sour pork, *goo lo yok* (ghost man's meat, or White man's meat, in a village dialect close to Cantonese), or sweet and sour *anything,* for that matter, gestures towards the creation of a Chineseness specifically manufactured for the White Canadian, a surrogate for the "authentic, timeless and unchanging other of settler colonial consuming desires". Cho maintains that:

> In thinking that he is eating Chinese, the settler colonialist will actually consume *goo lo yok,* whiteman meat, a version of himself, and will engage in a moment of symbolic self-cannibalism. Serving back to the settler colonialist his own excessive desires, the story deflects the violence of colonial identification and incorporation from the Chinese

> subject and back towards the settler colonial one. This narrative suggests a way in which the Chinese migrant escapes the dialectic of self-otherness. Chinese migrants did not need whiteness or Europeanness to define themselves. Right from the beginning, there was another register of emplacement. (2010, 39)

As Cho suggests in her thoughtful study, the gooey, shiny, orangey, "plasticity" of sweet and sour pork places it in a paradigmatic geography that is inauthentic and suspect, and certainly "un-Chinese". As she maintains: "After all, we all know that this isn't Chinese food. It is Chinese and not Chinese, at once impossibly full of ethnic meaning and yet strangely meaningless in that excess." This discourse of un-Chineseness also carries in its belly a subversive narrative where the "native informants", Chinese restaurateurs like Lee-Kung, use their agency to deprive the White Canadian from the "real" Chinese experience—something the Canadian cannot fight and win, since he lacks the episteme of Chinese culture. As Lee-Kung reveals to Su-Jen: "You know what your mother calls the Chinese food on the menu? Fool-the-*lo-fon* food" (Fong Bates 2004, 139).

Cho is lucid in her statement that the menu in Canadian Chinese restaurants "functions on this order, delivering or serving up palatable Chineseness at the same time that it jeopardizes its own authority as a text of Chineseness. Chinese food on the menu betrays the version of Chineseness that White communities can consume, revealing more about Whiteness than Chineseness" (2010, 70-71). The decision by Chou and Lee-Kung to serve the White clientele at the Dragon Café items familiar to the White Canadian palate (like chow mein and sweet and sour pork) reveals to us the acts of manipulation that diasporic minorities perform, thereby deciding how much and what kind of Chineseness should be made accessible to the White Canadian. A kind of cultural nationalism is performed by the Chinese restaurateurs in Canada, which becomes a counter-narrative.

Colour is central to the alterity argument in *Midnight at the Dragon Café*, since the novel enfolds at least a dozen instances of racial discrimination which might be read as a subliminal narrative that runs through this novel. The litany of violations is long: Su-Jen's encounters with White children, who call her "Chink" repeatedly, make her aware of her different skin colour and dark hair. She cannot perform in the school play "Sunflower Sal" is because the heroine needs to have "blonde hair and blue eyes". The disrespectful treatment of her gentlemanly father by some of the White customers of the Dragon Café, to which Su-Jen is witness, as well as her father's own accounts of how he and his contemporaries were racially profiled when they first came to Canada—all highlight the endemic discomfort of invisible borderlands where multiculture stumbles disastrously.

> In 1923, the Canadian government had passed a law that wouldn't let any more Chinese into Canada, and a lot of the men who are already here had to leave their wives and children behind. After the Second World War, the Government changed its mind and allowed the families to come over, but some of them were too old...and the communists made it hard for them to leave China. The old-timers in Canada...had grown used to a life suspended between a country that offered only hardship and a homeland they no longer knew. I was struck by how much they reminded me of my father. (Fong-Bates 2006, 188)

The reiteration of the swing door that forms an unstable border and divides the public space of the restaurant from the private space of the inner lives of the Chou family offers a reading that suggests this same kind of cultural resistance by a minority community to lay bare what is the core of its identity—a Chineseness that inexorably belongs to its own.

The resistance extends to Lai-Jing and Lee-Kung cooking and consuming traditional Chinese dishes with impunity—not merely as a statement of racial distinction but also as an act of insurgency against Lai-Jing's husband Chou, who stands for all that is good and wholesome but also represents the older generation of *lo wah kew,* Chinese men who came to China to break out of their cycle of poverty. Servile and poor, they paid head-tax and were subject to a defunct judiciary and the horrors of racism. Father Chou, representing the older Chinese immigrants who were resigned to their fate and attempted to acculturate in small ways to be more acceptable to the White Canadian "host" population, is "built on memories of my own father" says Fong Bates (in Mehta 2011).

Su-Jen's father and Fong Bates' father are conflated in the character of Chou. In a touching description in the novel, Su-Jen realises:

> The old-timers in Canada, the *lo wah kew*, as Father called them, had grown used to a life suspended between a country that offered only hardship and a homeland they no longer knew. I was struck by how much they all reminded me of my father and of Uncle Yat, partly because they seemed around the same age, all dressed in white shirts and dark pants worn thin, but mostly it was a way they had about them, a resignation to their lives in the new world. (Fong Bates 2004, 188)

and again, as Lai-Jing describes them:

> That's the way these old men are.... No imagination, just doing the same thing over and over, for years and years. Every penny goes in the bank. At least the old man's not washing clothes—some of these old men do nothing but wash and iron for fifty, sixty years.

Growing her own Chinese vegetables in her White Canadian patch was one of the few pleasurable and empowering acts performed by Su-Jen's mother. Every spring Lai-Jing looked forward to planting her Chinese garden. She would have saved some seeds from previous years or would buy seeds from Pock Mark Lee's mobile Chinese grocery: Bok choy, fuzzy melons, snow peas, and winter melons were her prized produce.

Lai-Jing feels exiled in Canada, but as the reader soon begins to realise, she also feels superior. The fact that almost at the moment of her arrival she expresses the view that the White Canadian knows little about nutrition and food, suggests her conviction that her Chinese culture is a more "informed" one. Her superiority comes not from a misinformed cultural arrogance but from a place of pride and an intricate and intense knowledge of her own tradition. As Su-Jen observes: "For her here were two things that were essential to a meal. One was rice, and the other was soup. I think she understood that *lo fons* substituted potatoes and bread for rice, but the thought of a meal without soup was unthinkable" (Fong Bates 2004, 70).

The idea of belonging to a certain community is blended with what the community consumes and how it consumes it. Lai-Jing's insistence that soup be the mandatory mantra for every meal at the Chou household is her way of establishing a Chineseness that is reflected in her active resistance to learn English. A spirit of solidarity is created at meal times within the Chou family. And though it might be a fractured spirit, with Su-Jen's mother and stepbrother having an affair in the household, the cultural value accorded to eating together under the most tense conditions, keeps that sense of family intact at least on the outside. The precision and love that were ingredients in her mother's kitchen still resonates with Su-Jen when she confesses that whenever she eats wilted greens with amaranth drizzled with soy sauce and sesame oil years afterwards, when she is an adult, she still tasted "a hint of soil, reminding me of my mother's garden".

As Mary Lukanuski explains, nostalgia is often influenced by psychological and ontological formations of foodways:

> How food is consumed is a powerful method of further defining a community.... A sense of order, place and discipline is created: the tacit understanding, beside any divine command, is that without such regulations the community would fall victim to its individual appetites. Once members of the community were pursuing their own desires, the community would disintegrate. (1993, 113)

The traffic of food from without to within the body also seeps into the discourse of difference. Su-Jen's observation as a young girl that "however warm it was no one in my family sweat like some of the *lo fon* customers who come into the restaurant", incorporates an otherness. Further juxtaposition of the White body and what it ingests becomes an interesting location for signposting Chinese physiological superiority:

> My parents commented on the men, dripping with moisture, and the women with the dark, wet patches spreading under the arms of their blouses. My mother also complained that the *lo fon* aunts and uncles smelled different, stranger than we Chinese. My father said it was because they drank too much milk and their bodies had more hair. I asked him how he knew. "Look at their arms. Look at Hardware Store Uncle", he answered. (91)

For Fong Bates, food is a smorgasbord of complexities and one that she uses deftly to visit the ingestion-digestion-excretion metaphor in order to distinguish between *lo fon* food habits and their consequent body smells. Early in the narrative, Lai-Jing is very clear about the importance of balancing a diet according to the principles of *yin yang,* and warns Su-Jen about eating too much of "heaty" *lo fun* foods. She looks at the White Canadian diet with derision and urges her daughter to remember the serious pitfalls of adopting Western food habits. Lai-Jing lives on the border that separates the mainstream White and the minority Yellow, and prefers to err on the side of her Chineseness, actively rejecting crossing over to the other side.

This is the kind of self-alienation that is reflected in Said's idea of travellers: "There are many sorts of travellers, some live on the borderline, the border between two states....The States could be feeling and thought, private and public. They have a foot in each camp. These may be migrants who don't want to give up their own culture or assimilate with the new group" (1991, 360).

In *Midnight,* Lee Kung is a rebel within the Chou household and it is manifested through desire on several levels. His having an affair with his father's wife, Lai-Jing, his stepmother and Su-Jen's biological mother, is the central act of insurgency in this work. It is strongly under-girded in his creation of the Boston Cream Pie which signposts a generational conflict within the Chou household between father and son. But the Boston Cream Pie is more than an assertion of Lee Kung's ushering in a new order where he challenges the older Chinese ethic of "keep your head down and work, work, work". The Boston Cream Pie, in its inherent hybridity, is a register of a new Chinese-Canadian agency where a Chinese cook in a small town greasy-spoon restaurant is able to create an essentially Western dessert that shatters the myth of *lo fon* supremacy in Western culinary creations.

The muddled identity of the Boston Cream Pie itself adds an interesting dimension to our exploration of hybrid identity in the novel. Historical trivia tells us that cooks in New England and Pennsylvania Dutch regions were known for their cakes and pies and the dividing line between them was very thin. This cake was probably called a pie because in the mid-nineteenth century, pie tins were more common than cake pans. The first versions might have been baked in pie tins. Boston Cream Pie is a remake of the early American "pudding-cake pie" (Stratley 2004).

Fong Bates nimbly inverts the symbol of power from *lo fun* to the Chinese, and hands the sceptre to Lee-Kung:

> The Boston Cream Pie sat behind the glass sliding doors. On the top shelf of the stainless steel cooler behind the Formica counter, like the queen of desserts for everyone to see. My mother said that it made the restaurant a little classier now that we were serving something so exotic—a cake filled with vanilla pudding, iced with soft peaks of whipped cream and decorated with maraschino cherries. (Fong Bates 2004, 79)

Eric Ing, a third generation Chinese-Canadian student who enrolled in my Asian Cultures class (2011), came from a family which owned a Chinese restaurant in Ontario. He volunteered an anecdote which shares parallels with Su-Jen's story:

> In my family, the Chinese frying pan, or "wok" is a symbol of tradition and transformation of identities. Traditionally, in the village, the wok is never washed so that the seasoning is not scrubbed away.... In our modern home, we wash and dry our wok every time we use [it].... As a Third Generation Chinese-Canadian, I find myself particularly distant from my roots when I am in my kitchen cooking Canadian bacon in a Western frying pan with chopsticks, while watching rap music videos on television.

Frying bacon with chopsticks represents a reinvention of tradition and history, as represented also in articulations of food in *Midnight at the Dragon Café*. It showcases how "inventing" tradition becomes a means to preserve tradition.

Taking a leaf out of diasporic author Meira Chand's meditations on the deep-seated urge for a diasporic writer to reconstruct—what Salman Rushdie had configured as—a "homeland of the mind", we might understand a little more clearly how culinary fictions will always compel us to forge territorial connectivity across borders in an age of globalism, so we remember our ties of blood to where we once came from:

> It has been argued that the past is a country from which we have all emigrated, that its loss is part of our common humanity. We are out of country and out of language. But perhaps this loss, and its subsequent search for an identity and the healing of a fragmented self, may enable the writer to speak even more concretely on a subject of universal significance. We are intent on inventing ourselves anew and of inventing imaginary homelands, recalling lands we barely know, searching for roots through ourselves and our stories, forging new and original roots, in countries far from our ethnic origins. And adapting and adopting new identities. (In Mehta 2004)

Theorising foodways in diasporic Asian literature in Canada is a relatively new field, and beckons invitingly as a road relatively untraveled. Unlike American theorists of foodways such as Wenying Xu (*Eating Identities: Reading Food in Asian American Literature,date*), Anita Mannur (*Culinary Fictions: Food in South Asian Diasporic Culture date*), and others, Canadian Studies on diasporic representations of food in Asian-Canadian writing is only recently beginning to be explored. Lily Cho's seminal work *Eating Chinese: Culture on the Menu in Small Town Canada* (2010) has been one of the first most comprehensive explorations of Chinese cuisines in Canada. With a growing interest in diasporic Asian Culture and the impetus given by many cultural initiatives like the annual Asian Heritage Month seminars, and cultural festivals in major Canadian cities, there is now an acknowledgement that food is a crucial component of cultural imagination and its performance in the Asian-Canadian diaspora.

With the publication of the formidable tome *Edible Histories of Canada* in 2012, which is conceptualised by historian Franca Iacovetta, *et al.*, the first consummate publication about food histories of different immigrant communities in this nation, the Canadian academy will hopefully seek out more spicy morsels embedded in the literary articulations about food in the narratives of subversion and citizenship by Asian-Canadian writers, to understand better the reality of immigrant lives in Canada.

Works Cited

Ashcroft, Bill et al. 2002. *The Empire Writes Back*. London: Routledge.

Badami, Anita Rau. 2007. *Can You Hear the Nightbird Call?* Toronto: Vintage.

Bhabha, Homi K. 1994. *The Location of Culture*. London and New York: Routledge.

Cho, Lily. 2010. *Eating Chinese: Culture on the Menu in Small Town Canada*. Toronto: University of Toronto Press.

Fong Bates, Judy. 1997. *China Dog and Other Stories from a Chinese Laudry*. Toronto: Sister Vision Press.

———. 2004. *Midnight at the Dragon Café*. Toronto: McClelland & Stewart.

———. 2010. *The Year of Finding Memory*. Toronto: Random House.

Iacovetta, Franca, et al. Ed. 2012. *Edible Histories, Cultural Politics: Towards a Canadian Food History*. Toronto: University of Toronto Press.

Kogawa, Joy. 1981. *Obasan*. New York: Anchor.

Lukanuski, Mary. 1993. "A Place at the Counter: The Onus of Oneness." In *Eating Culture*. Eds. Ron Scapp and Brian Seitz. New York: State University of New York Press.

Mannur, Anita. 2010. *Culinary Fictions: Food in South Asian Diasporic Culture*. Philadelphia: Temple University Press.

Mehta, Julie. Conversation with Joy Kogawa, April 2011. Unpublished.

———. Interview with Judy Fong Bates, November 2011. Unpublished.

———. Interview with Meira Chand, November 2004. Unpublished.

———. 2012. "Toronto's Multicultured Tongues: Stories of South Asian Cuisines" in Franca Iacovetta, et al. Ed. *Edible Histories, Cultural Politics*.

Online sources: www.toronto.ca/toronto_facts/diversity.htm[1]; www.40.statcan.gc/101/cst01/demo50a-eng.htm[2] both accessed on 19 May 2010.

Stratley, Linda. 2004. http://whatscookingamerica.net/

Said, Edward. 1993. *Culture and Imperialism*. New York: Vintage.

———. 1991. "Reflections on Exile." *Out There: Marginalization and Contemporary Culture*. Ed. Russell Ferguson. MIT Press.

Xu, Wenying Xu. 2008. *Eating Identities: Reading Food in Asian American Literature*. Honolulu: University of Hawaii Press.

CHAPTER 13

'Ethnonationalism', 'Strategic Essentialism' and Aboriginal Identity Formation: *Corroboree* as Case Study

Arindam Das
Heritage Institute of Technology
Kolkata, India

Critics like Haraway (1991), McDowell (1992) and others have vociferously argued for the requirement of clarifying the 'positionality' of researchers in the process of conducting research. Indeed, as a non-Aboriginal and as a person from an entirely different socio-cultural milieu (I am a middle class Bengali Indian), I acknowledge my being an 'outsider,' who may run the risk of not being able to fully empathise with the Aboriginal people's situation in Australia. My essay runs the risk of being a derivative discourse that rests primarily on secondary sources. However, my sincere attempt in this essay, given such an uneven relation between the researcher and the subject, is to bring to the fore a strategised/appropriative artistic expression of a hitherto a 'fringed' culture in a modern globalized world.

The very theme of the conference—"Vanishing Borders in the Age of Globalism: Australian/Asian Perspectives"—seeks to explore and theorise the impact of globalism and emphasises the importance of an Asian-Australian exchange of perspectives. In this essay, I will discuss the revival of ethnonation and identity formation of the Aborigines in their post-European contact period and highlight how it takes place through a prime 'narrative' tactic—the Spivakian 'strategic essentialism'. This resistive tactic—as a positivist cultural politics—is employed by the Aborigines to expose the power structure and subvert the hegemony of the

European both in the colonial and neo-colonial White Australia. At the very outset, to delineate the theoretical frame for this essay, an explanation of the concepts of 'ethnonation', 'ethnonationalism' and 'strategic essentialism' is necessary. As a case study, I will deal with the Aboriginal song-dance ceremony—*corroboree*—and underline how this 'essential' cultural element in the Aboriginal life is 'strategised', from time to time, by its conscious appropriative use in social life, Aboriginal literature, and music videos by Aboriginal groups like Youthu Yindi, to reclaim Aboriginal 'ethnonation' and identity.

'Ethnonation', 'Ethnonationalism' and 'Strategic Essentialism': Theoretical Premises

> It is in it that we were born, it is our mother
> We are men because it reared us
> We are free because we move in it
> If we are angered, it soothes our pain...
> Through it we talk today to our parents who lived thousands of years back
> Through it our descendants and posterity thousands of years later will know us. (qtd. in Connor 1994, 205)

It was David Riesman, as Glazer and Moynihan and Connor remind us, who first made the sociological use of the term 'ethnicity' in 1953. Speaking from a sociological perspective an "ethnic group" has been defined by Schermerhorn as:

> ...a collectivity within a larger society having real or putative common ancestry, memories of a shared historical past, and a cultural focus on one or more symbolic elements defined as the epitome of their peoplehood. Examples of such symbolic elements are: kinship patterns, physical contiguity (as in localism or sectionalism), religious affiliation, language or dialect forms, tribal affiliations, nationality, phenotypical features, or any combination of these. A necessary

> accompaniment is some consciousness of kinship among members of the group. (1970, 12)

A non-discerning analysis of nation and nationalism, at times, runs the risk of finding no dissimilarity between 'perennialism', 'primordialism' and 'ethnicity'. The 'perennialists' and the 'primordialists' are much narrower and extremist in their versions of ethnic nations than the 'ethnicists'. The first two groups are of the opinion that the nation is not a construct of modernity, but is rather a unit that has been shaped out of the incessant progressions of society and therefore a natural evolution. On the other hand, the 'ethnicists' perceive the contemporary nation to be an outcome of the past, formed through a definite and continuous process of self-realization. The confluence point of all three approaches lies in the fact that all envision nation to be rooted in its ethnic origins.

If the previous two groups did expound the theory of an ethnic nation through an emphasis on socio-cultural givens, the ethnicist Fredrik Barth's contra-distinguished stance highlights the fact that ethnicity is an ever fluid entity with a persistent alternation in its identity: "The human material that is organized in an ethnic group is not immutable" (Barth 1969, 21). His view is that the identity reformations and safeguards are interactive processes among people of different ethnic groups. The conclusions to be drawn from Barth's views are:

1. that ethnicity is all about the ethnic boundary that defines the group, not the cultural stuff that it encloses (Barth 1969, 14);
2. that the definition of this ethnic boundary is primarily concerned with the relationship with the other (Barth 1969, 21).

It is the "value standards" (Barth 1969, 19) of the ethnic groups that keep them from getting subsumed by another group. According to Barth, the cultural content of this social unit may undergo a change and what will remain unperturbed are the markedly distinguished 'boundaries' defined by its 'value system'. This cohesiveness in its 'value standards' and a sense of belongingness of its members become imperative in order to strictly differentiate the 'us'/'them' logic in one ethnic nation's interaction with another. Yet, a 'value system' which promotes a sense of belongingness cannot be compartmentalized from its cultural substances. Further, what connotes an ethnonation is not its 'value standards' which may also re-modify, if not change itself, but rather its worldview—a more cognitive and essential orientation of an ethnic group regarding its knowledge, outlook, perception, normative postulates, values and ethics.

Echoing Barth, James A. Armstrong avers that "groups tend to define themselves not by reference to their own characteristics but rather by exclusion, that is, by juxtaposed comparison to 'strangers'" (1982, 5). In trying to modify the Barthian 'boundary' concept, Armstrong talks about a host of symbolic factors—"mythomoteurs"—that had created an awareness of belongingness towards a single ethnic group from time immemorial. This sense of profound allegiance is made possible through a collective belief system that is sacred in its moorings and religious in its extensions. These nostalgic faiths in the mythical constitution of a group whether in its divinely derived origin, religious laws and customs, sanctity of an ancient language or collective wistfulness over a 'Golden past'—have hugely contributed to the making of an ethnonation. So myths primarily engender an ethnic consciousness which in its wake leads to the creation of a national consciousness. Thus, no wonder for Armstrong, *Nations before Nationalisms* is the ultimate conclusion. Ultimately what evolves is Armstrong's Barthian observation in a non-Barthian emphasis over unchanged myths and 'mythomoteurs'-based cultural identity. These mythomoteurs arouse intense affects by stressing individual's solidarity against an alien force, that is, "by enhancing the salience of boundary perceptions" (Armstrong 1982, 9).

The other ethnonationalist theorist of repute is Anthony D. Smith. In Smith's comparatively recent book—*Chosen Peoples: Sacred Sources of National Identity*—he states "it has been the general trend to dismiss the role of religion and tradition in a globalizing world, and to downplay the persistence of nationalism in a 'post-national' global order" (2003, ix). The notion of "authenticity", a key concept for him, links nationalism and religion, and is derived substantially from heroes, messiahs, and prophets (Smith 2003, 40-42).

The area where all three—Barth, Armstrong and Smith—make a basic structuralist mistake is assigning relative differentiating signifier(s) to denominate an identity. But any identity is equally slippery too and that being the case no 'ultimate' identity formation can take place. Moreover, even if we insist on certain essential ethnic qualities that are imperative to the making of a minority nation, it requires an amount of politicized and positivist strategizing from time to time.

To prevent ethnicity from becoming totally essentialsed and at the same time pervasive, Gayatri Spivak creates an approach that she terms as "strategic essentialism" (Spivak 1995, 214). Such essentialism has a politicized positivist approach and as Spivak holds: "I think it's absolutely on target...to stand against the discourses of essentialism...but *strategically* we cannot" (1990, 11). This strategically formulated and agenda driven essentialism challenges the dominant power structure and undercuts it from within. Therefore, for Spivak, the essentialist 'givens' of an ethnic group are accepted as far as they are strategically used in creating its own nation and identity and 'narrating' the dominant nation-state intermittently.

Within the limited scope of this essay, it is impossible to analyse all the cultural contents of the Aboriginal worldview that is contained in the concept of ethnonation. The cultural elements that are imperative in the consolidation of an Aboriginal ethnonation may comprise its language, myths, stories of Dreamtime, art, *corroboree*, socio-religious Laws, kinship pattern, etc. I will only choose *corroboree* as an example to show how in a Barthian manner it helps in 'boundary maintenance'; how in an Armstrongian manner it is a 'mythomoteur'; and how in Smithian way it is a moral-social force that reifies the said theorists' definition of a nation. I will also highlight how *corroboree* has been strategised from time to time—whether in real social life, literary spaces or in music videos—to avoid getting essentialised and pigeonholed and is thereby most strategically displayed with a positivist political edge.

Corroboree: Examples from Social Life, Literature and Music Video

The word *corroboree* as Jewell informs us (2011, 38), is an English word derived from the Dharug word 'ca-rib-ber-re' which signified a particular mode of dancing at the time of colonial settlement. For the Whites it was largely an indigenous dance form with 'bizarre' and 'mysterious' body-movements, songs, music and body paintings. Such an 'othering' obviously fails to incorporate the intrinsic spiritual attachment of the Aborigines with *corroboree*. *Corroboree*, contradistinguished from White fetishising, is an accompaniment to the oral narratives of 'Dreamtime' that gives expression to the stories of totemic icons and their transcendental powers. An age-old tradition most peculiar to the Aborigines, *corroboree* is a collective belief system that distinguishes the Aborigines from the rest. Thereby it is a 'mythomoteur' (Armstrong) that helps to awaken ethnic consciousness and 'maintain a boundary' (Barth) for the community. It is also the core of a sacred tradition—a moral-social force, an expression of a worldview that gives vent to the sentiments of nationalism (Smith). It is a display of common Aboriginal culture, myth and Law that reconjures their glorious past and consolidates their historic territory (Smith). Whether the enclosed group events or private 'Business' matters of men or women, these theatrical dance and music performances were in the post-contact period secularised by the modern White nation-state to make them more of a tourist events. However, as Barth would have it, their cultural content has undergone a change but not the significance and 'value standards' attached with it.

Melinda Jewell observes:

> Candice Bruce and Anita Callaway highlighted a similar dynamic in their article on the representation of the corroboree in paintings by white artists (1991). In the title of this article they pose the question of whether these depictions are 'Black Corroboree' or 'White Spectacle?' This question highlights an interaction between the act of seeing, the formation of knowledge and articulation of power. According to Bruce and Callaway, in colonial Australia corroborees often became instances of white spectacles as colonial people appropriated the Indigenous events for white benefit. The appropriation was a means to tame the potent sexuality of black performances and to rein in the power of what they imagined to be unknown and unknowable mysteries. In their discussion of paintings by white artists, Bruce and Callaway highlight that this appropriation is shown by common inclusion of white spectators who disarm the power of Indigenous dances and show little interest in what the ceremonies meant for Indigenous people. (2007, 33-34)

However, Jewell chooses a stance that rather than pitting the Aboriginals as 'objects' of colonial/neo-colonial gaze gives the former control over their own representation in the performance. She turns the power/knowledge table (mainly with the representations of *corroboree* by Aboriginal novel writers in the latter half of the twentieth century) to dub the supposed *seeing* of the colonisers in actuality as a *failure* to see (Jewell 2007, 34). But, Jewell does not theorise the oppositional act or speak about the ethnonational identity formation as a result of such resistive moves. It is this gap that my essay will address through examples from real social performances, literary representations and music video presentations.

Michael Parsons in his essay "The Tourist Corroboree in South Australia to 1911" discusses how these *corroborees* in South Australia successfully penetrated the settler economy. These dance performances were strategised as a resistive political move amidst a settler colony where Aboriginal entrepreneurial spirit was summarily dismissed and the 'sub-humans' were denied any access to any business. In Adelaide and its suburbs such *corroborees* were organized by the Aborigines themselves on Sundays to attract the colonial spectators who "certainly contributed something for the performance" (Parsons 1997, 49). Parsons further writes:

> Certainly by 1847 payment for the Sunday *corroborees* was an established practice. Complaints from the North Adelaide residents had continued through the 1840s, and in 1847 Matthew Moorhouse, the Protector of Aborigines, was ordered by the Colonial Secretary to tell the 'Natives encamped near Adelaide' that 'this is now a Christian Country' and the Sabbath must be kept holy; that they were therefore to 'abstain from making noise on Sundays'.

Exasperated, Moorhouse replied that:

> I have told them repeatedly not to corrobory (sic.) on the Sabbath, but crowds of Europeans visit them on this day, and offer them money, also the Natives find it more profitable to listen to them than to me. Last Sunday I believe they made nearly two pounds by their performances. (Letter from

Moorhouse, Protector of Aborigines, to Colonial Secretary, 10 November 1847) (Parsons 1997: 49)

If this was one of the strategic moves to use cultural artifacts for survival, then 'peace' or 'tourist' *corroborees* at least got a chance to perform amidst stringent Protection Laws of the colony, where such performances were dismissed as pagan nuisance. Such *corroboree*—'mythomoteurs' were also used to strategically counter the colonial presence and subvert its hegemonic structure and assimilative logic. Such 'mythomoteurs' do not merely add to the value standards but can confer on the community a common national objective and create an ethnic solidarity that helps them fight the oppression and aim towards a better future.

Moving from real social life to literature, *corroboree* has been variously used by Aboriginal authors in their writings. Jewell examines a host of such novels with a special emphasis on the ones written by Aboriginal authors: Mudrooroo's *Doctor Wooreddy's Prescription for Enduring the Ending of the World* (1983) and *Master of Ghost Dreaming* (1991), Doris Pelkington's *Caprice: A Stockman's Daughter* (1991), Philip McLaren's *Sweet Water—Stolen Land* (1993), Kim Scott's *True Country* (1993), Alexis Wright's *Plains of Promise* (1997) and Steven McCarthy's *Black Angels—Red Blood* (1998). In my analysis I will only dwell on Scott's *True Country*.

I have already discussed how *corroboree*, in real social life, was strategically commercialised by the Aboriginal communities themselves, especially in South Australia, to act as a source of earnings. What remained unsaid, both for such tourist/special performances generally and as mentioned in Scott's *True Country*, was another strategy where authentic performances were never put on display or their profound latent meaning disclosed to the Eurocentric tourist gaze. The uncertainty of positioning the locus of power/knowledge within the realm of *gazer* and *gazed* is properly resolved in the resistive acts of the characters who dance the *corroboree* in *True Country*. The mainstream's articulation of power through its acts of scopophilia is thoroughly appropriated in the instances of *corroboree* in the novel. The White viewers who invested money and idealistically thought they could have gained knowledge/power by gaining a penetration into the unfathomable mystery of Aboriginal *corroboree* in reality encounter a failure.

Jewell in her analysis of representation of *corroboree* in Scott's *True Country* observes:

> Indigenous ceremony as ocular commodity is similarly portrayed in Kim Scott's *True Country* (1993), although in this case it is within the contemporary context of tourism.
>
> ...
>
> In this case the spectacle is not the dancers but the ignorance and stupidity of the audience who have lost any colonial authority they once held in their gaze. (Scott 1993: 46-47)

The novel states three instances of *corroboree*. Fatima while narrating about her being taken away during her childhood, along with her sister Mary, by the European missionary to instill modern Enlightenment tells Billy—the narrator—how both of them did dance the *corroboree*: "Out on the water we used to dance corroboree for them. We were happy to do that. I used to sing. Mary dance. She used to sing for me, and I used to dance. Well we were children. We didn't feel shame or anything like that you know" (Scott 1993, 31). If such dance form was the sole source of expression of happiness that nostalgically reminded these little girls of their parents, family, community and country; then the White ladies on the board of the ship for whom such dances were organized remained totally unaware of such profound attachments that such dances conjured up. Though unconsciously, the *corroboree* performed by the girls succeeded in maintaining a cultural boundary which excluded the Whites from it—in participation and in comprehensibility of the performance. For the colonisers on board, the *corroborees* of the young girl remain a mere song-dance spectacle as they fail to figure out the ritual of remembrance that these girls associate with it. It is through this that the 'mythos' of an Aboriginal ethnonation counters the 'logos' of a rationalist modern foundations of a mainstream Australian nation.

Though an original *corroboree* was performed by these girls, the colonial gaze could not go beyond sight to reach an insight. Further, just after mentioning how such dances made both the sisters happy, Fatima immediately talks about the physical comforts that were handed down to these girls by the ladies in the ship: "They used to come and make our beds, clean nice underwear, shower. They used to be good to us. Nice food they used to give us, nice bed. They were nice people" (Scott 1993, 31). Such basic care of the Aboriginal inmates of the ship would not have taken place if these girls refused to *corroboree*. Though consciously such *corroborees* at that moment were not strategically molded to serve a purpose, yet they do bring about the desired result.

In the second instance, the expectations of the tourist are thwarted by the reluctant school girls who are made to perform the *corroboree*. This group of Aboriginal girls shy away and hide their face. However, Samson, an elder of the community, still demands money for the show and the photographs taken as he believes that this cultural manifestation would be sold at high price elsewhere. In the last instance, Aboriginal resistance to the anthropological colonisation in museumising or 'othering' Aboriginal *corroboree* is markedly evident. Billy finds out that *corroboree* is no more hosted in the traditional camps, rather in exotic locations like beaches to suit the tourist taste. At the same time, the White tourists expect to see essentialised versions of 'original' *corroboree*. In this "last tourist dance of the year" (Scott 1993, 214) the performers are reluctant: "The tourist corroboree was a messy affair, and embarrassing for most. Several of the dancers had stayed at the beach with their families, and others just did not come. So, many of the dancers were not there" (Scott 1993, 216-17).

But, resistance goes beyond mere reluctance. The show of the untrained small boys is criticised by their own family and community, which further siphons off the enthusiasm and involvement of the dancers and makes the show even a more pathetic one:

> Many of the smallest boys were recruited for the dancing, which began in the rapidly fading light. The boys were sullen, and their painted faces were smeared with tears. They watched a few older dancers and copied them, and so the dancers did not move together and it was all wrong. The families of the boys, perched on and draped over the vehicles parked on the edge of the area, whooped and jeered, and the dancers grinned or hung their heads. Some swore loudly and would have liked to fight. (Scott 1993, 217)

Understanding that the performance was becoming too inauthentic, Samson makes another strategic move. In "wheedling for audience's sympathy" he "growled at the tourist and posed a shaking spear at their cameras and appreciative laughter" (Scott 1993, 217). The motive behind posing such 'original' way is obviously pecuniary—a stance of Samson that has been discussed in the second example of *corroboree* in the novel. Even if the show is a complete flop, the cameras of the audience still flashed at times. With the setting in of the dusk headlights of the vehicle are turned on as traditional campfires seemed inadequate for the tourist gaze/cameras. Amidst such spotlights the dancers appear "like kangaroos caught in the shooter's light and staring, puzzled, at the source of their death" (Scott 1993, 217).

Jewell rightly observes: "this image suggests not only the damage imposed on the sacredness of the indigenous cultural practice as the result of thoughtless appropriation but the folly of attempting to stage Indigenous ceremony within a western theatrical context" (Scott 1993, 47). Even Penny Van Toorn in her article "A Journey Out/Back: Exploring Kim Scott's 'True Country'" critiques the White tourist tendency of commodifying the Karnama *corroboree* "within a non-Aboriginal semiotic" (qtd. in Jewell 2007, 47). Whatever be the case, the age old Power/Knowledge relationship is destabilized and the hitherto ocular commodity—the Karnama *corroboree*—defies colonial authority through subtle resistive acts of strategising the essential givens and thereby revives the ethnic identity.

The third example that I wish to examine is the widely circulated *corroboree* song/dance video "Timeless Land" by Yothu Yindi released in 1994. Yothu Yindi, a Yolngu nation of North-east Arnhem Land, when translated into English means 'child and mother'—i.e. to say if the land is their mother the Aborigines are its children. The band strategises the ancient song cycles and dance of north-east Arnhem Land by using and appropriating western musical rock form in their video. Further, the very performance that is so private and community centric is made public through recording and marketing by the same group worldwide. Essential ethnic elements of the Yolngu group, that were once meant for celebrations in a *corroboree*, become in this video resistive moves in the context of the condition of the Aborigines in a modern Eurocentric nation-state. This is a positivist political move that was done with the consent of the Elders of Yolngu nation. This strategic move of the band consolidates and revives the Yolngu ethnonation. The song sings the place that has Smithian (i.e. Anthony Smith) "historic territory"—edge of the mountains to the valley, snowy river to the ocean—a land to which the Yolngu people had their rights from time immemorial to recent date. Their myths, that they try to revive in the song, comprise stories handed down by "the great sisters" and "wise men". Such Armstrongian "mythomoteurs" that create the Yolngu nation's ethnic boundary are then juxtaposed with the communities (here obviously the White or Eurocentric communities) beyond their boundary. This is evoked by the "me"/"you" and "our"/"your" dichotomy. Thrice the refrain occurs —"This is a timeless land. This is our land."

Thus, we come to understand the concept of the Aborigine's ethnic identity and ethnic nation and a revival of the same by strategic methods hurled against the White modernist constructs. Such politico-cultural resistance, as evident in the performances of *corroboree*, goes on to 'narrate' the Australian nation-state in its own way. Such 'performativity' and positivist strategization not only gives the marginalized subjects an authority over their own representation, but even subverts and appropriates the modern Anglo-centric hegemony of Australian nation-state. The essay was never an attempt to offer an infallible theory or a grand narrative method, as there is none. Every strategy or subversive method is ever-changing and situational. Cultural fixity being hegemonic, a constant *difference*, even in *corroboree* representations and performances, is ever maintained.

Works Cited

Armstrong, James A. 1982. *Nations before Nationalism*. Chapel Hill: University of North Carolina Press.

Barth, Fredrik, Ed. 1969. *Ethnic Groups and Boundaries: The Social Organization of Cultural Difference*. Boston: Little, Brown and Co.

Bruce, Candice and Anita Callaway. 1999. "Dancing in the Dark: Black Corroboree or White Spectacle?" *Australian Journal of Art*. 9: 78-104.

Connor, Walker. 1994. *Ethnonationalism: The Quest for Understanding*. Princeton (NJ): Princeton University Press.

Glazer, Nathan, and Moynihan, Daniel P. Eds. 1975. *Ethnicity: Theory and Experience*. Cambridge (MA): Harvard University Press.

Haraway, D. 1991. *Simians, Cyborgs and Women: The Reinvention of Nature*. London: Free Association Books.

Jewell, Melinda Rose. 2007. "'A Vision through a Smokey Haze'—Viewing Corroboree in Selected Australian Novels." *Australian Studies*. 20. 1 & 2: 31-54.

———. 2011. *The Representation of Dance in Australian Novels: The Darkness Beyond the Stage-Lit Dream*. Berlin: Peter Lang.

McDowell, L. 1992. "Multiple Voices: Speaking from Inside and Outside 'The Project'. *Antipodes*. 24: 57-80.

Parsons, Michael. 1997. "The Tourist Corroboree in South Australia to 1911." *Aboriginal History* 21: 46-69.

Schermerhorn, Richard A. 1970. *Ethnic Relations*. New York: Random House.

Smith, Anthony D. 1991. *National Identity*. London: Penguin.

———. 2002. "When is a Nation." *Geopolitics* 7.2: 5-32.

———. 2003. *Chosen Peoples: Sacred Sources of National Identity*. Oxford: Oxford University Press, 2003.

Spivak, Gayatri Chakravorty. 1990. "Criticism, Feminism, and the Institution." *The Post-Colonial Critic: Interviews, Strategies, Dialogues*. Ed. Sarah Harasym. New York: Routledge.

———. et al. *The Spivak Reader*. London: Routledge, 1995.

Scott, Kim. 1993. *True Country*. Fremantle: Fremantle Arts Centre Press.

Yindi, Yothu. 1994. "Timeless Land." *Freedom*. In <http://www.youtube.com/watch?v=O7TWJMO4k3k> Accessed on 1 March 2012.

CHAPTER 14

Beyond Borders: Dalit and Australian Aboriginal Myths of Origin

K. Suneetha Rani
University of Hyderabad, India

While globalisation is opening up the geographic and territorial borders between countries, the invisible boundaries between cultures, communities and peoples within the countries are also becoming stronger and deeper. However, people marginalised in their native regions may discover that they have something in common with similar groups in other regions through their stories that emanate from their experience of exclusion. The oral literature of a community reflects its early experiences, discoveries, beliefs and imaginary worlds. These imaginary worlds cross all boundaries and borders as they visualise the past, analyse the present and foresee the future. Construction of the past is an important element in oral literature. It represents the efforts of the people to locate themselves in history and also trace the history of the universe itself. In their attempt to locate themselves, they re-create the universe in their stories, songs and rituals. Such "histories" of origin are most significant in the context of communities that have been destabilised, displaced and discriminated, for various reasons, in the contemporary context.

Despite their diverse contexts, similarities in the predicament of these peoples and the resistance they demonstrate against their situation establish connections between such peoples. Their oral literatures not only help erase larger international boundaries but also promote connections between them. This is one facet of globalization in which developments in communications technology seem to have effected a shrinking of the globe and the tyranny of distance has undergone erasure. Comparisons between the Indian Dalit and Australian Aboriginal myths of origin are made possible in a way that would hardly have been thought possible earlier. It is a fact well understood that each group has its own version of creation myths and understanding of creation but there is an interest in noting the parallels and also to present an alternative readings of those myths. It is more important to also note the element of re-writing of the community's history with the help of creation myths.

Indian Dalit and Australian Aboriginal stories of creation besides demonstrating their power of imagination, also hold a mirror to the anxieties and resistance of dispossessed peoples. This essay examines a few tales of creation from the Dalit and the Aboriginal contexts. It will study how these tales reflect their culture and tradition, speak of the colonial influence (internal as well as external), reveal gender bias, and become means of self-respect and human rights in the context of globalisation. This essay will use examples of stories of origin of the Australian Aboriginal and the Dalit communities to show parallels as well as dissimilarities.

Although the contexts and stories are widely different, the underlying spirit of resistance and reconstruction matches in a thought-provoking manner. Some obvious points of comparison between these two myths of origins are: both emerge from Indigenous knowledge and perspective; both are expressed in oral form but recorded in written form; both have acquired new dimensions with changing times sometimes forcibly influenced by the colonising/dominating origin myths; both have been mediated by people of the dominant sections; both aim to protect self-respect and announce resistance; both record and reclaim the past in their own terms.

In India, each caste, whether it claims to be in the fold of Hinduism or not, has a creation myth of its own. The caste system in India is designed so cleverly that each caste believes in its supremacy over the other castes. Each caste has a *purana* which elevates its position and generally this *purana* is narrated by a dependent caste and each caste has a dependent/satellite caste of its own. In such a context, it would be interesting to read the *kula puranas* of the lower castes who have no recent history to boast of. At the same time, these are the castes that need the narratives of self-respect the most. Ironically, these sections that protest against the caste system have to go back to the Hindu origins in order to write their resistance narratives as well.

Though Australia has no caste system, colonisation has written a similar story of discrimination and exploitation. Dalits revisit Hinduism, the colonising religion to confront the institutionalised segregation of Dalits, Australian Aboriginals use English, the coloniser's language to question the racial hegemony of European Australians. Dalits trace their history of untouchability to the Aryan invasion of India (1500-100 BC) thus arguing for their status as the Indigenous people of India and also tracing their racial hegemony in Indian history (Rani 2003, 17-25).

The texts chosen for this essay from Dalit and Aboriginal contexts are oral in tradition but the Dalit texts are performative texts which are now documented and are available in print. Similarly, Aboriginal texts are also available in print. The basic point stressed here is that these texts, though chosen as texts of marginalised people, go through the mediation of language, form and other agencies.

This is also closely linked to the fluidity and spontaneity of Dalit performative texts which, as this essay will illustrate, have adopted many contemporary beliefs. These narratives that subvert mainstream versions and beliefs offer alternative origin myths emphasizing these people's proximity to nature. Multiple versions of these narratives also become an important area of study. For instance, the story of Adi Jambava, the ancestor of the Madigas, is performed by different sub-castes and there are different versions of it as well. Madiga Mashteedus sing the song, Baindlas perform it in the folk tradition on twin *pambas*, Dakkalis make it a picture story and a street performance, Nukkala Chandayyas (Madiga Jangas) recite it as a *purana* and Chindus perform it as *yakshagana*.

The primary focus of this essay is on *Dakkali Jambapuranam* edited by Jayadheer Tirumalarao. The editors mentiones that it is a documentation in print of the performance of *Jambapurana* as *yakshagana* in 1995 and 1998 in different parts of the Telangana region of Andhra Pradesh. The book was published in the hope that it would provide new tools for studying the parallel traditions of sub-castes. The main editor Jayadheer Tirumalarao, though not an insider to the Dakkali caste, has completed remarkable research in the field of folk forms and cultures and has published a significant work.

In the "Introduction", the editors observe that *Dakkali Jambapuranam* unveils four of its major issues: (1) ridiculing the hegemony of the upper caste (2) declaring the self-respect of Madigas (3) relationships between Malas and Madigas, and (4) co-existence along with other labouring classes. The above four issues stand for the most important aspects of the protest movements of the marginalised people. The purpose is not so much to attack and destroy the upper caste hegemony as to ridicule it which is also a powerful form of protest. Rather than using violence, they use humour, sarcasm and satire in order to inflict humiliation on the upper caste hegemony. The system may not give them a chance to retaliate for the violence that they have suffered at the hands of upper caste people. Closely connected to this is the second purpose that is to declare, proclaim and establish the self-respect of Madigas.

This aspect is important for this essay as well because the oral literature of most marginalised peoples seems to be inspired by a need and commitment to establish their position in the society. These tales also reveal the relationships between the sub-castes in contrast to the contemporary situation of conflict between the sub-castes. These tales in multiple versions woven from different perspectives bring others from similar classes into the narrative, probably to connote the bonding between people of the toiling and exploited classes.

Interestingly, the editors propose that the "sacred narratives" of the downtrodden sections should be recognised as "secret narratives" as they have been protected and preserved from the hegemony of the upper castes for generations as alternative traditions while the privileged sections have declared their sacred stories as solely owned by themselves and made it sinful for others to even listen to them. The editors, Tirumalarao and Prabhakar, also comment on the transformation that has dawned on Dakkali lives:

> In fact, sub streams and origin streams are losing their existence in this age. The families that sing *Jambapurana* are converting into Christianity. In Nashkal village, Dakkali women are going in crowds to the Karunapuram church every Sunday with a bound copy of Bible in their hands. As never before, Dakkali men performers are leaving their women at home and going to sing *Jambapurana* by themselves. (Tirumalarao 2011, xxix)

This observation points to a crucial debate on the advent of globalisation and urbanisation in the Dalit context. It is true that the rural set up provided occupational security to all the villagers. But, it also perpetuated the caste system, especially the stigma of untouchability. So, urbanisation and globalisation could provide some relief from caste discrimination and could make economic mobility possible though social mobility which otherwise is not possible in a society steeped in casteist ideology.

Aboriginal people who were forced to become "westernised" had to adapt to new language, culture, lifestyle, etc. though these did not really help them to regain their pre-colonial status in their country. Claire Smith and Graeme Ward rightly observe in their introduction to the book *Indigenous Cultures in an Interconnected World* (2000) that Indigenous people are taking advantage of every means to help them keep in touch with one another and to tackle the problems posed by globalisation through radio, film, video, recorded music and the internet. This is a convincing argument as the written word in English has helped them connect with their own people who, like them, are left only with English as they have lost Indigenous languages and also to reach out to people from similar contexts in different regions of the world. It will be interesting to look at the positive response of Dalits and Aboriginals to the World Social Forum which has emerged as a response to the spreading tentacles of globalisation.

Dakkali performance has five parts—*Adi Puranam (Srushti Puranam), Parvathi Kalyanam, Mala Chennaiah Puranam, Aranjyothi Kalyanam and Balabhadra Vijayam.* This essay concentrates on *Adi Puranam* which narrates the creation of the world. According to the Dakkali narration, Jambava proclaims himself as the first person on the earth born six months before the birth of the earth. There was only water in the world then and a floating lotus in that water. Jambava was born in that lotus. The lotus opened when Srimannarayana in the form of an insect flew over the sea flapping its wings. When there was no earth, sky, sun, moon, stars, angels, rakshasas, humans and nature, the Ekonarayana was floating like a bubble on water and created Adi Shakti. They turned into peacock and peahen and Adi Shakti laid three eggs. Adi Shakti created the entire universe from these three eggs. She proposed to have sex with her sons, the *Trimurtis* (trinity—Brahma, Vishnu, Maheswara) to continue the world. Brahma and Vishnu angered her by not heeding her suggestion. Shiva, on his uncle Jambavantha's suggestions, tricked her, appropriated all her powers, burnt her to ashes and rejuvenated his brothers. The death of Adi Shakti and the birth of *Trimurtis* is the main theme of this part. In the later part the ashes were divided into three parts and made into Lakshmi, Saraswati and Parvathi who were married by the *Trimurtis*.

This story is narrated differently in different versions. In these narrations, various influences come to the forefront. One such influence becomes obvious when Srimannarayana says that he took out fistful of mud from his chest and a part of his bone and dropped into the ocean. The woman who is born out of it has thirty-two weapons, ten arrows, a sacred thread (a *shaiva* sign), lotus feet, fins on her back, and a miraculous third eye on the forehead. We can clearly see the *shaiva* influence here and an attempt to brahmanise the woman Adi Shakti.

Although the creator is called Sreemannarayana, it is Shiva who plays a crucial role in destroying Adi Shakti . Adi Shakti herself is described as one with Shaivaite features. It is interesting to see how these typical traits of Adi Shakti have gone on to become Shiva's powers. Jambavantha is also created in a similar manner. Srimannarayana calls Adi Jambava a *Harijan*. We see Jambavantha and Adi Shakti meeting Buddha. But this Buddha is none other than Srimannarayana/Ekonarayana. This has a very clear resonance of Advaita—the difference between Shiva and Vishnu is erased. Ekonarayana echoes the one and only God principle.

In the Chindu version of *Jamba Purana*, we come across Vemana who is called a people's poet vehemently condemning the caste system. Srimannarayana of *Dakkali Purana* becomes Paramatma here. Similarly, Chindu *Jamba Purana* says that village goddesses, especially worshipped by Dalits and lower castes, such as Ellamma, Maisamma, Sammakka and Saramma were born out of the ashes of Adi Shakti. This shows how Dalits wanted to include their goddesses who were considered evil goddesses by the mainstream society as the incarnations of Adi Shakti. It is an attempt by Dalits to claim acceptance not only for themselves but also for their gods and goddesses.

Interestingly, these origin myths have women who are all powerful and who create men. But these women either withdraw or disappear and are destroyed by men. Again, women are created by men. But, the qualities of women who were creators and women who were created are obviously very different. These women raise very radical questions and propose very different concepts. For instance, Adi Shakti comes across as a strong, firm and powerful woman who knows her power and is the source of power. She can create, give birth, change her form, propose, curse, and kill. However, all her power vanishes due to her aggressive sexuality. The instance of Shiva tricking her into surrendering her powers to him carries an important suggestion of the need to repress woman's active sexuality. Adhi Shakti's youth turns into old age once she loses all the weapons that she possesses and even her third eye does not help her see through Shiva's designs.

Similarly, she interprets relationships in a very different manner. When men try to convince her about her asexual relationship with them and warn her against incest, she says she has not given birth to them but has only laid eggs. They came out of eggs. So, they become her grandchildren but not children. She asserts that sexual relationship between grandmother and grandchildren is permissible. She does not merely rule out the moral aspect of relationships but tries to give them a reason for acceptance. The patriarchal turn to a matriarchal story opens up a discourse about the influences that changed the course of the story. Not only does the trinity take birth from the Adi Shakti but it also borrows, or rather snatches, the powers and weapons from Adi Shakti. Also, one Adi Shakti is divided into three as her womanhood and sexuality are unmanageable even for three men. Vishnu gets the conch, chakra, gada and other weapons and Shiva gets the trident from Adi Shakti.

The entire creation myth emphasises the superiority or acceptability of Jambavantha, who is the ancestor of the Madigas. Not only does the story say that Jambavantha was created by Srimannarayana but also that Jambavantha is a guiding force for others in the story. While it emphasises his creation by God who has created others, it also borrows the Gandhian concept of *Harijan*. It is not a violation of the caste system but a re-interpretation of the caste system.

Chindu *Jamba Purana* narrates that Manuviswabrahma blest Jambavantha with a son who was born from Jambavantha's right ribs. When Manuviswabrahma asks him for a leather bag, Jambavantha hesitates to kill the animals and kills his son. Before dying, the son curses his father with untouchability, but, when the father pleads with him, the son commutes the sentence to last for five thousand years after which the society will embrace him. His son is revived but Jambavantha declares that since he was reborn, he cannot be one with him but will be of a sub-caste of Madigas, that is Dakkali.

Kalyana Rao begins his novel *Untouchable Spring* with a version of *Jamba Purana* which is called the story of Kamadhenu. The trinity guards the Kamadhenu born out of the churning of the ocean of milk. Parvati hides her sari soiled with her menstrual blood in a tree on her journey to river Ganga. Shiva's shadow falls on the sari and a son is born. He is called Chennaiah as the tree in which the sari was hidden was the *chennangi* tree. Shiva appoints him to guard the Kamadhenu. Chennaiah desires Kamadhenu's milk which is forbidden for him. When Kamadhenu hears his desire, it falls dead. As the Kamadhenu's meat is being cooked, Chennaiah and his grandfather Jambavantha eat part of it instead of guarding it. Shiva curses them to be born as untouchables on the earth, that is as Malas and Madigas. In both versions, we note a similar attempt to convince themselves and the society of their original respectable lineage and acceptability. It is their making of a mistake which brings punishment. This echoes the mainstream belief that to be born into a lower caste is a punishment which is the result of some sin committed by them.

Let us now look at the parallels in Australian Aboriginal mythology. I have drawn here from two collections of Aboriginal tales edited by A.W. Reed titled *Aboriginal Stories of Australia* and *Aboriginal Myths: Tales of the Dreamtime*. We are told here of Yhi, the sun goddess in the Aboriginal tales a creator, nurturer who loves the world. Her power is established again and again. She is almost on par with the Great Spirit. Her absence creates chaos in the world. In the beginning she chooses to be away at night and present in the day, as she is the sun goddess. But, later once she thinks that the world is self-sufficient, she decides to step out. The story presents an interesting concept again of the woman playing a crucial role in the creation. This also presents a convincing division of responsibilities of creation between man and woman. In the beginning when the world was quiet and dark without any vegetation or life, Yhi was waiting in her sleep for the whisper of the Great Spirit. When the whisper came, Yhi floated down to earth and began a pilgrimage that took her far to the west, to the east, to north, and south. Wherever her feet rested on the ground, there the earth leaped in ecstasy. Grass, shrubs, trees and flowers sprang from it, lifting themselves towards the radiant source of light. Yhi's tracks crossed and recrossed until the whole earth was clothed with vegetation (Reed 1998, 10).

Let us also look at another story that talks about the origin of the universe, "The Making of Mankind":

> In the Centre the primal cause of creation was believed to be the goddess of the sun. Not the sun itself, but the spirit of the sun, the Great Spirit, the

> Mother, richly endowed and fecund, but yet spirit, whose power was manifested in thought and, through other agencies, in action. According to the wisest men, the agency through which she worked before her departure was one known variously as Baiame, Spirit Father, or All-Father.
>
> Baiame, the male counterpart of the female Yhi, the Sun goddess, was not only her representative, but her alter ego, created by her, partaking of her divinity. To him she had entrusted the task of forming and caring animal life in its infinite variety. One thing only was lacking—the form and intelligence of man. This task, too, was entrusted to the Father Spirit. (Reed 1999, 32)

But, interestingly, "The First Man" later talks about a romantic image of a woman who takes birth from a flowering tree:

> The loneliness was ended; the duty and obligations of Man began. Woman came slowly to full life and communion with her husband. He hunted food for her. He sought shelter for her. He showed her love and tenderness, which are the fruits of the spirit. He taught her the names of birds and animals and their ways. She learned to love him, and to work for him, to be the other part of him that he needed for the satisfying of his longings and needs. (Reed 1998, 18)

Certainly there is an echo here of the Biblical story of creation of a woman to be the companion of the man. It is not from the body of the man that she is made but from creation, which is a crucial factor here. In another story, "Bunjil the Creator", the man findsa woman's body submerged in a lake and rejuvenates it. But, the story "Baiame and the First Man and Woman" begins by saying, "And again the Lord God, Baiame walked on the earth he had made, among the plants and animals, and created man and woman to rule over them" (Reed 1999, 4). Reed observes in his Introduction:

> A certain 'westernisation' of the traditional tales must be admitted. In some cases they are the retelling of twice-told tales; in others the story may be adapted and enlarged from the transcript of a myth or legend recorded directly from an Aboriginal teller of tales. In such circumstances, particularly in more recent times, the original myth may already have suffered a number of changes. Again, it should be remembered that a favourite tradition may have been preserved in song and dance rather than or in addition to the spoken form. (Reed 1999, viii)

He comes up with an interesting explanation for his collection of Aboriginal tales:

> Every writer who ventures to retell Aboriginal myths and legends must adopt his own style and presentation. For my part, I have rewritten a variety of myths and folk tales with sincere admiration for the men of old who gave pleasure and inspiration to their fellow tribesmen. Profiting by the research of others I have retold them simply, as they appeal to me, and with only sufficient change to make them acceptable to present day readers. If by chance they give enjoyment to others and a little insight into the treasury of Aboriginal lore, something will have been gained. (Reed 1999, ix)

The intentions of the editors of *Dakkali Jambapuranam* are much more political as they identify this tradition as a subtle subversion of the Brahminical traditions and this documentation as an important milestone in the Dalit movement.

"Baiame and the Land of Women" refers to a valiant women's land and the story "The Seven Sisters" narrates an account of girls who wanted to go through the tests to show that they were ready for womanhood and marriage just as the young men had to prove themselves for manhood. These valiant and independent women give rise to similar constructions of women in other tales. One version of this story concludes as follows:

> The whole tribe came out to greet them and congratulate them on the triumph of mind over body. On that day even the gods and spirits of the high heaven were present. The girls, now entered into full womanhood, were snatched from the midst of their friends and taken up to the sky where, as the Seven Sisters of the constellation of the Pleiades, they shine down serenely on the world, encouraging every successive generation to follow their example. (Reed 1998, 71)

The Dalit story about seven sisters also brings in seven strong women who like Adi Shakti argue for their sexuality. While the Aboriginal story about seven sisters presents the young women's urge to prove themselves and attain womanhood, the Dalit seven sisters vehemently prove their individuality, power of creation as well as their sexuality.

The question that arises is, why is it that most creation myths begin with a powerful creating woman and end by establishing created women who are powerless, subservient and dependent? Why do these powerful women either disappear or get destroyed? What influences contribute to this transformation? The people who rewrite the mainstream stories are from sections that are marginalised and colonised. These stories come out of their resistance and urge to deconstruct the existing hierarchies. Yet, one wonders why these stories betray a tendency to subjugate and ridicule powerful women. It would be interesting to study the creation myths from feminist perspectives that argue for a sisterhood among women informed by various specific contexts.

The topic of this essay and the issues it has discussed open up new areas of research that need to be explored further. They provide opportunities for research connecting Indigenous peoples who share certain similarities despite the wide differences between their socio-cultural contexts. The two groups whose myths have been studied here have both survived challenges to their existence and adapted to changing situations. Their written literatures in "the other tongue" and "the other form" underline their battling spirit and the long history of their creativity. The characteristics of their mythologizing suggest that these marginalised people will, despite the new challenges, retain their unique place in a globalised world.

(I gratefully acknowledge the contribution of Prof. Ghanta Chakrapani, the co-author of a version of this paper that was presented at the ASAA international conference held at OUCIP in Dec 2011).

Works Cited

Blaser, Mario, Harvey A. Feit and Glenn McRae. 2004. *In the Way of Development: Indigenous Peoples, Life Projects and Globalisation*. London: Zed Books.

Chakrapani, Ghanta. 2009. *Pambalas: The Vanishing Dalit Priests*. Hyderabad: Aneka Publications.

———, (ed.). 2009. *Globalisation and Social Exclusion in India*. New Delhi: Milind Publications.

Kalyanarao, G. 2010. *Untouchable Spring*. Tr. Alladi Uma and M. Sridhar. Hyderabad: Orient Blackswan.

Rani, Suneetha K. 2003. "Protest as Theme and Resistance as Technique: Australian Aboriginal Poetry and Dalit Poetry", Cynthia vanden Driesen, and Satendra Nandan, eds. *Austral-Asian Encounters: From Literature and Women's Studies to Politics and Tourism*. New Delhi: Prestige. 17-25.

———. "Deconstructing the Caste Hegemony: Lambada Oral Literature". *The Journal of Alternative Perspectives in the Social Sciences*, vol. 2, no. 1, May 2010: 455-67.

Reed, A.W. 1998. *Aboriginal Stories of Australia*. Sydney: Reed New Holland, (1963).

———. 1999. *Aboriginal Myths: Tales of the Dreamtime*. Sydney: Reed New Holland, (1978).

Smith, Claire and Graeme Ward. 2000. *Indigenous Cultures in an Interconnected World*. Vancouver: UBC Press.

Srinivas, M.N. 1995. *Social Change in Modern India*. Hyderabad: Orient Blackswan.

Tirumalarao, Jayadheer. 2011. *Dakkali Jambapuranam*. Hyderabad: Janapada Prachurana (1998).

CHAPTER 15

Fluid Borders and Continuous Displacement: Partition Stories from Talbagicha, Kharagpur

Sharmistha De
Dr. B.C. Roy Engineering College
Durgapur, India

Anjali Gera Roy
Indian Institute of Technology Kharagpur, India

Ambreem Hai maintains that in recent years, the problems and possibilities of borders and boundaries have become an increasing preoccupation for theoretical discourses in a wide variety of fields (2000, 380). The emergence of border studies during the past decade has been characterized by a crossing of disciplinary borders This growth in border studies runs contrary to the globalisation discourse of the late 1980s and early 1990s, positing a new 'borderless' world in which borders became obsolete (Nikolov 2009, 262).

Boundaries, borders and frontiers may be defined as the 'creative' markers used to retain and preserve the identity of a specific place. In distinguishing traditional and modern states, one important aspect to stress is that traditional states had 'frontiers', while modern states have borders which are more sophisticated and internationally accepted and thus less contested than frontiers. The history of borders in Western Europe dates back to the Roman Empire, during which emperors regulated the 'practice of boundaries' through frontiers in order to control territory. With the introduction of cartographic mapping during the

Renaissance, the drawing of borders continued and reduced frontiers to lines on maps.

Maps, according to Ashcroft, "not only represented space, they represented the power of the fixed, all-seeing viewpoint: the power to create a universal space" (2001, 129). Ashcroft argues that "the physical occupation and control of space have been crucial to British imperialism" (2001, 124). Paula Banerjee agrees that "liberals and Marxists alike agree that boundaries are made to manipulate a certain distribution of power and that there is a clear connection between imperialism and the demarcation of state borders" (2002, 28). The mapping of the world and spaces thus asserted European dominance over "other ways of experiencing" and also the "dominance of imperialist language". According to Ratzel, borders are "expressions and measures of state power (...) dynamic aspects of a state, since stronger and vibrant ones aspire to expand their spatial range, while declining ones lean to shrinking themselves within smaller area" (Nikolov 2009, 263). However, Ratzel and other 'geographical determinists' failed to develop a holistic theory of borders that can incorporate their physical and metaphoric aspects.

According to Avtar Brah (1996) borders are "arbitrary dividing lines" which function on a social, cultural and psychic level. As such they are always "metaphors and part of the discursive materiality of power relations" (198). In her seminal text *Borderland La Frontera, The New Mestiza,* Gloria Anzaldua actually refers to the US-Mexico border and uses the term 'border' not only pertaining to physical boundaries but also to other boundaries, which encompasses race, gender, status and other considerations. In addition, the 'border' also serves as an allusion to the boundaries that exist between the physical and spiritual realm. The concept of borderland as a way of thinking about identity, according to Katherine Pratt Etwing (1998), has emerged "through the process of metaphorical extension" based on the works of Gloria Anzaldua and Renato Rosaldo, which has focused on the negotiation of identities while considering the border as a metaphor.

We might, therefore, well understand that borders drawn to divide spaces are "not some innate traits of sovereignty, but merely human constructs built on an amalgamation of geography, cartography, theories of sovereignty and the prevalent system of power" (Banerjee 2002, 38). The crossing over of boundaries that are not merely physical or natural but are artificially created has led to a rethinking on movement across borders. Migration or moving over from one place to another, therefore, has come to be associated with the notion of borders. As a result of this movement, the issue of crossing the 'border'—both literally and metaphorically—has been foregrounded and the fixity of the 'border' interrogated. Recent postcolonial writings also emphasize the flexibility of border-crossing and contest essentialist notions of borders. The *leitmotif* in these writings is that political borders are really 'shadow lines' and that all cultures and human beings reach out to others defying divisive lines.

Borders and the Partition of India

The Partition of India in 1947 is probably the most recent act of the physical demarcation of place in the history of British imperialism that caused large groups to be displaced from their 'homeland'. Sir Cyril Radcliffe, entrusted with the responsibility of drawing the borders of Pakistan and India, himself "confessed to the impossibility of trying to construct a contiguous boundary between eastern India and East Pakistan". As a consequence, the lines that were drawn were "too static and too simple" (Banerjee 2002, 37). Ishtiaq Ahmed analyses the arguments of the Punjab Boundary Commission to show "the political and cultural implication of the religion-based division of Punjab between India and Pakistan for post-independence South Asia" (1999, 118). Following Ahmed, Lucy Chester, in "The 1947 Partition: Drawing the Indo-Pakistani boundary", examines the problems in the drawing of the political boundary line between India and Pakistan and analyses the reasons for the violence and trauma caused by the drawing of the boundary line (2002). Tan Tai Yong and Gyanesh Kudaisya point out, "the boundary line was drawn arbitrarily, mostly ignoring factors such as communications and railway links, water channels, cultural and pilgrimage sites, location of industries and vital strategic factors" (2000, 144).

Partition-in-the-West and Partition-in-the-East

The Partition of India caused unprecedented violence and mass displacement leading to large-scale displacement that produced in survivors the traumatic experience of being alienated, rootless and homeless. Partition studies have largely focused on survivors who crossed from the west side of the border consisting mainly of Hindu and Sikh Punjabis but also Sindhis and Kashmiris. Historians like Mushirul Hasan and Gyanendra Pandey have made significant contributions in conceptualizing the event of Partition in the West by moving its focus to the lived experiences of violence and displacement. In his essay "Memories of a Fragmented Nation", Hasan contests both imperialist and nationalist histories of Partition through presenting a revisionist history of Partition. Partition scholars like Ishtiaq Ahmed, Ian Talbot, Urvashi Butalia, Veena Das Nonica Datta and a few others, have added to the study of the politics of resettlement in the West. Following Hasan, this group of Partition scholars has focused on personal narratives and oral histories of Partition.

The trauma of women affected by the division is brought out poignantly in the form of oral testimonies compiled by scholars like Urvashi Butalia, Veena Das, Ritu Menon and the like. Butalia, in her book *The Other Side of Silence: Voices from the Partition of India,* begins with her own family's traumatic experience of the Partition and brings out the untold violence and suffering which the 'division' (Partition) brought. However, Butalia's archival work (1998) is based on the testimonies of the survivors from West Pakistan who moved to the province of East Punjab and parts of Northern India. A similar study by Ritu Menon and Kamala Bhasin (1998) also draws attention to the trauma of women who were victimised during the Partition violence especially in the West. Veena Das, in her essay "The Act of Witnessing: Violence Poisonous Knowledge and Subjectivity", argues that women who didn't encounter Partition violence became indirect victims of Partition. Das (2000) takes up the personal testimony of a woman called Asha who must live with "the poisonous knowledge" of relations of kinship within the family turning sour with the drawing of boundaries.

These historical documents, oral narratives, personal testimonies, along with fictional texts, that testify to the trauma, displacement and the politics of resettlement related to communities directly affected by the event have led to a new understanding of the cross-border movement and migration of refugees during and after the drawing of the new borders in 1947 (Ishtiaq Ahmed 2004, Ian Talbot 2007, Nonica Datta 2001).

However, the violence, trauma and displacement experienced by the affected communities in East Bengal was no less distressing. The Durand Line that led to the division of Bengal into two halves in 1947 led to the forced migration of Bengali Hindus from their 'homeland' in East Pakistan. The trauma, violence, displacement and/or migration of the East Bengali survivors of Partition remained undocumented except in cinematic and fictional texts. Among many are films like Ritwick Ghatak's "Meghe Dhaka Tara" (1960), "Nagarik" (1952), "Ajantrik" (1958), "Subarnarekha" (1965) and fictional texts like Sunil Gangopadhyay's "Purba Pashchim" (1989), "Arjun" (1988), Jyotirmoyi Devi's "Epar Ganga Opar Ganga" [translated as *The River Churning* (1995)]. It is only recently that Partition scholars, including historians, social and political scientists, have turned their attention to the study of the Partition in the East by documenting the oral histories and testimonies of migrants.

In their anthology entitled *Trauma and the Triumph* (2003) Bagchi and Dasgupta have attempted to document women's memories and struggles during the Partition, through oral histories, literatures and critical analyses. Thakurta (2006) adds a new dimension to Partition historiography by reconstructing family histories in reconsidering the "case of Bengal Partition". Another study examines the ideological differences between the relief and rehabilitation measures offered by the State government to Bengali refugees in the years after Partition and critiques the West Bengal government's policy of dispersing the refugees in the guise of resettlement and rehabilitation and failure to rehabilitate the refugees of Bengal (Chatterjee 2001).

However, the displacement of communities in the East are not only restricted to the 'event' of Partition but continues as subjects continue to cross the borders between the two countries (India and Bangladesh) both physically and psychologically. Tasleema Nasreen's *Phera* (1993) Amitav Ghosh's *The Shadow Lines* (1988) have documented the Partition of Bengal and its impact on people, culture and society. As Renuka Roy, in her essay "And Still they come", states, "there was no immediate interchange of population, nor even panic.... It was not until December 1949 that it became obvious that an influx of refugees from East Pakistan had started" (2006, 80). Similarly, Meghna Guha Thakurta, in her essay "Uprooted and Divided", admits that "even after two generations the migration across borders continues" (2006, 98). The displacement due to Partition in the Eastern part of the country is, therefore, a 'process' which continues even sixty-five years later. As Nilanjana Chatterjee aptly points out,

"Partition was predated by sectarian violence in 1946 in the case of Bengal, which spurred the initial two-way movement of Hindus to West Bengal and Muslims to East Pakistan. She argues that the flight of Hindu refugees eventually outnumbered that of Muslims and has continued sporadically from the brutal civil war in Pakistan in 1971 and the birth of Bangladesh into the present (2008, 4). This continuous crossing of the boundary line, especially in the eastern part of the country (West Bengal), testifies to the porousness of borders.

Dipesh Chakrabarty (2002) drawing on his reading of *Chere Asha Gram*, a nostalgic compilation of essays written by East Bengali refugees, suggests that the home/homeland remembered by them was one where the 'bastu' or 'bhita', meaning, the foundation was located (Chakrabarty). Manas Ray (2000), in his autobiographical essay "Growing up Refugee" relies on the oral narrative and anecdotal mode to document the trauma of being displaced and homeless due to the division of Bengal. In her essay "Re(Creating) the Home", Rachel Weber (2003) relies on the oral histories of residents of a refugee colony in South Calcutta called Bijoygarh and demonstrates how Partition redefined social spaces and enabled women's participation in public activities in an effort to 'place' themselves after the trauma of displacement.

Kharagpur as a Locus of the East Bengali Hindu Community

Kharagpur, a major Railway town established at the beginning of the 20th century, has been largely absent in the histories of East Bengal Partition. But the Railway Town happened to be the natural choice of re-placement/ resettlement for the many East Bengali Hindus who were in the service of the Indian Railways (previously BNR) and opted for official postings from East Bengal to India (West Bengal) before and during Partition. Gradually, after Partition, a number of East Bengali Hindus unconnected with the Railways moved to Kharagpur. Subsequently, after Partition and during the rehabilitation programme, the West Bengal government granted a few acres of land to East Bengal refugees on the periphery of the railway colony and Kharagpur grew into an important rehabilitation/ resettlement site for the displaced East Bengalis who did not belong to the category of the educated '*bhadralok*'. Kharagpur has since been "home" to the East Bengali Hindu refugees who have made an attempt to re-establish themselves in their new home after being displaced from their old homes in Bangladesh during and after Partition.

The section that follows throws light on the unheard voices of Partition survivors from an undocumented region of resettlement, namely Talbagicha, located on the outskirts of Kharagpur, which is the second largest Government sponsored resettlement colony after Taherpur (Nadia district) in West Bengal (personal communication with Palchowdhury 2011). Based on qualitative interviews with twenty residents of Talbagicha, this essay records the causes of migration and displacement due to Partition varied from communal unrest to economic stability and was not limited to a particular time frame. It argues that Partition-in-the-East remains an ongoing process with continuous inflows of migrants from Bangladesh confirming the porosity of borders. It also complicates the understanding of Partition as ethnic cleansing by demonstrating that although ethnic riots might have produced the initial impulse to migrate, the time of migration varied from person to person or family to family in this region of Bengal. Through uncovering the institutional processes and state apparatuses through which migrants were resettled in Talbagicha, it corrects the common understanding that East Bengali refugees were marginalized in the rehabilitation process as compared to those from Punjab. Finally, it shows that home continues to be imagined by the displaced on the other side of the border more than 65 years after Partition.

Tales from Talbagicha

76-year-old Shobha Rani Ghosh from Barisal District, Kaunia Branch Road, Kotwali Thana, recalls many incidents from her childhood days while reminiscing about her past:

> I can talk about many incidents in my childhood. For instance, when I was ten years old, I used to accompany my father to his shop. I used to carry goods back and forth from Father's shop. On my way back home, the neighbourhood Muslims boys would tease me by chanting hori bol hori bol. However, I flew into a rage at their jeers one day. When the Muslim youth were shouting the same standing in front of the shop owned by a distant relative I used to address as 'Meshomoshai', I complained to him that they should be told not to shout hori bol hori bol on spotting me. Then they stopped troubling me.... We came here (India, West Bengal) much before the riots. We came because—as I told you—the Muslim boys used to taunt us... And then we also saw people from our neighbouring areas leaving. We would not know where they were going until they boarded the van [vehicle] and then they would say that they were leaving for India. Then, we thought how we could stay back when there was no one to be trusted. If the Muslims were to attack us, then we would become helpless.... (Personal Interview, December 2010)

Shobha Rani became nostalgic while remembering her journey to India:

> We first crossed the river in a steamer and reached Khulna. Bangladesh is full of rivers. We sailed overnight and reached Khulna in the morning. From Khulna we took a train and reached the Sealdah station. Then everyone asked us to 'become' refugees. But we did not 'become' refugees. We took a house on rent. In order to become refugees, we would have had to register our names as refugees. But we did not

> become refugees. ...Then, one of our relatives from East Bengal suggested that if we were to continue staying in a rented house, we would not be able to have our own land or house. Then, we again came to Sealdah and enlisted our names as refugees.... Those who were registered as refugees were given jobs on the basis of their surnames—like 'Ghosh, Guha, Mitra, Sarkar' were given jobs and so on by providing evidence of their origins in the other des. As our surname in the documents was listed as Ghosh, he [her husband] could get into IIT. Like many people got into the Railways.... Many joined the Railways. In the same way we got into IIT. Jobs were given on the basis of one's refugee status, the interview was a mere formality. After my husband got the job, we were allotted plots in Talbagicha by the Rehabilitation Committee. They would make groups and then make a lottery for the allotment of plots. Each family would get 10 kottahs of land. So, in that manner, we got this 10 kottah plot. Then we gradually started living here initially by making huts and then a concrete house. And am still living here. (Personal Interview)

The reason for displacement for Shobha was of course the fear of communal riots. The time of displacement was, according to her, "after Partition". It is interesting to note that Shobha and her family represented a group of early migrants who had to "become" refugees to avail themselves of Government relief and rehabilitation. As she says, she (along with others) was transferred to the rehabilitation site in Talbagicha from the refugee relief Camps in Ranaghat. Thereafter, their refugee status helped her husband to get a job in the newly opened IIT.

However, 75-year-old Bokul Chakraborty became a "refugee" and acquired a plot of land in Talbagicha. She migrated to India from Noakhali with her husband who was working with the Railways and opted for a posting in Jamshedpur before eventually moving to the Kharagpur Railway workshop. Bokul also narrated her experience of the Noakhali riots relying on her memory. In her words:

> I am from Laxmipur village in the Noakhali district. My father was a school teacher. He used to teach Maths and Sanskrit. We were getting along quite well in Laxmipur village until the riots began. I don't remember the details. All I can recall is that the riots took place a year or two before Gandhi (Mahatma Gandhi) died. Gandhi had visited our place during the riots. I must have been 14 or 15 years old when the riots began. During the riots, Muslims would not kill grown up females. They would "take" our girls with them professing that they would "marry" them and would murder the male members of the family mercilessly. (Personal Interview)

Despite witnessing riots in Noakhali, Bokul and her family did not move to India immediately. They stayed on in Noakhali as her father did not want to move to a new land leaving his ancestral home. She explained the migration:

> Father was under the impression that half the people would die in any case. If one didn't have a job or a place to stay, it would have been much wiser to stay put here in Noakhali. He reasoned that here we had our own home and land and there we would become homeless. So things were like that and then the year after Gandhi died I got married. I was married in Maijee village in Noakhali district. My husband was then working in Tata [Jamshedpur]. He left as soon as we got married. I remained with my in-laws and after eight months I also left for Tata. I was in Tata then. But then in Jamshedpur, the railways withdrew rations—they wouldn't provide us anything at all—and he was going to be transferred elsewhere. As soon as that happened he found himself a job in Kharagpur

> Railway Workshop store. We stayed initially in Midnapore in one of my cousin brother-in-law's house when I got pregnant. We were in the house of this Kanungo. We stayed there for 14 years and from there I moved to railway A-type quarter in Mathuraghati in Kharagpur and stayed there for another 12 years and moved after that to here in Talbagicha and it's been 30 years since then. (Personal Interview)

For Bokul, the displacement was not directly triggered by communal violence. But to resettle in a place meant for the refugees, she had to exploit loopholes in the rehabilitation policies in a refugee resettlement colony. She had to prove her Bangladeshi descent with documentary evidence. According to her:

> If we could produce any "evidence", any documents proving that we were East-Bengalis, for example, some papers like passport, etc. (cannot specify), then there was no problem. That would be adequate proof of our being Bangladeshis.... (Personal Interview)

However, Bokul's father stayed back in Bangladesh as he was a schoolteacher. He came to India only after his retirement where his sons and wife had migrated earlier. Bokul asserts that her father "came back with self-respect. What would he do there? My brothers had already migrated to India way back along with my mother. We have no faith in that place anymore. There is no trust in that place. My sister is still there...the one next to me she is still in Bangladesh".

Irrespective of the reason for their displacement, Bokul continues to imagine home in Noakhali's Laxmipur: "No dear, would I ever forget that place until my dying day? I was born there, reared there...how can one forget? (weeps). Now it comes to my mind that this place was like this. I think of the food there. My children have not seen the place when they were children. They went a few times, three of my sons visited but not my three daughters."

Similarly, both Shobha Rani Ghosh and Bokul Chakraborty moved from their native place almost during the same period. Both crossed the borders almost immediately after the Partition. But for 55-year-old Arati Majumder, displacement was induced by communal riots during the Bangladesh Liberation War in early 1970's. Arati incidentally is also a resident of Talbagicha. Originally from Golokpur village in Bangladesh's Bhola district, Arati came to stay with her elder brother-in-law who had a house in Talbagicha because they had arrived there earlier, probably in 1969. Arati preferred to remain in her native village with her in-laws. However, she says that she and her family faced continuous disturbances. She vividly narrates her experiences:

> While we stayed on, we could never be at peace. We had land, pond, orchards...but everything was taken away. You can't imagine the number of times we were robbed. Whenever they found a chance, they would steal from inside as well as outside the house. A year after my marriage, when my son was barely six days old, our house was looted by the Muslims. Leave alone gold and silver, they did not even leave behind a sari I could change into the next day that was the situation. They did not even leave a handful of rice that I could cook. I had to go to other people's house to beg for rice and put together a meal. They left nothing but only the clothes that we had on. While leaving, they strictly warned us that if we squealed, they would return the following day and slaughter us. They left flinging dirty abuses on us. After this incident my heart broke. I was heartbroken since then and urged my husband that I wouldn't stay there any longer and move to where my elder brother-in-laws were already staying. I said that we'd rather live on

just plain rice with all of us together. I kept persisting and when my son turned seven there was so much trouble there. Every month or two or even every fortnight. I couldn't live in peace. Couldn't dress up. I was not at peace. And my household was such that my father-in-law could not manage without me. He packed his three sons and daughters away but kept me and my husband behind with me. My father-in-law would say that we could leave only after he was dead. Even when I tried to send my son to my brother-in-laws in Kharagpur, he repeated that we could do that only after his death. I could not go against his word. When my son was seven years old, my father-in-law passed away and I sent my son along with my brother-in-law who visited us. As I was not sure whether I would live or die since no one can survive such oppression, I begged him to keep my son or else at least get him admitted to some boarding school so that he could complete his schooling. After this, a few years passed by. I did not succeed in persuading my husband to go to Kharagpur.

With my father in law's passing away, my husband found it difficult to cope with the pressure of managing the property. The three brothers decided to divide the property and my husband sold off his brother's share of the property and kept sending them money, 20,000 or 10,000. I would urge him not to send such unaccounted money and to put it in a post office or bank account. In Talbagicha, too, my brother-in-laws were allotted 10 kottah plots. My elder brother-in-law owned a house in Talbagicha. They—my brother-in-law and his wife—had probably arrived in 1969. My husband and I stayed back with my in-laws. I even sent my mother-in-law away after my father-in-law died. My husband would not come because of the land and property. But we could never be at peace. This was due to the fact that though we had land, property, pond, orchards and a lot more we were robbed so many times that you can't imagine. Whenever they [Muslims] found an opportunity, they would steal paddy. Days were passing by like this with riots and chaos every other day. ...My kitchen and verandah were set ablaze.

After that incident, I became adamant about moving to India [Kharagpur]. I told my husband that if he were not willing to go then, at least, he could escort me [Kharagpur]. I took my younger daughter along with me and took shelter in Lalmohan police station as I knew someone there. When I reached the police station, it was again another horrifying scene. Numerous women who had been rescued by the police from the Muslims (some were even raped), queued up to take refuge in the police station. I was very shocked to see that. Yet, we stayed in the police station for about six months and then came to Kharagpur leaving my village, the three ponds, and the betel nut trees. My husband returned back to Bangladesh leaving us here. He insisted on guarding his share of property and said he would come to India (Kharagpur) only when he could arrange to sell off the property. When he came to drop me here, he stayed for eight days. I asked him to build me a separate hut because there were too many members in the house already (my three brother-in-laws, my sister-in-law, and their children). So, on that plot I built a hut and stayed with my three children along with my sister's children. It was a difficult life as there was water problem. I stayed like that for eight long years with my husband coming once after every two or three months and sending money from Bangladesh. I would keep on pleading with my husband to come but he was waiting for a good price for the property.... Then I decided to go to Khulna to bring him with me....

The border, however, was not rigid and there was no difficulty in transborder movements. For according to Arati, there was no difficulty in crossing the border. She explains:

> I did not face any difficulty crossing the border. There were agents ("dalals"). They helped us crossing the border. I also crossed the border and reached Khulna as I vowed I would not go to my village house after that incident [when the Muslims burnt part of the house]. I called my husband and my mother and they came to meet me in Khulna [Doesn't specify where she had put up in Khulna]. I tried to convince my husband to come with me to Kharagpur with whatever money he had been able to get from selling off the lands and plots. But he was not prepared to come to Kharagpur unless he got back the full worth of the property. Then I told him that if he was not willing to come to Kharagpur, I would stay in Khulna itself but that I would neither return to Kharagpur to look after my children nor would I go to the village house. Then after much persuasion, my husband promised to come within six months. Eventually, he came within a few months but then we had to face a dire financial crisis. As my husband was reluctant to work, we bought cows and would earn for a living by selling milk. My elder son now runs a catering business and now we are doing well. We have left my brother-in-law's plot and have purchased neighbouring plots in Talbagicha itself and have built our own house here. We did not come here as refugees like my brother-in-law did. They came during the Partition (or maybe after that) and "became" refugees and, hence, got the 10 kotta plot in Talbagicha. Since we did not become refugees, we purchased a separate plot from another person and built our house there.

When asked if she had thought of ever going back again, Arati replied:

> No way we can go back there again. The kind of terror and torture that I have witnessed is painful and traumatic. Although it is after all my own land, my desh. My mother is still there. But the last time I met her was in Khulna. Now we talk over the phone once in a while. But I can never forget my desh. Everything is still so fresh that I still cannot control my tears.

Thirty-year-old Shyamali Ghosh from Kutba village in Bangladesh's Bhola district moved with her family as late as early 1990's during the Babri Masjid riots. The reason of displacement was once again demonstrated as communal violence. Shyamali recalled:

> Our house was set on fire when the Babri Masjid trouble started. Several people fled during the trouble and when the tension subsided, they went back to the village and rebuilt their houses because they had lands which they tilled. But we came here and never went back because we were four sisters and my father feared that the Muslims would attack us again and 'dishonour' us ('izzat').

She went on to mention the mode of transportation: "We crossed the border taking help from the *dalals* (agents) who brought us here (Talbagicha)." She confessed that she felt like moving to a 'foreign' land and clings back to the memory of the lanes and houses back home in her native village. When the author asked: "Did you feel that you had moved to a foreign land?" the reply was:

> Yes, of course. Amader bhasha alaada chilo. Our language [probably she meant dialect] was altogether different. Like here, the language was more like that of Kolkata. Ours was a different one because we used refer to men as byadaah and women as byedeeh while here they used chhele (boy) and meye (girl). I feel strongly about leaving the land because it was my

> birthplace (amar jonmosthaan) and we lived well there. Now I have to live here—that's a different issue—but that's my native land and we have left our land, which are still there. But now they must be occupied by the Muslims. My uncles are still there. They say that we will not leave our place and if the Muslims don't allow us to stay, we'll prefer to live like the Muslims (amader jodi musalman ra thakte na daye to amra tader shonge tader moto hoye thakbo). But they would not come to India because they would not like to leave their birthplace. But my father said that I have daughters and cannot afford to take the risk. My father expired within a few years of his coming here in an accident. So now I am looking after my mother and two younger sisters. One of them is working as domestic help and another is studying in school. My elder sister is married in our neighbourhood. I am earning to provide for myself, my sisters and my mother.

When asked whether she feels at home in Talbagicha, Shyamali is quick to deny the idea of home in India. She promptly replies:

> No. This is not my place. (Ekhono jani j eta amar onno desh. Jodio thakte thakte bhalo laagche tobe prothom prothom ekdom bhalo laagto naa.) It is out of habit that I have started to like this place. But when I got here I did not like the place at all. Still I cannot consider this as my home. I was born there and I still remember even the lanes of my village. If I am able to cross the border and get there, I can go to my village.

But with the passage of time, she yearned to go back but did not wish to stay there for more than a few days as it was not safe for women. Moreover, she says,

> Here I am able to earn a living. There we don't have this much of independence and liberty. My mother, of course, would want to go back because she doesn't

feel at home here even now. And that's natural because if we have so many memories, then obviously my mother will feel a stronger longing for the lost homeland. So now even if we want we cannot go back.

Conclusion

In view of the need to archive the stories of displacement and resettlement, this essay has put together the stories of migrants who resettled in Talbagicha to examine the impact of political borders on border crossing. From the narratives of East-Bengali migrants resettled in Talbagicha, it is evident that cross border flows in Bengal preceded and continued after the Partition of 1947. Secondly, while communal riots might have been a major factor in influencing the displacements of the East-Bengali migrants, movements to Talbagicha were not always directly triggered by actual riots but apprehensions about safety. Talbagicha in West Bengal appeared to be a safe haven as many migrants already had family settled in the region. The stories, thus, confirm that although Partition was neither a one-time event nor were the drivers of migration identical and that Partition survivors continue to imagine home across the border.

(Editors' note: Because of the exigencies of space, the individual narratives of refugees have had to be edited considerably. Sufficient substance has been retained to illustrate the basic thrust of the authors' argument.)

Works Cited

Ashcroft, Bill. 2001. *Post Colonial Transformation*. London: Routledge.

Bagchi, Jasodhara and Subhoranjan Dasgupta, eds. 2003. *The Trauma and the Triumph: Gender and Partition in Eastern India*. Kolkata: Stree.

Banerjee, Paula. 2002. "Frontiers and Borders: Spaces of Sharing, Spaces of Conflict" in *Space, Territory and the State: New*

Readings in International Politics, Ed. Ranabir Samaddar, Hyderabad: Orient Longman, 27-42.

———. 2010. *Borders, Histories, Existences: Gender and Beyond.* New Delhi: Sage Publications.

Butalia, Urvashi. 1998. *The Other Side of Silence: Voices from the Partition of India.* New Delhi. Viking Penguin.

———. 2003. "The Nowhere People" in *The Trauma and the Triumph: Gender and Partition in Eastern India.* Jashodhara Bagchi and Shubhoranjan Dasgupta, ed. Kolkata: Stree, 113-22.

Carter, Paul. 1987. "Spatial History", from *The Road to Botany Bay: An Essay in Spatial History.* London: Faber.

Chakraborty, Bokul. 2009. Personal Interview. 30th December.

Chakrabarty, Dipesh. 1998. "Remembered Villages Representations of Hindu-Bengali Memories in the Aftermath of Partition" in *Freedom, Trauma, Continuities: Northern India and Independence.* Ed. D.A. Low and Howard Brasted. New Delhi: Stage.

Chatterjee, Joya. 2001. "Right or Charity? The Debate over Relief and Rehabilitation in West Bengal, 1947–50" in *The Partitions of Memory*, ed. Suvir Kaul. New Delhi: Permanent Black.

Chatterjee, Nilanjana. 2008. "Interrogating Victimhood: East Bengali refugee Narratives of Communal Violence". www. swadhinata. org.uk/misc/ chatterjee EastBengal%20 Refugee.pdf 14th Jan.

Chester, Lucy. 2009. *The 1947 Partition: Drawing the Indo-Pakistani Boundary* http://www.sscnet.ucla.edu/southasia/ default.html Accessed on 16th Jan.

Datta, Nonica. 2001 "Partition Memories: A Daughter's Testimony" in *The Unfinished Agenda: Nation-Building in South Asia.* Eds. Mushirul Hasan and Nariaki Nakazato, New Delhi: Manohar: 17-48.

Ghosh, Shobha Rani. 2009. Personal Interview. 30th December.

Ghosh, Shyamali. 2009. Personal Interview. 12th April.

Hai, Ambreem. 2000 "Border work, border Trouble: Postcolonial Feminism and the Ayah in Bapsi Sidhwa's *Cracking India*". *Modern Fictional Studies,* 46.2 (Summer): 380.

Kaul, Suvir, Ed. 2001. *The Partitions of Memory—The After life of the division of India.* New Delhi: Permanent Black.

Majumder, Arati. 2010. Personal Interview. 10th January.

Mehdi, Syed Sikander. 2003. "Refugee Memory in India and Pakistan" in *Divided Countries, Separated Cities*, Eds. Grislaine Glasson Deschaumes and Rada Ivekovic. New Delhi: Oxford University Press: 85-95.

Menon, Ritu and Kamala Bhasin. 1998. *Borders and Boundaries: Women in India's Partition.* New Delhi: Kali for Women.

———. "Recovery, Rupture, Resistance: Indian State and Abduction of Women during Partition." 1993. *Economic and Political Weekly* 24 April, WS-2—WS-12.

Md. Mahbubar Rahman and Willem Van Schendel. 2003. "I am not a refugee", *Modern Asian Studies*, 37.3.

Nikolov, Stephan E. 2009. "Borders: Which in Between Most of Our Lives Has Gone" in *Armed Forces, Soldiers and Civil-Military Relations Essays in Honor of Jürgen Kuhlmann.* Eds. Gerhard Kümmel, Giuseppe Caforio and Christopher Dandeker, II, 261-88. Web. 10.04.11 <http://www. springerlink.com/ content/ k55249p821g81572/>

Ray, Manas. 2002. "Growing Up Refugee". *History Workshop Journal.* 53.1 Spring: 149-79.

Roy, Renuka. 2003. "And Still they Come" in *The Trauma and the Triumph.* Eds. Jashodhara Bagchi and Shubhoranjan Dasgupta. Kolkata: Stree: 80-97.

Soja, Edward W. 1999. "Reassertions: Towards A Spatialized Ontology" in *Postmodern Geographies: The Reassertions of Space in Critical Social Theory,* London: Verso: 118-37.

Talbot, Ian. "A Tale of Two Cities: The Aftermath of Partition for Lahore and Amritsar 1947-1957", 2007. *Modern Asian Studies,* 41.1: 151-85.

Tan, Tai Yong and Gyanesh Kudaisya. 2000. *The Aftermath of Partition in South Asia.* London: Routledge.

Thakurta, Meghna Guha. 2003 "Uprooted and Divided" in *The Trauma and the Triumph*. Eds. Jashodhara Bagchi and Shubhoranjan Dasgupta, Kolkata: Stree: 98-112.

Weber, Rachel. 2003. "Re(Creating) the Home: Women's Role in the Development of Refugee Colonies in South Calcutta" in *The Trauma and the Triumph: Gender and Partition in Eastern India*. Eds. Jashodhara Bagchi and Shubhoranjan Dasgupta. Kolkata: Stree.

SECTION 3

Globalisation: Literary Insights

CHAPTER

16

Negotiating the Local and the Global in Adib Khan's *Seasonal Adjustments*

Jackie Highland
Chisholm Catholic College, Western Australia

Salman Rushdie, in his essay "Imaginary Homelands", quotes these well known words from L.P. Hartley's novel *The Go-Between*: "…the past is a foreign country, they do things differently there", but suggests that the idea should in fact be inverted: "...it is the present that is foreign and the past is home, albeit a lost home in a lost city in the mists of lost time" (Rushdie 1991, 9). For the migrant, the experience of disorientation and loss is particularly acute on account of being "out-of-country" and even "out-of-language" (Rushdie 1991, 12). Rushdie goes on to state that individuals in diaspora become hybridised, radically altered in translation, but it is through this hybridisation that innovation can surface.

The migrant experience occupies a central position of scrutiny in contemporary literary studies in an increasingly globalised world where the movement of peoples and individuals to regions far removed from their origins is recognized as integral to the phenomenon of globalisation.

Adib Khan was born in a different geographical and cultural space, constrained to negotiate the tensions between nostalgia for the past in Bangladesh and the needs of his present situation in Australia.

Iqbal Chaudhary, the protagonist Adib Khan's *Seasonal Adjustments,* moves across spatial and cultural boundaries, reconfiguring notions of home and locatedness in what Homi Bhabha refers to as the "Third Space" which can be considered as an "interstitial space" where a "profound process of redefinition" of identity begins (1994, 5). With the collapse of his marriage to Michelle, a Catholic Australian schoolteacher, Iqbal Chaudhary returns to his homeland Bangladesh after an absence of eighteen years to find himself floating between two spaces, homeland and adoptive land. He is now "a variable without a constant...a changing shadow unable to determine where he belongs" (Khan 1994, 9). His relationships with his family and friends seem to have changed irrevocably. His family embraces his young daughter, Nadine, but counts him "a traitor" for betraying his country and family in their hour of greatest need, a betrayal further exacerbated by his long silence in reconnecting with them.

The negotiation of the local is highly problematical for this protagonist who registers a deep sense of rupture from his original context. Paradoxically he is also acutely sensitive to the place, the people and the cultural nuances that underpin the society from which he originated. The question to be asked then is, at what point does the host country become the local, and what does this mean for the individual who inevitably sets down roots in another space, that now becomes home with new affiliative links that bind him to it.

This essay will suggest that the arrival at the "Third Space" is neither a benign experience of adaptation to a different sense of home nor is it a sense of permanent loss and alienation. Rather it will be apparent that the experience of migration is more mosaic than formulaic, with individual characters poised amongst differing configurations of cultural allegiances and identities within the Third Space. The representation and perception of the Third Space "in relation to the performance of identity as iteration and the recreation of self... [particularly in terms of] the desire for recognition" is destabilised (Bhabha 2004, 12).

Stuart Hall asserts: "cultural identities come from somewhere, have histories. But, like everything which is historical, they undergo constant transformation. Far from being eternally fixed in some essentialised past, they are subject to the continuous "play" of history, culture, and power" (quoted in Ang 2001, 150) Khan's novel traces constant shifts and accommodations as the protagonist moves back and forth between his original homeland in Bangladesh and adoptive home in Australia interrogating notions of cultural allegiances, home and nation. For second and ensuing generations of migrants like the child Nadine, who moves confidently through the Australian landscape and culture, there appears to be a clearer sense that the move back to her parental homeland of Bangladesh is only temporary, constituting yet another formation in belonging not acccssible to the original migrant. Therefore, Bhabha's "Third Space of Enunciation" appears to be a contentious concept, always and already open to multiple interpretations.

The focus of this essay is to interrogate the paradoxes, the ambivalences and the challenges of the border crossings particularly as these surface in the reflections and memories of the first 'home' as the protagonist moves between two spaces. The strategies undertaken in investigating this novel are broadly based on Edward Said's suggestions for evaluating the Orientalist ideology of a text as he describes these in his classic work *Orientalism* (1978): the gaze turned on the landscape (of former home as of adoptive place), its flora and fauna, the sights, the sounds, the smell impinging on the experiencing consciousness; the positioning of the protagonist; the gaze turned on the Australian by the migrant and the returning gaze of the native Australian on the migrant. Finally the use of language—the motifs and epithets circulating in the text. Tracing contrasts and synergies will enable the exploration of the evolution of cultural identity in another space and the possible transformations that ensue in the negotiation of the local and the global contexts.

The 'thesis' of this essay is that in the novel *Seasonal Adjustments*, the protagonist Iqbal Chaudhary is not at-home in both spaces demonstrating that the migrant experience does not lend itself to a pattern of neat binary oppositions but rather presents a kaleidoscope of changing, fluid impressions which do not permit of tidy resolutions. The representation and perception of the Third Space "'in relation to the performance of identity as iteration' and the recreation of self, particularly in terms of 'the desire for recognition" (Bhabha 1994, 12) is therefore problematized on both the local and global levels.

Writers like Khan recuperate the tensions and struggles of migrant subjects in claiming a space in this nation. Castles states unequivocally that "for Australia, immigration has been a crucial factor in economic development and nation building ever since British colonisation started in 1788" (Castles *et al.* 1993, 57). The decade between 1960 and 1970 which had witnessed the dismantling of the infamous White Australia policy, saw huge numbers of Asian migrants particularly from Vietnam, Cambodia and other conflict zones such as Bangladesh (which became a nation in 1971) arrive in Australia. This is the scenario in which Adib Khan's protagonist, Iqbal Chaudhary, also arrives in 1972, as a refugee entering a vastly changed national environment that articulated the principles of ethnic diversity and of cultural and structural pluralism. Nevertheless, several attitudinal studies in the 1980s and the 1990s indicate "the continuation of earlier unfavourable and negative attitudes towards ethnic groups and migration". The Hansonite backlash against Asians and indigenous Australians continues to shadow the national agenda right up to the present day (Jayasuriya 1997, 71).

Adib Khan's *Seasonal Adjustments* (1994) also recreates the turmoil and violence that marked the creation of

Bangladesh. At the time of Partition in 1947, following the end of the British Raj, the Muslim minority vociferous in defending their interests against a predominantly Hindu population demanded a separate state which led to the creation of Pakistan, 'the land of the pure' However from the outset several issues including linguistic, economic and cultural differences between the two ancient cultures of the Punjab in the West and Bengal in the East—separated by a distance of 2000 kilometres plagued the nation. In the ensuing tensions, the Bengalis vigorously affirmed their "linguistic and cultural identity against the Punjabi oligarchy" (Jaffelot 2004, 60). It was a situation poised for conflict, which erupted in the formation of the *Awami League*—led by Sheikh Mujibur Rahman—in the wake of the 1971 general elections. Student activists, trade unions and a disaffected peasantry launched a mass movement of non-cooperation demanding autonomy for Bangladesh which was met with the brutal repression.

This is the context of Adib Khan's protagonist, Iqbal Chaudhary, in *Seasonal Adjustments*. As a refugee, he is plagued by the memory of "a nation born in agony, its soul deformed by loathing". He is haunted by grim memories:

> [In] a world turned upside down one dark night in March 1971...Pakistani troops "tumble[d] onto the streets to unleash the demonic wrath of Yahya Khan" against a people who dared to dream of freedom from the yoke of Pakistani military rule. (111)

Writer Khan highlights the fate of various marginal groups encountering sporadic encounters with racism and exclusion even in a multicultural Australia, re-inscribing their stories into the history of the nation.

Sneja Gunev argues for the particularity of migrant writers to be acknowledged in terms of ethnicity and cultural difference, in order to "explore other landscapes (spatial representations) and literatures to rediscover the cultures and languages in which such concepts as the nomadic, displacement, identity and gender are figured differently" (1992, 43). Khan appears to be engaged in precisely this articulation, demonstrating a resistance to an essentialised or homogenous notion of their positionality within Australia. Khan recognises that his writing emerges in a "kind of no-man's land, wedged between polarised cultures"...which prohibits "any sense of permanence or belonging" (2001). Yet there are episodes that register what Paul Carter identifies as a "haptic connection" to the land in the protagonists' perceptions of their new location within Australia.

In *Seasonal Adjustments* there is an interweaving of vastly different perceptions of the foreign and the familiar, the local and the global, particularly in the representations of the land. The motifs of flora and fauna at 'home' are interlaced with descriptions of another landscape that is at times hostile and at others reassuringly familiar and recognisable, lending an almost palimpsest-like quality to the text. The remembered homes of the protagonist Iqbal Chaudhary in Bangladesh seem to pervade his psyche long after he is re-located within the urban centre of Australia—in Melbourne and Ballarat. Indeed, as Russell West-Pavlov asserts, "there is a continuous intersecting, shifting and colliding of cultural boundaries which one could assume is inevitably a part of the migrant condition—'inside, outside, crisscross, inside out'" (2007, 11).

The environing landscape seems to operate dualistically as a place of exile as well as a place of nurture and acceptance. Carter comments that "the meaning and significance attributed to our life are closely bound up with a sense of place and places and spaces...[which] gives us a sense of orientation" (1992, 9). Iqbal Chaudhary, Khan's protagonist, ruminates over the "vast emptiness of the continent...like the microcosmic eye of the universe—mysterious and full of wonder... [affording] the expansion of [his] vision" (124) thus suggesting a haptic connection to the landscape.

> To be unhomed is not to be homeless, nor can the 'unhomely' be easily accommodated in that familiar division of social life into private and public spheres. The unhomely moment creeps up on you stealthily as your own shadow and suddenly you find yourself...taking measure of your dwelling in a state of incredulous terror. (13)

The major point to be considered here is that 'home' for migrants in the Third Space, in the words of bell hooks, "is no longer just one place":

> It is locations which people settle in temporarily en route to other destinations [accepting] 'dispersal and fragmentation as part of the construction of a new world order that reveals more fully where we are, who we can become. (Qtd in Ashcroft 2005, 49)

In *Seasonal Adjustments*, Iqbal Chaudhary's attitude to home in Bangladesh is characterized by the vacillation between the familiar and the unfamiliar, between Australia and Bangladesh. It is Bangladesh which has become the unknown territory after two decades of absence. He ruefully admits:

> I am uncomfortable here in the village of my birth. I can discern no changes in the years I have been away. Yet there is unfamiliarity about everything I see and hear. It is like looking at life with borrowed eyes. (7)

This novel differs from other novels of migration, in that Khan seems to be writing what Aijaz Ahmad calls a "nationalism of mourning" (quoted in George 1991, 2). Like Rushdie, he is engaged in exploring what the process of decolonisation has meant for a subject people and the gains, if any, since independence.

Iqbal is a descendant of the affluent landlord class and seems intent on following the footprints of power from the period of *zamindari* privilege to the constant surveillance of the local populace of dissenters by a vigilant, revisionist government. At the same time he is aware of, and appalled by, the continuing legacy of poverty, corruption and violation of minority rights that have continued unabated in a nation born with such a tremendous vision for the future.

In Shopnoganj he notes the "sprawling, double storeyed ancestral home surrounded by lychee and mango trees standing like an abnormal growth...(as) a mirage...an awesome symbol of the Chaudhary empire" (11) but stops short of visiting the graves of his ancestors whose brutality had traumatised the village population for decades. Travelling through the "crazy, cart-wheeling world of man-made chaos" to visit, the Imam he observes the:

> ...narrow dirt lanes which branch off the main road and end like amputated limbs of undernourished war children. The thoroughfare pulsates with the 'discordant jangle of blaring horns, bells, smoke-belching vehicles and brittle tempers. (43)

The Imam lives in a massive "triple-storeyed mansion... the waxed mosaic floor...covered with a vinaceous Shiraz carpet...satin-covered bolsters" (46) and ninety-nine framed photographs of dignitaries and political leaders highlighting the social divide in Bangladeshi society. Iqbal is riven with guilt and an overwhelming sense of powerlessness at the nation's (and his own) betrayal of the values of social justice and equity that were at the forefront of the idealistic student movement that he had supported in his youth.

The trip to Wari to meet his old boyhood friend, Iftiquar, is a grim journey into his guilt-ridden past as his visit to the newspaper offices of *The Voice*, once the hub of left-wing journalists and student activists, reveals a building gutted by fire a "neglected godown...with cobwebs hanging from the ceiling" (264). Everything about the place speaks of impermanence. If Iqbal needed any further sign of the insidious manifestation of power, then the empty room in the office with a noose dangling from the ceiling is the tangible reminder of the failure of the glorious promise of a new society. It was the place where their friend Ajit, a Hindu and a Communist, was strangled by the investigating officers after the death of Mujibur Rahman.

Iqbal's isolation and loneliness in Australia, particularly after the breakdown of his marriage to the schoolteacher Michelle appears to be marked by a similar process of "deterritorialization" and "displacement" (Appadurai 2009, 16). His recollections of his home in the "wintry city" of Ballarat with Michelle and Nadine are imbued with a palpable sense of nostalgia. Said in *Orientalism* quotes the French philosopher Gaston Bachelard in describing what he calls the "poetics of space", where "the inside of a house acquires a sense of intimacy, secrecy, security, real or imagined, because of the experiences that come to seem appropriate to it" (1978, 54). Thus the home acquires "an imaginative or figurative value" that can be named and felt and consequently experienced as "haunted or homelike, or prison-like or magical...[thus] acquiring an emotional even rational sense by a kind of poetics of space" (Said 1978, 55).

Juxtaposed with these are the flashbacks to Iqbal's father-in-law's home in Camberwell, where he feels the outsider in an Anglo-Celtic world. Michelle's fateful conversation about their imminent separation takes place at the Jam Factory on a "tempestuous Melbourne day...[as] the wind howled and tore through the streets" (67). These memories are mitigated, however, by his trip with his good friend Theo to Geelong along the Great Ocean Road and the balmy September in Apollo Bay. Intermingled with these memories are his impressions of another place and another time, of "the insecurity of curfewed nights. The darting shadows. Gunfire and explosion. The dreaded knock on the door" (119). All of these plague him like grim voices from a benighted place.

However, despite his aversion to the blatant displays of wealth and his acute awareness of his family's insulation from the grim realities of poverty, he registers a strong objection to the sale of the ancestral estates at Shopnoganj. He experiences "anguish and frustration, a frantic desire to claw and destroy the intruders...[and a longing] for a restoration of the pristine order and the ancient cycle of life" (Khan, 279). It is also in this final return to the home of his childhood that he visits the graves of his ancestors "cordoned off by a low cement wall, cracked and broken at the top and the sides [with] weeds and grass [sprouting] from crevices". Here he contemplates the headstone of "the most notorious of the Chaudharies, fabled for his wealth and arrogance" who now shares a resting place with his "lesser known relatives" (289). For Iqbal this appears to mark conciliation with his past and he makes his decision to return with Nadine to Australia.

In Nadine one observes the confident ties to Australia that are evident in the second generation. While conceding that she is still too young to forge strong affiliations with Bangladesh, it is equally apparent that for her this was a merely a visit to another place. Except for her one encounter with a woman breaking stones in the street, her experience of the place is confined to shopping sprees and celebrations in the ancestral homes of her family. Home for her is most definitely Australia and it is apparent that Iqbal's decision to return here is predicated on his own desire to provide her with the security that this implies.

This novel seems to present contradictory understandings of the local and the global. Ledgister (2001), in an incisive analysis entitled "Growing up in Two Elsewheres" states:

> I found myself struggling to explain that where my parents live was not "home", that where I was born was not "home", that the places I had lived had never been "home". In clearer words, that home for me was

> wherever I happened to be.... Home is what I carry with me...elsewhere is everywhere.

However, there is need for a more nuanced approach to this move of drawing boundaries between homeland and diaspora, between citizens and displaced persons, between home and away, for in a transnational world, border crossings appear to highlight far more complex entanglements and interdependencies than is offered by polarities. Homi Bhabha asserts that understandings of cultural displacement of various minority groups do not always "follow a centre and peripheral mode but rather in another's country which is also your own [you] encounter yourself in a double movement" (2004, xxv).

There are definite congruencies, resonances and dissimilarities in the perception of the diasporic individual—the gaze turned by the alien *Other*—on the dominant cultural group and the returning gaze of the Australian on the migrant *Other*. Equally, this perceptual gaze is also trained on a network of family and friends in the former homeland as also on parallel figures in the new context. Vanden Driessen states that "within these texts the Australian is not only construed as the antagonistic and rejecting Ugly Australian but also as friend, neighbour, lover, wife, surrogate parent or teacher, an important acculturating factor inducting the Asian into the Australian way of life" (2005, 224).

In *Seasonal Adjustments*, Iqbal Chaudhary is a complex representation of the dislocated individual, whose responses to people in his native Bangladesh are as problematic as his perceptions of Australians. His experiences with his in-laws, particularly his father-in-law, Keith Harrington, are negative and mistrustful. He notes the latter's barely concealed prejudices:

> As for the rest of us, from the dark unknown regions of the north, we are lumped together as Asians, recognisable by [the] absence of Christian principles

> which outweighs any discernible difference in ethnic characteristics. (86)

He is aware of being "in conservative territory... discuss[ing] the stock market...or antiques...furniture restoration or beach houses or cars" (145) all of which do not interest him in the least.

Counterpoised with this scene is his recognition of his distance from his former friends on his return to Bangladesh after eighteen years. At his parents' home he observes former friends with almost clinical detachment.

> [It is] a group of men locked in animated conversation...Munit, Haroon, Shafiq, Naseem, Taufiq, Khorram...most of them from university days... intelligent, ambitious and dedicated in their pursuit of bureaucratic prestige. (138)

Both Bhabha (1994) and Rushdie (1991) perceive the migrant position as being at the vanguard of cultural borderlines representing "innovative potential...for change for their access to several cultural traditions" (Alexander 2008, 86). However, Iqbal's is not the voice articulating a "happy hybridity" with the "felicitous suggestions that the term conveys" (vanden Driesen 2005, 231). Rather it foregrounds the ambivalence of positionality with reference to both 'here' and 'there'. His eighteen-year separation from Bangladesh, from family and friends, has created a vacuum about where he belongs or more precisely how to conceptualise a valid identity in the in-between space between homeland and adoptive land.

This pervasive feeling of alienation highlights the areas of tension arising from belonging to both opposing sides of the cultural divide. Malak asserts that "the structural framework of *Seasonal Adjustments* is informed by a binary conception of the hero's experiences shifting contrapuntally between two societies of diametrically diverse ethos" (2005, 83). In fact, while it appears at first that the novel is foregrounding "perceived irreconcilable polarities" between two vastly different and differing cultural contexts—namely Catholic/Muslim, insider/outsider, Australian/migrant—the text gives way to a multiplicity of affiliations and a "profound preoccupation with liminality and shifting boundaries". Malak says of these "ambivalent affiliations" that they are embedded in the consciousness of the central protagonist (2005, 66).

Iqbal's objection to his daughter Nadine's baptism in the Roman Catholic rite, on the grounds that adherence to a single tradition "could impede her development as an adult", appears to be predicated on his earlier experiences of the "sustained" proselytising attempts of the "Brothers of the Holy Cross" at the Catholic school he attended as a boy. In fact it could be said that his antagonistic responses to followers of Christianity are echoed by an equally fierce repudiation of institutional Islam and its adherents. He recalls a Peshwari *Mullah* employed by his parents "to indoctrinate" his brother Hashim and himself in Koranic lessons "at his family home". Iqbal appears to be advocating a humanism that transcends dogma and ritual to engage meaningfully with the poor, the disenfranchised and the downtrodden.

His representation of Colin, a "very old friend" of the Harrington's is similarly characterised by his own sense of alterity from the mainstream culture. His derisive judgments of the "rich, balding accountant...with the fake accent and a perpetual pining for jolly old England" (71) ironically shows the same arrogance that he objects to in his dealings with his father-in-law. It can be asserted that "his splintered life...as a result of migration" and his colonial legacy have skewed his sensibility of his position within a society that deems him different (3).

There appears to be a characteristic ambivalence in the reactions to characters in both spaces. Ironically, both his wife Michelle and his younger sister Nafisa diagnose a similarity in his reactions to people, an emotional distance "from people who should matter" to him. Nafisa's accusation that he "has become callous...selfish... emotionally stagnant" (47) is juxtaposed with Michelle's censure that he "never expresses [his] affections..." (48).

He acknowledges an affinity with the Harrington's family pastor, Tom, who constantly mediates in the heated debates between Keith and his son-in-law; affection for his friend Claire, whose "migrant's...spirit is forever tormented...by childhood songs [from Ireland she] had never forgotten" (1994, 1) and his Australian friend Theo: "garrulous...full of cynical wisdom. Authoritative and irritatingly smug. A verbose school master" (54).

Interestingly, Iqbal strikes no connections with other Muslims in Australia to afford him a community. Recalling the frosty reception he receives during a visit to the Preston mosque in Melbourne earlier; he believes that he was viewed as "an untrustworthy distant cousin the family preferred not to know" (196). During a confrontation with 'a red-haired man' who pushes a *burqa*-clad woman against a fence taunting her with racial abuse, he muses that in the scheme of things "dark-skinned foreigners" were expected to "subject themselves passively to verbal insults and physical abuse for the privilege of living in his country. They were not expected to retaliate and yell" (196). He admits that his awareness of Australia and Australians has undergone a dramatic change over the years. Perhaps his sense of alienation can be traced to this changed perception of his own position as an outsider in Australia inhabiting the periphery of society.

Iqbal's encounter with a policeman represents the mainstream Australian at his racist worst. He recalls not only the confrontation but his resistance to the homogenising stereotype that brackets all Asians as 'Other' on the basis of colour:

> Of all the days to be stopped by an aggressive weekend cop on the prowl.... "Put you blokes in the

> driver's seat and you're a bloody danger!" he sneers. "You darkies are all the same, aren't you?" "No we're not" I reply tonelessly. "There's mahogany, walnut, teak and ebony. The variety is great." ...The bulldog jaws open...I have offended him by contradicting a sacred belief. (145)

Khan (2001) notes that the conceptual and emotional difficulties that a migrant faces in coming to a singular understanding of the term *identity* is akin to standing in the middle of a chamber of mirrors that are in constant slow rotation. One catches glimpses of transient reflections without ever settling on a 'fixed image.' He goes on to state that mainstream perceptions of a single 'heroic' identity undermine meaningful explorations of these issues (Khan 2009).

Iqbal's marriage to Michelle is clearly problematic. On the one hand, he acknowledges that their relationship was initially characterised by a sense of enhanced freedom. They share similar interests and acknowledge their many differences. "She confesses her ignorance about Bengalis" (242) although she had followed the events in the subcontinent with interest. He accepts that "all Catholics didn't share the cloistered, sanctimonious world of nuns and priests" (243). This negotiation of difference initially enables them to create "a private space to let [their] individuality grow" as they come to view "the future as an extension of the present" (244). Even after their relationship deteriorates, he asserts: "No...she had never been unfaithful to me in our married life" (72). When difficulties arise over their differences, their inadequate cross-cultural communication appears to exacerbate their marital conflicts. This seems to be apparent in Michelle's decision to separate, citing that they have "few common interests". There is a certain ambivalence towards his wife, as he finds it "impossible to react to [her] with any degree of consistent hostility" (66), an ambivalence that goes some way towards explaining his decision to return to Australia with the slim hope of a reconciliation.

The constant use of flashback and flash forward in the recording of specific events gives the impression that the recording consciousness is in a constant state of flux—never completely 'here' and most definitely not 'there'. Iqbal's perception of his family is one of estrangement bordering on alienation appearing to be predicated on the childhood apprehension that "failure of any kind was not permissible in our family. We were the Chaudharies—rich, clever, industrious. Infallible. Without human weakness" (45). Iqbal's reunion with his family is an encounter filled with bitter recriminations on the one hand and a heavy burden of guilt on the other. He acknowledges that "eighteen years is a very long time, long enough to realise that for a migrant, the word *home* is fraught with ambiguities" (61).

He is "troubled by [his] lack of tenderness for the portly, grey-haired woman", his mother. Nafisa his youngest sister berates him for his lack of respect in not informing the family of his marriage, and insists that he has "always been cautious about loving" (47). Iqbal's aged father is "a fragile and suffering symbol of mortality", his face "etched with lines of disappointment... buffeted by the tidal strengths of pity and guilt" (236). On his return to Bangladesh, Iqbal is curious about his brother Hashim's conservatism and religious fervour wondering if this is indicative of his "craving for the communal acceptance" that he was deprived of during his years in England (198). Hashim scornfully dismisses his brother's "undergraduate stance of anti-religion" demanding to know whether he is an atheist summarily dispensing with his explanation that he is a "zetic...a skeptical inquirer" (197) who demands the fundamental right to choose his identity. Hashim insists that Islam is Iqbal's culture because it "defines him as a man and [he] cannot escape from his religion" (198).

However, Iqbal's most savage portrayal of religious hypocrisy is reserved for the Imam whom he describes as "a huge, urceolate man with a belly which juts out in front of him like a balloon...[and] a grotesquely small head in proportion to his massive torso" (49). Iqbal does not interject when his mother launches a diatribe against Michelle, his wife, whom she believes has "trapped [him] into marriage and then heartlessly initiated the break-up" (51). He acknowledges silently that he should "accept a significant proportion for the blame" for the broken relationship (51).

Iqbal's attitude to Islam appears to be mediated through his memories of the ethnic conflict that preceded the birth of Bangladesh as a nation. He attributes the acceptance of abject poverty and deprivation to a failure of Islam to create a just and equitable society, evidenced in Amjad, the leper he encounters outside the mosque, and in the emaciated old woman breaking bricks for a living. He muses:

> I recall the Koranic words I struggled to understand as a young boy. It was drummed into me from an early age that submission was the defining quality of Islam. I have never reconciled myself to the notion of arbitrary suffering as a trial of faith. (41)

It is apparent that his disenchantment with his homeland and the abject conditions he encounters has led to reductive assumptions about the role of religion in initiating social reform. Iqbal's response to his closest friend, Iftiqar, is tinged with regret and shame over his affair with Shabana, the girl his friend had hoped to marry. While Iftiqar joined the *Awami League* to fight for the freedom and independence of his country from West Pakistan, Iqbal chose to leave the carnage and devastation for the safe haven of Australia, a move that was seen as a betrayal of his ideals and his family. Iftiqar remained in his native land, championing the cause of the persecuted minorities, especially Hindu *Biharis*, stating: "This is me. I am not resilient enough to take on another identity. I would feel as if I had betrayed myself" (118). It is apparent that Iftiqar represents the "moral centre of the novel" (Malak 2005, 115).

Iqbal also confesses to a weary disillusionment with his life in Australia, which he had initially believed to be "a humane society, a just society—generous and friendly" but with time he has become aware of its flaws and come to realise that "behind its ornate façade of wealth lay the weaknesses of any human society" (123). It is Iftiqar who offers him an insight into his present condition: "as a first generation migrant you probably sacrificed the right to belong" (117). Iqbal is adrift, in the in-between space of belonging neither 'here' nor 'there'; unable to make sense of who he is or where he really belongs. Iftiqar, by contrast, is home.

However, Iqbal is also brought face to face with the "infinity of traces" that Said identifies as being embedded in all identities (1978, 25). The faultlines of patriarchy and elitist thinking are apparent in his response to his cousin Alya. His dismissal of "her intellectual puerility" and her anxiety to secure a new husband is devoid of compassion or even understanding of the precariousness of her position in a traditional society where a woman's identity and her security is dependent on her marital status. His sister Nafisa's confession of her sexual orientation shakes him to the core. (221). This realisation of his own prejudices is perhaps one of the few moments where Iqbal confronts his own frailties, realising that he is powerless to comfort his loved sister.

Iqbal's encounter with Nadira Hussein, his brother's friend and probably soon-to-be second wife after his divorce, proves remarkably productive. Unlike Iqbal, she has chosen to return home to Bangladesh to practise medicine and perhaps marry Hashim. She states:

> Life can be such a creative act if you make the effort. I no longer treat living as if it is a treacherous enemy. It is subtle and full of obtuse meanings. I intend to devote my life to their discovery and understanding. (173)

Nadira's purpose is in sharp contrast to Iqbal's own indeterminacy and ambivalence. Her choice to return home is an example of another choice within the Third Space. It is more reasoned, born not of nostalgia for the lost homeland but of what Bhabha calls "the emergence of another sign of agency and identity" (2004, 331).

This encounter with Nadira and understanding of her decision to return home has a profound effect on Iqbal, especially in mitigating his adversarial attitudes to his family and his homeland. When his child Nadine falls ill, the family strength helps to almost will the child back to health. Iqbal then rediscovers the value and importance of family in grounding him to his reality, but despite their urgent pleas that he should remain in Bangladesh he decides to return to Australia after receiving a letter from Michelle that she too, is returning home. Iqbal's visit to his homeland has offered him productive insights into his own life, opening up a new space that is neither marginal nor estranged but a focus of hope for the future. His maturing insight is clearly represented in his altered perspective and his choice to return to Australia.

> It makes me think that perhaps the terms of life are negotiable. Maybe life was not meant to be a linear, one-way motion. There may be opportunities for U-turns and diversions, for slowing down, for pausing to search for a previously missed niche in the haste to keep going. (173)

For Iqbal, his Third Space of Enunciation appears unclear, but he returns to Australia with a new vision "that [he] must not merely change the *narratives* of [his] histories but transform [his] sense of what it means to live, to be in other times and different spaces, both human and historical" (Bhabha 2004, 367).

It is clear that this novel records multiple pulls and allegiances, which are fundamentally and inextricably part of a hybridised life. He recognizes that

> Now I know that the fabric of my life cannot be separated into...individual strands. They must remain interwoven in a complex texture....(296-97)

It is clear that the Third Space of Articulation as envisaged by Bhabha is not just one position but a continuation of spaces calibrated by the life experiences of this protagonist. It seems that approaches to the *Third Space* are circuitous, even fraught:

> The borders between home and world become confused...a vision that is as divided as it is disorientating, while paradoxically also opening up 'a vision...of what it means to live, to be, in other times and different places, both human and historical. (Bhabha 1994, 13, 367)

In his novel *Seasonal Adjustments*, Khan has shown that the local and the global are not polarities to be negotiated in a single linear fashion but rather in a globalised world these are fluid, collapsing into each other, merging and re-emerging in a complex and ever changing dynamic relationship.

Works Cited

Alexander, V. 2008. "Worlds of Disenchantment" *Alienation and Change in Adib Khan's Seasonal Adjustments*. Amsterdam: Rodopi. 375-84.

Ang, I. 1993. *On not Speaking Chinese: Living between Asia and the West*. London: Routledge.

Appadurai, A. 2009. "Disjunctures and Difference in the Global Cultural Economy". In J.M. Evans and A. Braziel. (Eds.), *Theorising Diaspora Keyworks in Cultural Studies*. Oxford: Blackwell Publishing. 25-48.

Ashcroft, B. Griffiths, G. and Tiffin, H. 1989. *The Empire Writes Back, Theory and Practice in Post-Colonial Literatures.* London: Routledge.

———. 1995. *The Post-colonial Studies Reader.* London: Routledge.

Ashcroft, B. "Home and Horizon". In Cynthia vanden Driesen and Ralph. Crane (Eds.), *Diaspora: The Australasian Experience.* New Delhi: 45-58.

Bhabha, H.K. 1994. *Location of Culture.* London: Routledge.

———. 1996. "Cultures In-Between". In S. Hall and P. du Gay. Eds. *Questions of Cultural Identity.* London: Oxford University Press.

Braziel, E.J. and Mannur, A. Eds. 2003. *Theorizing Diaspora: A Reader.* Oxford, U.K.: Blackwell Publishing.

Carter, P. 1995. "Naming Place". In B. Ashcroft, G. Griffiths and H. Tiffin, (Eds.). *The Post-colonial Studies Reader.* London: Routledge. 402-406.

Castles, S. and Miller, M. 1993. *The Age of Migration: International Population Movements in the Modern World.* (4th Ed). London: Macmillan Press Ltd.

Gunew, S. and O'Longley, K. Eds. 1992. *Striking Chords.* Sydney, Australia: Allen & Unwin.

Hall, S. and du Gay, P. (Eds.). *Questions of Cultural Identity.* London: Sage Publications Inc.

Jeyaratnam, W. 1997. *Immigration and Multiculturalism in Australia, Selected Essays* (Vol. 1). Perth, Western Australia: School of Social Work and Social Administration of the University of Western Australia.

Khan, A. 1994. *Seasonal Adjustments.* Australia: Allen & Unwin.

———. June 2001. "In Janus' Footsteps". *Australian Humanities Review, Journal 1.* <www. australianhumanitiesreview.org/ archive /IssueJune2001/ khan> Accessed on 13 Oct. 2010.

Ledgister, F.S. 2001. "Growing up in Two Elsewheres". *Jouvert.* 6.1, 1-2 <http://englishclass.ncsu.edu//jouvert611-2/ledgis, htm>

Malak, A. 2004. *Muslim Narratives and the Discourse of English.* New York: State University Press of New York.

Ommundsen, W. 2004. " Floating Lives: cultural citizenship and the limits of diaspora". *Life Writing, 1*(2):101-21.

Petersee, J. 2001. "Hybridity So What?" *Theory, Culture & Society*. 182-83.

Rushdie, S. 1982. "Imaginary Homelands". In *Imaginary Homelands, Essays and Criticism* (Revised ed). London: Granta Books in association with Penguin Books. 9-21.

Said, E. 1978. *Orientalism*. England: Routledge & Kegan Paul Ltd.

vanden Driesen, Cynthia 1995. *Centering the Margins: Perspectives on Literatures from India, Africa, Australia*. New Delhi: Prestige Publications.

vanden Driesen, Cynthia and Ralph Crane. Eds. 2006. *Diaspora: The Australasian Experience*. New Delhi: Prestige.

CHAPTER 17

'International Regionalism' in the Age of Globalisation

Glen Phillips
Edith Cowan University, Australia

Globalisation spares no country in the contemporary world. Every year, under its pressures, populations have moved not only between regions of the world but also within regions. Poets and fiction writers these days live more commonly in the great cities of the world and these cities and the life-styles of their citizens become daily more and more like each other The inhabitants of Australia, which the rest of the world regards as famously identified with rural or outback lifestyles, have begun to move steadily from the country to the city (Stehlik 2009). Only a small segment of our population, apart from Indigenous Australians, dwell in rural areas. In fact, the Australian countryside (glorified as 'the bush' in so much Australian literature of the past, and the source of so much Australian mythology) is losing many of its farmers and stockmen to the city.

With the mobility of modern life the old borders both physical and psychological between the country mouse and the town mouse (to remind ourselves of Aesop's famous fable) are disappearing. Even those who continue to live in the country in modern times expect air conditioning, television and access to the internet. The age of the automobile has immensely increased personal mobility and contributed to the vanishing borders or distinctions between the town life and the country life. The city lifestyle from country to country is growing steadily more homogeneous around the globe. How do poets react to this contemporary situation?

In this essay I wish to consider this movement across rural-urban borders in a poet's homeland through looking closely at the poetry of Western Australian poet John Kinsella. I will also look at the writer's movement across regional and continental boundaries. These journeys as reflected in his writing could be held to contribute to a sense of the vanishing of global borders, at least in a literary sense.

More than most Australian poets perhaps, Kinsella has found himself challenged to live for extended periods overseas in India, Britain and the USA (Kinsella 1999). He has developed a concept he calls 'international regionalism' which applies to his mode of retaining his strong identification with the West Australian wheat growing region, while at the same time developing new and powerful sensitivities to the fenlands of Cambridgeshire, the open farming lands of Ohio or the crowded cities of India, such as in Kolkata. Kinsella's poetry demonstrates the relative success of his progress towards an 'international regionalism'. The lands of his Australian forebears become connected with the local particularities of the landscape of other regions whether in India, Britain or the USA.

Evidence of this surfaces in a typical poem by Kinsella about the 'Wheatbelt', a region larger than Britain in the south-west of Australia. It is where Kinsella chooses to live today when he is in Australia, close to family roots and, as already mentioned, it constitutes the centre of his world of 'international regionalism'; and it is from here that in all his work he reaches out to and interacts with the global landscapes. Every schoolchild who has held a model globe of the world sees that any point on its surface could be chosen as the centre of the global surface. We have a poet making this pre-emptive claim on the basis of a feeling of sheer identification and familiarity with landscape. John Kinsella also seems to see certain qualities in his Western Australian homeland (or birthland) that can be found nowhere else, and which make him a fortunate and faithful son of this point on the Earth:

Wild Radishes

Across the dark fields the family is spread
While overhead the sky is haunted,
In the dull light they scour the crop
Never looking up as the day seems to stop.
Wild radishes missed will destroy the yield—
Bills to be paid, deals to be sealed.
But the plover's refusal to lift and drop.
And the absence of crow and parrot talk,
And the immense racket as stalk rubs on stalk,
Register somewhere deep in the soul.
And as the sun begins to uncoil—
The deep green of the wheat uneasy with light
The golden flowers of wild radishes bite
Just before they are ripped from the soil.

(Kinsella 2004, 63)

Some would observe the reminiscences here of Thomas Hardy's rural scenes, with its celebration of the communal farming work. Yet it is happening in the remote Wheatbelt of Western Australia, on the other side, the 'underside' if you like, of the globe.

Kinsella is not just a vegetarian but a Vegan and even though the wild radish weed is a curse to the farmer, the poet feels compassion for its removal: it reminds him of the legendary mandrake plant, which was supposed to cry out when uprooted. Like a pebble dropped into a pool the reverberations in this poem seem to spread all the way from Western Australia to Europe. This scene of working farmers also evokes reminiscences of the French naturalist and post-impressionist painters of peasant life in the 19th century, such as Millais, Bastien-Lepage or even Van Gogh. Yet it simultaneously also evokes a scene in the Australian pastoral tradition, with its rural setting, its seemingly uncomplicated country folk at work and especially the apparently necessary task of getting rid of the weeds that would spoil the growth of the coming wheat crop. But we would be wrong to categorise the scene as a conventional pastoral one. Kinsella's known objection to killing animals for food or even taking birds eggs and his fierce defence of the rabbit and the fox (and other introduced species) which farmers and naturalists have tried to eliminate as vermin, is here extended even to the feral foreign weeds, the wild radishes. These weeds are not merely fancifully resistant as was the mandrake to being uprooted; they are symbolic of the whole exploitative rather than caring use of the land in Australia since the time of white settlement.

Kinsella himself has lived from time to time in urban situations for work in various universities. Indeed he has spent lengthy periods living in suburban parts of Perth, the city where he was born. It was only in the university holidays that he was able to spend time in the Wheatbelt, working on the rural 'wheatbins' where the harvest was collected before shipping overseas. Even when describing these suburban streets in *Peripheral Light* (2004) his mind notes the increased use of native shrubs such as the melaleuca or bottle brush as an alternative to previously fashionable trees imported from Queensland, England or other overseas countries:

> **The Bottlebrush Flowers**
> A Council-approved replacement
> For box trees along the verges
> of suburban roads, it embarrasses
> with its too sudden blush—stunning
> at first, then a burning reminder
> of something you'd rather forget.

(Kinsella 2004, 19)

What he means here is that even the natural or native plant which would be admired in its wild habitat is too poignant a reminder of the truly rural in this city landscape. Kinsella may have crossed the border from country to city life but his yearning for the rural or bush environment remains strong.

Later poems of Kinsella's written during sojourns abroad show how he adapts his poetry to these new or 'foreign' landscapes in a way analogous perhaps to the learning of a second language, a sort of 'second landscape learning' as I have termed it in previous essays. Does he abandon his regional landscape learning in Australia or does he retain connections as he crosses these global borders? Kinsella's first settled 'foreign home' was Cambridge at the University's Churchill College where he is an elected Fellow for life. I visited him there to give poetry readings and a lecture in 1999 and toured the flatland marsh country, which Kinsella wrote about in *Fenland Pastorals* (*Prest Roots* 1999). In the book's opening poem, "Prologue" he mentions the historical invasions of England via this east coast of the British Isles near Cambridge:

> fenlanders...birds and eels...
> might in instinct know the way through channels of water and growth
> or augur the storms that would
> have driven six-foot waves
> against a small king and his mobile hoard.
> Somewhere out there in Centralia,
> they find the wrecked boat of an explorer,
> so sure of finding that greatest
> of inland oceans.
>
> (Kinsella 1999, 9)

The explorer referred to in the last lines of the poem is Charles Sturt, born in India in 1795. In 1929 on his second journey to find the great inland sea expected to exist in central Australia (perhaps because of the Mediterranean climate of much of Australia) he took a boat with him and followed the major river systems of eastern inland Australia, expecting to be able to sail into this body of water. Instead, he found that all the westward flowing rivers eventually joined into the Murray River, which flowed into the sea south-east of where Adelaide now stands. But still Sturt yearned to find such a sea or large lake and from Adelaide many years later, in 1838, he travelled north again with a boat on a series of largely disastrous explorations which in the end cost the life of his second-in-command and almost his own. He went back to England to die in 1869. Many years later his horse, still alive, and the abandoned boat were found in desert country near the centre of the continent.

Kinsella's segue from the English Fenlands back to Centralia illustrates his 'international regionalism'. From one 'lost cause' to another, he makes a comparison, the connection between the wetlands of Cambridgeshire immediately before him and the dreamed-of, recollected wetlands in the outback of Australia. Incidentally, Lake Eyre was eventually discovered north-west of Adelaide. When filled by cyclonic rains in western Queensland it is in fact a very substantial body of water and breeding ground for thousands of water birds including seagulls and pelicans, a fact compounding the irony of Sturt's tragic failures. If we move back to the Fens, the small king is presumably Hereward the Wake with his hoard (or does he mean *horde*?), who, like Robin Hood of legend, against great odds, roamed the Fens attacking the Norman invaders of England in the early eleventh century.

As we leaf through this slim volume there are many signs of Kinsella's 'international regionalism' at work. In the "Triptych: Poems From Churchill College" we experience the sound of plant seedcases opening at the end of summer, a reminder of similar sounds heard in the Australian Wheatbelt:

> ...that crackling
> like fire in undergrowth,
> or water exploding on hot metal.
> A partial collusion of the elements—
> only the fifth element missing,
> as if the eponymous has no part

in the moment. You hear the seed cases
opening and searching your memory
for a name, a species, find nothing.

But it's a familiar sound—brings back
Dryandra Forest in the South-West
of Australia. Even the hemisphere
is with location....

(Kinsella 1999, 12)

All through this British collection Kinsella's imagination is constantly moving from one hemisphere to another. A hedgehog run over by a car evokes the road kill of Australia and the 'equivalent' echidna (or spiny anteater). A drive at night in the fenlands:

...The first badger
and hedgehog you see
in this, your New Country,
should lie dead upon the road—
at night you might say "At least
there aren't any kangaroos
to worry about!" the impact
potentially fatal.

(Kinsella 1999, 25)

If we remember that the second word in the title of this small collection is 'pastoral', and Kinsella even quotes from Ovid's *Metamorphosis* at one stage, we can be sure he is conscious that here too, in the literary heartland of English pastoralism, we find the same violence, bloodshed and horrors he takes pains to expose in *The Silo* and his other works—subverting myths or misperceptions of pastoralism commonly attached to Australian rural settings. Kinsella used to liken his "anti-pastoral" approach to that of the Trojan Horse of Greek legend, penetrating the cities of aesthetic romanticism in the Western poetic genre and then seeking to reveal the unpleasant truths that are the focus of his environmental concerns. A consciousness of the poet's moving across borders can be observed again in the poems of *Peripheral Light* (2004) the return movement, just as we saw it in the context of the poet's movement from city back to rural landscapes:

> **The Road to Brookton**
> Back from England and fenland
> we drive into the wheatbelt—
> warm weather with the possibility
> of a storm late in the day.
> Or maybe it is cool, but warm when compared with where we came from....
>
> (Kinsella 1999, 76)

Kinsella's American poetry was written during the period 2001 to 2005 following his appointment from to the Richard L. Thomas Chair of Writing at Kenyon College, Gambier, Ohio. In the volume *Peripheral Light,* edited by the distinguished American critic and academic Harold Bloom, in the poem "Location Triggers" a corn farm visited by the poet is inevitably compared with the Australian farms of his childhood and adult experience back in Western Australia:

> ...but suddenly
> undercut, we resist calling it revenge,
> colluding with indifferent Nature,
> visa and permit, green card
> as crops spread: they won't let me
> into their pastoral entirely,
> invited to ride the header
> to harvest cobs and interiors
> that exchange chemical appearance;
> protectionist policies and markets
> fill supermarket aisles, fill
> hunting and trapping magazines,
> fur around collars, covering
> cold ears,

addressing steers
in Texan clichés, clinging
like ideas of Kansas...
...I track these infinitudes,
connect nouns from an uncle's paddocks
in places threatened by closure,
the tariff, sucked into global
silos and temptations...

(Kinsella 2004, 178)

In this poem Kinsella lists something of a litany of the failures of the West's once brave manifestation of the Arcadian dream, the American pastoral. The new world of mechanised farming and clean red barns of Ohio are depicted but so also Kinsella's pet hates—the wearing of animal furs, overt gun use (or misuse), chemical sprays for crops. All this echoes the similar evils he finds lying beneath the surface of Australian rural life and which made him anti-pastoral in the first place. True to his 'international regionalism', Kinsella returns very quickly to his Wheatbelt centre of the world and the negative underbelly of monoculture in large-scale farming—with its silos of grain already in the power of the global supermarket chains to buy produce at tempting prices to the farmers, only to put pressure on them later to take much lower returns until many are forced into the closure of their properties. What we have seen so far in Kinsella's work is an awareness of the environmental problems created by the misuse of the ecology and that mankind's interference with nature is conducted on a global scale. What worries him is that the deterioration of landscapes is even more prevalent in the rural areas of the countries visited.

Kinsella's encounter with Indian landscapes took place much earlier, in fact while he was still an undergraduate. On a return trip from Britain and Europe in 1985, he travelled from Mumbai through much of India to Bangladesh and Kolkata before turning north to Nepal.

Kinsella released some of the poems from these Indian journeys in *Night Parrots* (1989). I have been told that most of the poems from this journey have never been published but are held in an archival collection at the University of Western Australia.

Kinsella's Indian poems bear the hallmarks of a young but brilliant poet making his way through the flood-tide of American youth drug culture after the example of the Beat poets such as Ginsberg and authors such as Kerouac. There is an attraction to Indian culture which had perhaps started with T.S. Eliot or perhaps with later promptings by the Beatles. All of this had made travelling through the Indian subcontinent something of a rite of passage for many of Kinsella's generation. We can see it in his "In the City of Kaks":

> you walk down the street to be
> shot up by a pharmacist
> your room is littered with food
> broken ampules, books, cigarette butts,
> foils of mandrax, dexedrine, shots of hash
> your chest is so tight that you can
> barely speak or move
> you lie on your bed, always waiting
> it is overcast, and as you
> glance into the street below
> the last glow of a discarded sun
> catches eye and window
> and you think of Ted Berrigan
> who said that he died of Pepsi and pills,
> and of Robert Adamson, who was quite taken
> with the idea that Berrigan had died
>   of Pepsi and pills.
> the kaks, on the windowsill, always laughing,
> at these, your small crimes.
>
> (Kinsella 1989, 67)

On the whole, these Indian poems of Kinsella's youthful era can be seen to be less concerned with landscape and more concerned with the people of India and Bangladesh and new and exotic cultural experiences. We may note this in the poem above and also in the following Bangladeshi poem, also published in *Night Parrots*:

Asham
I watch my friend move across
his bed towards his 'Bengali boy',
the shadow of roof fan chopping
their faces, parting their bodies.
Neither is 'master of the situation'.
Theirs is to leave things up to
the breeze blowing in through
the fly screens, to follow its
wavering intensity, the
sounds of Dhaka it carries—
slow sordid movement of rickshaws
as they pedal through the cries
of Asham, horns and kaks.

(Kinsella 1989, 68)

At least there is more landscape (or cityscape) here but one does not sense the developed 'international regionalism' of the later poetry of Kinsella. There is none of the deliberated connections back across the borders from the new surroundings to those of his homeland, the Wheatbelt of Western Australia.

However, six years later in a much more stylistically distinctive work, *erratum/frame(d)* (Fremantle Art Centre Press, 1995) perhaps there are some slight touches which suggest the making of connections to Australia and Kinsella's home territory. In a poem entitled "Every now and again thoughts of Bombay [sic] enter the heads of those in Bangalore":

this place
is pure(ly) structures lists of unbuilt & un-

finished like languages evolving
with social predicaments so new stories are added
well and truly lived in
satellite dishes like orbits of images
beggar bowls aimed to heaven—
becoming clearer
they neglect groundswell(s)
as Ta-Ta trucks ARE their own trend
passing luminescent (but) smog-washed [?] BUT glowing
Boulevards of optimism, the script
as clichéd as eucalypts
around Bangalore University...

(Kinsella 1995, 21)

The mere mention of the iconic Australian tree here, the eucalypt, immediately recalls his native habitat. Can we conclude, therefore, that it is in the blossoming of Kinsella's great pastoral trilogy (*The Silo, The Hunt* and *The New Arcadia*) that we see the omnipresent Wheatbelt region being more amply presented to an international readership?

Kinsella's concept of 'international regionalism' seems unique to his own work and as such appears to be a relatively new development in regional poetry. Other Western Australian poets such as Randolph Stow and Dorothy Hewett, who too have acquired international reputations, also show the predilection for landscape of the Wheatbelt region that distinguishes so much of the work of the poets from this region of Australia; but, when their imaginations reach beyond the local it is with a singularly different effect with each. There is not sufficient time or space to expand these points in this discussion beyond stating here that with Stow, landscape is always vested with heavy symbolic significance as in "The Land"—a poem included by Kinsella in his selections for *The Penguin Anthology of Australian Poetry*—as can be illustrated even by the short excerpt given below:

...And the question (applauded, derided)
falls like the dust
on verandah and bar; and in pauses, when
thinking ceases,
the footprints of the recently departed
march to the minds horizons and
endure.

(2009, 249)

With Dorothy Hewett the tendency was rather to bring in European allusions, fairytales, legends and literature which work towards creating a kind of 'Wheatbelt Gothic' not dissimilar to effects created also by Kinsella in some of his work. Unsurprisingly, he admired Hewett's work and included three of her poems in the Anthology mentioned above. Below is an extract from one:

Yealering* in the Mind
...outside the cool drink shop
the silos shine
silvered in the moonlight
the wheat ears glow

on spindly legs with wings
and a cardboard crown
the old woman
perched on a spring cart
steers a crooked wheel rut
out of town

(qtd. in Kinsella 2009, 211-12)

* A small Wheatbelt town.

My own practice has perhaps been closer to Kinsella's. Since I was also born and raised (at least for the first 12 years of my life) in the Western Australian Wheatbelt, much of my poetry reflects these same landscapes. Closer to Kinsella in terms of my time of developing as a poet, I have also travelled widely in Europe and China, and I found my own regionalism challenged by new landscapes and languages. I have worked closely with Kinsella and travelled with him into almost every region of the Wheatbelt. I have included here an extract of a poem of mine to illustrate the echoes which suggest the impact on still another Western Australian poet of the pressures of globalisation:

> **Sweeping my Paths of Leaves**
> (for Fei-fei)
> when I think of the misty early mornings
> years ago in Firenze or Perugia,
> Guangzhou or Xi'an, I remember
> insistent whisper of sweeping
> brooms in the cool pre-dawn hush.
> ...they still used the old brooms then—
> swatch or thatch of twigs gathered tight
> on the long broom handle's end.
> that was how we made them as children
> in the mallee country of the wheatbelt
> of my distant west of Australia.
> that was how we made them as children
> when we played by the salt lake
> making trails among sparse bush growth....
> back now under banksia, hakea or gum
> each new day I see more fallen leaves
> to sweep clean from proud new paths;
> each day new paths to extend my maps.
>
> (Phillips 2003, unpublished)

My focus must remain on Kinsella's work. I set out to explore in this essay how poets today respond to the communication revolution which has created our 'global village' and whether or not, in particular, Kinsella is justified in claiming that his work is reflective of 'international regionalism', that his birthplace region remains the effective centre of his world no matter through what geographical locations his travels in the world may take him. In this sense, all other locations are simply proximate or distant global extensions of what the poet recognizes as truly his 'place in the sun'. Within the context of this limited discussion, I believe it is possible to claim that Kinsella's poetry most certainly is a contribution to 'vanishing global borders'.

Works Cited

Kinsella, John. 1989. *Night Parrots*. Fremantle: FACP.

———. 1995. *erratum/frame(d)*. Fremantle: FACP.

———. 1995. *The Silo: a Pastoral Symphony*. Fremantle: FACP.

———. 1999. *Fenland Pastorals*. United Kingdom: Prest Roots Press.

———. 2004. *Peripheral Light: Selected and New Poems*. Harold Bloom [ed]. New York: W.W. Norton.

———. 2005. *The New Arcadia*. Fremantle: FACP.

———. 2008. *Disclosed Poetics: beyond landscape and lyricism*. Manchester: Manchester University Press.

——— [ed]. 2009. *The Penguin Anthology of Australian Poetry*. Melbourne: Penguin.

Stehlik, Daniela. 2009. "Intergenerational Transitions in Rural Western Australia", in Merlan, F. (ed.), *Tracking Rural Change*. Canberra: ANU Press. 135-50.

CHAPTER 18

Glen Phillips' Poetry and Kinsella's Concept of 'International Regionalism': Western Australian Poets and Globalisation—A Discussion

N. Bindu
SS Government Arts College
Tamil Nadu, India

Introduction

Born in 1936 in the remote Goldfields Centre of Southern Cross in Western Australia, Glen Phillips in his formative years lived in numerous small towns where his father was a headmaster. His mother hailed from a family of farmers and this streak of feeling for country landscapes and sensitivity to the situations of country folk must have been inherited from this lineage. Glen Phillips confesses: "I believe my guiding philosophy in writing is in tune with recent American theories of ecocriticism and the comparatively recent British rethinking of the traditional pastoral mode in literature". He has expanded these ideas in his 'Introduction' to his doctoral thesis (Phillips 2006).

The pastoral influence is exhibited in a journey back into time in the poem "Amphora" (1999). Glen Phillips grasps the vivid images of his 'then' immediate surroundings and ponders on their survival in the Australia of tomorrow:

> Picking over barren fields: the past,
> The disturbed, convoluted roots, the stones,
> And now and then the splintered weathered bone;
> I raise my eyes to the dark line of scrub at last.

A low fertile mound surfaces with a few sprouts of vegetation. The Australian landscape, barren and flat, conveys a silent communication. A picture of the homeland is foregrounded with the 'then' and 'now' intricately woven to proceed towards a vision of a shrouded future. Urbanisation is the symbolic image of the "disturbed convoluted roots", with stones being upturned to accommodate new ventures. Yet the explicit change cannot drive away the implicit message of nature being all powerful and its inherent wisdom is grasped by the poet:

> What is it in the curve and rack of land,
> This flatland homeland, speaks to me
> Out of this same earth, familiar mystery,
> The spinning clay leaps to the potter's hand.

In a poet's artistic imagination lies a mystery that unfolds only with the completion of a work of art. The clay in the potter's hand takes its final shape only after the potter has given his best and decides to rest the wheel. Is this then behind the fascination which draws the poet to nature, for both his art and nature remain a mystery until introspection leads to clarity? Glen Phillips also wonders at how ultimately his creativity would be received by the judgmental critics.

> I draw an analogy in the poem to creation of poetry itself as resembling the way in which a potter might make an amphora on the potter's spinning wheel. The way ancient amphorae are found thousands of years later are really unlikely to happen to my poems so my final question is evidently self-mockery.
>
> (1999)

Despite these doubts he continues

> Secrets hover close in sheoak's songs, tuned
> By dry inland sweep of air: songs of death.
> If I spin words from present time on earth,
> Shall I expect them to be found?
>
> (1999)

The Australian landscape is not all green and fertile. The description of the dryness, barrenness of the land subverts the traditional pastoral theory of the countryside being brushed only with positive elements of beauty, peace and romance. Further the poet in the lines contemplates the stark reality of death in the form of urbanisation of the land, and death, for the human being and the artist particularly also in the form of oblivion overtaking his creative work. Works of art with a desire for immortality finds only temporary anchors in fleeting life. For Phillips, the memories of his native Australia have given him assurance and respite during his extensive travels abroad. Along with his undying fascination for the landscape of his birthplace there is a note of anxiety regarding the encroaching changes of modernity.

These aspects of Glen Phillip's work will involve a longer study which I hold in reserve for a later date. Here I will focus particularly on how Phillip's work could also serve as grist to the mill of the 2011 ASAA conference theme of globalisation as he spoke of this in his own presentation on Kinsella's work at the conference. The synergies are best illustrated through the reproduction here of a written exchange between Glen Phillips and me.

N. Bindu (NB): You have studied the work of John Kinsella very closely and have discussed his work in many contexts, including at the ASAA Conference of 2011. Your focus was Kinsella's concept of 'international regionalism' and your closing comments mentioned some of your own work as reflecting this concept. Do you feel this is something that has evolved naturally in your own work or has it been a development influenced by your acquaintance with Kinsella's work?

Glen Phillips (GP): Kinsella and I share one particular special interest, writing poetry about the West Australian Wheatbelt. I mean serious poetry based on our detailed knowledge of the landscapes, the people who choose to live there and the blighted example of the classic 'pastoral' mode which we Europeans brought to these Australian shores a couple of hundred years ago. Until I met Kinsella and read his early poetry in the 1990s I had not found another poet (with the possible exception of Dorothy Hewett) who felt it was a worthwhile region for poetry that could or should be meaningful to the rest of the world.

Here is a poem that is illustrative of the 'international regionalism' you referred to. The immediate context is a Chinese scenario but this becomes most intimately connected to an Australian past:

Sweeping my Paths of Leaves

(for Fei-fei)

When I think of the misty early mornings
years ago in Firenze or Perugia,
Guangzhou or Xi'an, I remember
insistent whisper of sweeping
brooms in the cool pre-dawn hush.
...they still used the old brooms then—
swatch or thatch of twigs gathered tight
on the long broom handle's end.
that was how we made them as children
in the mallee country of the wheatbelt
of my distant west of Australia.
that was how we made them as children
when we played by the salt lake
making trails among sparse bush growth....
back now under banksia, hakea or gum
each new day I see more fallen leaves
to sweep clean from proud new paths;
each day new paths to extend my maps.

(Phillips 2003, unpublished)

NB: Can you comment on any synergy that you perceive between your work and Kinsella's?

GP: Apart from field trips to the WA Wheatbelt (all areas) with Kinsella and recording our conversations over ten years, I have spent time at Cambridge University at his invitation and also taught with him in Ohio at Kenyon

College. I have presented papers on his Indian poetry as well as responding myself to the Indian landscapes. However, we differ in our attitudes to Australian rural life, I think, in that I retain greater warmth, perhaps, toward the farming people and their struggles to make a modest living with great privations yet with real feeling for and understanding of their beloved (if stolen) landscapes. Kinsella, a committed Vegan, began as an 'anti-pastoralism' activist in terms or what he sees as willful destruction of the natural landscapes as a result of monoculture. Now he describes himself as an 'international regionalist' and a dissident or activist in terms of destroying the rural myths of classical pastoralism. The two following poems might illustrate our differences:

The Silo

The sun has bleached the walls
bone-white while the path to the heavily
bolted door was of red earth, a long thin
stream of unhealthy blood. Before those storms
which brew thickly on summer evening
red-tailed black cockatoos settled in waves,
sparking the straw like a volcano, dark
fire erupting from the heart of the white
silo, trembling with energy deeper
than any anchorage earth could offer.
And lightning dragging a moon's bleak halo
to dampen the eruption, with thunder
echoing out over the bare paddocks
towards the farmhouse where an old farmer
consoled his bitter wife on the fly-proof
verandah, cursing the cockatoos, hands
describing a prison from which neither
could hope for parole, petition, release.

(Kinsella 1995, 59)

Autumn Sestina

This country breathes. Always a leaf, or loops
of bark stir when the evening seems calm,

perfectly calm, with the salmon gums dark
parachute shapes against a scarlet sky.
But the wind rises, thin mallees rub dry
Shoulders. Grains roll from the crests of sand drifts.
Presently a gold coin of a moon driftsup from the east
horizon. Its strong light loops
and searches stubble of paddocks
long dryin this lingering autumn...
They eye the sky,
these farmers in paddocks, thumbs through belt loops
as they lean back, find ithard to be calm,
who waited to sow seed through the long dry...
rain, bucketing rain will break autumn's calm.
So be it. The dust at my feet, once calm,
is suddenly exploding as black sky
fires its warning shots. A cold shudder drifts
across wodjil and tor. Now there are few dry
patches as the drops join up into dark
mapped continents; puddles mark lines and loops.
Out here they calmly say: end of the dry;
as farmers eye skies, returning home near dark;
change of season drifts in; while life loops and loops.

(Phillips: 1994)

NB: Perhaps it would be most appropriate (in view of the fact that this conference is set in India) to ask you to talk about your recollections of works written in India?

GP: I have now made four visits to these regions and have been conducting landscape research and reading of Indian literature in order to equip myself to write competently and in depth a poetry collection which would represent these places as a form of 'second landscape learning', a theory I have been espousing since the early 1990s. A planned volume of poetry reflecting my Indian responses (is being assembled for publication and translation).

The following poem, "Hyderabad Sweeping", written during my first visit to India on the occasion of the inaugural ASAA conference (about 1997) would be a good poem to recall here. I wrote it during a visit to India several years ago. I had seen street sweepers in China often enough but did not quite expect they would also be so common in Hyderabad. Following a visit to Hyderabad in late 2011, the image of an elderly street sweeper in safety jacket and sari connected with my memories of other sweepers, not only of streets, in other countries and cultures. It was also a time of farewells to my many dear Indian friends of academe who had attended a conference at Hyderabad University with me. Immediately I began mentally comparing the Indian woman street sweeper with those in my past experiences in Europe, China and other countries. Strangely enough, I found myself remembering my mother and grandmother sweeping the brick paths and other areas of the farmyard or other household environs in past years. There is a universality to be discovered in the actions of the street sweepers which can also be connected with the domestic sweeping we all witness especially in childhood.

Hyderabad Sweeping

(for Bindu)

She swept the streets there daily
outside our Secunderabad hotel
in her orange safety vest, worn
askew over that modest hued sari.
To her, perhaps her own home-yard
extended, this whole stretch of street?
Pride in her slow strokes sweepingdetritus of her neighbours' disregard
And sweeping women fill my past.
My mother as a child had swept
the square of brick at the back door
of the farmhouse, always in protest.
Married she swept her own home

and yard for her husband, beating
new dust devils back. And did so down
the paths of married life to come.
Mother chased me once with a broom,
her straw yard broom, because I'd failed
to do some chore. Now each day I sweep
my brickyard driveway in gathering gloom....
Yet now back on dusty streets stroke
of the twigged broom whispers a history
ancient as human presence on this earth
and all that gender, class or caste evoke....

(Phillips 2010)

A much earlier poem, is set in Trivandrum:

Trivandrum
From the dark window, ten flights
up from the seethe of evening streets,
bullock carts, buses, bicycles, lights
of lines of stalls and shops, I glimpsed
a sable wall, a carved cliff face
that was outlined against last glow
in the west of the sun's fierce race
across spinning ancient Earth.
This must be the holy place where
Krishna, Vishnu and Kali are hallowed
by the followers. I won't dare
to place an unbeliever's foot in there...
...
Slowly the risen red sun boiled
away nightfall's mists and cast long
shards of light on wet grass. We toiled
from green to green with dew-webbed words.
Later, at table, lunch for two
amid spice and curry scents, in last
conversation, words withdrew,
as two boats in an ocean apart.
Life is like struggling waist deep

along palm-crowded waterways
in light and shade with the steep
banks forcing you forever on....

(Phillips 2003, unpublished)

The lines depict the routine scenes of an Indian evening in the city, the colours of life and society alien to his own, but the Australian poet conveys a response which reveals an empathy with the magnificence of a tradition and culture not part of his own existence.

NB: What of your travels in China?

GP: My Chinese poetry began after our first visit to China in 1985 when I wrote a number of poems and one short story. In 1990 after the Tianamen massacres I spent half a year teaching in South China and researching the landscapes of Guangdong province. Some fifty poems resulted from that very powerful experience, particularly seeing captured dissident students being taken away for probable execution.

While the poem discussed at the beginning of this essay invokes and older way of life in China, many later poems deal with the emergent new modern China of expressways, high-rise cities, and university campus life. I have visited China annually, usually to teach Australian literature I Shanghai, Mudanjiang or Qingdao. All these landscapes have produced an immense number of new poems. My publications "Shanghai Suite" and "Heilongjiang Summers" have been the result:

He pointed Out Hai'an Road
Maybe he thought I paused
at the cross road lost in space
of this megapolis? Touched
by the sun as I peered from
side to side? So he rushed across
red-faced to point to the sign: Hai'an Lu.
Peaceful sea road, I knew it said
for I was about to step in inferno

of a dockside street where the mega trucks
and motorcycle combinations, articulated
trolley buses, hell-bent black cars
and blind tri-cyclists come at you
from every corner of the earth, even
when the lights went green. I thanked
him for his concern as best I could,
and thought wistfully of a peaceful sea

(Phillips 2009, 25)

The differences surfacing from a Chinese landscape is treated with tolerance and patience. In the last line of the poem, the image from the past evokes the desire to be embraced yet again by the familiar landscape of his birth, Australia.

Cement Sleepers
Thunder of guns in Jungong Road?...
And then the lorry load of cement
in bags. Among the bags what looks
like grey rags but it's a man, no.
Two men lying on their backs, one
with a dirty dust mask half over
his mouth. One thing sure, from
my own childhood years in Perth
down wind of Portland Cement, their lungs will be well and truly dusted.
Lucky I got away in the South west
forests where I breathed with the trees.

(Phillips 2009, 36)

The chance observation from my high-rise apartment in a busy Shanghai street of a couple of napping workers lying in the back of a lorry full of cement powder took me instantly from the urban environment in China to the urban environment I had temporarily lived in during the Second World War, unfortunately, in the lee of a very large cement works. Perhaps I was also rather oppressed at the time of writing the poem by the noise and squalor of Shanghai docklands and wishing to escape to the beautiful countryside of Zhejiang province with its shaded waterways and green rice paddies? And in my memory of my unfortunate encounter with the serious pollution from my WA cement factory, I pitied those sleeping workmen even more. And thought of my own narrow escape those years ago when the family moved to the deep forests of the southwest, well away from industry.

NB: Apparently you have also have a special tie to Italy —would you like to enlarge on this aspect of your experience?

GP: My wife is Italian-born, and this inspired me to study Italian at Italian universities, I have responded strongly to the landscapes in both the north and south of the country (including two visits to Sicily). I completed an intensive research project in Tuscany in 1991 and have had one collection of poetry published in Italy. I will shortly publish a new illustrated set of my Italian poetry entitled "Etruscanini: Little poems of Tuscany".

NB: You have written a poem on which you published an interesting commentary (in a previous ASAA publication on a group of Italian miners who were entombed in a mining accident in W. Australia. Could you regard that episode and the fact of your writing on it as another aspect of the impact of globalisation on your writing?

GP: I wrote a lengthy narrative poem based on the 'Entombed Miner' incident that occurred at the Bonnieville goldmine near Southern Cross (incidentally my birthplace) in 1907. Modesto Varischetti was a Valtellinese zinc miner from Gorno in Lombardy who migrated to WA during the great WA goldrush. His dramatic rescue with the aid of a pearl diver from Broome made world headlines and was possibly the first human story from WA to 'go global' as they say. My wife belongs to the very large group of Italian migrants who have become a permanent part of the WA population (one in ten is of Italian origin) and they represent a living example of a very specific diaspora (itself another global phenomenon).

NB: You must be conscious of Indigenous attitudes to the Australian land and landscapes. How would your concept of the Australian landscape as 'home' compare with theirs?

GP: Indigenous poetry in English is only of relatively recent growth, though of course there is a long and ancient tradition of Aboriginal art that celebrates the land. I have presented studies of the Indigenous author Kim Scott and have taught appreciation of his work abroad. In my own writing I seem to have focussed more on various Indigenous personalities I encountered very early in my young life. Very early in my poetic career I began to write about my earliest encounters with the Indigenous people of our shared homeland:

STATIONS: 4

Lake Grace

I looked at her ankles coming out
of her old sandshoes as we sat
on the back verandah of the schoolhouse
that stands no more by the lake.
Daisie Mundi ate from her enamel plate,
like a child's bowl, that we kept for her.
and our oldest knife and fork,
the brass showing on the worn prongs,
the handle of the knife yellowed with use.

As the propped clothes-line flapped
with her wash I looked and looked again
at her ankle's silky black. Suppose
after all she wore black stockings? For it was true
the palms of her hands, as she scraped
the last of sausage and mash, were almost white.

But it puzzled me. Just as the black
beast of a train that had thundered from night
into the prim little eau-di-Nil station

(with its marseille orange-tiled roof,
all art nouveau fashionably bespoke)
had thrown me into confusion with its fuss.

There, as the blackness blazed into roaring light
I was overcome. So I turned my face to the wall
while my dad searched lighted compartments
for sign of mother's best friend, come to help.
In the morning Daisie Mundi was gone.
I missed taking her dinner plate out.

This poem has been translated into several languages and published many times but I always feel uneasy and even condescending in my depiction. In terms of describing the landscapes, I must defer always to the Aboriginal culture's superior depth of feeling for and understanding of our landscapes, wherever I encounter evidence of these in Western Australia. I have tried to express this in the poem quoted below:

Among Friends
these other ones
moving mostly in the shadows
among the soft bush shapes
shadowed like the shadows
We who move boldly through their lands
smiling distribute bright cloth and tomahawks,
fat bags of flour and tea in our tempting hands.

but they remain
further off
stricken mortally by our fevered touch
shadowed like the shadows

On the strange rock outcrops we hammer pegs,
the leases and the farmlands measured and shared out;
our flocks trample the billabongs to muddy dregs.

soft bush voices
calling from the red wastelands
speak urgently to our instincts buried in the shades

beyond dynasties of greed

But our cities spear their windowed crystals upwards;
growths of roadway networks multiply
searching in patterned grid for treasure hoards.

the shadows do not
stir our memories of the great forests
cough of sabretooth or pungent taste of woodsmoke
shadowed like the shadows
Compassionate churchmen led our encounter,
our language now includes dingo, boomerang and wombat;
this has been a great endeavour.

in secret places
the shadows are singing
the dust shuffles and ochre and pipeclay stamp
the song is sacred like the shadows
They sit, the tribal elders, heavy with dread perhaps;
we prefer to stand, planes waiting, promising at least...
we know about Judeans, Sioux, Esquimaux, the Lapps.

but those other ones
moving mostly in the shadows
among soft bush shapes
shadowed always like the shadows

(Phillips 1980)

Or here is another in which I acknowledge the Indigenous culture and presence in the land.

Fire on Wet Granite
Like a fire lit on wet granite rock
I am burning through this brief
enough life of mine on the edge
of the great south land. We stole
it from those runners in the woods
who are our human Nyungar cousins
still stricken by our force today.

....
A great circle of our world
Separates us now. As I am
distanced from my Celtic past,
the cut hay on mountain slopes,
the gathered berry fruits, bread
baked from grain, the blackened
metal forged as cooking pots.

In this, your culture is nearer
yet so far from mine. So, light
your hearth fire, and wish me
at your fireside too, my friend.

(Phillips 2008, 70)

Works Cited

Born, Anne and Glen Phillips. 2008. *Singing Granites: Poems of Devon and Gondwana Land*. Devon: Oversteps Books.

Phillips, Glen. 1999. *Spring Burning: New and Selected Poems*. Fremantle: Salt Books.

———. 2003. "Trivandrum", unpublished.

———. 2009. *Shanghai Suite & Other Poems*. WA. The International Centre for Landscape and Language, Edith Cowan University.

———. 2011. "International Regionalism in the Age of Globalisation: A Revaluation of the Poetry of John Kinsella". Paper presented at the Vth International Conference of the ASAA, Osmania University, Hyderabad, December.

CHAPTER 19

'Representational Waste': Refugees, Writing and Affect in this 'Restless Epoch'

Tony Simoes da Silva
University of Woollongong, Australia

> Refugees, the human waste of the global frontier-land, are the 'outsiders incarnate', the absolute outsiders everywhere and out of place everywhere except in places that are themselves out of place—the 'nowhere places' that appear on the maps used by ordinary humans on their travels.
>
> (Zygmunt Bauman 2004, 80)
>
> How come we respond emotionally to artwork, when we know it is mere fiction?
>
> (Matravers, in Palencik 2008, 259)

I start with these two statements because together they encompass the main concerns this essay will pursue. Working out of the field of literary studies, I am interested in the way much fiction so often sets out to harness the power of emotion as a catalyst for change and transformation. In this essay, I explore the increasingly visible role literary fiction plays in debates about refugees and asylum seekers, and displaced people more generally through work that overtly draws on the power of emotion as a political instrument. Drawing at once on the poetic license of the work of fiction and on its unique way of connecting image to feeling, this essay examines some of the ideological work that much contemporary literature is being compelled to undertake on behalf of refugees. For, the 'production' of the refugee, both as embodied and as representational self, is a far more complex issue than social scientists and historians, driven by an empirical and factual impulse, will allow for.

Thus, rather than concerning myself with refugees and refugeeness with reference to well-established and researched points of origin, the empirical evidence of cause and effect, that characterises much work by historians and social scientists, here I want to consider how imaginative literature can help bridge the gap between the *imagined* refugee and the *real* refugee in ways that go beyond the diagnosis offered by the social sciences. To put it differently, I seek to explore literature's ability to create a space for acts of empathy with characters who might not be real people but who are *like* real people, 'like us'—in a sense literature that suggests that we are all refugees *in potentia*.

In an insightful comment on how the 'effects of affect' are mobilised, and manipulated *in* and *through* the work of fiction, literary critic Suzanne Keen posits that "readers' perception of a text's fictionality plays a role in subsequent empathetic response, by releasing readers from the obligations of self-protection through skepticism and suspicion" (2006, 220). For Keen, working out of a relatively recent cognitivist movement in literary studies, the power of fiction resides in its paradoxical ability to draw on *unreal* (imagined, represented) worlds and situations to make *real* a wide range of experiences that readers may not know first-hand. Although Keen's concern with the impact of literature highlights the emotional *effect* it has on a reader—how it may induce self-change or the willingness to work to enact change on behalf of or for the sake of others—her discussion is especially relevant in the context of long-standing debates about the meaning and purpose of literature. These debates, as Keen notes, are hardly new, and in her study she reviews a body of critical work spanning three hundred years; what is new is the potential for radically innovative work on the workings of the human brain made possible by recent technological developments in the fields of neuroscience.

As literary critic David S. Miall asserts, in an essay entitled "Emotions and the Structuring of Narrative Responses", "the literary texts we read evoke emotion in us, enabling us to match fictional or poetic situations to episodes in our previous lives, although this most likely occurs unconsciously—we often do not know why we weep during reading, or feel pleasure at a particular moment" (2011, 339). Working across disciplines, in *Empathy and the Novel* (2010) Keen posits for the literary text, as *representation*, a concrete, *material* role.

Work such as that of Suzanne Keen and David S. Miall is typical of this recent trend that draws on ongoing developments in cognitive theory and applies them to the reading of fiction, an approach that Ruth Leys describes as "the turn to affect" (2011, 434), in an essay of that title. Setting out a critique of "the general turn to affect, particularly the turn to the neurosciences of emotion, that has recently taken place in the humanities and social sciences" (434), Leys' essay appears in an issue of *Critical Inquiry* that coincided with a double issue of *Poetics Today* published also in 2011 devoted entirely to this topic (volume 32, 1-2). The double issue brings together a body of work concerned with what Suzanne Keen describes in her editorial as a *re*-turn to affect, since she argues that the concern with the emotions and literature has a long history in literary criticism. Perhaps it is not surprising that, given the coincidental publication dates, Keen should make no reference to Leys' work, though the omission nevertheless is remarkable. Ruth Leys has now been working in this field for many years, largely centring her seminal work on the literature of the *Shoah*.

Keen's editorial essay offers an extensive survey of the interplay between literature and psychology in particular, and of the ways fiction's re-presentation of the real can be harnessed to good effect. As she points out, psychologists long have sought to understand the power of literature to access the life of the mind, while literary critics have turned to cognitive theory in order to understand how readers respond to literary texts. Ironically, while in some ways the collection builds on the work of I.A. Richards, many of the contributors seem unaware of his views. Keen herself writes in her editorial that "it is not even clear that most of the emotion researchers involved in the affective turn are even alert to the work of others outside their fields" (8).

In response, Keen sets out to link much of the current work inthis field to Richards' influential work of literary criticism, *Principles of Literary Criticism* (1926). Identifying in Richards "a not unfamiliar, hopeful expression of the powers of literary reading to renovate and elevate the emotions", Keen proposes that what his work lacked was "a thorough account of its operations" (2011, 4), the kind of theoretical mapping found in the two issues of *Poetics Today*. "Far from banishing emotions from discussions of literature", Keen avers, "Richards elevates them as 'signs of attitudes' (132) and gives them a central place in theories of art" (2011, 2). She quotes Richards' view that "a theory of feeling, or emotion, of attitudes and desires, of the affective-volitional aspect of mental activity, is required at all points of our analysis" of works of fiction (Keen 2011, 2).

My own take on the work of Keen, Leys, Miall and others seeks to consider the possibilities raised for a reading of contemporary fiction concerned with the life stories and the experiences of refugees, asylum seekers and displaced people in a more general sense. For at the heart of most of these texts is an overt attempt *to act* on behalf of refugees by appealing to readers' emotions in ways that will *affect* them and then in turn *compel* them also to act on behalf of refugees. In this way the work of art, here the novel or life writing text, overcomes the dense and often inscrutable web of political, legal and social discourses set in place to control and even to define refugees. If I may return to Miall, "[i]n reading,...we try out environments made available to us in the texts we read: although we may never encounter them in reality, feeling enlivens our experience of their implications for developing or modifying the self" (2011, 337). My concern here is with the way literature and particularly the literary work that thematises the life experience of refugees, allows readers "impressionistic expressions" of refugeeness, as it were, in words used by Suman Gupta in a recent study of the representation of globalisation in literature (2009, 3). This vicarious embodiment of the experience of (an)Other is articulated through a twining of the effects of emotion and affect, in the kind of pact with a reader that literature is especially well-equipped to propose.

As David Attridge has noted, in words that are quite apt in this context, the "singularity of the literary work is produced not just by its difference from all other works, but by the new possibilities for thought and feeling it opens up in its creative transformation of familiar norms and habits: singularity is thus inseparable from *inventiveness*" (2004, 11). The kind of work of fiction with which I am concerned thus is at its most powerful when it succeeds in creating "new possibilities" for political and material action by drawing on the complex ways in which "thought and feeling...open[...] up in its creative transformation of familiar norms and habits" reaching out to a broader collective of individuals, the *actors* who may then take up in their lives the work that fiction alone cannot perform. To Miall the last word: "while actual doing is not possible for the literary reader, feeling in this way alerts us to the implications of potential action—whether narrative implications or implications for our own interactions in the world. Feeling provides the signals by which potential courses of action can be judged, and does so often well in advance of our ability to appraise a situation cognitively" (2011, 336-37).

I believe that David S. Miall's comments are particularly relevant here in Australia because the debate about refugees, the validity of their experiences and the country's responsibility to recognise them has become so impossibly politicised and polarising. It is an issue of extra poignancy because of the fact that the numbers in question are almost insignificant in the context of Australia's demographics. Indeed, the very word 'refugee' is now so over-signified that it too "provides the signals by which potential courses of action can be judged, and does so often well in advance of our ability to appraise a situation cognitively", to borrow and take out of context Miall's words (2011, 337). 'Refugee' alone evokes emotion and response in ways that cannot always be explained rationally, for the term has long been used to describe hugely diverse bodies of people and experiences. The overt engagement in much recent work by Australian novelists in un-mistakenly political interventions on behalf of refugees highlights both this dimension and the power of literature as a "shaping force" of public opinion through an appeal to emotion and affect (Boehmer 2007, 6).

Writing about refugees often by retelling stories shared with and by refugees and asylum seekers themselves, authors such as Blanche D'Alpuget, Eva Sallis, Thomas Keneally, Caroline Brothers, Morris Gleitzman, Alice Pung, Shaun Tan and Linda Jaivin, among others, have sought to bring into the intimate spaces where readers and texts interact "the new possibilities for thought and feeling [that fiction] opens up in its creative transformation of [*un*]familiar norms and habits", to quote and reinterpret Attridge's words cited above. All draw on literature as a cultural act to undertake the kind of work to which Miall, Leys, Attridge and Keen refer. Some writers go even further, resorting to complex affective discourses that encourage readers to donate to a nominated charity working on behalf of refugees, *here* or *elsewhere*. Such gestures, however diverse, and perhaps precisely in their diversity, signal a recognition that the writer of fiction who engages in *literary* action on behalf of refugees will, sooner or later, be co-opted into a culture where the pain and suffering of others can be easily commodified. In Australia these writers have been at the forefront of a campaign to counter what Suvendrini Perera described as a "demonisation of asylum seekers" that she saw as "once again a popular sport" (Perera 2009).

My own response to these texts is marked by a concern I share with these writers about human rights and the rights of refugees more specifically to be treated like the human beings. As a literary critic, I hold a strong belief in the power of literature to affect readers into active responses that are as much emotional as they are material. Yet, in an insight that has become core to a postcolonial critical viewpoint, I wonder if it is possible to consider how some of this writing on the refugee experience may echo Karl Marx's famous dictum:"They cannot represent themselves; they must be represented" (in Said 1978). In an uncannily topical comment on the vagaries of ideology, the risk is that the well-intentioned novelists seeking to put their literary work to work on behalf of refugees will come to rely on refugees merely as 'representational waste' in need of recycling, as it were. For in a world where the commodification of culture is all but complete, works about—and *for*—refugees are not exempt from the demands of the market place. Their function in an economy of affect and emotion is inseparable from their place as artefacts to be traded for profit. Both points are picked up by Binyavanga Wainaina in an essay entitled "How to Write About Africa" published in *Granta* magazine in 2002, where he instructs fellow but non-African writers, tongue in cheek:

> Among your characters you must always include The Starving African, who wanders the refugee camp nearly naked, and waits for the benevolence of the West. Her children have flies on their eyelids and pot bellies, and her breasts are flat and empty. She must

> look utterly helpless. She can have no past, no history; such diversions ruin the dramatic moment. Moans are good. She must never say anything about herself in the dialogue except to speak of her (unspeakable) suffering. (Wainaina 2002)

As the title of the essay implies, Wainaina directs his satire at a symbolic archive that is explicitly associated with the representation of Africa and Africans in a Western imaginary, one that Chinua Achebe (1977) traced to the work of European writers and for which he so castigated Joseph Conrad's *Heart of Darkness* (1903). Indeed, focusing on the the refugee as abject figure—"'outsiders incarnate'", (Baimun 2004, 80), Wainaina raises the spectre of the colonial encounter so aptly summarised by Gayatri Spivak's assertion about white men working to save brown women from brown men (1985). For the refugee emerges in Wainaina's view as the stock figure so dear to Western, Eurocentric discourses—always and *essentially* a signifier of hopelessness, of suffering, of despair, of pity, of charity. The point he seeks to drive home is that *this* refugee cannot exist in the work of fiction other than as a recipient of much deserved empathy that is essentially a correlative for the (Western) reader's capacity to give, and to give of his—or herself. Writing in the era of relentlessly mediatised celebrity benevolence, Wainaina puts his finger on one of the most fraught ethical dilemmas of all time—to do good is not without its perils and the agent of kindness may just as well be the harbinger of pain, suffering and destruction. And the benefits of doing good rarely travel in one direction alone and the point he makes is that self-interest often is better served than the interest of its intended objects. His attention to the work of literary representation is especially relevant because in many ways fiction plays by its own rules, in a universe semi-disconnected from the rules that apply to the relationship with the Other.

Finally, it is interesting to note too that Wainaina's refugee is no ordinary refugee—she is gendered, for one, and racialised, because African. The camp in which she lives itself whips up an ideological mini-storm, as it were, depending on whether it exists on the border with (an)other nation(s), or whether it stands at the heart of the nation. Although at one level the "non-places" Marc Augé (1995) suggests that are refugee camps exist simultaneously as powerful geo-political irritants, catalysts to transnational wars and fratricidal conflicts they forever remind us of the arbitrariness of national boundaries. The refugee as sign foregrounds the complex ideological forces at play in globalisation. Synonymous with an embrace of cultural diversity and of a cosmopolitan consciousness, and the erasure of literal or figurative boundaries, globalisation is simultaneously at heart synonymous with strengthened border controls and restrictive flows of peoples.

This is a point I want to pursue in what follows, working with reference to a couple of works by Australian novelists, Thomas Keneally's *The Tyrant's Novel* (2003) and Nam Le's *The Boat* (2008). In very different ways, both authors are concerned with refugees and their stories, and their writing intervenes in countering the cyclical "demonisation" of refugeesWhile Keneally goes so far as to add an authorial note that positions the fiction(alised) with reference to the real, and *vice versa*, critics have reacted to Nam Le's work in ways that signal the importance of such work. Indeed, in the book's opening story, the narrator engages in a frank discussion with his father about the need for narratives that inscribe the experience of refugees: "This is important, Ba. It's important that people know" (Nam Le 2008, 25).

I

Thomas Keneally's, *The Tyrant's Novel*, is not overtly concerned with the thematisation of the refugee experience as such, for while the story it tells is that of a man who will become a refugee in Australia—more accurately a detainee—it is set before that moment. It is set in an unnamed country, though the identifying codes are easy to decipher. The novel's 'refugee dimension', its function as a refugee narrative, is defined by the author in a brief but crucial preface where he describes being impelled to write this work by the *effect* of meeting the real person behind his fictional character. The preface also informs readers about the role played by Keneally himself as a refugee advocate and the fiction is the product of the emotional impact of that work. Without this preface, a *parergon* in the best sense of Derrida's discussion of the concept (1979), readers could be excused for engaging with the novel as essentially an absurdly allegorised treatment of the political situation in a far-off land that is coded as 'the not West' by such *endemic* conditions as corruption, nepotism, dictatorship and the ease with which people are killed.

However, Keneally reveals in the Preface that the fiction was based on a real story told him by a man detained in a real camp somewhere in Australia, a camp Keneally visited regularly in his capacity as an activist working to improve the conditions of would-be-refugees in Australia. It was there he met a real Iraqi refugee who, in an act redolent of the colonial and slave foundations of contemporary settler societies such as Australia, has taken on the name of 'Alan Sheriff'. Rather than weight to be given a new self by assimilationist policies, Sheriff takes it on himself to adopt these beforehand. In the kind of *caesure* I have in mind as an instance of 'representational waste', the nameless Iraqi refugee provides Keneally with a ready-made narrative strategy that frees him from any concern with the ethics of representation—the refugee *fictionalised* himself and the novelist thus is free to do likewise. Keneally writes of Sheriff's decision as a sign of a detainee's desperation to accelerate the process of becoming Australian in a way detainees might believe will improve their chances of acceptance and resettlement. But...?

The Preface details how, over time, Keneally and a friend who shares his interest in the plight of refugees developed a strongly empathetic relationship with Sheriff, and, in a move that provides the novel with its second 'freedom card', the latter confides in Keneally how he came to be in Australia, in his present condition. Thus the story, when it gets going, *is and is not* made up by Keneally as a fiction; he mediates a story that otherwise might not be heard. Before that, though, Keneally's friend, Alice receives from Sheriff a letter that she interprets as a declaration of his love for her. As a 'Western' woman familiar with how non-Western men behave, she politely makes herself scarce, both for the sake of making clear that the feelings are not reciprocal and to save Sheriff's pride. As a liberal-minded Western woman, she recognises the stereotype of the male Other—chauvinistic, hypersexual, demanding, insensitive—and gently defuses it. When Sheriff himself wonders what may have happened to Alice, he is told the full story by Keneally and then it is his turn *to read* Alice as the debauched and ingénue Western woman his symbolic archive of Western people allows him to construct.

Put this way, the Preface appears to offer a naive, even absurd picture of cross-cultural and cross-gender relations; but that is precisely what it does and it is difficult to imagine that Keneally is unaware of this aspect. In some weird sense, Alice in particular becomes a surrogate reader-figure in the text; like her, readers are challenged to doubt their ability to make sense of the chaotic existential consciousness of the refugee, for the Preface seems to endorse Sheriff's interpretation of Alice's actions. As a liberal-minded man Keneally offers this misunderstanding as an illustration of how easy it is to fall prey to bias and bigotry while he himself is not immune to the risk. Hence, as if to confirm his awareness of how easy it is to do as Alice (a fiction, too?) did, he has Alan Sheriff tell his own story, and the Preface merely opens the stage for the arrival of Sheriff as author-cum-narrator.

Ironically, in another uncanny slippage—intertextual, ideological, ethical—Keneally resorts to a strategy inextricably associated with Conrad's *Heart of Darkness* and Sheriff becomes a Marlow-like narrator, *in* the novel and *of* the novel, but also outside of it. In one of the countless instances of self-referentiality in a novel that seems determined to prove to readers that they are *and* are not reading a work of fiction, Keneally takes on the role of mediator, allowing the Alan Sheriff who in his country was a 'Mediationist' (clearly not the same thing but it is hard to avoid the resonances) to tell *his* story, *without* interference from the author. Hence when all of Allan Sheriff's 'characters' appear with Anglo-Saxon or Celtic names, in a narrative strategy typical of works that aim to touch readers by offering them a mirror-image of their own humanity—it is worth recalling that the novel is written by an Australian author, for Australian readers, about Australia's treatment of people who arrive in the country in search of refuge. It is possible to argue, as has been done about Conrad's Marlow, that it is the narrator and not the author who speaks thus. If the move strikes the reader as a hegemonic sleight of hand that betrays Australia's strong mono-cultural residue, one never too far from the surface in popular and official life practices, the author might conceivably argue *Sheriff did it*.

I may be labouring the point a bit, not least because Keneally intelligently anticipates the critiques readers may offer of the novel. Repeatedly, he draws on burlesque detail to evoke, for example, the ordinary extraordinariness of the life in Iraq under Saddam Hussein, seeking in this way to foreground the extraordinary ordinariness of the likes of Alan Sheriff (am I alone in wanting to read it as 'Omar Sharif'? No doubt it is 'an age' thing and younger readers will not be subject to the trick of the tongue but Keneally knows well the meaning of the Egyptian actor as stereotyped Other). Yet, as a reader I am rarely inclined to empathise with Sheriff—it is, I concede, perhaps a name thing—but most of all it is the utter unreliability of the literary construct through which I meet him as a fellow man. Miall tells us that "the literary texts we read evoke emotion in us, enabling us to match fictional or poetic situations to episodes in our previous lives, although this most likely occurs unconsciously—we often do not know why we weep during reading, or feel pleasure at a particular moment" (2011, 339). But I would argue that the key to this affinity, this moment of recognition, is the work of fiction's ability to take us into an unreal world that is real—momentarily, contingently, but powerfully so. The secret to this experience, one that Suzanne Keen (re)defines when she avers that the work of fiction detaches us—protects us?—from our own narrow-mindedness by exposing us to the possibility of dis-interested empathy, in the way the work of fiction takes itself seriously. That, I want to argue, is something that Keneally's novel refuses to do.

There is something profoundly strange in the way Keneally the novelist is so concerned with distancing himself from his activist self that he forgets that the function of art is to make readers respond "emotionally...to mere fiction", in the words of Matravers. That, in a sense, is the 'transactional contract' to which author and reader commit. In "Emotion and the Force of Fiction", Joseph T. Palencik follows on from a brief discussion of Matravers' interest in the didactic potential of fiction by quoting the psychologist Robinson's view that "the message of a great [work of art] is inextricable from the...experience of it" (in Palencik 2008, 260). Although Palencik goes on to challenge this view that emotion offers access to the work of art because he thinks that it fails to explain how this allows for a developed, textured response, he concludes by proposing, via Keith Oatley, that as "fiction's 'muscles and joints'", the latter "set stories in motion and help us make sense of events" (2008, 273). The challenge *The Tyrant's Novel* fails to meet is precisely this—the stories Alan Sheriff tells are never set in motion for they are constantly undermined by an authorial desire to show how hard Alan Sheriff, and 'other Alan

Sheriffs' in Australian detention camps, have had it. In the end, the refugee emerges on the page merely, or primarily, to be a sign of Thomas Keneally's goodness but not, ever, as the fully fledged human being that might make readers inhabit the condition of the refugee. Sheriff is Keneally's own 'woman refugee' as identified in Wainaina's typology.

Ultimately, there is in the novel little of the individual refugee's consciousness, of the intimate feelings that bespeak the vulnerability of genuine 'outsiders incarnate'. Rather, we are left with an arrogant, delusional, self-serving character who fails to make us feel like him. If he is like 'us', I for one would rather not discover that part of myself. The challenge the novel fails to meet is to create a figure of empathy rather than of pity, and it is hard to conceive of a neurobiological monitoring graph that would 'capture' much empathy between reader and character.

Nam Le's *The Boat* (2008) is an ambitious collection of seven short stories on a series of themes focused on place, identity and restlessness, the kind of work that has come to reflect a certain view of life in the postmodern, postcolonial world. It is not overtly about refugees yet two of the stories resonate closely with the writer's own background as the child of Vietnamese refugees who travelled to Australia. Nam Le, a brief biographical note printed on the back cover, "was born in Vietnam and grew up in Melbourne". I want to concentrate here on the work's opening story, its title already redolent of an 'intention' to channel the effects of cloyingly powerful emotions: "Love and Honour and Pity and Pride and Compassion and Sacrifice". At once ponderous and subtly ironic, the story's title hints at the complex emotions that obtain in the relationship between the two main characters, the narrator and his father and gain an extra layer in the context of the characters' ethnic background.

In "Love and Honour" the narrator reflects on the unravelling web of feelings he experiences as he and his father meet after years away from each other. Crucial to the story, theirs is not an unusual relationship among diasporic ethnic minorities, haunted by past traumas and golden dreams, and bitter disappointment. Success for the narrator, to have been selected to attend a residency at the prestigious Iowa Writers' Centre, means little to his father, but for the narrator too the earlier satisfaction has given rise to frustration, a writer's block of sorts that has seen him produce very little in the time he has been at the Centre. The father's visit both accentuates this awareness and acts as a catalyst that will see the writer start creating again.

Nam Le draws on this rather straightforward conceit to explore issues we found also in *The Tyrant's Novel.* Unspoken here as in Keneally's novel are questions that have long marked much contemporary writing: "Who can speak for the Other?" but also "Who can speak as Other?" The narrator's insight into a possible answer comes when he finally gives in to fellow writers' encouragement that he delves into his ethnic background to write an 'ethnic story': "'It's hot', a writing instructor told me at a bar. ... Ethnic literature's hot. And important too" (8). A literary agent tells him, "slowly as though intoning a mantra" that what sells is "Your *background* and *life difference*" (8). Others dissuade him from seeking refuge in this kind of writing, dismissing it as flat and unsophisticated in its mimetic emphasis. A friend, also a fellow writer, reminds him that "Faulkner...said we should write about the old verities. Love and honour and pity and pride and compassion and sacrifice" (9) and while the words hit home, as it were, the narrator resists the easy temptation to quarry his ethnic self. Then, as the father's arrival triggers a flood of memories, he produces two stories in quick succession, both centred on his father's experiences as a Vietnamese refugee but even earlier as a combatant in the Vietnam War. Both moreover, are stories about his own ethnic self, un/consciously crafted from his personal background and life experience.

Yet, while these are also the son's stories, in the way that all familial identities are produced relationally, Nam Le suggests that to narrate these stories, *to represent* these experiences is to render them alien, and to cheapen the value of lives and experiences whose meaning is inherently personal. This is made especially visible when the narrator's father comes across one of the stories and challenges the son's recall of past events and experiences: "There are mistakes in it" (22), the father tells him; and again: "There were mistakes in your last story too" (23), prompting the narrator to inform his readers: "I had sent him my refugee story" (23). The point here is not that the refugee story is not also *his* to tell, rather that it demands he recognises the father's view that no *re-presentation* will ever do justice to the kinds of experiences father and son shared. The father's gentle insistence that the story he has read cannot be meaningful because it is only ever an act of representation returns us to ideas about the limits of fiction. Yet by re-presenting the past on the page, Nam Le returns us to the possibilities that literature opens us to meaningful empathy, as posited by Attridge.

The secret, Nam Le seems to imply, rests in how a story that is not and cannot ever be individual, can be made singularly meaningful. Keneally's work illustrates that there are risks in having fiction effect empathy and perhaps even compassion and in Nam Le's story the father points that what the son wants his "refugee story" to do is to engender "*their* pity" (25; my emphasis), that of readers who are imagined as external to the background and life experiences of father and son. Despite the lack of a Preface in the manner of Keneally, Nam Le's story also seeks to record the in/visible stories and experiences of people caught up in a vortex of self-interested political debates they are powerless to inflect and in which so often they exist as mere contested signs, 'representational waste' for the good of others.

In some ways both writers employ fiction to the same effect and with similar intentions—these are important stories and it is important that *we* know about them, even if *we cannot ever know what it is to be like them.* If the moment of empathy, that encounter between us and them, readers and characters, a real imagined reader and the fictional act of re-presentation is to endure and to foster a new ethics of writing and reading, the writer needs to be aware of the risks of literary activism. What distinguishes Nam Le's story from Keneally's is the unflinching lens it turns on the act of writing and on the writer's ability to lay open the innermost self of the refugee self, not as a figure of pity and compassion but of genuine empathy. In "Love and Honour" he does it by having the violent, painful and traumatic relationship between father and son laid bare, the refugee not the stereotype identified by Binyavanga Wainaina but a fully fledged subject—vulnerable but equally capable of doing harm to others; a victim but equally a perpetrator. In comparison to Thomas Keneally, Nam Le's use of emotion is understated, almost detached, an experience that both draws readers into the text and pushes them away in a manner that foregrounds the point made by Wainaina—for most readers, the experience of the likes of Nam Le's characters, and indeed Sheriff, is only ever one they consume in a vicarious manner.

In conclusion, I want to dispel any sense that I view literary activism as, *per se*, always politically and ethically compromised; neither am I arguing that all acts of representation necessarily lead to the objectification and the commodification of the life experiences of people Other to the writer. That is not the point Wainaina sought to make and what attracts cognitive researchers to literature is precisely its ability to create the conditions for a restaging of authentic acts of empathy and in turn of genuine commitment to action and change. But as a reader I struggle to relate to the work of fiction where the background and life experiences of Others serve merely (and I grant it that it can often happen unwittingly) as a means to political activism, just as often cannily grafted onto a web of celebrity discourses.

Works Cited

Attridge, David. 2004. *J.M. Coetzee & the Ethics of Reading: Literature in the Event*. Chicago: University of Chicago Press.

Bauman, Zygmunt. 2004. Identity: Conversations with Benedetto *Vecchi*. Cambridge, UK: Polity Press; Malden, MA: Blackwell Pub.

D'Alpuget, Blanche. 1981. *Turtle Beach*. Ringwood, Victoria: Penguin.

Derrida, Jacques. 1979. "The Parergon." *October*, 9: 3-40.

Jaivin, Linda. 2006. *The Infernal Terrorist*. London: HarperCollins.

Keen, Suzanne. 2006. "A Theory of Narrative Empathy." *Narrative* 14.3: 207-36.

Keneally, Thomas. 2004. *The Tyrant's Novel*. London: Sceptre.

Leys, Ruth. 2011. "The Turn to Affect: A Critique". *Critical Inquiry*. 37.3: 434-72.

Miall, David S. 2011. "Emotions and the Structuring of Narrative Responses." *Poetics Today* 32.2: 323-48.

Nam Le. *The Boat*. 2008. Melbourne: Hamish Hamilton (Penguin).

Palencik, Joseph T. 2008. "Emotion and the Force of Fiction". *Philosophy and Literature*, 258-77.

Perera, Suvendrini. 2009. "What gain in stopping the boats?" *The Sydney Morning* Herald, November 13. www.smh.com.au/opinion/politics/what-gain-in-stopping-the-boats-20091111-i9y1.html

Pung, Alice. 2006. *Unpolished Gem*. Melbourne: Black Inc.

Said, Edward. 1978. *Orientalism*. London: Routledge.

Spivak, Gayatri C. 1985. "Three Women's Texts and a Critique of Imperialism." *Critical Inquiry*, 12.1: 43-61.

CHAPTER

20

The 'Poetics' of Borders in Amitav Ghosh's *Sea of Poppies*

Jane Fernandez
Avondale College, NSW, Australia

A fundamental feature of globalisation is the phenomena of migration and displacement with its many attendant complexities. Accordingly, there has been much discussion in recent years on "the poetics of borders". Indeed, borders have come to the foreground of our attempts to articulate the point of tension between reaching, staying within and transgressing spaces, spatially and imaginatively. Borders provide an exploration of a new form of aesthetics driven largely by a discourse that circulates around themes of "mobility", "movement" and "performance" in the face of a globalised world which has seen the emergence of a whole new body of performers who agitate against established paradigms. For many, these "border-crossers" and "border zone dwellers" speak for the collective urge in a globalised world to overcome the subversive forces of politics and economics which militate against our common freedoms (Schimanski and Wolfe 2010, 43). Refugees and migrants continue to loom large in the physical and social imaginary as people who, by transgressing borders, open up and expose the superficial layers of historical notions of ownership and politics of place and home. Ghosh's novel, *Sea of Poppies* raises the spectre of borders only to transgress or diminish them.

This essay will explore the boundaries the novel evokes and transgresses to provide a route beyond nation-spaces to a more globalised sense of place and self. What *Sea of Poppies* encourages is an interrogation of the presumed purity or sanctity of a nation's borders and a celebration of the ruptures and breaches of its contained or hegemonic spaces, pointing us to somewhere beyond the here and now. Set in India, the novel evokes the British exploitative and expedient presence as a contaminating element of the Indian landscape. English power and greed is symbolised through the motif of the poppy plant; its prolific grip over the land suggested through the title: *Sea of Poppies,* which by yoking two elemental and opposing images, superimposes connotations of volatility and unpredictability with the poppy-ridden land. In so doing, Ghosh subverts the usual connotations of fertility and productivity associated with the land by alluding to its contaminating power in the context of the opium trade. The metaphoric representation of the land's Other raises on the one hand the prevalence of the British presence in India as well as highlights the magnitude of the corruptibility of the opium trade on Indian soil. The enslavement of Indians is treated through the breakdown of both physical and moral barriers. This breakdown is suggested in the former through the implied oppositions of the symbols of the land and sea. Indeed, for most of the novel, the reader recognises the semiotic relationship between the land and sea, each dependent on the other for its identity. If the title of the novel provides an arresting image of colour and movement, it more importantly evokes also the connotations of cleansing and renewal through the reference to the sea.

Yet, the usual connotations associated with the sea are revoked here by the connotations of death conveyed through the poppy-ridden land. The scope of this reversal is treated through the sweeping image of the flow of the land's colour spreading across the drug-infested landscape. What this reversal achieves is to breach any comfort we may be tempted to succumb to from Ghosh's reference to the sea. Rather, it foreshadows the pervasive scope of the opium trade in the light of the British preoccupation with opium and the enslavement of Indians to the British cause. This pervasive power is extended further through what the title implies, that the land's corruptibility also encroaches upon the sea. This is reinforced by the fact that the land's harvest must be transported through the sea, in search of victims.

Accordingly, what the title achieves is to reinforce the entangled subjectivities of the oppressor and the oppressed, each dependent on the other for survival. In this sense, the novel reduces the connotations of master and slave to the same common denominator. Both are equally oppressed so long as they choose nothing beyond their inherited destinies. What the novel calls for then is for a border-crossing ritual. Oppression and victimisation can only be broken as men and women stand against the tyranny of their own fates. The novel brings readers to the borders of our imagination in exposing the spaces within which we confine our fears. It provides no real escape for the players on either side of the spectrum, reducing the political and the social to the same level. In this sense, the novel's political borders are absorbed into the social and cultural frame of the novel.

So, while it can be argued that *Sea of Poppies* is concerned about "political borders", our reading of borders should not be confined to the customary sense of "the separation of territories" (Schimanski Geenhuizen and Rietveld 2002, 60) but rather, it should be read in the Derridean sense of borderlands as "cultural production". Whereas traditionally we have perceived of culture as fixed and unchanging, a form of archival inheritance that demands our allegiance, Derrida asks us to think of culture as subversive, driven by ruptures "based around difference, division and borders" (qtd. in Schimanski and Wolfe 2010, 36). Derrida also provides a mode of interpreting the novel's seemingly "unfinished" ending, as will be seen at the conclusion of this discussion.

This subversion is treated in the novel through the depravity of the indentured labour system highlighting both British greed and Indian helplessness but more importantly through Ghosh's applied treatment of domestic and social relationships. While the novel exposes India's role as a breeding farm for the British exploitation of the earth's resources, it also evokes ecological and environmental concerns in as much as it appeals for an understanding of the terrible cost of human enslavement in the face of the costs for human survival. The novel establishes, through its treatment of the opium trade, the paradox that existence and living are opposing categories and that the individual must ultimately choose one or the other, just as the individual must awaken to the seamless trace of the political and the social.

Accordingly, the novel's interest is in the ways in which we are subjected by historical and social forces to participate and perform within restrictive and oppressive frameworks. It asks how and why we succumb to such forces and why we should break through those forces. The question of how individuals are subject not just to the exercise of sovereign/state power but also to the power wielded by traditional domestic, social and family structures bring the many threads of the novel into unity.

If the novel traces the state's control over its subjects, it highlights also, the equally pejorative control exercised by social forces over the individual. Through the theme of poppies, the novel brings together these two trajectories, namely the British control of the Indian nation through the exploitation of the land made subject to British interests, and the human toll on the Indian mind and body. This toll is highlighted early in the novel through the central character, Deeti, through whom the descriptions of the poppy farms are provided and through whom also the impoverishment of the Indian people is exposed and managed. This impoverishment is treated by Ghosh's casting Deeti as the novel's voice and eyes. She draws for us a vivid description of the potent power of the poppy planting she and others must endure.

The control the poppy plant has over their lives is suggested through Deeti's scrutiny of the plants, breathing "relief" only when "some of her flowers had at last begun to shed their petals" (5). Her over-dependence on the life of the plant is suggested also by the fact that her life is managed by the randomness of the plant's fruit and her forced and undivided attention to the plant's temperament, given the short lifespan of the "priceless sap" (5): "a day or two, this way or that, and the pods were of no more value than the blossoms of a weed" (6). Again, the novel returns us to the theme of borders by raising the labyrinth that Deeti must face each day as she negotiates the needs of her life in the face of the uncertainties and vulnerabilities exemplified through the poppy pods. The poppy plant becomes the prism through which Deeti's relationships are traced and audited, particularly her relationship to her husband, Hukam Singh. The fatal effects of opium are characterized through the figure of Hukam Singh, Deeti's opium-addicted husband whose failure as a husband and father signal the power of opium to destroy life, love and meaning.

Characters such as Deeti help define the element of choice in the articulation of boundaries that restrict our movement both physically and intellectually. Ghosh's treatment of Deeti, the central character in *Sea of Poppies* is significant in this regard. Deeti's employment in the novel as a figure of subversion is heralded in the first lines of the poem where she is framed as a prophetess, given a vision of the future through the image of the ship, which she comes to recognize later as the *Ibis*, an old slave ship, which paradoxically will enable her to choose freedom against all the odds of her gendered subjectivity defined by the land she turns her back on. The cost of her crossing the border between the land and sea is particularly poignant because for Deeti it involves her sacrifice of her daughter whom she leaves behind so that she can choose life.

Sea of Poppies in this sense parallels the quandary we are faced with in Morrison's *Beloved* (1987). How do mothers survive choosing and not choosing their children? Does Deeti like "slave mothers", like Morrison's Sethe, have a "special knowledge"? Can a realist account of identity spell out the claim that members of a diaspora often have a privileged, albeit sharable knowledge about their social world?" (Saldivar 2007, 343). How do we choose to forgive ourselves our most heinous crimes? These answers are treated in the novel's latter phase where Deeti's wisdom enables a recreation of self and community and a rewriting of the ocean's power in the lives of those who choose to cross borderlands, to become a wanderer. As Bhabha points out:

> wandering peoples of the world do more than alienate the frontiers of the modern state and disorient the borders of modernity. They articulate the death-in-life of the idea of the "imagined community" of the nation. It is in the disarticulation of the imagined community of the nation, and of the state, that a new imagined community, "postnationalist" and "deterritorialised" in life orientations, becomes possible. Wandering peoples of the world blast the world open to new horizons. (qtd in Soguk 2000, 425-26)

The elements of this quest for freedom are defined through the power of choice. By merely choosing, Deeti moves from death to life. The novel's preoccupation with death is treated through three points of contact: the opium pod, i.e. the kernel that bleeds life; the Ganges, i.e. the womb that receives death; and the *Ibis*, i.e. the womb that has witnessed death. My interest is in the novel's treatment of death as a "point of contact" between temporality and its Other in relation to its central character Deeti. Deeti remains the novel's prophetess and its future and Ghosh leads Deeti through several death encounters to enable her to finally recognize that life and death are as much about choices as they are about inevitabilities and risks that we cannot run from. Through Deeti, the novel encourages us to explore a "poetics" of borderlands by opening up the sealed, confined and private spaces of the conjugal home to scrutiny.

The novel provides us with the opportunity to touch the borders of both the sea and the land imaginatively through its evocation of the Ganges. Deeti's life as an oppressed wife, married while merely a child to an opium addict, Hukam Singh raises significant questions about the constitution of marriage in the context of women's gendered histories. The boundaries of homely and unhomely spaces are complicated in the characterization of Deeeti's plight as a young wife, neglected on her wedding night by her husband's "opium-induced somnolence" (37). It is complicated by her mother-in-law and brother-in-law's abuse of her mental and physical frame. The novel brings to the surface the concentrated focus in Indian society on issues of progeny and propriety expected of married women. The degree of helplessness and the extent of exploitation that is rationalized in the interest of progeny is raised in the novel through Hukam Singh's response to Deeti the morning after their wedding: "'Yes, everything was as it should be' he said. 'You gave proof of your purity to my family'" (37). The "proof of purity" that is raised here is ironical given that Deeti is violated by the family she had married into, for this supposed proof.

The novel satirises this through demonstrating the failure of the maternal models and raising the spectre of the deviant mother in the form of Deeti's mother-in-law. Her transgression of the social and psychological spaces entrusted to her care is shown through her facilitating the rape of Deeti. Through the malignant mother archetype, the novel opens up areas of enquiry regarding the sexual abuse of women within the marital setting, an issue that is regarded as "taboo" in the Indian cultural sense. In its treatment of sex, gender and tradition, the unquestionable hallmarks of patriarchal power and exploitation, the novel returns us to the motif of opium. Ghosh comments on how opium draws all the players into a vicious cycle of oppression reducing the external and internal politics of oppression to the same common denominator, i.e. through casting those closest to Deeti as traitors in the same way the British had turned traitors against the land it had colonised.

This maternal excess is treated by the connotations of the contaminated land whose wide fields of opium, are treated in the text as polluted, poisoned and bleeding. It is emphasised through the evocation of the "seedy, heady odour of the bleeding pods of opium" (29). Further, this bleeding of life is extended in the novel through Ghosh's treatment of the self-abuse of the Indian farmers, who by their complicity in working the farms, encourage their own victimisation. Accordingly, Ghosh's allusion to the morphing of life and death is suggested through Deeti's descriptions of the opium harvest. Notably, the "weight of the [opium] harvest" is presented in sacrificial terms alluding to the terrible cost of human life the opium trade will exact but in doing so, Ghosh does not minimise the complicity of both oppressor and oppressed, caught in the same web of self-deceit and death.

The fact that it is Deeti who conveys the haunting death ritual is significant because it is through her that the borders of death are raised and subverted in the novel's final analysis. Her descriptions of the potent power of the drug are prefaced by her description of the pods as "fleshy" and "plump" conveying connotations of fertility, ripeness and seduction. This is balanced by the allusion to the "bleeding pods" hinting also at the vulnerabilities of risk and death associated to the opium trade (29). The encroaching of the opium trade into Deeti's life is suggested also by her description of her hut which looked to her from a distance "like a tiny raft floating upon a river of poppies" (30). The vulnerability of home is suggested through the juxtaposition of the image of the floating raft against the river of poppies. In one sense, the novel reinforces the proximity of life and death and the terrible vulnerabilities which rule our lives. These are emphasised by Deeti's witness of the death ritual of insects drawn to the scent of the opium sap "many [of whom] would get stuck in the ooze" and whose bodies would eventually "merge into the black gum, becoming a welcome addition to the weight of the harvest" (29). The paralysing power of the opium trade is suggested further through Ghosh's allusion to the overpowering and "pacifying effect" of "the sap" on them which had in some strange way robbed "even...the butterflies" of their memory of flight: "The sap seemed to have a pacifying effect even on the butterflies, which flapped their wings in oddly erratic patterns, as though they could not remember how to fly" (29).

Deeti's witness of this is crucial as it is through her that the novel subverts the oppressive political and social elements that cripple Indian society. The fundamental aspect of this element is the question of caste which the novel resolves through the marriage of Deeti and Kalua. It is Kalua, the low-caste oxen driver who saves Deeti from the fires of *suttee*, which by her position of birth becomes an obligation. The bravery that Kalua demonstrates in risking his life to save Deeti is a central turning point in the novel and establishes the novel's concern with collapsing boundaries. The boundaries of caste are satirised by the novel's treatment of the Singh family who are depicted as depraved as discussed earlier. Deeti's ability to reinvent herself after she is saved from the funeral pyre suggests her capacity for renewal and is underlined by her alignment to the Ganges.

The Ganges becomes her witness at critical points in her encounter with life. It enables her to break free of her paralysing life, symbolized by her *suttee* identification, by enabling her escape from those rites and providing her with the means to a new life with Kalua. Her marriage to Kalua is witnessed by the Ganges, just as it is gifted by the elements of the Ganges. This is symbolised through the ceremonial flowers that Deeti collects from the river bed for her marriage garland and revokes the horror of her first-wedding-night through providing her with nature's pure elements as accompaniments to their love-making. Through Deeti and Kalua, the novel collapses the taboos associated with caste and brings together two human beings in their elemental natures celebrating intimacy and spontaneity without adherence to rules and rituals.

This crossing of boundaries is extended further through the space prepared for the couple aboard the *Ibis*. The ocean becomes the labyrinth through which Deeti demonstrates her own growth and maturity as she casts away her old life and chooses to risk everything for a life of hope with Kalua. The *Ibis* becomes the womb through which the couple find a new sense of home. Deeti's role as Bhauji, ministering to the people of different castes, nationalities and religion revokes the gendered submission and exploitation that had crippled her on land. The *Ibis* as home to slaves becomes now a home where caste and class are collapsed as evident through Deeti and Kalua's marriage and through the fact that the boundaries between Raja and peasant are also resolved through the figure of Neel.

Given the fear of crossing the *Kala Pani*, "Black Water", Deeti's ability to reflect on the sea's power to cleanse is significant as are her questions and her assumptions of fear and guilt associated to her conditioning on the land, which only the journey through the Black Waters enables her to process. It is significant that these fears and guilt over marrying Kalua and her fear of being punished for choosing happiness comes when Ecka asks her to facilitate his marriage to Heeru. For Deeti, this becomes a moral dilemma parallel to her own as both Ecka and Heeru had left behind wife and husband respectively. Given that

Heeru had been abandoned by her husband, she would never have been able to marry by Indian law.

But on the *Ibis,* it is Deeti who enables Heeru to choose marriage with Ecka, turn their backs on the past and choose a future together. And this, she is able to do only as she comes to terms with her own guilt and insecurities. The novel demonstrates that the struggle to choose happiness does not mean a total absence of fear and guilt:

> If the Black Water could really drown the past, then why, should she, Deeti, still be hearing voices in the recesses of her head, condemning her for running away with Kalua? Why should she know that no matter how hard she tried, she would never be able to silence the whispers that told her she would suffer for what she had done, not just today or tomorrow, but for *kalpas* and *yugas*, through lifetime after lifetime, into eternity. (448)

Deeti overcomes these fears by embracing and rewriting kinship, not one endorsed by birth but rather one built on the common bonds of pure human sympathy. These bonds of sympathy call for a focus on "the other as mortal", an understanding of our own mortality as a foundation for our shared kinship.

In *The Gift of Death* Derrida argues that death is the place of one's irreplaceability (qtd. in Kirkby 1995, 41) and the birth of responsibility: "my first and last responsibility... is that responsibility of responsibility that relates me to what no one else can do in my place" (qtd. in Kirkby 1995, 44). He cites Levinas' idea that "responsibility is not initially of myself or for myself", but is "derived from the other": "I am responsible for the death of the other to the extent of including myself in that death.... I am responsible for the other inasmuch as the other is mortal" (qtd. in Kirkby 2006, 462-63).

Deeti's journey both physically and psychologically invokes something of Derrida's politics of mourning. There is a sense of mourning as well as of promise which the novel balances through its treatment of the migration of the self from the old to the new world. Physically and ideologically the sojourners encounter a shift, a change, a death-rebirth encounter. Through Deeti's journey from her old to her new world, the novel traces this responsibility of the individual in transition from a closed to an open entity: that is, a self in touch with Derida's notion of responsibility "for the other inasmuch as the other is mortal". This connectedness to the other is a cathartic encounter with the self, one that Deeti experiences as a cleansing of the prejudices of the old world, an opportunity for a new sense of self and community: "And wasn't it she herself who had said, at the start, that they were all kin now; that their rebirth in the ship's womb had made them into a single family?" (449).

This celebration of renewal is epitomised in the novel through the symbol of marriage. The emergence of a new community bonded by their experience of displacement and suffering is endorsed in the novel through Heeru and Ecka's marriage. The fact that the entire community organises and supports the couple's wedding rites is significant. Of particular note is the fact that the wedding ritual is created and resourced by the community in the *debusa*. Each brings a personal gift for the couple and the emotional and psychological support the couple need and receive is portrayed touchingly through the fact that the new community actually lends the physical weight of their bodies to support the newly married couple, propping them up against the violent movement of the ship. The sea's ability to dissolve previously held prejudices and taboos is celebrated through the marriage rite and through the interconnected bonds of sympathy the inmates express and develop.

In this regard, the novel evokes several symbols that enable us to trace the trajectory through which Deeti eventually frees herself of the historical and socially-induced oppressive regimes that manipulate her existence. Deeti's journey through the novel is traced through several "contact points" which enable her to transit through each of these borders and eventually face the moment where she submits to rewriting her life and destiny in relation to the "common bonds of pure human sympathy" the novel invites us to participate in. It is through Deeti's confrontation of the Other, the sea, the community on board the *Ibis*, represented by different castes, class and language that she is reborn as a leader, *"Bauji"*, a universal sister-comrade, rewriting the codes of conduct and new marriage laws, subverting the oppression she had suffered on the land by embracing the future the sea provides her with through her confronting the "*Kala Pani*", the "Black Waters".

At the close of the novel, Deeti is left in the quandary between the borders of life and death. Shc watches silently from the deck as she and her husband are forced apart. Her acceptance of that separation is treated through her silent witness of his being taken from her so that his life may be saved. In that final witnessing, the distance between Deeti and Kalua reiterates a new border that is yet unchartered for each of them, an awakening to "mourning", "memory" and "responsibility".

Derrida points out that all our relationships are from the beginning tinged with mourning, for the unspoken truth of every friendship is that one of us will live to see the other die "there is no friendship without this knowledge of finitude" (qtd. in Kirkby 2006, 464). Derrida argues that "we are who we are because of the memory of those we have loved and carry within us" (qtd. in Kirkby 2006, 464). For Deeti, this is the border of mourning, a time of "responsibility" and waiting to know the future.

And if we were to attempt to make meaning of the parting of the two points of contact the novel closes on, i.e. with Deeti on the the *Ibis* and Kalua on a boat to somewhere else, we could "well ask like Derrida, what is the place of mourning and where 'might the politics of mourning reside'"? (Kirkby 2006, 470). To borrow Kirkby's observation, "I think Derrida's answer to this question would circle around his idea of the *aporia* as a gift for the future, a provocation to think new paths, new ways through apparent impasses" (Kirkby 2006, 470). To reach a border is a gift.

Works Cited

Ghosh, A. 2008. *Sea of Poppies*. John Murray, London.

Kirkby, J. 2006. "Remembrance of the Future: Derrida on Mourning". *Social Semiotics*, 16(3): 461-72.

Saldívar, J.D. 2007. "Unsettling Race, Coloniality and Caste". *Cultural Studies*, 21(2): 339-67.

Schimanski, J. and Wolfe, S. 2010. "Cultural production and negotiation of borders: Introduction to the Dossier". *Journal of Borderlands Studies*, 25(1): 38-49.

Soguk, N. 2000. "Poetics of a World of Migrancy: Migratory Horizons, Passages, and Encounters of Alterity". *Global Society*, 14(3): 415-42.

van Geenhuizen, M. and Rietveld, P. 2002. "Land-borders and sea-borders: An exploration of differences in border region development". *Journal of Borderlands Studies*, 17(2): 63-77.

CHAPTER

21

Travelling Cultures in Global Currents: A Reading of Amitav Ghosh's *River of Smoke*

Prantik Banerjee
Hislop College, Nagpur, India

Where are your monuments, your battles, martyrs?
Where is your tribal memory? Sirs,
in that grey vault. The sea.
...
The sea is History.
(Derek Walcott 1992, "The Sea is History")

In his writings, Amitav Ghosh 'relocates' the migrant from the margin and makes his hidden, suppressed history a corrective to national or grand, global narratives. He also signposts the historical and material differences that define the cultural provenances of varied groups of migrants. The people in Ghosh's histories are displaced from their original locations due to a variety of reasons: war, partition, riots, ecological disasters, economic compulsions, trade and commerce, or societal pressures. They traverse regions collapsing borders and boundaries, carrying with them their affiliations to country, community, caste, class and gender, and then attempt to renegotiate their local identities with global enculturation. Ghosh's narratives of travel and migrancy advocate the need to cultivate a cosmopolitan multiculturalism without resorting to teleological myths of unitary identities and discrete cultures. Enlisting the recovery of subaltern histories and analysing the continuing legacy of colonial and neo-colonial inequities in defining the contours of the modern world, Ghosh stresses the need to enter into an ongoing practice of intercultural dialogue, but without guarantees.

Sea of Poppies and *River of Smoke*, the first two parts of his '*Ibis* trilogy', seem to be, in particular, a searching examination of cultural borderlands at whose porous intersections alterity and diversity are negotiated at different levels, thereby presenting an outlook of what I would term "critical cosmopolitanism". My analysis of *River of Smoke* shows how the novel displays the familiar features of all diasporic writing—border crossing and immigrant experience—but will also show how it is distinctive in at least two significant ways.

Roger Bromley proposes that every diasporic narrative is "both an individual story and, explicitly, a cultural narrative" (2000, 21). This essay contends that in the *River of Smoke*, Ghosh, firstly, favours a more discriminating investigation of 'discrepant' travelling cultures and cosmopolitan identities by locating their "unresolved historical dialogues between continuity and disruption, essence and positionality, homogeneity and difference" in the "specific, often violent, histories of economic, political, and cultural interaction" (Clifford 1992, 108).

Second, Ghosh's writing in general, and the *Ibis* trilogy in particular, reflects a predilection for the intricate historical connections of trade, cultures and peoples that comprise pre/colonial cosmopolitanisms in South East Asian and Middle-Eastern histories. The location of his fiction, outside the "cartographic circle of Europe" (Dharwadker 2001, 3), is where cultural identities get re-located in diasporic spaces, in global movements of power and capital. The ship's travelling space in *River of Smoke* is for Ghosh a metaphorical extension of diasporic consciousness, wherein common bonds created by shared origins are sundered in dispersal and new ties are forged through co-option and collaboration. The focus of displacement being on people-centred migration 'from below' provides a critical alternative to reified notions of identity, difference and belonging.

'Mainstreaming' *River of Smoke*

The backdrop of the *River of Smoke* is provided by events leading up to the First Opium War between Great Britain and China (1838-39). The text exposes a colonial history of ruthless exploitation: its use of threat, force and subterfuge to drug a resistant nation to submission; its exploitation of colonies like India, Mauritius, Macau and Java; and, its unscrupulous use of the principles of so-called "fair" and "free" trade by Europe to make ill-gotten gains. Ghosh delivers a damning indictment of British colonialism by showing how millions of human lives came under its sway with tragic consequences.

The text reminds us that nearly one-fifth of Britain's colonial revenue was provided by the opium trade and that, without it, the Empire itself could not have been sustained. But when Britain's drug-peddling is resisted by the Manchu dynasty, she prepares to go to war to defend the financial engine of its empire. The novel exposes this duplicity:

> The Weiyuen says he cannot believe that any country would be so barbaric as to allow its merchants the freedom to harm and despoil the people of a foreign realm. This is not freedom—it is akin to piracy. No government could possibly condone it. (402)

The arrival in 1838 of Commissioner Lin Zexu to Canton brings the political crisis to a head. The Commissioner adopts a no-nonsense approach, and when his conciliatory measures fail to have any impact on the European factory owners, he enforces a blockade on their opium-laden ships and brings in soldiers to halt the activities of the Hong. The story follows an inexorable path of confrontation between the Empire and its trading agents, the East India Company and the Cantonese authorities.

Ghosh's *River of Smoke* makes Canton and Macau, China's trading outposts in the 19th century, the centre of its action. His vivid description of its ports, wharves, market places, streets, shops and houses, and his colourful portrayal of seamen, traders, merchants, coolies, lascars, colonial bureaucrats and Chinese mandarins, of every colour and race, capture the exotica that had made the Orient a place of fabulous "discovery" by colonial enterprise. Britain uses Chinese ports as conduits for smuggling drugs into the mainland. Like Cairo, Tunisia, Malay, Rangoon and Malabar in the earlier novels, Canton here is delineated as a space where international mercantile trade, imperial ambitions and multicultural exchange make for a complex and varied narrative. The novel is a nostalgic paean to the rise and fall of this Oriental city, capturing in fine detail its sights, sounds and flavours as an endless stream of people come and go. Its destruction, nevertheless, is wrought by imperial power and greed. The city is bombarded by British and French gunships as the First Opium War starts and Imperialism's triumph crushingly reduces the once bustling city to a "monument built by the forces of evil" (533).

The narrative is replete with hundreds of period nuances and trivia—from sartorial styles, cuisines and pottery to horticultural nomenclature and miniature paintings—meant to showcase the range of cultural exchanges that took place in Southeast Asia in the mid-1800s. The most arcane pieces of information become anthropological cues of transcultural fusion. How curious it is, for instance, to know that: "*chopsui*" the most famous import of Chinese cuisine to the rest of the world, was actually the handiwork of a steward serving the East India Company, who went to China as a boy; or that it was a Parsi cook who invented "*chai*" by adding milk, "*cheeni*" (another Chinese import) and clove, cinnamon and star anise to the *chah* that was commonly served in Canton. Or even the fact that Chinese porcelain, a craze with European households, was indeed made by Cantonese pottery makers, but whose "oriental designs" were actually supplied by Western traders who did business in Canton.

Ghosh seems to deliberately invert the process of what Gayatri Spivak calls 'worldling'. In contrast to Western meta-narratives, here it is Europe that is spatially located within a South Eastern region essentially constructed by a pre-existing network of connections. This kind of postcolonial inscription makes colonised places more than just an inert space that was overwritten by European intervention. Rather, Ghosh amply demonstrates how a colonial site was actually the hub of the most vigorous trade and cultural transmission long before it was colonised. This kind of revision of both history and historiography is consistent with Ghosh's imaginative reconstruction of other suppressed narratives throughout his fiction.

Alternative Modernities and Subaltern Cosmopolitanism

Like *Sea of Poppies* Ghosh's *River of Smoke* is also engaged with the critical theme of location, culture and identity. Issues of "home" and "belonging" in diasporic spaces are mediated through the dislocated lives of people caught in history's sweeping movements. Ghosh recreates for his readers a richly detailed phenomenon of cultural osmosis in the changing Eastern world of the period 1815-40. The convergence of merchants, traders, sea-farers, colonial administrators, missionaries, etc., belonging to different races, creed and nations to the port cities of Calcutta, Canton, Singapore and Hong Kong, establishes a locationary site for a complex and dynamic engagement of places, cultures and identities. That Western imperialism had caused serious ruptures in the historical tradition of a culture of accommodation and compromise in non-Western regions is a thesis that Ghosh had amply demonstrated in his earlier work, *In an Antique Land*.

What is proposed in *River of Smoke* is that homelands get inscribed into a new location in a curious paradox of de-territorialization and re-territorialization, where the material culture and spatial location is "foreign" while the metaphoric space is "home". The twining of colonial structures with global flows of labour, capital and goods leads to the production of a site where complex patterns of intra- and inter-cultural relationships are formed. The new socio-cultural formations recoup alternative modernities, other than the historicised version of Enlightenment's Modernity and project possibilities for subaltern cosmopolitanism.

For example, the novel shows the formation of several kinds of solidarities in a multi-cultural site: solidarity between two or more ethnic minority groups (Blacks, Armenians, Parsis, low-caste Hindus), solidarity of oppressed, marginal groups (migrants, refugees, coolies, sepoys, sea-farers), and solidarity of women (mainly of the lower classes). These unique social formations are a good example of subaltern cosmopolitanism or that considers the marginalized individual as the ultimate unit, and a unit "entitled to equal consideration regardless of nationality and citizenship" (Tan 2004,1). It is, nevertheless, a cosmopolitanism because of the nature of social collectivities that emerge out of transnational dislocations, of a cultural identity that is always in transition and in translation, and of subjectivities that are involved in a process of being and never becoming.

Not a "Collective Identity" but a "Collection of Identities"

River of Smoke begins with the storm that struck the convict ship the *Ibis* at the end of *Sea of Poppies*. *Redruth*, the vessel of a Cornish plant-hunter, Frederick 'Fitcher' Penrose, sails into Port Louis, Mauritius, two days after the *Ibis*, while the *Anahita*, belonging to Bahram Modi, a Bombay opium merchant, encounters the same storm on the other side of the Indian Ocean. The main narrative again brings in a large cast of characters, including the five characters who had in the prequel jumped ship, ridden the rough sea on a boat and found themselves on the island of Great Nicobar in the Indian Ocean.

The story recreates a small community of Indians in Canton in the mid-nineteenth century at a time of high imperialism—migrants who are "*khidmatgars, daftardars, khansamas, chuprassies, peons, durwans, khalasis and lascars*" (185). So, Fungtai Hong, the foreign enclave in Canton, significantly has "no flag of its own" (185), and is described thus:

> ...a world in itself, with its own foods and words, rituals and routines: it was as if the inmates were the first inhabitants of a new country, a yet unmade Acchasthan...on the face of it, the idea that the Achhas might form a family of some kind was not just improbable but absurd: they were a motley gathering of men from distant parts of the Indian subcontinent and they spoke between them more than a dozen different languages.... (192)

Acchasthan is Benedict Anderson's 'imagined community', a socio-political space where subjects in their ordinary lives must constantly arbitrate between the local and global, nation and transnational, and communal and community. It is the "Third Space of enunciation" (Bhabha 1994, 37), an in-between location that is contradictory and ambivalent, making all claims to a hierarchical purity of cultures untenable, and, additionally, overriding an enfeebled alterity in favour of an empowering hybridity.

Moreover, when migrants are compelled by the politics of colonial trade and global capitalism to form local communities in diasporic spaces, like the Indians in Acchasthan, their brokerage of place, identity and culture hints at a new-age cosmopolitanism that is a compromise between "sameness" and "otherness". One may argue that whereas globalisation weakens the putative nexus between nation and state, releasing ethnic minorities and allowing new social formations beyond borders, it also pluralises the world by recognizing the values of cultural niches and local abilities.

At the center of Ghosh's story stands a man who owes his life to Canton and to the opium trade: Bahram Modi, a Parsi merchant from Bombay. His fortunes are crucially tied to the fate of the *Anahita* which is carrying three thousand chests of opium, "the single most valuable cargo that had ever been carried out of the Indian subcontinent" (45). Entirely absent from the first book of the trilogy, he is almost everywhere in the second, and serves as the narrative's pivotal figure.

It is not without reason that Ghosh makes Bahram the helmsman of this travelling tale of epic proportions: he is a member of a Zoroastrian group in Bombay, descendants of Persian refugees who came to Western India in the 7th and 8th centuries. Bahram, then, has an ancestry that is the prototype of the wandering migrant, and whose own position in the country of his adoption is both of the insider and the outsider. His hyphenated identity escapes all essential ontological categories, and its instability and mutability is further complicated by his business location in China. The fact that he has taken a Chinese woman and has a child by her also marks him and his progeny as fated to move between ethnic and cultural borders.

In *River of Smoke* names change, castes are cast away, races get mixed, gender-roles are transgressed. The characters of Paulette, Robin Chinnery and Zachary Reid demonstrate a constant "slippage" from essential categories of race, class, and even gender. Chinnery's character is a prime example of this disorienting phenomenon. Like Baboo Nob Kissin in *Sea of Poppies*, Chinnery is a queer so far as his sexual orientation is concerned. During his stay in Canton he sets up with an oriental lover to whom he is obsessively attached. His letters to Paulette are filled with explicit details of this scandalous relationship. It is interesting that Ghosh makes the entire action in Canton unfold through the letters of Chinnery. This may be construed as a deliberate ploy to give the agentive power of history's representation to a 'deviant character', one who is traditionally marginalised in imperialism's gendered discourse and has no say in its articulation.

One important postcolonial move in Ghosh's text is to show how Indians, like Bahram Mody, "travel East". Here, Ghosh is cleverly subverting several stereotypes that have historically underpinned the imperial discourse. First, the journey of an Indian travelling East is meant to offset the classical trope of the European traveller as the Imperial adventurer setting out eastwards, in a bid to master hostile lands and a savage people. Ghosh has himself acknowledged that his imagination has always been deeply engaged with India's equivalent of the "near abroad", to correct the East-West binarism that is the foundational premise of western epistemologies. His counter-move as opposed to "going west" enables him to recoup other travel and cultural routes that make for "alternative modernities".

Linguistic Crossings

The location of subjects in Ghosh's *Ibis* triptych is a global arena marked by cataclysmic cultural interpenetration, one that provides layered linguistic *topoi* where migrant subjects construct an idiom that allows them to overcome cultural and political boundaries. With an acutely nuanced sense of historical detail, Ghosh recreates local variants of languages that made the diverse communities in Canton in the nineteenth century a *lingua communis*—a goulash of English, Hindustani, Gujarati, Parsi, Bhojpuri, Martinique creole, Portuguese, and Cantonese that enabled traders and lovers to simply communicate across boundaries of race, nation and culture.

We hear the musical lilt of Deeti's strange mixture of Bhojpuri and Creole that becomes her personal idiom as she relates events on the *Ibis* that fateful night: "I thought vreman I'd lost my sight. It was so dark nothing was vizib except when lightning flashed—and tulétan the rain [...] and the thunder, dham-dhamak-dhamakaoing as if to deafen you. [...] you can't imagine how difisil it was..." (21). Robin Chinnery's conversation transports us to Jane Austen's England. And we are charmed by the sing-song of pidgin as Chi-mei, the Chinese washerwoman and widow sympathises with Bahram: "Mister Barry trouble have got? Bhongi sadinside?" (70). The 'lob-pidgin' sessions between them are a delightful rendering of love in the time of transculturation.

Conclusion

In *River of Smoke* Ghosh reveals how colonial expansion and imperial capitalism in the 19th century formed the historical antecedents of the modern phenomenon known as globalisation and how the South China Sea became the colonial theatre, the fluid location on which colonial trade and transnational capital played out some its most fascinating scripts. This maritime mapping may thus be seen as Ghosh's attempt to break free of the territorial limits of nation-states defined by rigidities of land and explore the dynamic nature of cultural identity in the fluid, open spaces of the sea and the ocean. The use of "sea", "ship", and "boat" as metaphors for travelling cultures and plural identities disrupt the settled geographies of the self-imposed by nationalist traditions and celebrate cosmopolitanism as marked by cross-cultural transfigurations. To sum up, *River of Smoke* serves to locate the dislocation of people who are swept by the tide of global flows to constitute a flexible citizenship, a citizenry that stands across cultural borderlands.

Works Cited

Anderson, B. 1993. *Imagined Communities: Reflections on the Origin and Spread of Nationalism*. London: Verso.

Bhabha, Homi. 1994. *The Location of Culture*. London: Routledge.

Bromley, Roger. 2000. *Narratives for a New Belonging: Diasporic Cultural Fictions*. Edinburgh: Edinburgh University Press.

Clifford, James. 1992. "Travelling Cultures". *Cultural Studies*. Ed. Lawrence Grossberg, Cary Nelson, and Paula A. Treichler. New York: Routledge. 96-116.

Dharwadker, Vinay. 2001. *Cosmopolitan Geographies*. Ed. and intro. New York and London: Routledge.

Ghosh, Amitav. 2011. *River of Smoke*. New Delhi: Hamish Hamilton, Penguin.

———. 2008. *Sea of Poppies*. New Delhi: Viking, Penguin.

Tan, Kok-Chor. 2004. Justice Without Borders: Cosmopolitanism, Nationalism and Patriotism. Cambridge: Cambridge University Press.

Walcott, Derek. 1992. *Poems: 1965-1980*. London: J. Cape.

CHAPTER 22

Global Models, Local Products: Advaita Kala and Indian Chick Lit

Parimala Kulkarni
Osmania University, India

Advaita Kala's debut novel *Almost Single* (2007), first published in India by Harper Collins became a huge commercial success, with sales estimated at more than a 10,00,000 copies (Venkatesh 2011). The book did good business in other parts of the world as well when Random House published the American edition in early 2009. It was released in French by Hachette (*Love Masala,* 2009), and also in Marathi and Hindi (*Lagbhag Single*, 2010) by Harper Collins. Photocopies of her book were also distributed surreptitiously in Saudi Arabia (Chatterjee 2009). In this essay I examine Advaita Kala's *Almost Single* as a product of "chick lit", the global media empire which is anchored in the Anglo-American neoliberal ideology "that has moved beyond the economic dimension of maximized profit-making into the socio-cultural domain of subject formation" (Chen 2010, 243). I argue that the novel, *Almost Single,* considered an Indianised version of *Bridget Jones Diary*, produces a conception of female subjectivity embedded in a heteropatriarchal, racist, ageist and neoliberal capitalist ideology. However, while I argue that the novel endorses the normative order of the global neoliberal ideology, I also argue that it is imperative not to disregard the resistance that *Almost Single* offers to the primacy of patriarchal institutions like the traditional family and the arranged marriage both of which, despite claims to the contrary, enjoy a robust presence in most Indian middle class communities not only in rural but also in urban spaces.

The essay is divided into two sections: the first part provides an overview of the origin and growth of the chick lit genre in Britain and America and traces its trajectory across the globe. This section also reviews the critical response to this genre in and outside Britain and America by both hegemonic and transnational feminisms. The focus of the second part is on Kala's *Almost Single*. This section attempts an analysis of the novel to examine how it adheres to the conventional Anglo-American chick lit formula while simultaneously breaking away from some of the conventional institutions like arranged marriage and family which are deep-seated in the Indian patriarchal thought and which aid in reinforcing and perpetuating gender stereotypes and unequal relations between the sexes. The paper concludes that *Almost Single* articulates a heteronormative, patriarchal, neoliberal capitalist sensibility, and is embedded in postfeminism which simultaneously embodies entangled discourses of feminism and antifeminism (Gill 2007).

'Chick lit' is the genre of popular literature that arose in the UK and the US towards the close of the twentieth century. Chick lit continues the legacy of the romance tradition's preoccupation with heterosexual romance. However, chick lit departs from the traditional women's romance by emphasising the female characters' sexual assertiveness and financial autonomy. Unlike the passive, virginal and domesticated heroines of traditional romance who are fixated on their own private romance and wait patiently for marriage with the one dominant male (Modleski 1982, 21), chick lit protagonists are sexually active, inhabiting a fashionable cosmopolitan scene, seeking to balance personal and professional lives. From objectification the female characters have moved to subjectification. But it seems "the codes of traditional romance are reinstated 'through the backdoor'" (Gill 2006, 494) and further, as argued by Gill, chick lit, like traditional romance, offers precisely the promise of transcendent love and sexual satisfaction discussed by Modleski (1982). Thus the chick lit genre appears to be a mutation of the romance genre.

The term 'chick lit' was originally employed ironically by Cris Mazza and Jeffrey DeShell in their anthology *Chick Lit: Postfeminist Fiction* (1995). The anthology contained some fictional works intended to project a new approach to contemporary women's experience; one that both echoes the influence of feminism as well as addresses questions feminism is supposed to have ignored or neglected. But what they had not anticipated was that less than two years later their "tag would be greasing the commercial book industry machine" (Mazza 2006:, 18). And the term subsequently emerged as a brand name for a particular type of commercial fiction frequently described as 'by women, for women and of women'.

In the United Kingdom, Helen Fielding's *Bridget Jones's Diary* (1996) is frequently considered to have launched the multimillion dollar publishing phenomenon of the chick lit genre contributing to what publishers termed a "commercial tsunami" (Ferriss and Young 2006:, 2). The phenomenal success of its film version set a benchmark in British film success. But more significant than the economic gains however, was the explosion of discourses about Bridget Jones. She turned into "an icon, a recognisable emblem of a particular kind of femininity, a constructed point of identification for women" (Gill and Herdieckerhoff 2007, 489). As pointed out by Gill and Herdieckerhoff, *Bridget Jones's Diary* spawned huge numbers of "copycat" novels focusing on the life of a 'thirty something' female who was unhappily single, appealingly neurotic, and preoccupied with the shape, size, and look of her body, and with finding a man (489). *Bridget Jones's Diary* remains for most the "touchstone of what chick lit is" (Whelehan 2011). Candace Bushnell's *Sex and the City* (1996) published in the United States also proved to be hugely popular, spawning an equally popular television series and a deluge of chick lit fiction followed. By the late 1990s the genre was well-established.

The initial era of the Anglo-American 'white' chick lit was followed by the emergence of a wide variety of sub-genres, appealing to distinctly segmented markets, crossing the divides of generation, ethnicity, nationality and gender. The genre sub-morphed into Hen Lit, Mommy Lit, Matron Lit, Teen Lit, Bride lit, Bridezilla Lit, and Christian Lit or Church Lit. Then it crossed the racial divide in Ethnic Lit like Chica Lit, Sistah Lit, Jewish Chick Lit, South Asian Chick Lit, etc. The genre also traversed the gender boundary with the rise of the Lad Lit or Dick lit. Now, chick lit is on a global trot, expanding beyond the borders of the UK and the US, making inroads into different parts of the world, including those of highly conformist societies like Saudi Arabia. The global publishing tsunami unleashed gigantic tidal waves targeting markets in the developing and ex-communist countries which are experiencing the expansion of global capitalism and the increasing influence of the Anglo-American neo-liberal socio-economic and cultural standards and values. The mushrooming of the global chick lit in South America, Asia and Eastern Europe is evidence of what Paul Virilio (1997) in a different context, refers to as "globaritarian" mechanisms of the chick lit media empire, embedded in the neoliberal market rationality. Bridget Jones has "triumphantly ventured out of Britannia and colonized the world" (Misra 2011). The consequence is a "chick lit pandemic" seeking to capture new territorial markets and "tapping into larger social shifts in places...where traditional values collide in unexpected ways with a new economic order" of neoliberal capitalism (Donadio 2006).

Chick lit's foray into the Anglo-American commercial fiction category received two extreme responses of enthusiastic defense and harsh criticism. Defenders considered 'choice', 'freedom' and 'agency', "the magic words forever cited by chick lit heroines to symbolize their liberation and progress over women of the past" (Chen 2010, 253) while British novelists like Beryl Bairnbridge and Doris Lessing dismissed the genre as "trashy fiction", and "froth" (Ferriss and Young 2006, 1) and Maureen Dowd, in her *New York Times* column, complained about the spread of this "fluffy" genre. Much of the early chick lit criticism dismisses the genre as a symptom of commodification, retrosexism, patriarchy or antifeminist backlash. Recent discussions in the popular and academic spheres understand the genre in a framework of postfeminism. Such readings consider chick lit as an "apolitical" genre. Despite chick lit assuming diverse global avatars, most critical readings of chick lit either focus on novels written by and about white American and British women, or collapse the differences among distinct subgenres. However, as Pamela Butler and Jigna Desai argue, such readings reflect the limitations of the hegemonic feminist thought which "assumes chick lit to be a homogeneously white normative genre to be read primarily for its relationship to feminism and femininity, to the exclusion of other forms of social difference" (2008, 2).

In their readings of chick lit in general and of South Asian American chick lit as a particular women of color subgenre, Butler and Desai employ race and transnational feminist critiques to foreground questions of race, nation, empire, and political economy which "illuminates not only the operations of chick lit and the middle-class neoliberal subjects it produces, but also interrogates the ways in which hegemonic feminisms in the U.S. (as exemplified by chick-lit criticism) continue to disregard such questions" (2). Their critique highlights the ways in which chick lit works to produce a transnational racialized feminine subject embedded within neoliberalism, heteronormativity, and racism (2). In doing so, Butler and Desai shift the grounds for engaging chick lit away from those defined by dominant chick-lit criticisms (which emphasize the supposedly apolitical nature of chick lit or trace its feminist genealogies only to a Western liberal feminism originating with Jane

Austen), to a framework guided by critical race and transnational feminism (4-5). Eva Chen, in her reading of *Shanghai Baby* (1999) by Weihui Zhou, argues that global chick lit works in tandem with the economic policies of global capitalism that breaks down national/ geographical borders, and promises a desirable world order of universalized choice and freedom, where geopolitics and biopolitics combine together to aid the expansion of Anglo-American neoliberal ideas (2011, 1).

Chick lit arrived in India after nearly a decade since its inception in the Anglo-American media. India is a country of several languages (its 1.2 billion people share 22 official languages, each spoken by at least a million people; and more than a hundred regional languages), yet "it is English language publishing in India that gets international—and Indian—attention" (Urvasi Butalia qtd in Ogunlesi 2011). The scope of English-language publishing in India has expanded exceptionally in recent times. With an estimated 550 million people below the age of 30 (Pathak 2011), and a significant upwardly mobile neoliberal English-speaking middle class, book sales in the country have surpassed expectations bringing in massive profits. It is not surprising then that the publishers are trying new and innovative strategies to tap into this huge market. For instance, a country that had only a small number of authors writing in English a couple of decades ago, now prides itself on a book launch almost every day of the year; moreover, new literary awards are regularly being instituted, and there has been a recent proliferation of literary festivals (Pathak 2011). With an expanding market in the subcontinent, the argument of writing for a foreign readership is no longer applicable. The entry of the global publishing houses (following the post-1990s market liberalization process) ushered in neoliberal business models of production, distribution and consumption and the era of agents and commissioned writing in India. In this commercially flourishing English-language publishing industry in India, "ladki lit" to borrow Sunaina Kumar's term (2006) for the Indian version of chick lit, has captured the hitherto untapped market segment of the 'popular' writing targeting the young, urban, English-educated, middle-class females, living and working in the Indian metropolises.

Indian chick lit books, which use English as it is spoken by many Indians, spliced with Hindi, share many features of its western counterpart: typically Indian chick lit portrays cosmopolitan single women in their twenties and thirties, living in urban spaces, with jobs mostly related to media, public relations, fashion or film industry, looking for heterosexual love and romance and preoccupied with brand names, body image and addiction. However this "masala chick lit" is peppered with typically Indian themes like arranged marriage, matrimonial advertisements along with domineering mothers and interfering neighbours. Indian chick lit is embedded in the neoliberal discourses of freedom, choice and agency which are seen as central in the chick lit conception of female empowerment and emancipation. The desire for "liberation" is often seen as contained in individual choice and consumerist pleasure.

"Neoliberalism" is a term used to describe economic practices since the 1970s that include deregulation, the dismantling of social-welfare programs, and the privatisation of public service. Michel Foucault claims that neoliberalism posits a marketisation of all human spheres and perceives the individual as *homo economicus*, a subject who freely deliberates every action based on a rational cost-benefit calculation. Morality or ethics is now seen to reside in the responsibility which the individual must shoulder for his/her own marketized choices. Moreover, the neoliberal subject is one of competition. This subject is then obliged to adopt market values in all her actions in order to incessantly build up human capital and become an entrepreneur of herself. The subject is thus both compelled and enabled

(Foucault 2008, 12, 139, 226). As a political ideology, neoliberalism entails a re-envisaging of liberal individualism through the concepts of "choice" and "consumer sovereignty". A prominent discourse in both democratic politics and consumer culture, "choice", according to Inderpal Grewal, has also become fundamental to what she calls "neoliberal feminism" (2005, 28). While twentieth-century liberal feminisms sometimes used the concept of "choice" in appeals for rights ensured by the state, the notion of "having choices" increasingly signifies feminine agency (Grewal 2005, 28).

Advaita Kala's *Almost Single* posits a neoliberal feminist discourse based on the notion of "choice". Hailed as the Asian Bridget Jones (Bhowmick 2009), *Almost Single* perfectly fits into the formulaic fiction of the chick lit genre. It has all the essential features of global chick lit: a first person confessional narrative by a twenty-nine-year-old single woman Aisha Bhatia, living in the country's capital New Delhi away from her family, and working as a guest relations manager at the five-star Grand Orchid Hotel. Her "elective family" comprises a small group of close friends: a divorcee, an unmarried girl and a gay couple. She enjoys a cosmopolitan lifestyle complete with pubs, discos and blind dates. She has a philandering boss. She perceives herself to be flawed, as she is endowed with a "generous proportions" and unable to compete in the dating market, and therefore on a path of continual self-improvement which includes abortive diet regimes, neglected gym membership and fashion disasters. The future Mr. Right, Karan Verma, a handsome NRI is attracted to the innate virtues of the heroine, and loves her despite her perceived faults. The global recipe is peppered with local flavours: the archetypal over-domineering mother, astrologers, online matrimonial websites, inquisitive neighbours, *sadhus* and *sadhvis*, and *Karva Chauth*.

As Stuart Hall points out "popular culture is one of the sites where this struggle for and against a culture of the powerful is engaged.... It is the arena of the consent and resistance. It is partly where hegemony arises, and where it is secured" (1981, 239). Extending Hall's argument, I argue that Indian chick lit is an important site in the struggle for and against the cultural and ideological hegemony of the dominant groups.

Kala's *Almost Single* operates within the framework of the Anglo-American neoliberal ideology with its emphasis on choice, agency and conspicuous consumerism. Aisha's friend Misha is a typical neoliberal subject, her only ambition is to net a perfect NRI, for which she has moved from the small town Bhatinda to the country's capital, New Delhi known for unobstructed circulation of the top fashion brands, the latest trends, the freest capital flow and global lifestyle, and the most eligible, cosmopolitan men and women. She believes she has to take being single into her own hands and decides to go online shopping for a husband as she thinks she is too cosmopolitan for the local boys (8). Aisha Bhatia, marketed as Bridget Jones in a sari, however still retains a certain aura of the Mills & Boon (the novel actually recalls the type) romance heroines. She nurtures romantic ideas of meeting the right man and marrying for love. However it is also important to interrogate the sites where the book contests the hegemony of the dominant groups.

Two such sites of contestation are the traditional "arranged marriage' and "family" which are integral to the conception of Indian patriarchy even in the twenty-first century globalised India. A sociologist, Patricia Uberoi (2009) points out that it was widely expected that the custom of arranged marriage would decline as India modernised and individualistic thinking grew. The institution has no legal status according to the Hindu Marriage Act (1955) or the Special Marriage Act (1954).

Moreover, romantic love is a conspicuous motif in the popular mass media. Yet, the institution of arranged marriage has proved surprisingly robust, continuing to account for the vast majority (an estimated 90 per cent) of marriages in all communities and this is not restricted to the "traditional" sector of rural society (24). Though arranged marriage remains the rule, the idea of romantic love and courtship is socially acceptable, if at all, only if it leads to marriage (26). Nevertheless, romantic love provokes a great deal of concern. Uberoi points out the important reason for this is the "high premium placed on a bride's virginity" in accordance with the ideology of "kanyadana", the purest of all gifts (25). The institution of arranged marriage is at the core of the tension between surrender to the family and the aspiration for personal autonomy and individual freedom of choice.

Another site for contesting the dominant order is the "family', the "epitome of heteropatriarchy and heterosexuality" (Vasudevan 2008, 139) which has become an icon for the Indian nation. Nuclear families remain the predominant family form in India, though the joint family also continues to be an empirically significant household type (Uberoi 2009, 24). In this system daughters are undervalued and treated as temporary "guests" in their natal homes and post-marriage, they are required to move from their natal family to their marital family (30). In this context, it is also important to understand that marriage is projected not as a means of individual self-fulfilment but as primarily a union between families (31). Aisha of *Almost Single* resists both; choosing to stay outside of the patriarchal family and opting out of arranged marriage. Instead she prefers the single status (even if only temporarily) and though she moves away from her natal home, she lives independently with her "family" of friends before she can think of living in the conjugal home thereby subverting the patriarchal conceptions of the feminine. The emphasis on refusing the traditional passive roles assigned to women and actively seeking 'choice' and 'agency' in changing women's lives reflects a feminist sensibility and points to feminist concerns.

An increasing number of women in contemporary India are opting to remain single. Still, the number remains small. Traditionally single women have had no presence in most Indian cultures. It is significant that there appears to be no suitable term in any major Indian language to denote this status; there seems to be no equivalent for the English term 'spinster'. In India one is either a "kumari" (Sanskrit for unmarried girl) which does not indicate maturity or middle age, or a "shrimati" (married woman), and the marriage institution is the only means to respectability for most Indian women. Women opting to remain single are viewed as socially subversive and threats to the patriarchal family structure. Therefore heterosexual marriage is the norm for Indian women cutting across socio-economic and cultural boundaries in different parts of India. 89.5% of Indian women between the ages of 25-59, are married. As for the unmarried women in that age range, the "never married" account for 2.5% in India, while the percentage of divorced women in that population is 1%, and the percentage of Indian widows is 7% (2001 Indian Census). The data reveals marriage as the norm for most Indian females though these numbers may vary in the case of urban and rural female population.

In such an intensely marriage-centric Indian society, especially so for its female population, it is significant that the novel's title centralises the discourse of singlehood. The novel, Kala claims, sets out on the "daunting task of making a single and happy woman palatable to society" (Bhandaram 2012). Aisha considers herself a part of "what is, tragically, a small minority" (Kala 2007, 4), perhaps due to the privileging of a married woman as "fulfilled" or the negative stereotypes of the unmarried woman. Aisha's boss warns her not get into the "bitchy spinster mode" (33). In fact, she declares she is neither discontented nor lonely (277). However, the single status for a woman is seen only as a temporary phase until Mr. Right enters the scene. As Aisha declares, "I'm okay with being the oldest bride in India just as long as when I do get to be a bride it is to the right man" (282). The author makes an important point when she states, "Rather than the right age, they are looking for the right time to get married" (Bhandaram 2012). So, though singlehood for a financially independent urban female is not the socio-cultural curse it used to be, heterosexual marriage as the normative female destiny remains unchallenged.

Marriage is seen as normative for females, yet, the novel conceives the middle class marriage as oppressive, and based on unequal gender relations. The novel portrays three marriages: that of Aisha's older cousin, Lata Didi who is the "privileged" married woman, and presumably is in an 'arranged marriage'. Early in the novel, the "'I'm-married-and-hence-my-life-is-perfect'" (41) Lata Didi, is seen pitying the unmarried Aisha. By the end of the book, there is an ironical reversal when the happily "married" Lata Didi is actually envious of Aisha's single status, her "job, a life, friends, an identity..." (276) and confesses the loneliness she experiences in an oppressive marriage with her alcoholic husband, but her lack of financial independence compels her to remain married. The second is a portrait of a failed 'love marriage' ending in a divorce. Aisha's close friend, Anushka, an attractive thirty-year-old woman who works in a garment export house, marries Anuj after dating him for six years. Later she files for divorce when on the eve of her anniversary, she discovers her husband in bed with another woman. The third marriage is that of Aisha's philandering boss, who Aisha thinks is cheating on his wife by having an affair with his wife's sister. But to her bewilderment she discovers that the wife is not unaware of the situation. Although Aisha finds it difficult to reconcile with the social reality, she realises, "Strange as it is, I don't need a man to pay my bills, but I do need him to give me his last name" (190). Economic independence does not entail socio-cultural and political emancipation for the urban middle-class female in India.

The refusal to perform the socially assigned gender roles may point to a feminist awareness, but in *Almost Single* as well as in many other global chick lit novels, the credit is inevitably due to the Western style of consumerist culture and the significance it attaches to individual pleasure through satisfaction of personal desires. The local tradition and custom is disguised as backward, conservative and conformist and the Westernized lifestyle as modern, progressive and emancipatory reflecting the limiting and racial views of hegemonic feminism contained in the observation made by Mallory Young: "in countries where feminism hasn't fully taken root, chick lit might be offering the feminist joys of freedom and the post-feminist joys of consumerism simultaneously" (quoted in Donadio 2006). In *Almost Single* one finds an endorsement of the hetero-normative order of the neoliberal ideology with its emphasis on freedom, choice and agency and in achieving the Anglo-American standards of beauty and body image which privilege youth over age. The postfeminist style of individual responsibility is privileged over the feminist ideal of collective responsibility in bringing about transformation and achieving the goals of socio-economic, cultural and political emancipation and empowerment of women belonging to different race, class and sexuality. Rather than challenging the hegemony and unequal relations of race, class, gender and sexuality, *Almost Single* like other Indian chick lit novels, reinforces the status quo, while only seeming to exhibit a new paradigm of a liberated female subject.

(Note: I am grateful to Dr. T Vijay Kumar, Professor of English, Osmania University, for suggesting the title of this paper.)

Works Cited

Bhandaram, Vishnupriya. 2012. "Successful, Single, Happy and 30!" *The Hindu*. February 1.

Bhowmick, Nilanjana. 2012. "Almost Single, but Most Eligible." *Little India*. March 5, 2009. http://www.littleindia.com/ arts-entertainment/4582-almost-single-but-most-eligible.html. Accessed o February 12.

Butler, Pamela and Jigna Desai. 2008 "Manolos, Marriage, and Mantras Chick-Lit Criticism and Transnational Feminism." *Meridians* 8.2: 1-31.

Chatterjee, Madhushree. 2009 "*Almost Single* author turns Bollywood scriptwriter." *Hindustan Times* March 20. http://www. hindustantimes.com/News-Feed/Author Profiles/Almost-Single-author-turns-Bollywood-scriptwriter/Article1-391406.aspx. Accessed on February 15, 2012.

Chen, Eva Yin-2010. "Neoliberal Self-Governance and Popular Postfeminism in Contemporary Anglo-American Chick Lit." *Concentric: Literary and Cultural Studies* 36.1: 243-75. http://www.concentric-literature.url.tw/issues/ Transnational Taiwan/11.pdf. Accessed on December 5, 2011.

———. "Shanghai(ed) Babies: Geopolitics, Biopolitics and the Global Chick Lit." *Feminist Media Studies*. 2011. doi:10.1080/ 14680777.2011.597102. Accessed February 16, 2012.

Donadio, Rachel. 2007. "The Chick-Lit Pandemic." *The New York Times* March 19, 2006. http://www.nytimes.com/ 2006/03/19/books/ review/19donadio.html. Accessed on November 21, 2011.

Dowd, Maureen. 2007 "Heels over Hemingway." *The New York Times* February 10, http://www.nytimes.com//02/10/ opinion/10dowd.html. Accessed on 11 February, 2012.

Ferriss, Suzanne and Mallory Young. 2006. *Chick Lit: The New Woman's Fiction*. New York: Routledge.

Gill, Rosalind and Elena Herdieckerhoff. 2006: "Rewriting the Romance: New Femininities in Chick Lit?" *Feminist Media*

Studies 6.4: 487-504. http://dx.doi.org/10.1080/14680770600989 947. Accessed on December 2, 2011.

Gill, Rosalind. 2007: "Postfeminist Media Culture: Elements of a Sensibility." *European Journal of Cultural Studies* 10.2147-66. DOI: 10.1177/1367549407075898. Accessed on December 3, 2011.

Foucault, Michel. 2008. *The Birth of Biopolitics: Lectures at the College de France, 1978-1979*. Trans. Graham Burchell. New York: Palgrave Macmillan.

Grewal, Inderpal. 2005. *Transnational America: Feminisms, Diasporas, Neoliberalism*. Durham: Duke University Press.

Hall, Stuart. 1981. "Notes on Deconstructing 'the Popular'." *People's History and Socialist Theory*. Ed. R. Samuel. London: Routledge. 227-41.

Kala, Advaita. 2007. *Almost Single*. New Delhi: Harper Collins.

Kumar, Sunaina. 2006. "The Rise of Ladki Lit." *The Indian Express* October 8. http://www.indianexpress.com/news/the-rise-of-ladkilit/14234/. Accessed on December 5, 2011.

Mazza, Cris. 2006. "Who's Laughing Now? A Short History of Chick Lit and the Perversion of a Genre." *Chick Lit: The New Woman's Fiction*. Ed. Suzanne Ferriss, and Mallory Young. New York: Routledge.

Misra, Manjul. "Ladies Special." 2011http://expressbuzz.com/magazine/Ladies-special/329631.html. Accessed on November 6.

Modleski, Tania. 1982. *Loving with a Vengeance: Mass Produced Fantasies for Women*. New York: Routledge.

Ogunlesi, Tolu. 2011. "Going Local: Indian Lit Focuses on Native Languages over English." *Publishing Perspectives*. October 18. http://publishingperspectives.com. Accessed on February 21, 2012.

Pathak, Akshay. 2011 "Publishing in India Today: 19,000 Publishers, 90,000 Titles, Many Opportunities." *Publishing Perspectives* July 6. http://publishingperspectives.com. Accessed on February 21, 2012.

Uberoi, Patricia. 2009. *Freedom and Destiny: Gender, Family and Popular Culture in India*. New Delhi: OUP.

Vasudevan, Aniruddhan. 2008. "'What Do We Know (Not)?': Alternative Patriarchies—Alternative Female Sexualities—Anti-essentialisms". *Redefining Feminisms*. Ed. Ranjana Harish and V. Bharati Harishankar. New Delhi: Rawat.

Venkatesh. 2011 "Do I need that agent?" http://www.foreword.in/ /12/20/do-i-need-that-agent. Accessed on February 11, 2012.

Virilio, Paul. 1997. *Pure War*. Tr. Mark Polizotti. New York: Semitext(e).

Whelehan, Imelda. 2011. "Chick lit and Lad lit." *The Encyclopedia of Twentieth-Century Fiction*. Ed. Brian W. Shaffer. Vol. 1. Oxford: Blackwell. 68-71.

CHAPTER 23

An Insight into Facets of a Globalised India: Aravind Adiga's *The White Tiger*

Rano Ringo
IIT Ropar, India

Globalisation is one of the most fiercely debated issues today as it affects people, institutions and societies all over the world. For some, it is a cover concept for global capitalism and imperialism and is accordingly condemned as another form of the imposition of the logic of capital and the market on ever more regions of the world and spheres of life. For others, it is the continuation of modernisation and a force of progress, increased wealth, freedom, democracy, and happiness. Its defenders present globalisation as a beneficial force, generating fresh economic opportunities, political democratisation, cultural diversity, and allowing entry into an exciting new world. Its critics see globalisation as harmful, bringing about increased domination and control by the wealthy over the poor, thus increasing the hegemony of the "haves" over the "have-nots." In addition, supplementing the negative view, globalisation critics assert that globalisation produces an undermining of democracy, a cultural homogenisation, and increased destruction of natural species and the environment. It generates new conflicts and new spaces for struggle, and there is a need to distinguish between globalisation from above and globalisation from below (Brecher, Costello, and Smith 2000, 168). Some imagine the globalisation project—whether viewed positively or negatively—as inevitable and beyond human control and intervention. The processes of globalisation are highly turbulent and have generated new conflicts throughout the world.

It is important to present globalisation as a strange amalgam of both homogenizing forces of sameness and uniformity and heterogeneity, difference, and hybridity, as well as a contradictory mixture of democratizing and anti-democratizing tendencies. On the one hand, globalisation unfolds a process of standardisation in which a globalised mass culture circulates the globe, creating sameness and homogeneity everywhere. On the other hand, globalised culture makes possible unique appropriations and developments everywhere, thus encouraging hybridity, difference, and heterogeneity to proliferate. Every local context involves its own appropriation and reworking of global products and signifiers, thus encouraging difference, otherness, diversity, and variety (Luke and Luke 2000, 112). Grasping that globalisation embodies these contradictory tendencies at once—that it can be a force of both homogenisation and heterogeneity—is crucial to articulating the contradictions of globalisation and avoiding one-sided and reductive conceptions. This essay proposes to analyse the Aravind Adiga's *The White Tiger* in the context of globalisation as manifested in India.

The White Tiger, which won the Man Booker Prize for 2008, foregrounds an India that is undergoing the process of globalisation, and is subjected to its opposite pulls of prosperity and poverty. Aravind Adiga is himself a child of the era of globalisation. While he was born in India, he was educated in Australia, the U.K. and the U.S., and currently holds the citizenship of Australia. Exposure to different cultures has given him an added insight into the forces of globalisation as exhibited in an underdeveloped country like India. The novel critically analyzes the effects of unbridled capitalism on an emerging economy like India, and the social injustice and inequalities that it entails. *The White Tiger* throws into relief the discrepancy between the crushing rural poverty from which the protagonist Balram emerges, and India's new-found status of a modern global economy. About his novel, Adiga says, "At a time when

India is going through great changes and, with China, is likely to inherit the world from the West, it is important that writers like me try to highlight the brutal injustices of society (Indian). That's what I'm trying to do—it is not an attack on the country, it's about the greater process of self-examination". He further explains that "the criticism by writers like Flaubert, Balzac and Dickens of the 19th century helped England and France become better societies" (English Sahitya.net).

The novel is written in the form of a letter of confession to the Chinese Premier, Mr. Jiabao, who is scheduled to visit India shortly in order to learn more about its successful entrepreneurs. Balram believes he is the most suitable person who can acquaint the Chinese Premier with the reality of India by narrating the story of his own rise in life from a rural simpleton to a successful entrepreneur. Balram Halwai aka Munna aka Ashok Sharma is born in the Darkness, i.e., in an impoverished village of Laxmangarh in Bihar. The village has the misfortune of being controlled by cruel feudal lords. The young Balram is not the one to take his destiny lying low. He rebels against the system by finding himself a job as the feudal landlord's driver. Very soon he is transferred to Delhi where he serves the landlord's son, Mr. Ashok. Delhi provides him with a whiff of liberty and before long he breaks free from the mental shackles of loyalty that tie him to his US returned master. He murders him, steals his money and escapes to Bengaluru where he emerges as a successful entrepreneur, running taxi services for BPOs.

Adiga has attempted to delineate aspects of the contemporary globalised society of India. One of these aspects is education. At the very start of the novel, the narrator writes to the Chinese Premier, "Neither you nor I can speak English, but there are some things that can be said only in English" (3). Adiga wishes to highlight the enormous significance that English has acquired in the age of globalisation. On the one hand, there are those like Balram's America-returned master Ashok and his wife Pinky Madam who speak English with facility thanks to their education; and on the other there are those like Balram who have to leave studies unfinished and who are thus placed at a disadvantage in the capitalist society. In his letter to the Chinese Premier, Balram voices the gaping loopholes in the country's education system which emphasises on rote learning and produces half-baked Indians. "Open our skulls, look in with a penlight, and you'll find an odd museum of ideas: sentences of history or mathematics remembered from old textbooks, sentences about politics read in a newspaper, triangles and pyramids seen on the torn pages of old geometry textbooks—all these ideas, half formed and half digested and half correct, mix up with other half-cooked ideas in your head" (11).

To make matters worse, the teachers in government schools such as Balram's teacher are not paid their salaries on time. Balram's teacher, in order to make ends meet, resorts to dubious means to make money. He resolves not to teach until his pay cheque arrives and sells off the school uniforms that the government has sent for the students in the neighbouring village. Without education, most Indians have no chance of securing meaningful work. In the Darkness, "every morning, tens of thousands of young men sit in the teashops, reading the newspaper.... They have no job to do today. They know they won't get any job today. They've given up the fight" (45-46). Even though Balram is a brilliant student, the financial constraints of his family force him to quit studies, but not before the school inspector impressed by his mental prowess gives him the eponymous title of "The White Tiger".

The novel also focuses on the role religion plays in modern day India. According to Balram, religion is a travesty. In India there are 360 million gods, plus the Muslim God and the Christian trinity. God asks the Indian:

"Isn't it all wonderful? Isn't it grand? Aren't you grateful to be my servant?" (75). Balram imagines a little black man wearing a khaki uniform who is "spitting at God again and again" out of anger that the world was created "in this particular way, instead of all the other ways it could have been created" (75).

Balram's cynical attitude towards the religious beliefs he has been raised on is perhaps one of the reasons for his success. He is not bound by constraints, such as the caste system, that are associated with Hinduism, and emerges as an independent thinker. According to him, "in the old days there were one thousand castes and destinies in India. These days, there are just two castes: Men with Big Bellies, and Men with Small Bellies" (64). The novel also throws light on the mistrust between the followers of the two major religions in India—Hinduism and Islam. Ram Persad, the chief driver of the family is a Muslim who has concealed his religion from his masters as that would entirely block all his chances of getting a job with them. He has even taken up a Hindu name and placed several idols of Hindu gods and goddesses in the servant quarters where he resides. Balram finds out the truth when he follows him and sees him enter a mosque during the days of Ramdan.

Balram uses the prejudice of his master as a pretext to blackmail the trusted Nepali servant. Ram Persad leaves the place without telling anyone and consequently, Balram is made the chief driver of the family. Earlier, it was Ram Persad alone who was allowed to drive the luxury car Honda City that Balram had set his heart on, but he was only given access to "a battered old Maruti Suzuki" (69). Through his blackmailing, Balram realised one of his many dreams of escaping from the Darkness and going to Delhi to start a new life as the Honda City driver for the landlord's son, Mr. Ashok. He repents for barely a moment:

> I thought, what a miserable life he's had, having to hide his religion, his name, just to get a job as a

> driver—and he is a good driver, no question of it, a far better one than I will ever be. Part of me wanted to get up and apologize to him right there and say, *You go and be a driver in Delhi. You never did anything to hurt me. Forgive me, brother.*
>
> I turned to the other side, farted and went back to sleep. (110)

Thus, Balram exploits the prejudices inherent in the society against members of a certain community to advance his personal interests. The novel also shows that if men like Balram hold a religious position that is expedient, there are others like the landlord (referred to as "Stork" throughout the novel) who adhere to an intransigent religious position. The tenacity with which certain people such as Stork cling to their religious and communal identity is also a facet of the era of globalisation. India is witnessing the conflicting forces of homogenisation and heterogeneity.

Another point that needs to be noted in connection with Balram is that he is a representative of the new breed of Indians in the age of globalisation who put self before the family. Unlike his brother Kishan, Balram does not bow to family pressure to get married. Balram's brother Kishan is prematurely aged, already resembling their late father, showing the physical signs of exhaustion. Kishan's family obligations are "eating him alive" (74), but Balram decides his own fate, and is not very regular in sending money back home. When he murders Mr. Ashok, he knows his family will be exterminated by the powerful Stork, but he does not let it get in the way of his plans. His desire for freedom and success surpasses his love for his family. Family is a burden, especially in the persona of Balram's domineering grandmother. Balram's aversion to his family underscores Adiga's message that in India the family is the problem, not the solution. In India loyalty to family is so intense that "'You were rude to your mother this morning' would be morally the equivalent of 'You embezzled funds from the bank this morning'" ("An Interview with Aravind Adiga".net). It is by breaking free from his traditional value system that Balram is able to climb the social ladder.

Adiga painstakingly describes the impact of uncontrolled urban expansion and its impact on the ecology and environment:

> There was a fierce jam on the road to Gurgaon. Every five minutes the traffic would tremble—we'd move a foot—hope would rise—then the red lights would flash on the car ahead of me, and we'd be stuck again. Everyone honked. Every now and then, the various horns, each with its own pitch, blended into one continuous wail that sounded like a calf taken from its mother. Fumes filled the air. Wisps of blue exhaust glowed in front of every headlight; the exhaust grew so fat and thick it could not rise or escape, but spread horizontally, sluggish and glossy, making a kind of fog around us. (157)

The novel satirises the senseless development and construction going on in urban areas and the face of poverty hidden behind urban glamour:

> Even at night, the construction work goes on in Gurgaon—big lights shine down from towers, and dust rises from pits, scaffolding is being erected, and men and animals, both shaken from their sleep and bleary and insomniac, go around and around carrying concrete rubble or bricks. (192)

It is evident that the lavish luxuries of modern life that the rich enjoy are based on the endless miseries that the poor and the impoverished masses have to suffer in order to procure two meals a day. The Darkness is a cesspool: the rivers are contaminated with "feces, straw, soggy parts of human bodies, buffalo carrion and seven different kinds of industrial acids" (12). The deprived ingest the waste that is dumped into the rivers by those industries that produce the goods to be enjoyed by the affluent. Indian radio boasts that

India will defeat China, even though it does not have sewage or drinking water, because it is a democracy (Adiga 2008: 20). Sardonically, Balram remarks that "if I were making a country, I'd get the sewage pipes first, then the democracy, then I'd go about giving pamphlets and statutes of Gandhi to other people, but what do I know? I'm just a murderer!" (80).

Corruption is rife in twenty-first century India. There is the village school teacher who steals money meant for students' uniforms from the state. But Balram supports this act by saying "you can't blame a man in dung heap to smell sweet" (33). In this case, corruption is a means to supplement low income. Growing up, he comes across higher levels of corruption that businessmen like his master, Mr. Ashok and the politicians in power indulge in. Balram is "corrupted from a sweet, innocent village fool into a citified fellow full of debauchery, depravity and wickedness" (197). Despite the government's claims of a shining India, Balram has only known an India of "defunct electricity poles, broken water taps, and children too lean and too short" (19-20).

Among the economic changes that have taken place in recent years, privatisation has been most closely linked with corruption. There is no question that public or state enterprises have been a major source of corruption and especially of political corruption because funds have been used to finance the activities of political parties and to provide jobs to the clienteles of particular political groups. Individuals have become enormously rich because of these abuses. By citing the unholy nexus between politicians and businessmen, Adiga expresses his skepticism about the virtues of a market economy. In fact, as depicted in the novel, some proceeds of corruption go to finance the activities of the political parties.

There is another face of India that belongs to the middle and upper classes of the country. Under the effects of globalisation, the society that consists of people like the Stork's US-returned son, Mr. Ashok is also undergoing a transformation, and becoming more liberal. Ashok's wife, Pinky Madam is westernised in her outlook and lifestyle, and is very different from the traditional women that Balram was accustomed to in his village. About Pinky Madam, Balram says, "I assumed at first she was an American, one of those magical things he had brought home from New York, like his accent and the fruit-flavoured perfume he put on his face after shaving" (76). Ashok has married Pinky Madam despite the fact that she is a Christian and in opposition to the wishes of his family. Adiga highlights the new trend of preference of love marriages to arranged marriages among the youth of today's India. A traditional Indian marriage is based on considerations of caste and family status. The qualities sought in a wife, apart from social background, are virginity and good behaviour. Good behaviour means that she should be able to fit into the normative pattern of the Hindu joint family. The worth of a woman is in the contribution she makes to the household economy and her skill in the traditional occupation. Women are viewed as repositories of knowledge, especially with regard to cooking, healing, including mid-wifery and women's ailments.

However, marriages are undergoing a transformation in the era of globalisation. As pointed out by Gullestead (1993, 159), in modern marriages the increasing independence of women from men, who continue to be emotionally dependent on women, and in most Indian families on their domestic skills as well, renders "definitions of masculinity particularly problematic". In India the man is often dependent on his wife as a social partner. Thus in an urban middle class household, a wife is needed to teach children the school curriculum, accompany her husband to "parties," act as a symbol of his "modernity" by dressing up and looking western and fashionable, all roles that were totally absent in the traditional set up. A man requires a wife who would complement his individual social position and not that of his joint family.

The constant bombardment from the media of global aesthetic and cultural images have led to the construction of imagined ideals of both masculinity and femininities that men and women find hard to realize, especially as such imaginary constructions are a blend of the old and the new. Thus men have as their fantasies, slim and svelte beauties, able to carry off high fashion western clothes, articulate and educated yet nurturing and submissive to the interests of the husband and his family. The fantasies of women have undergone more radical transformations. Women visualise kind men, cooperative partners, who would not stand in their way of progress. Women also understand that they have to live up to standards of physical perfection that modern husbands demand, a concept totally alien to Indian culture. Physical beauty of a wife is a value that is creeping in very slowly and standards of beauty are also changing. While earlier, families would look for a sturdy girl who could produce children and do household work, now the standards of beauty are tilting towards western models projected by global advertisements. The novel also portrays the increasing trend of divorces and separations among couples in the urban metropolis. Pinky Madam leaves Ashok for good as she finds the marriage incompatible. The new-found confidence among women makes them more assertive about what they expect from their partners, and their failure to meet those expectations often results in separation.

After his separation from Pinky Madam, Ashok starts using the services of white-skinned call girls. His master's conduct and his exposure to global media that brings up provocative sexual images incite Balram all the more because he comes from a rural and remote area where the women he is accustomed to addressing by respectful kin terms are visually different from what he sees in the cities. In their haste to project India as a modern society our leaders were in a hurry to introduce such items of global consumer economy as were viewed necessary for India to be seen as a progressive state. Thus massive efforts were made to have televisions, satellite television and computers to reach remote corners of the country. What it really achieved was to send across images quite contrary to what could be digested by the people. The soft pornographic images broadcast from American television, the hard pornography that one could come across on the internet, damaged irreparably the traditional respect that Indian society had for women.

It especially damaged those who were not otherwise exposed to western education and western culture and to whom such images could only come across as extremely stressful and provocative. No doubt other factors also operate in the rising demand for call girls and prostitutes but one cannot underestimate the power of images bombarding people, creating conflicting messages. While Balram himself emulates his master, he loses respect for Ashok for seeking out call girls after his wife had left him. When Ashok goes to pick up a whore, Balram gives him an insubordinate, disparaging look that says, "Are you sure you want to do this?" (185). As Ashok's own personal conduct deteriorates, the authority of the supposed superior is undermined and Balram's relative sense of power increases. The loss of respect proves fatal for Ashok, as it emboldens Balram to first cheat his master and eventually murder him.

Balram's tale is one of gradual deterioration from Edenic innocence to Satanic corruption, aided and abetted by a scheming mind and the overwhelming inequality inherent in urban life which defeats all theories of social justice. Entry into a mall is like a peep into the world of the privileged: "I was conscious of a perfume in the air, of golden light, of people in T-shirts and jeans who were eyeing me strangely" (152). Balram has caught a glimpse of the world of the rich, and desires to have the same comforts and luxuries which he knows he cannot afford. Balram first apes his master in superficial ways—drinking the same Scotch and seeking out blond women—but then comes to the realisation that the only way to accomplish his goals is to kill his master and steal his money. Balram commits a crime of theft as well as a crime of violence when he steals 700,000 rupees that Ashok was taking to the hypocritical leader (the "Great Socialist") to avoid payment of taxes. Balram rationalises that in a sense he is not stealing but reclaiming the funds that would be his but for corruption and tax evasion. Given the corruption of today's India, dishonesty is the only path to success, and violence replaces constructive protest. Significantly, the weapon of murder is a broken bottle of Johnny Walker Black Label whisky—the drink of India's elite. The choice of the murder weapon symbolizes the violent outcome that is a possibility in a consumerist society characterized by severe inequalities in the distribution of wealth.

Neither religion nor family checks Balram's criminal impulses. Through violence, Balram breaks the shackles that hold him in bondage: "I pierced his neck and his lifeblood spurted into my eyes. I was blind. I was a free man" (246). The act of killing gives him back his manhood: "All I wanted was the chance to be a man—and for that, one murder was enough" (273). Balram revels in his existential act: "I'll never say I made a mistake that night in Delhi when I slit my master's throat. I'll say it was all worthwhile to know, just for a day, just for an hour, just for a minute, what it means not to be a servant" (276). Balram thrives after the murder/robbery by embracing the role of an entrepreneur with the money he stole from Ashok. In defiance of the remorse, one might expect, Balram asks, "Haven't I succeeded in the struggle that every poor man here should be making—the struggle not to take the lashes your father took, not to end up in a mound of indistinguishable bodies that will rot in the black mud of Mother Ganga?" (273).

The injustice and corruption of twenty-first-century India is so deep-rooted and so pervasive that the only way a poor man can better himself is by an act of aggression, indeed the extremes of theft and murder. But what has Balram's violence really achieved? Balram has bettered his own condition, but he has not created a better society. Adiga's vision remains dystopic: he foresees a world where one thing will have changed, the colour of the ruling class, but nothing else, because the Manichean division of master/slave will persist.

Adiga writes in an era when Marxism has been discredited and he is hardly optimistic that modern India will escape the snares of family and the deathtrap of corruption. Balram's rhetoric is more capitalist than Marxist. He recognizes that although there are "lots of self-made millionaires in India now" and "lots of successful entrepreneurs", those who succeed are a small minority (287). "Getting to the top" takes something like what Balram has done. It is a rare breed of cat, the white tiger, who can escape the coop. Balram's story is indicative of a social upheaval in an India which is witnessing a conflict between the traditional and the modern. India, in this globalised era, is a country of political corruption where the law enforcement can be bribed, politicians can buy votes, the upper-class can live a life in luxury, and poverty hangs on like an epidemic in large parts. Adiga's searing portrayal of the social divisions in present-day India reveals that the fruits of globalisation have benefited just a small minority of the country's population. Balram is a type of the lucky few who will make it big in the context of a globalised India and Adiga has presented an unforgettable insight into the process through which that success is achieved.

Works Cited

Adiga, Aravind. 2008. *The White Tiger*. New Delhi: Harper Collins Publishers.

———.Adiga,Aravind.EnglishSahitya. http://isahitya.com/index.php/english-sahitya/160-aravind-adiga

"An Interview with Aravind Adiga". www.bookbrowse.com/author_interviews/full/index.cfm/author_number/1552/aravind-adiga

Brecher, Jeremy, Tim Costello, and Brendan Smith. 2000. *Globalisation from Below*. Boston, MA: South End Press.

Gullestead, Marianne. 1993. "Home Decorations as Popular Culture: Constructing Homes, Gender and Classes in Norway". In *Gendered Anthropology*, edited by Teresa Del Valle. London, Routledge, 128-60.

Luke, Allan, and Carmen Luke. 2000. "A Situated Perspective on Cultural Globalisation". In *Globalisation and Education*, edited by Nicholas Burbules and Carlos Torres. London, England, and New York: Routledge, 275-98.

CHAPTER 24

Beyond Borders and Across Cultures: Writing Other People's Stories

Pat Lowe
Writer, Australia

When I was invited to write a paper for this Conference and was considering whether and how my work would fit into a symposium on Globalism, I was struck by the thought that this phenomenon really began with colonialism and the movement of European nations across the globe in search of markets and raw materials. Subsequently, their acquisition of and settlement in territories far from their original homelands and the consequent displacement of so many other peoples from their original possession of those lands brought consequences which are still being worked out today. My own personal story, which is the focus of my essay, records aspects of my relationships and work with individual Australian Aboriginal people, and is an outcome of that history in Australia.

No one nowadays wants to be seen as a colonialist, but my very presence in Australia is the direct result of that country's colonial history or (perhaps more accurately) Britain's policy of imperial expansion. I migrated to Western Australia from England in 1972 without any need for preliminary screening or submission of an Application for permission to enter the country. On my immigration form I simply ticked the box indicating my intention to migrate permanently. When I disembarked at Fremantle docks, I proffered my British passport and I was allowed into the country without being asked a single question.

I spent my first seven years in my new country in Perth, working as a psychologist for what was then the

Department for Community Welfare, and later for the Department of Corrections, at Fremantle maximum security Prison. I requested a transfer to the small northern town of Broome, and arrived there in February 1979. Until then, none of the three northern prisons—at Roebourne, Broome and Wyndham—had had the benefit of the usual prisoner services; there was no welfare officer, social worker, psychologist or teacher. It was my job to start setting up such services in the three prisons. Almost all the prisoners in these three prisons were Aboriginal, and one of the first educational activities I started in Broome Prison was the 'Art Class'.

This was a small project and was conducted in the prison yard by a local man, who soon found that he didn't have to do much teaching. It appeared that most of the participants had a natural, unselfconscious artistic sense, and only seemed to need the opportunity to develop it through practice and experiment and with occasional guidance. Further classes were introduced and eventually, a classroom was built to accommodate the students and a full-time educational officer appointed. I was even allocated my own office.

In 1986, I went on Long Service Leave, in the course of which I visited one of the former prisoners, Jimmy Pike, who had already made his reputation in prison as an artist and was now serving three years on parole at his bush camp on the edge of the Great Sandy Desert. I came to an important personal decision during that visit. Ten days later I went back to Broome to sort out my personal affairs and let my house. I had decided to join Pike at his camp. From that date we remained together for the next sixteen years, that is until Jimmy's death in 2002. In keeping with the theme of this Conference, I think you could say that as far as our relationship went, the borders between two very different cultures had vanished.

Jimmy Pike was born in the desert as a hunter and gatherer, probably around 1940, at a time when his people were gradually moving from the desert to the riverside and ranges, to work on cattle and sheep stations which had been set up by white settlers in the Kimberley and Pilbara regions of Western Australia. He left with a small group of relations sometime in the 1950s, when he was still a boy. The young Jimmy had never worn clothes or travelled anywhere other than on foot. In fact he had not seen anyone of a different race. He knew nothing of cars, houses, horses or cattle. Nevertheless, he learnt quickly and soon took to life as a stockman on Cherrabun Station.

In 1967, following a historic referendum, Aboriginal people obtained full rights as citizens of their country. Besides political rights which allowed Indigenous persons the right to vote, they were also allowed a range of social rights which had been denied before. Among these which was the right to earn equal wages for equal work and to purchase and drink alcohol. Pike took to drinking and it wasn't long before he fell foul of the law and began serving sentences in prison. [This was soon to become almost a rite of passage for most Aboriginal youth afterwards]. I already knew Pike from a previous sentence in 1981, when I was working at Broome Prison. When he arrived the next time, he had been convicted of murder and sentenced to life imprisonment.

He served most of this sentence in Perth, and 1986 was released on parole, on condition that he live in the bush on the remote desert outstation where I later joined him. Note that, under Western Australian law at that time, there were different categories of murder and of life sentences, and Pike was released at his first parole review—largely, I believe, because of his gifts as an artist, which the Parole Board saw as his passport to a better future. Certainly, this is what it proved to be.

Pike had not returned to a fully traditional life in the desert—he could hardly do that as a man on his own and without the support of his community group. However with a two-way radio and a few other basic requirements, he had set up camp under a tree and spent his time hunting for survival and carving artefacts as an occupation. Shortly after I arrived, a four-wheel drive vehicle was delivered, in lieu of royalties for the reproduction of his designs on fabric, and he was then able to travel back to the remoter parts of the desert, where he had lived as a child. It might be said that globalisation had invaded the life-style of the traditional Aboriginal world. Pike's life would never be the same again. My own life and world-view was also radically changed. My energies were directed to trying to ingest the enormous new range of experiences that were opening up to me.

I was fascinated not only by the situation in which I found myself but also by Jimmy's world and facets of his history. As we explored his country, he told me how his people had lived through the different seasons, as well as accounts of incidents from his own childhood. I wrote down his stories, along with words and sentences in his language, Walmajarri. Our first book, *Jilji*, embodies a description of the material conditions of the hunting and gathering life as I was told about them. It was illustrated by Jimmy's paintings and my photographs. Jimmy knew exactly what I was writing in this book, having provided most of the content through practical demonstrations and explanations, and answered my many questions while I made copious notes. When I was transforming these *ad hoc* notes and experiences into chapters for the book, I often checked things with him or asked him to fill in details. I therefore faced none of the usual ethical dilemmas about describing another culture; I regarded myself as a recorder of Jimmy's experiences in a context of mutual trust. I did not have to feel constrained by the formal requirements of academic ethics committees.

The next book we worked on together was a collection of stories. Again these narratives were set out as Jimmy recounted them to me about his childhood. An important purpose I now had in mind was to assist in the teaching of English literacy to Aboriginal children through stories and characters they could identify with. There were very few at that time. Because of the nature of Aboriginal storytelling, and all the background information that Jimmy took for granted when telling his stories, I rewrote them in the third person and fictionalised them, giving all the real-life characters fictitious names. Yet I stayed true to Jimmy's accounts, even to recording most of his original dialogue. For example, in the first story, "Yinti goes hunting," his second mother's scolding him for accidentally setting fire to the tree she was climbing is quoted as follows: "You nearly burnt me! How would you get back home if I was burnt up?" is a direct version in English of what Jimmy told me she said at the time.

Similarly, in "Yinti goes training," when Yinti inflicts wounds on his young brother and nephew, he tells them: "Don't cry! You must laugh!" These anecdotes were related to me by Jimmy and confirmed by his victims when they retold the story, amidst much laughter, decades later. However, in all the stories I provided descriptions and information which I felt were essential to an understanding of the events and actions, missing from Jimmy's versions. He understood what I was doing and got into the spirit of it, telling me about things his alter ego, Yinti, had got up to. When he wanted to recounts something from the past he would say with a smile: "Yinti bin have trouble, one time", and launch into a tale about his own childhood misdeeds. He also drew one illustration for every story.

Looking back on this effort, I can see that it could be viewed by some as representative of colonialist interventions: here was I, one of the colonisers, not only writing down the stories of the colonised, but taking it upon myself to use these stories to assist the children of the colonised to learn to read and write the colonisers' language—my language. There are certainly people in Australia who would argue that only the original verbatim record has any validity and that white people have no business imposing their own order on the way stories are told. David Milroy said words to that effect at the launch of our book *Desert Cowboy,* at Yirra Yaakin theatre (he did, however, state that our work was an exception).

While I understand this point of view, I don't agree with it altogether. I take the view that, for better or worse, the legacy of colonialism is now inescapable. While there is no going back to pre-colonial days, and few would want to do so, the continuing appropriation of land and the privileging of mainstream law and worldview can and must be resisted; however, a mastery of the imposed system of education is necessary for Aboriginal people's survival in the present world. In addition, I believe that recording stories from the last generation of people who lived traditional lives is important in order to preserve even a small part of such a significant and interesting era of Australian history for the benefit of future generations. I have observed at first-hand the pleasure with which—otherwise disaffected—Aboriginal school students respond to books that portray characters they can identify with.

Jimmy and I produced two other books based on his youthful experiences, one of which, *Desert Dog*, I took more liberties with and turned the bare bones Jimmy had told me into a novelette. I wrote the first part of the story from the point of view of the dingoes, though without anthropomorphising them, and incorporated into the book other incidents concerning dingoes that Jimmy had told me about. I also added to this material my own intimate knowledge of the behaviour of these animals acquired during my own experiences in the desert. For instance, a dingo Jimmy's mother had once speared became the male dingo in my story. The puppy she had subsequently taken into her care and brought up became the dingo pup we adopted, in my story.

The other book, *Desert Cowboy*, was a sequel to *Yinti*, covering incidents in Jimmy's later life on cattle and sheep stations. Each chapter was based on a real incident, but instead of simple narration, I dramatised it by adding dialogue between characters and description of the landscape, as well as describing in detail activities which conveyed knowledge of the actual lifestyle such as making a fire and cooking game. I built into the narrative the common European literary device of building events and action to a climax. The traditional Walmajarri way was often to relate the climax first and then to proceed to fill in the events leading up to it. Jimmy illustrated all three of these books.

A niece of Jimmy's, Ngarta, just a few years his junior (she is also one of the characters in *Yinti*) was with the very last group of people to leave that part of the desert, in the early 1960s. Ngarta's experiences in the year or so before she left, when most of her remaining family members were murdered, were so extraordinary that I asked her if she would be willing for me to write them down and she agreed.

Unfortunately, my knowledge of Ngarta's language was rudimentary, consisting of not much more than a basic vocabulary; I was therefore unable to string together her account into grammatical sentences. I recorded or wrote down the details in her own words at various times and places and managed to render into plain English. The piece was published in *Westerly,* (the literary Journal produced by the University of Western Australia). Friends complained that Ngarta's account was hard to follow without some knowledge of her background, and urged me to write her story again in the third person, providing the necessary information. With her consent I did so, but the final product was not long enough to be published as a book. Meanwhile,

Ngarta's older sister, Jukuna, who had worked extensively with linguists and was literate in Walmajarri, had written an outline of her own life story in her own language. With the help of linguist Eirlys Richards, Jukuna developed her draft further, and Eirlys then translated it into English. The stories were eventually published together by Fremantle Press, as *Two Sisters*.

Both Ngarta and Jukuna were keen for their stories to live on after them, and for future generations to learn something of the desert way of life, which they would never have a chance to experience fully for themselves. Ngarta had no way of writing her own story and was happy for me to do it for her. I remember when the first draft was complete and I started to read it back to her; she laughed and said, (after only a few paragraphs) 'You got it!' and didn't want to hear any more.

Jukuna did have a written language to express her thoughts, and she made good use of it. It could be said, therefore, that Jukuna's story, published with its Walmajarri text and English translation, has greater integrity than her sister's, which I had extensively rewritten, and I think Jukuna's reads beautifully. I would prefer Ngarta's story to have been written in the first person in Walmajarri too, and translated into English. On the other hand, rewriting it allowed me to inquire and write about the two men who had killed so many members of her family.

Now all three of these protagonists are gone. When Jimmy died in 2002, I was working on the first part of his biography—his desert childhood. Again, I wrote it in the third person so that I could have the freedom to tell the story in sequence and to provide background descriptions and information. Wherever I could, I included quotes from Jimmy, which I had either recorded on tape or, more often, written down. I added cultural information in a foreword and an introduction.

Once Jimmy was no longer there to advise me, I had to make decisions about what to include in his story and what, if anything, to leave out. He had been generous in telling me stories, but would he have expected all of them, even the most personal, to go into print? What about the stories that revealed aspects of his culture that outsiders might well find confronting, or seize on to justify their own prejudices: the killings and abductions, the violence, even the occasional abandonment of children? I came to the conclusion that any offence my writing Jimmy's story without being able to consult him could cause could only be compounded by my attempts to censor parts of it, and so I included everything. The result, for better or worse, is the Penguin book, *In the Desert—Jimmy Pike as a Boy*.

Jukuna, who died in 2011, had for a long time been telling me stories of her own desert childhood, vignettes not included in her biography. A few of them were of incidents that Jimmy had told me about, which I had rewritten for the book *Yinti*, but from a different perspective (the victim's rather than the perpetrator's!). We were putting them together for publication. As with the Yinti stories, I had rewritten Jukuna's in plain English and given the characters who had previously appeared in *Yinti*, the same names. A question for me now was how to sequence the stories. A broadly chronological sequence, showing the main character's growing maturity, seemed a reasonable approach for a book that I hoped would be used in schools. I had started to work through the stories with Jukuna, and found that my guess had been way out. However, if I followed her sequencing, various anomalies arose: characters appeared again after they were supposed to have died, or the children seemed younger in the later stories than in the earlier ones. Had Jukuna lived, we might eventually have been able to sort out these problems , but now that she was no more, it was up to me—and if I made mistakes, I doubt if she would have worried; she was much less interested in chronology than I was.

There are many other dilemmas and uncertainties about the interpretation of Jukuna's stories, particularly since our communication has been mostly in English—a language that was my own but which was totally alien to Jukuna. It would be easy to have lost courage and abandoned the task as too hard. What kept me motivated was my belief in the importance of recording, however faultily, a way of life now gone forever, and of keeping faith with those people who had entrusted their stories to me, trusting that they would be transmitted to future generations.

Works Cited

Lowe, Pat with Pike, Jimmy.1990. *Jilji—Life in the Great Sandy Desert*, Broome, Magabala Books, republished as *You Call it Desert—We Used to Live There*. 2010. Broome Magabala Books.

———. 1992. *Yinti—Desert Child*. Illustrated by Jimmy Pike, Broome: Magabala Books.

———. 1997. *Desert Dog*. Illustrated by Jimmy Pike. Broome: Magabala Books.

———. 2000. *Desert Cowboy*. Illustrated by Pike, Jimmy. Magabala Books, Broome.

Bent, Ngarta Jinny, Jukuna, Mona Chuguna, Pat Lowe, and Eirlys Richards. 2004. *Two Sisters*. Fremantle, Fremantle Arts Centre Press.

Contributors

Ameer Ali lectures in economics in the Business School at Murdoch University. His teaching fields relate to The Economy of Modern China and the Economics of Globalization. His research interest, however, lies in the Development of Muslim Minorities. He has published a series of articles on this subject in a variety of international journals. His article on "The Sri Lankan Ethnic Morass and China-India Geopolitical Manoeuvres" was published in *Economic and Political Weekly of India* (Aug 2011). Among his other recent publications is "Assimilation, Integration or *Convivencia*: The Dilemma of Diaspora Muslims from 'Eurabia' to 'Londonistan', from 'Lakembanon' to Sri Lanka" in *Journal of Muslim Minority Affairs* (June 2010).

Bill Ashcroft is Australian Professorial Fellow at the University of NSW. A founding exponent of post-colonial theory, co-author of *The Empire Writes Back*, he is author and co-author of sixteen books including *Post-colonial Transformation*; *On Post-colonial Futures*; *Caliban's Voice*; *Intimate Horizons: The Post-Colonial Sacred in Australian Literature* and over 150 chapters and papers.

Prantik Banerjee is Associate Professor of English at Hislop College, Nagpur, India.

N. Bindu is Assistant Professor of English at SS Government Arts College, Tiruttani, Tamil Nadu. Her doctoral thesis was on Australian poetry of Judith Rodriguez, Jennifer Strauss, Fay Zwicky and Ania Walwicz.

Arindam Das is an Assistant Professor of English at Heritage Institute of Technology, Kolkata. He has recently submitted his PhD in Australian Studies to Vidyasagar University, West Bengal. He was Australia-India Council's Australian Studies Fellow (2010-11) at Australian National University, Canberra. He represented India and presented a paper at the 1st World Conference on Australian Studies at Monash University, Prato Centre, Italy. He has published more than a dozen research articles and book chapters. He has co-edited the book *Colonial Spectre and Beyond* (Booksway, Kolkata) and is currently co-editing two books on Raja Rao and Mulk Raj Anand (Authors Press, New Delhi). He is currently translating (from Bengali to English) the first Australia-travelogue by an Indian.

Sharmistha De received her PhD degree from the Department of Humanities and Social Sciences IIT Kharagpur in 2013. She is an Assistant Professor in Dr. B.C. Roy Engineering College, Durgapur, India.

Jane Fernandez-Goldborough is vice-president, teaching and learning at Avondale College, New South Wales, Australia. Jane's research interests are in the areas of postcolonial literature, the English classroom, diaspora, and the interface between literature and religion. She has edited an e-book of conference proceedings entitled *Diasporas: Exploring Critical Issues* (2008).

Julia Gross is Research Data Management Librarian at Edith Cowan University. She specializes in blog writing, travel writing, Web 2.0 and emerging technologies, teaching and learning in tertiary settings, information literacy, usability studies, research in libraries and universities, data management.

Nicholas Hasluck has a distinguished career both in law and literature. He is a former judge of the Supreme Court of Western Australia and a well-known novelist. He has served as Chair of the Literature Board of the Australia Council and later as Chair of the Commonwealth Writers' Prize from 2006 to 2011. His eleven works of fiction include the prize-winning novels *The Bellarmine Jug* and *The Country Without Music.* His latest novel *Dismissal* (2011), published by Harper Collins/4th Estate in hard copy and E-Book formats, centres upon the 1975 constitutional crisis in Australia that led to the sacking of the Whitlam government.

Jackie Highland is a senior teacher in the Department of English at Chisholm Catholic College, Perth. She has an abiding interest in bringing in innovative teaching areas into the secondary school curriculum and has introduced her students successfully to new writing in English from India and Africa, Australian literature, and also the writing of theorists like Said and Bhabha. She completed a Masters' Degree at Edith Cowan University in the area of Migrant Writing and intends to continue her research in this and allied areas.

Parimala Kulkarni is Assistant Professor of English in Osmania University, Hyderabad, India. She has been teaching English (language and literature) for the past twenty years. Her interests are Women's Writing, Women's Studies, Media and Culture Studies and English Language Teaching.

Serge Liberman is a medical doctor, independent scholar and writer from Melbourne. He has been an editor and co-editor of diverse literary periodicals and is author of six collections of short stories. His most recent publication is the definitive third edition of *The Bibliography of Australasia Judaica* (Hybrid Publishers, 2011).

Pat Lowe was born in England and began her career as a secondary school teacher in France and East Africa. She obtained a first class degree in psychology from the University of Liverpool in the UK and migrated to Western Australia in 1972. She completed a Master's degree in clinical psychology and started work in Western Australian prisons, moving north to Broome in 1979. There she met Aboriginal artist Jimmy Pike and some years later went to live with him at his camp in the Great Sandy Desert, where she also began her own writing career. She collaborated with Pike on a number of books until his death in 2002. Pat's most recent book is *In the Desert: Jimmy Pike as a Boy* (2007).

Harish C. Mehta has taught history at McMaster University, Trent University, and University of Toronto. He has written three books on Cambodian politics and media, and his articles on U.S.-North Vietnamese diplomacy have appeared in *Peace and Change, Diplomatic History,* and *The Historian.* A new and expanded edition of his 1999 book, *The Strongman: Rise of Hun Sen from Pagoda Boy to Prime Minister of Cambodia, An Oral History* (co-author Julie Mehta) is being published in 2013 by Marshall Cavendish. He is working on another book: *People's Diplomacy of North Vietnam.*

Julie Mehta teaches the Chancellor-endowed course "Asian Cultures in Canada", under the Canadian Studies Program, University College, University of Toronto. She is the author of *Dance of Life: Mythology, History and Politics of Cambodian Culture* (2001), and co-author with historian Dr. Harish C. Mehta of *Hun Sen: Strongman of Cambodia* (1999). She has published extensively on Postcolonial Literatures and Cultures and works on exile and identity in representations of food and language, among Asian diasporic novelists. Born and brought up in Kolkata, Julie recently translated Tagore's play *Dak Ghar* from Bengali into English as *The Post Office*. Julie was dedicated to promote cross-cultural understanding while she lived and worked as a correspondent in Australia, Singapore, Thailand, Cambodia, and India. She now lives in Ontario, Canada.

Glen Phillips is a reputed Australian poet with a special predilection for writing about the landscape of his native Western Australia. He serves on the Board of *Writing WA* and is Patron of the KSP Foundation. His books include *A Show of Colours* (2011), *Redshift: 42 Name Day Poems* (2009), *Shanghai Suite* (2009), *Singing Granites: Poems* (2008) with Anne Born, and *Spring Burning* (1999). (His latest, *The Moon Belongs to No One* is in press.) Additionally he has co-edited *Contrary Rhetoric* a collection of Kinsella's landscape lectures (2008), and (also co-edited) *Lines in the Sand* (2008). He is represented in more than 20 anthologies and is author or editor of 20 books. Glen is Director of the Landscape and Language Centre at Edith Cowan University.

Mohan Ramanan is a Professor of English at University of Hyderabad, India. He has been a British Council Scholar at Oxford and a Fulbright Scholar at Amherst MA. He has specialized in Modern Poetry and his publications include *The Movement: A Study of Contemporary Poetic Tradition* (1989), *Nineteenth Century Indian English Prose* (2004), and he has edited *Ah! Columbus: The Indian Discovery of America* (1993), and *English and the Indian Short Story* (2000).

K. Suneetha Rani teaches in the Department of Womens' Studies, University of Hyderabad, India. Her PhD was on Australian Aboriginal women's autobiographies. Her research interests include Indian literatures, literatures of the marginalised, women's studies, comparative literature, and translation. She translates literature from Telugu into English and from English into Telugu. She is currently working on translations of Sri Lankan women's short fiction from English into Telugu and of Dalit women's writings from Telugu into English. Her book *Dalit Women's' Writing* was published in 2011 (New Delhi: Prestige).

Dieter Riemenschneider's PhD thesis (1971) was on *The Modern Indian Novel in English*. He, taught Commonwealth literature/English Language Literatures at Frankfurt University (1971-99), and in 1993 set up the centre for "New Literatures and Cultures in English". He founded and edited the bi-annual newsletter *ACOLIT* (1977-99) and was Chair of "The Association for the Study of the New Literatures in English" (1989-93). His main research areas are: Indian, African, Australian Aboriginal and New Zealand/Aotearoan Māori literature and culture. His publications include: ed. *Postcolonial Theory: The Emergence of a Critical Discourse: A Selected and Annotated Bibliography* (2004); *The Reception of the Indian Novel in English* (2005); *A Survey of Indian English Literature in Germany* (2006); essays on Māori Biculturalism/Glocality (2002), Māori Poetry (2004), Theatre (2004) and Film (2007). His bilingual (English/German) anthology of poems from Aotearoa New Zealand, *Wildes Licht* [*Wild Light*] (Tranzlit: Kronberg) was released in 2010.

Rano Ringo is Assistant Professor of English at the Department of Humanities & Social Sciences at IIT Ropar, Rupnagar (Punjab). Her research interests include Gender Studies, Postcolonial Studies and Modern Fiction. After completing PhD from IIT Roorkee, Dr. Ringo joined Mody Institute of Technology and Science, Laxamangarh (Rajasthan) as Assistant Professor of English and worked there from

July 2007 to June 2010, before joining IIT Ropar in June 2010.

Anjali Gera Roy is Professor in the Department of Humanities of Social Sciences at the Indian Institute of Technology, Kharagpur. She has published essays in literary, film and cultural studies, translated short fiction from Hindi, authored a book on African fiction, edited an anthology on the Nigerian writer Wole Soyinka and co-edited another on the Indo-Canadian novelist Rohinton Mistry. Her new publications include a co-edited volume (with Nandi Bhatia) *Partitioned Lives: Narratives of Home, Displacement and Resettlement* (2008), and a monograph *Bhangra Moves: From Ludhiana to London and Beyond* (2010). She is now researching the transnational flows of Bollywood cinema and has recently co-edited with Chua Beng Huat an anthology *The Travels of Indian Cinema: From Bombay to LA* (2012) and edited *Bollywood's Soft Power: Across Five Continents* (2012).

M.A.B. Siddique is a development economist and is Director of the Trade, Migration and Development Research Centre and Chair of Economics at the University of Western Australia. His research centres on development economics, particularly environment, good governance and international migration in the Asia-Pacific region. He has published in international journals such as *Environment International*, *Mathematics and Computers in Simulation*, *International Journal of Social Economics*, *South Asia* and authored and edited numerous books including *International Migration in to the 21st Century: Essays in Honour of Reginald Appleyard*; *Regionalism, Trade and Economic Development in the Asia-Pacific Region*, *Handbook of Sustainable Development Planning: Studies in Modelling and Decision Support*, and *Tourism and*

Economic Development. He has won numerous national and international research grants and is a consultant to several national and international organisations.

Tony Simoes da Silva teaches in the English Literatures Program at the University of Wollongong, focusing primarily on Afro-diasporic writing. He is the author of *The Luxury of Nationalist Despair* (2000), a study of George Lamming and has completed a monograph on southern African life writing, tentatively titled *Narrating a White Africa: Life Writing, Memory and History*. Current research in progress examines representations of refugees and refugee selfhood in world writing. Tony co-edits the *Journal of the Association for the Study of Australian Literature* (*JASAL*) and *La Questioners Meridionale/The Southern Question*.

Amritjit Singh is the Langston Hughes Professor of English at Ohio University and the senior editor for the MELA (Multi-Ethnic Literatures of the Americas) Series. He has held visiting positions at New York University, Wesleyan University, and the University of California at Berkeley. An internationally known scholar of African American and Migration Studies, Singh has lectured and/or taught in more than a dozen countries in Europe, Africa, and Asia. He has authored or edited many books on American, Postcolonial, and Indian Literatures, such as *The Novels of the Harlem Renaissance* (1976, 1994); *India: An Anthology of Contemporary Writing* (1983); *Conversations with Ralph Ellison* (1995); *Postcolonial Theory and the United States* (2000); *The Collected Writings of Wallace Thurman* (2003); *Interviews with Edward W. Said* (2004) and *The Circle of Illusion: Poems by Gurcharan Rampuri* (2011). Recipient of the 2007

MELUS Lifetime Achievement Award, he is currently the Creative Writing Editor of *South Asian Review*.

Rita Tognini currently works in the State-wide Services Directorate of the Western Australian Department of Education. She has a PhD in Applied Linguistics. She taught foreign languages and English in primary and secondary schools, has worked at tertiary level as a teacher educator. Her research interests include second language acquisition, classroom interaction, policy development and teacher beliefs in linking theory and practice.